'Follow an unforgettable cast of characters as they navigate the System in Ryan Gattis's pacy, polyphonic, hyperreal crime novel. Gripping, meticulously researched, and smartly plotted, I devoured this brilliant novel over the course of a weekend.'

Paula Hawkins, author of *The Girl on the Train*

'*The System* is an odyssey through a legal system you know but you don't know. It goes beyond the lawyer shows, cop shows, expert opinions, and headline cases. The dialogue isn't dialogue; it's what you'd actually hear – on the street, in a courtroom, on the prison yard. And so it is with the entire book, its relevance and insight transforming an excellent thriller into a historical document.'

Joe Ide, author of the IQ series

'Gripping, fascinating, moving, and so very, very real. *The System* is one of the best books I've read in years. Told from multiple perspectives, it's the story of life on the street – for gang members, fringe players, cops and lawyers – told in all its gritty, authentic detail. It grabbed me by the heart and mind from page one and never let me go. I'll be thinking about Dreamer, Angela, Wizard, Little – and all the rest of the vividly drawn, incredibly compelling characters – for a long time to come. *The System* is a thrilling, brilliantly written and profound work of art.'

Marcia Clark, author of *Final Judgment* and former
Criminal Prosecutor in the L.A. District Attorney's Office

'An heir to Richard Price and Upton Sinclair, Ryan Gattis ingeniously casts deeply researched novels of social protest as page-turning crime fiction. *The System* is grade-A Gattis, by which I mean totally authentic, whether we're cutting corners with a conflicted cop or following a reluctant gangster into a terrifying prison war. This book blew my mind.'

Dan Slater, author of *Wolf Boys: Two American Teenagers*

'*The System* is as real as it gets – often brutal, but a beautifully written reality of not only life on the street, but also getting caught up or working in the justice system. Absolutely brilliant how Ryan Gattis was able to accomplish such streetwise authenticity. It makes one wonder whether he lived the life on one side or the other.'

David Swinson, author of *The Second Girl*

'*The System* is a tour de force that shatters all the usual categories: It is a page-turner, but one you will want to read slowly in order to savor every gorgeous sentence. It's got bad guys and good guys, but you're never quite sure who belongs in which category. And if a novel is magical when you feel like you know the characters intimately and like them despite the fact that they are mostly people you would ordinarily cross the street to avoid, then Ryan Gattis is a magician.'

David R. Dow, author of *Confessions of an Innocent Man*

'*The System* took me back, powerfully, to my incarceration in the early nineties. Wow. I relate so much to this book, it's painful. I could swear I did time with one of these characters in County. That's how real this novel is. I had to keep reminding myself it was fiction. Front to back, it's not just an incredible work, it's an experience. Especially for those with no idea what it's like to be inside.'

Gustavo "Goose" Alvarez, author of *The Pawn* and coauthor of *Prison Ramen*

'A stunning and unique achievement. *The System*'s panoramic approach – eschewing one main character for a whole set of people associated with a crime – sets it apart and shows how a single crime reverberates through a whole community. At the center of this dark story is a tale of redemption, an examination of loyalty, and a love song for family bonds. It's brilliantly done.'

Patrick Hoffman, author of *Clean Hands*

THE
SYSTEM

THE
SYSTEM

Ryan Gattis

PICADOR

First published 2020 by MCD Books,
a division of Farrar, Straus & Giroux, New York

First published 2020 by Picador
an imprint of Pan Macmillan
The Smithson, 6 Briset Street, London EC1M 5NR

Associated companies throughout the world
www.panmacmillan.com

ISBN 978-1-5098-4383-1 HB
ISBN 978-1-5098-4384-8 TPB

1 3 5 7 9 8 6 4 2

A CIP catalogue record for this book is available from the British Library.

Printed and bound by CPI Group (UK) Ltd, Croydon, CR0 4YY

Visit **www.picador.com** to read more about all our books
and to buy them. You will also find features, author interviews and
news of any author events, and you can sign up for e-newsletters
so that you're always first to hear about our new releases.

For Roger Cortez

For neither life nor nature cares if justice is ever done or not.

—PATRICIA HIGHSMITH

THE SYSTEM

In the United States, the term *criminal justice system* refers to the institutions through which an accused offender must pass—until the accusations are either dismissed or proven, and punishment is assessed and completed.

The system consists of three distinct entities:

1. Law enforcement, e.g., police and sheriffs.
2. Adjudication (courts), e.g., judges, prosecutors, defense lawyers, and clerks.
3. Corrections and supervision, e.g., jail or prison staff, probation officers, and parole agents.

They operate together in order to maintain the rule of law in civilized society.

*****

When you are caught up in the system in Los Angeles County, you are at its mercy.

While in custody, your body is not your own. It belongs to the county.

Your necessities are county-issued. Your food. Your toothpaste. Even your clothes.

You sleep where they tell you to sleep. Get up when they tell you to get up.

If you or your family have no money for bail, you remain in jail until trial.

Depending on the backlog of pending cases, this can last months.

*****

In 1993, California housed 15 percent of the U.S. jail population—more than any other state—and within its correctional institutions, a shift was occurring.

One that had been building for many years.

Organized prison gangs sought to direct the criminal activities of street gangs from behind bars, and as they became successful in doing so, power moved from the streets to jails and prisons.

These prison gangs offered an affiliation model, and its reasoning was simple: if they could control the environment behind bars—the worst possible consequence of criminal behavior—then they could control almost anyone, anywhere.

This is the story of one such crime—those accused of it, those who witnessed it, the law enforcement who investigated it, the lawyers who prosecuted and defended it, and those left behind on the outside.

PROLOGUE

THE ALIBI

and this is no dream

just my oily life

where the people are alibis

and the street is unfindable for an

entire lifetime.

—ANNE SEXTON, "45 MERCY STREET"

Jacob Safulu, a.k.a. Dreamer

Angela's never sat me down and looked at me like I'm a problem she finally solved before. She hasn't said anything yet, but I feel her words on their way to me like how I can feel a punch is coming. Inside, I'm already trying to get out of the way.

"This isn't easy for me or anything," she's saying, and I know it's the windup before she hits me with, "but I need you to move out, Jacob."

That's the knockout right there. It's over. Done.

When Angela makes decisions, they stay made.

What she's doing right now is dumping me and making me homeless in the same swoop, but all I can think of is how the microwave's beeping. This new one I got off a homie last week. It's from Japan. Good shit. Digital. It's got this thing where it reminds you if you don't get your food out. That's what it's doing right now with her macaronis. It's beeped twice already. The sound of it reminds me how that monitor sounded on my homie before his heart just stopped.

Tiny Gangster, R.I.P. Southsider. A real Lynwood rider. Un matón grande.* Toughest fool I ever met. And remembering that mixes into right now, and this hot hard pain sticks in my chest. Like a fire rock.

Angela snaps her fingers in front of my eyes.

"Hello?" She's getting heated. "You paying attention to me, or what?"

Beep.

I come back with, "Or what."

She rolls her eyes at me. She used to love how I made her laugh. Now she's got a look like me even trying is just . . . sad.

"You see how this isn't working out, right? You get all immature when you should be serious. Is everything a joke with you? Cuz I need somebody who can be more than one thing, like somebody who can deal with real shit *and* be all romantic with me."

---

* A glossary of terms can be found at the back of this book.

"Listen." I grab one of her hands. It's cold. It don't want to be between my palms, I can tell. "I can be better. I can be all that. Buy you flowers."

Angela pulls her hand away. All I ever heard from homies is how she's too good for me. How she's older. How she's the prettiest around by far. How she's going places. Even Wizard says all that. Over time that messes with you. And I'm regretting ever leaving Little's house, ever having that big-ass fight with his mamá about how I wasn't ready for this type of thing yet. Living with a girl, at seventeen? She wasn't about it. I did it anyways.

Beep.

I smile again. Not at her tho. At my feet this time. I talk at them too, like, "So, if all of a sudden I was serious, this wouldn't go different?"

"No," she says to me, "we already crossed those bridges."

"So why you want me to be different when you're pulling the plug?"

She's leaning forward. She's looking me hard in the eyes. "But *is* this you? Or is this just what your homies want from you?"

I kind of retreat, like, "Whatever."

She ain't letting it go. "Remember that time you got caught up moving those TVs?"

I got to trip on that for a second. It was after the riots. After I maybe helped burn down that Jack in the Box on MLK. There was a storage shed in the hood, one full of shit we'd rounded up. Homies were coming all hours to fill it. That was laughs.

She's saying, "Remember how you acted like you could be the one to find a buyer since Jellybean wanted to see who'd step up? You came with this big smile like you could fix it."

Shit. I remember. I tried to sell everything to this old Korean lady with an appliances shop on Long Beach and that lady called the sheriffs on my ass. What Angela's not saying is how Wizard's advice came in real good. Not having tattoos. Not being on a gang card. Not being photographed or FIed. There's no evidence of me being affiliated. Sheriffs didn't even pick me up, cuz I'm a sleeper like that. And, besides, Mrs. Hong couldn't pick anybody out of a lineup, anyways. She picked some pineapple-headed paisa, I heard.

Angela's staring at me. Wants me to say something. I don't have the right answers for her, so I don't. I just wait for a beep. There isn't one tho.

She puts her head down and brings it back up by pushing all her hair away from her face in a wave. She's all, "Thanks for making this easier."

All I got left is hurt. That's the shit making me say, "I mean, at least I can do that, right? You're welcome."

She gets this wiggly look on her face like she's not sure what to say. And I get that. It's how I feel too. I know I fucked up. A lot. I messed around on her with Tiny's cousin Giselle when I was high. It's more than that tho. Angela's always been after me to change it up, to be up out of the streets. Get a job. Or go to school.

"It's like you're still wearing a mask around me," she says, "of what you think I want to see."

The beeping's done for good, I think. I'm remembering how all it ever does is five. It doesn't go on forever or anything. That gets me thinking how maybe everything's on a timer. Not just me and Angela. Everything. Ticking down. Running out.

So I figure why not be real with her if . . . if that's what she wants?

So I'm leaning forward, saying, "All I got is this burning feeling right here since the moment you said what you had to."

She nods, like whatever, she don't believe me.

"I'm serious," I say. "Just . . ."

She bites her lip at me, wondering where I'm going with all this.

I say, "I wish you luck. In life, you know? All that suerte. For real. Just please don't be messing around with no homies. I can't handle that. For real, that's not . . . I mean, nobody needs that. Not me. Not you. Not Wizard. Not whoever the fuck ends up being next. Okay?"

She don't need me to say that nobody needs another Tiny Gangster situation. Shot six times. Lying up in St. Francis till his body gave up. No match for some bullets that his girl's ex put in him.

I say, "So I'm gonna go now, all right? I'll grab my shit some other day."

She blinks. And I see how she's crying. And that gets me. Cuz this whole time she's been so cool and calm and grown with dropping this on me. A couple tears letting go, running down her cheek. I wanna wipe them off. That's not for me to do anymore tho. She's looking at me now in a way that says how she's feeling my pain and feeling bad for causing it at the same time. But fuck that. She did it. And it's done. And it's been burning me inside how Little's mamá was right all along.

"I guess," Angela says.

"Okay," I say.

And I just get up, like a man, and I carry the weight of all the stupid shit I done, cuz there's no other choice. Cuz you have to. Always.

And I turn my back on her and walk out that front door. I bounce.

And I don't fucking look back . . .

PART I

THE CRIMES IN QUESTION

When citizens destroy neighborhoods because of rage and we are asked to "understand" and "sympathize," what we are being asked is to have compassion for rage. Well, what about the rage of the cops who see their efforts thwarted daily by a system that returns an endless parade of human debris to the streets to commit more crime? . . . How about a little "understanding" and "sympathy" for them and what they face every day? At present, there is less than one chance out of a hundred that a criminal who commits a serious crime will serve time in jail. Law-abiding people are fed up with this.

—RUSH H. LIMBAUGH III,
THE WAY THINGS OUGHT TO BE (ABRIDGED)

1

I'm standing on the corner of Josephine and Long Beach Boulevard saying to myself how I need to walk eight houses down Josephine or I'll die. And right then is when this earthquake goes off inside me. It bends me in half. Feels like my bones are breaking from the inside. I got to use the sidewalk to hold myself. I got to put two hands on concrete and it's cold and I'm looking like I'm trying to be an animal on all fours.

These earthquakes I got are major. Every one's like a mouth in the middle of my body trying to eat what's left of me. And this one's swallowing me up.

It lets me go and I know I need to be moving before another comes. I wipe my nose on my shoulder when I feel wetness going down my lip and I'm real glad when I find it's not blood.

A car rolls up slow. Lights hit me in my eyes and I flinch out of them. It's got the windows down and some girl singer's singing out the speakers. I can hear it. But I can't tell the words.

"The fuck's wrong with this fool? He's got them malias or what?"

I hear that from the driver. And then he's gone. The lights too.

Me and him both know how this's no neighborhood to get caught in being dope sick. South of the new 105 like this? Off Long Beach like this? This is gangtown shit. After dark? That's asking for bad things to find you.

And I sure as hell'd not be here if I had other types of options.

But this is what happens when you sleep for a day and a half and you wake up and you need fixing up worse than you ever needed anything.

I feel the next earthquake coming in shaky at first. Like a little aftershock. So I lean on a wall I got next to me and ride it out like I'm in a storm. I'm five houses down now. Almost there. Holding a wall and looking like I'm trying not to get picked up by some hurricane winds.

The smell of beef comes at me. Meat. It's Tam's. Or it's Tacos Mexico.

And my stomach's acting like it's grabbing on that just to mess with me. The earthquake right after is the worst one ever. So bad I think I'm gonna scream right there.

I would. But it wouldn't make the pains better. And it wouldn't fix this calling I got inside me. The calling's more major than major.

It's above the pain. Around it.

The calling pushes my steps and I fight right through some type of spaz move that makes my legs go sideways but I somehow keep walking. I'm used to these pains. I hate them. But I know them. And always the calling's on top of me. It's a need. Up there with breathing.

I worked nights in the port. Till my accident. I know how the night sounds of the boats go. And these feelings are like the front ends of foghorns. All up. No down. Not *beeeee-uhhhh*. Just like a *beeeeeee* that trails off. *That's* how dope calls me. How it keeps calling me. How it's out there in the night and telling me to come to it. Telling me if I get there I can keep floating after.

And that's what makes me get to this door right now. And knock on it. I know better than to do it at night. Than to do it here. But I got to. It's do this or die. It's talk to Scrappy or die. That's what my stomach's saying. What my brain's saying. They're both agreeing on how I got no options left.

So I knock on the metal screen door and it rattles and then I lean all over the house and tell it to hold me.

The first person opening the door is a little kid. A boy with no shirt on. Behind the screen I see him with a popsicle in his mouth and he blinks at me.

That's when I hear somebody shouting, "No!" and coming at us from the living room.

And me and him both know how he's in trouble for opening the door at night. And the little boy turns in time to catch a swat across his butt from Scrappy.

Scrappy's looking pissed too. Only in a T-shirt and shorts. No bra. But she got a game face on. All types of anger come at me through the holes in the metal screen.

"Bitch, get on," she says. "I got nothing for your hype ass."

She slams the door in my face. I feel the air from it hit me and I know then that this's what it feels like when you're drowning and somebody motors up to you in a boat and looks at you sinking and then rides off.

It's fucking humiliating. It's sad. It's embarrassing. It's everything at once.

But then another earthquake hits me and nothing else matters.

Fuck Scrappy. I decide that right now. I'm here. I'm gonna do whatever till she comes out. I don't even care. You kill me? Fine. You're putting me out my misery.

I go to the window and start tugging on that wood shutter it's got attached. I'm yanking on it. I'm putting my weight on it. And it makes this goddamn terrible sound. This sound that's like teeth scraping when one of the hinges decides to break out of the stucco.

I feel bad about that. I do. But I keep going.

I see bodies through the white curtains at the windows and then the curtains open. And it's got to be Scrappy's mother or whatever. And it's Scrappy behind her looking horrified and telling me to get the fuck out with her eyes but knowing I'm not about to. Knowing I'm all the way in and she better deal with me before I fuck shit up for her worse.

Right then I fake like I'm about to upchuck everywhere. Like I'm about to be Scrappy's big problem if she leaves me out here. She sees in my face how I'll be on this lawn all night. I'll use her mom's bushes like a bed. And maybe I'll be there in the morning to deal with. I'll either be dead and she'll need to call an ambulance and have authorities through here and answer questions or just run my ass out right now.

We have this moment right after another earthquake hits me and I got to stare at her grass and how it's had no water in weeks. How it's mostly dirt. And then I look up and we stare at each other and we both know how we hate each other but we know how it goes.

This's the game. I need something bad. So bad I'll do whatever has to be done for it. She knows that and she knows she has what I need to get fixed up. And she knows she better give it to me because I definitely got nothing to lose. I'll fuck her whole house up from outside. What's she gonna do? Call some sheriffs?

She points at me and slings her arm like she wants me to go across the street and then she pulls the curtains closed fast and I walk back a little.

I lean on the mailbox. I got a stitch going in my side from my hip to my ribs. It's real quiet outside too. And I'm feeling eyes on me but fuck them. I look left. I look right.

I see a car down the block turn the front lights off but I don't know if it was the car from before or a new car or a neighbor or what. Don't care either.

When I look up again? Scrappy's coming at me from the side of the house. She's got a hoodie on now. And jeans. And she's coming at me *hard*.

She's whisper-shouting, "What the fuck you thinking, trying to come at my pad like this?"

BAM. She gets me good in the stomach with a fist I don't even see swinging and I go down on where there should be grass but there isn't. And the funny thing is how it feels good almost. How it's not so bad as the quakes. It takes my mind off them. And I laugh.

She hates that shit. She kicks out at me and gets me good in the ribs where my stitch was. That I don't laugh at. I just lose everything I got in my lungs and collapse into the dirt of her shitty front yard. I go into a ball till she gets sick of kicking at me. And she's trying to catch her breath.

"You fight like a fucking closed envelope," she says. And she spits next to me.

I pull out a wadded-up twenty and I hold it out to her. Like some flag of surrender.

She scoffs at that shit.

I unwad it. I try to make it flat between my hands before she snatches it and turns like she's trying to go back inside that house. And you know I can't let that happen.

"I'll break the rest of your shutters off. I'll fuck your garbage cans all up," I say around some groans.

"You do that shit and I'll kill your ass, Augie. Dumbass fucking gabacho!"

But she doesn't step up to me. She's shaking her head. And me? I hang on her every little move when I see her go into the pocket and rattle out a plastic bag with my name on it. When it's out in the air, I don't see anything else. Not streetlights. Not her. Nothing.

Only that plastic. Only that little bit of what's inside it.

She throws it on the dirt and I go after it hard to get it in my hand. Like it's a World Series catch and I fucking won the whole thing for making it. I smile so hard after that it's like my face is gonna fall off.

Scrappy's above me. Kicking at my foot but not hard.

"Hey. You ever walk up here again and you're going in the hat. I don't even care." She puts both hands in her pockets and turns.

I get another quake where I'm sitting on my knees but I don't feel it so much anymore. Not when I'm holding.

Because I'm up right after that and I'm walking back the way I came as fast as I can.

I don't get too far when I hear some running footsteps and at first I'm thinking how they're for me and I'm throwing the baggie in my mouth and getting it wedged up against my cheek but then I hear a guy's voice.

"Scrap!"

That's all he says. It's not much. But it's loud.

And it's enough to get Scrappy to turn. And I'm turning too. Back up the street to face Scrappy's house. And that's when I see two people walking at her and one of them's raising up a hand and there's a pistol in it and I'm flinching back quick. But it's too late.

I saw the guy's face. It's Wizard. And I'm fucking mad I just had to see that and mad he's not covering his face or anything because that's not good shit for me to be knowing and I'm getting right up behind the wall I had to lean on before when that fire spit comes from the barrel and goes white in the night.

One bang from the sidewalk. And Scrappy spins from that.

One from the middle of the dirt where I fell before. And she's going down.

One from up close. When she's already down.

I'm thinking how that was major when the gun's getting dropped at her feet. Still smoking. My ears're ringing. Dogs in people's backyards are barking as loud as they can.

And Wizard and the other guy are running for a car. The other guy with a hoodie on. It's a yellow Lakers one. The car's starting. And that girl's singing again. And then they're gone. Not fast. Not screeching. Slow. Like they'd done it before. And that makes sense because Wizard's real cold. He's done all this before, I heard.

And I got adrenaline buzz all over me. It's pushing my pains down. It's making me run to stand by Scrappy and see how she ain't moving but she's breathing. So I roll up close to tell for sure.

But when I get there is when the door opens and her mother starts screaming. I try to tell her how there was dos muchachos here just now but that shit gets tangled up in my mouth.

"Telefona ambulanza!"

That's what I end up saying. I say it twice for her to get me. But it helps with her knowing how I'm just the same dumbfuck from before. I didn't do this. Couldn't have.

She leaves the door open behind the screen when she goes for the phone. And I see the kid seeing his mom. He's holding the popsicle stick. He's got orange on his mouth. I can see that from the lamplight over the porch. He doesn't even know what he's seeing, and that's good. That's lucky for him.

Because I'm trying to put myself between him and Scrappy because she's bleeding here right in front of me. And I'm seeing how she got one in the leg now. And one in the stomach. And one in like the upper shoulder by her neck. She's got all types of bloody mud around her when I push both her hands onto her stomach.

"Hold there." It's like an order when I say it. "Hard as you can."

A knife's in the grass by her that she must've had and it fell out somehow. I grab that up and cut off some of the lower leg of her jeans and rip it into a strip and from the cuff. Baggies fall out and then I tourniquet the thing onto her thigh pretty good and fast.

"You'll be okay." I tell her that.

I count the baggies on the ground. There's three.

And I tell myself how she doesn't need them now. Look at her!

She shouldn't have opened that door up late at night.

"You'll be okay," I say again.

She knew better.

And bleeding like that? Look! She's not needing anything anymore!

But I do.

My heart's going like crazy. I feel it every other place in my body. In my ears. In my throat. In my toes.

She's got tears going. She's closing her eyes.

"Motherfucking Wizard." She says that.

And that's making my stomach drop right then. Because of course she had to see him from that close.

"You'll be okay. This ain't shit." I don't see her react to what I'm saying.

She ain't gonna be okay but I don't say that.

And I'm going through those pockets of hers and I'm grabbing up every baggie in there but that's not enough. My lip has got the itchies. So I bite it when I'm unrolling her other jean cuff and more baggies are falling out and I'm pocketing them till I don't have enough room anymore and then I'm putting them in my socks.

I'm thinking about how I should've gone all up in her underwear to check her for more but there's no redoing that tourniquet now, so I'm ripping her shoes off and pulling the liner things out and there's two more baggies each and I'm scanning after that and not really thinking because then I got the gun in my hand.

And I don't even give a fuck about fingerprints till I'm holding it and thinking how that's probably bad and how I probably shouldn't have but it's also too late. So I got to do what I got to do. And then I'm thinking how even that doesn't matter so much as what it's worth.

What I can sell it for. If I clean it up. If I don't say where it's been. Or how I got it.

I'm thinking on that when I try to run. Try to make one leg go in front of the other fast.

Because it's just a gun I found. And anybody'd pay something for that.

Anybody.

2

When I park and turn the car off, Rush Limbaugh's tape cuts out. The first stop on my shift is Augustine Clark, a new case I got saddled with because Martinez (supposedly a hard-charger) is away on maternity leave, and she isn't married or even *with* the baby's father anymore, which is just complete nonsense. Frankly, any feminazi is welcome to explain how Martinez deserves to get paid as much as me when I have to do twice the work to make up for her being gone for months when I get no extra time off. Sure, she's got two years' seniority on me, but do I get overtime working her cases, at least? Nope. Budget restrictions mean I'm expected to handle four of her parolees in addition to what I've already got in terms of caseload. This is what happens in America now. White men pick up after everybody else. We fix things, quietly, while the lazy complain and get handouts. I'm sick and tired of it.

I open my door and get out. I thumb through Clark's Parole Field File with my head on a swivel, checking my immediate vicinity for threats (the parking lot of the Islands Motel on Long Beach Boulevard in Lynwood, but nothing is stirring just yet, too early), as I familiarize myself with the man: CDC# is R19237, height is five-foot-seven, weight is one hundred and thirty, born 1953, street address is the same as this one but most definitely not the halfway house Martinez recommended (which she should've caught, frankly), place of employment listed on his Initial Interview Form is *Working on it* (no shit, he actually wrote that), listed monthly income is worryingly low even with *for 15 years in the Navy and disability* written beneath it, description and license of vehicle is *Not applyable*, and I can only assume he misspelled it. His rap sheet is: possession of a controlled substance '87 (six months served), possession '88, possession '90, burglary '90 (two years), and possession '92, which resulted in his latest stretch, from which he was released five months early, likely for overcrowding, but they're calling it *good behavior* on paper, what a joke. None of these scumbags do real time anymore.

I flip the paperwork back down and close the Field File. When I get out of the car, I open the trunk and drop the manila folder on top of my field book binder before slamming the trunk and locking it. I finish my coffee and leave the disposable cup sitting on the trunk when I don't see a nearby trash can, because I'm no animal.

I knock hard, because this scumbag on the other side needs to know it's time to get checked by a pro.

When the door opens, a smell comes out first. Rank staleness is how I'll describe it in the write-up, likely an accumulation from re-wearing clothes without washing and food waste. These are not good signs for sobriety or doing parole the right way. Already I'm liking his chances for recidivating.

This feeling is compounded when I see Clark behind the door, bowing his balding head. He's unshaven, hasn't had a haircut in weeks. It's a Tuesday, and he's not ready to go out and look for work (obviously), which calls into question what he was up to last night.

I say, "What's your CDC number?"

"R-one-nine-two-three-seven." He says it hoarsely. "You can call me Augie."

"Augie, I'm Agent Petrillo from the South Central Parole Unit. You can call me Agent Petrillo. Don't confuse the fact of me being friendly with being your friend. I'm here to do a homecall. I'm handling Agent Martinez's cases now. I see you didn't report to the parole office last week as instructed. Why not?"

"I-I was sick," he says.

"Failing to report is a serious violation. That alone is enough to issue a PAL warrant. That could mean a year in custody. And with your criminal history, that would be straight time."

He's been on parole three times. He knows PAL is short for parolee-at-large. I don't need to explain it.

I look around the room: piles of clothes in each corner, empty Gatorade bottles around the television, food wrappers everywhere. It's a rathole.

I say, "This isn't the halfway house my partner recommended to you. Is it, Clark?"

When he doesn't respond immediately, I step into the room, extract a penlight from my pocket, and shine it in his eyes.

He jumps back, hits the wall by the bathroom door, and essentially sticks to it. He's got his palms over his eyes when he says, "C'mon, man!"

"What's going to happen if you test?"

He's been using. No doubt in my mind. Still, I always have to ask first. Give them a chance to be honest. It's only fair.

"I-I don't know, Agent Petrillo."

"You're lying, Clark."

"It's Augie. Just Augie. Please?"

His pupils are constricted. I'm near the light switch, so I flick it off, and I flash Augie in the face with my penlight.

"I'll be noting for the purposes of my report that your pupils appear nonresponsive to direct light, and I have reason to believe you have been using a controlled substance and violating your terms. I need to search the premises."

"C'mon, Agent Petrillo, man!"

He's busted. He knows it. It's just a matter of how long it takes me to find what's worth finding. For my own safety, I pick a wooden chair for him that's out of reach of the dresser and the bed, and far enough from the door that I can fuck him up if he tries to run.

"Sit," I say.

He does, so I glove up. I consider cuffing him, but decide not to. I survey his immediate surroundings for a weapon: a knife, anything. There's nothing. I keep one eye on him as I toss the bed. I check inside the pillows, between mattress and box spring, and every drawer of the nightstand. Nothing. I do the big dresser. I pull it out. I go behind the television. I do the closet. Nothing. In the bathroom, I find his kit: a rig-needle, a bent spoon with some residue, some dirty cotton that looks like he tore it off a Q-tip, and his tie-off.

This alone is enough to cancel his vacation from prison. He's looking at a year flat. No good time. No work credits. And he does the whole 365.

"You're fucked, Augie," I say. "You're going back for a bullet."

"I-I know," he says.

I'm not done, though. I kick at the carpet. The far corner comes up and I pull. Underneath is the glue and white bits of carpet base, but nothing else. I flop the carpet back, but something's not right with how it goes down. It's not entirely flat. I kick at it again, but it doesn't sit, and what's more, the baseboard moves, so I kick that too, and it jiggles.

I look to Augie. He's frowning, and looking like he's about to cry.

"What am I going to find, Augie?"

He digs his knuckles hard into his forehead.

"Fuck," he says. "Fuck!"

I pull the baseboard back with my fingers, careful not to poke myself on any nails still attached to it. When I've got it all the way off the bottom of the wall, I can see into two little hidey-holes, roughly eight inches long and two inches high. Inside one is ten plastic baggies. Inside the other is a gun.

I pull my weapon and am gun-pointed on Augie. My heart thumps up in my chest as I go from zero to high-order violence. "Get the fuck down, now!"

Augie slides out of the chair and collapses onto the carpet face-first. He prones out and I cuff him hard. That's what he gets for not telling me.

"You knew I was going to find that! Why the fuck didn't you tell me it was there? You're lucky I didn't shoot you!"

I holster up. I take a few breaths to calm down. It doesn't work.

I say to him, "You're sitting on a sales case for that many baggies *and* a felon-in-possession charge. That's definitely double-digit time."

Augie doesn't have an answer right away, and that's okay. He doesn't have to, but I need to call this in to the sheriffs. I cross the room to the phone, and I'm about to pick it up when he turns his head, opens his mouth to spit out some carpet twine, and says, "What if I knew something, man?"

I stop. I say, "Knew something about what, Clark?"

"A worse crime," he says. "Some major shit."

"That's not something I deal with. Now let's get you that ride and get you going."

There's a phone on the bedside table. I pick up the receiver.

"You know Wizard?"

When he says the name, I feel it in the base of my spine like somebody kicked me with a steel-toed boot, and then I feel a tingle. A tingle I know well.

I put the phone down. Everybody knows Wizard. You spend time in

Lynwood, you hear the name, but there's something else: he's one of my original parolees since I transferred here a year ago, after my incident.

I say, "What about him?"

"I-I saw Wizard and another guy kill a girl last night," he says, "with that pistol."

I don't hide my disbelief when I say, "You're telling me you took a gun from a crime scene?"

"I was gonna sell it," he says.

The second that's out of his mouth, I laugh at the idiocy of it, but then something else grabs me: the thought of having something solid on Wizard, and after that, it's all I can think about.

That little fucker, he's lied to me more times than I can count, but the most maddening thing about it is that I've never been able to catch him in one, because down here in the ghetto, everybody covers for everybody else. They see everything, these neighborhood people, but they don't say *anything*. It's the opposite of a civil society, because these little gangsters run a tight ship. Neighborhood people never give statements on the record, never aid prosecution. These Hispanics, they don't have values like we have values. They'll lie like breathing. They'll shoot you for nothing, too. They'll shoot you because somebody told them to. It's the law of the jungle out here. The only way anybody ever goes away for anything is—

An idea hits me then. It stops me cold, and it must make me pull a face, because Augie says, "You okay?"

"Shut it, Augie."

Straightaway, I know it's the best idea I've ever had. It could kill a few birds with one big stone. There's no way anybody stands up about this shooting, not even Augie, unless I make him stand up, because the only way anybody goes down for this is if he points fingers.

Damn, it could be sweet. It could be the sweetest move that ever got pulled.

It could be justice (*real* justice, for once), and a whole lot more. There could even be something for me to take out of it. I could get the best kind of reward. Two things at the same time (something I've always wanted, and something I could punish them with), because if I can get those little criminals out of that house, it'll be open season on Wizard's cousin.

She'll be vulnerable. She'll be alone. She won't have anybody to lean on close by. I've seen how she's looked at me. I know she's thought about me. It's in her eyes. Those eyes always told me something else too: she's the type of girl I can teach things to, and she'll appreciate it.

Augie's got his mouth open, and he's staring at me, so I say, "Who was the other guy, Augie?"

Augie gulps. "What?"

Say Dreamer. I'm trying to send the word across the room to him. *Dreamer. Please, God, just let him say that word.* He's not getting it, though. I have to say, "You said there were two guys. If Wizard was one, who was the other guy at the shooting?"

Dreamer. I'm practically saying it under my breath. *Dreamer. Dreamer. Dreamer. C'mon, Augie, say it. Give me the name of a thuggish little gangster who everybody knows is into bad things but has never gotten a felony on his record. Say Dreamer. Give me the name of Angela's boyfriend, the dipshit living in that house rent-free and getting pussy he never deserved, so I can take him off the board altogether, because whether he was there or not last night doesn't matter. If he didn't shoot somebody then, he'll do it next week, or next month, with no guarantee he goes to prison for it. No, sir. This way, they both get what's coming.*

"Don't know," Augie says. He's looking at the kicked-up chunk of carpet like it betrayed him.

This could mean he knows, but he's not telling me. I decide to prompt him again, but all the way this time.

I say, "Was it Dreamer?"

"I-I don't really know him, not to look at, and it was dark."

I don't say anything. I wait for Augie to bring his eyes back up to my face. It takes a few seconds, but it's enough time for him to know that things might be shifting between us, that maybe he has options after all. My mouth goes dry. My throat, too. What I'm about to say is risky, so risky I'd never even take the chance on it if I weren't telling somebody that nobody else would ever believe.

I say, "You're going to tell them it was."

He just leaves his mouth open. I nod to the plastic baggies.

"All of those bags but one go down the toilet. I only violate you for using. I take you in. You tell the sheriffs what you saw, which I'm sure will make things easier for you when it comes time for your discharge review. The only thing you add to your witness statement is: you tell them it was Wizard and Dreamer you saw last night. Both of them."

He's trying to get his head around it and failing. "But—"

I cut him off. "Get on the right side of the system, Augie. I'm your one shot. I want Wizard and Dreamer gone, and you want to stay out of prison. If we can agree on that, I will make sure this gun gets to the proper authorities so they can prosecute a couple of murderers."

Augie blinks at me. "How you gonna tell them where you found it?"

"Who says I need to tell them anything?"

He closes his mouth then, and he nods right there where he is on the carpet.

We have a deal.

"Good." I uncuff him and nod toward the bathroom. "Now get your kit and fix up a quarter dose, so you're not completely dope sick when they question you."

His eyes bug out at that. He can't believe I'm serious.

I am.

3

The drop goes smoothly. Augie needs one more pep talk to go over the details again, to get them sealed up tight in his brain, and then we go through the front doors and he gets taken into custody. They'll jail him in Firestone Park Station because it's where I bring him. I have better links to people here than the Lynwood jail, and besides, they're having some construction issues anyway. When the detectives are ready for Augie, he'll be in a chair answering questions about what he knows and how he knows it. He's not likely to be the most reliable key witness, given his past convictions and drug use, but if I do what I need to do with the gun, it will all work out by the time he gets to County Jail and gets PCed.

I check with the desk about the shooting. I'm still half expecting it not to be true, if I'm honest. To my surprise, Lucrecia A. Lucero, a.k.a. Lu-Lu, a.k.a. Scrappy, was indeed shot last night at approximately 2120 hours, outside her mother's residence. She caught three rounds. It was good aim, and her shooter was close, but it wasn't the best aim. She lived, just like a cucaracha. She's at St. Francis now, status: stable. The deputy on desk duty let me know that she went in with a tourniquet on her. It saved her life.

I ask if I can head back to the bullpen and leave a note for Montero, one of the detectives I know (not sure what their rotation is, or if he'll be assigned, but it's worth a shot to cover my ass), and I get told that's fine. My note details what I know regarding Augie's statement, that my parolee confessed it to me, and I brought him in on a parole violation as well as to give an official statement. However, since one of my other parolees may have been directly involved in this shooting, I write that I felt it was incumbent upon me to go check up on him with patrol. When I'm done writing, I head back to the front and request a unit.

It takes about twenty minutes to get cleared from above, so I use that time to sit and think about how I'm about to go into Wizard and Dreamer's place to hide that gun a few minutes before finding it there with my sheriff counterpart. If both suspects are there when it happens, okay, they go straight into custody, but that potentially complicates the plant. If they're not there, it's easier to plant, and then maybe I find it on my search because I'm a pro.

And with that in mind, I'm in enforcement mode now. Before I walked Augie in, I switched to my ballistic vest and a marked raid jacket to keep things going high-speed, but also because it is very easy to conceal the .38 pistol under my vest, where it is both accessible and secured.

"Petrilla?"

In front of me is a muscular deputy in the tan uniform they've all got. He must be six-foot, two hundred. He's a black, but he says my name like it's Spanish: the double *l* as a stupid *y*.

"Petrillo," I say as I stand. "It's Italian, and it's got an *o* on the end of it."

"Oh, right." His name tag says JACKSON on it. "What'd I say?"

I give him a look that means: *You know what you said.* "You said it wrong."

"I got you." He looks at me. "Petrillo."

I smile when he pronounces it rightly to show him he did better, but it's more out of relief that I don't have to sort him out. We shake hands. Jackson's got a shaved head that looks like a shiny piece of rock you'd never want to get hit with, and a hand that swallows mine up when we shake.

I say. "So, you got a partner coming along with us?"

He says, "No, he's got a case review thing. It's just us."

"That's fine," I say, and as I turn, I motion for him to follow.

We walk out together. From two minutes of talking to him, I gather that he's fresh off Central Jail duty in downtown, and new to these streets, which is just my good luck.

It's getting toward nine and the clouds have burned off. What's left is a sky that looks dirty-river-blue. I park on Virginia, across the street and five houses before Wizard's residence. Jackson parks behind me. I exit my vehicle. Jackson follows, one hand on his gun and one at his side. I slow my pace, allowing him to walk side by side with me. He's eyes up on the street, looking left and right as we cross. We mean business, and the neighborhood knows it. I feel someone looking at us, but there's no one else on the street.

The closer I get, the more I anticipate seeing her, and I feel queasy. She does this to me.

Across the sidewalk, there's a low chain-link fence with a gate blocking the driveway. It's on rollers. Behind it is what's left of a yard. I approach the gate and open it without hesitation. Jackson can tell I've been here before. We go straight up the walkway and I knock my knock on the front door. We wait.

A plane sails overhead on its way to LAX. The door doesn't have a spy hole in it, but vertical shades in the window next to it shake and then a voice from the other side says, "Who is it?"

To my relief, it's Angela. It's been a week since last I saw her.

I clear my throat. "Parole search!"

Two locks unbolt, and she fumbles with the one on the handle before it turns. She's nervous, I think. I wonder if she knows what her cousin and her boyfriend got up to last night. I think it unlikely, because she's a good girl, but anything is possible. I've seen enough by now to know that. As the door swings open, Jackson rocks back slightly on his heels when he sees Angela standing there in front of us, the soft yellow light hanging above the kitchen table shining through her curls. She's a ten and he knows it.

She's five-six and a former local track star (hurdles).

Every time I see her, I think: *She's better than this. She doesn't deserve this place. I can save her from it.*

Her hair is wet (from the shower, or a bath?). She's wearing a Lynwood High T-shirt, loose white sweatpants, no shoes. Her toenails are painted silver and black.

She works at Tom's Burgers most days, and attends night school for her nursing certificate for elderly care.

Jackson doesn't know any of that. He just knows she's a knockout living with a couple of gangster scumbags.

"Agent Petrillo," she says, gathering her wet hair into a ponytail. "What is it you need today?"

She heard me say search before she opened the door, but now she can see my hand is on my holstered weapon.

I say, "Is anyone else home?"

"No," she says. "Just me."

More relief: it's the best-case scenario for doing what I need to do. I let go of my sidearm.

I say, "We are here to do a parole search."

She steps back from the door. I go first. Jackson walks in behind me and shuts the door.

Angela has seen searches like this before. She's used to the fact that parolees do not have private space. This is the third such search I've conducted since Wizard was released for his conviction of assault with a deadly weapon (ADW) months ago. However, Angela's eyes are wary this time. Never have I brought a deputy with me to do it. She moves to sit at the nearest place at the table, one where a textbook sits open next to a bowl of unfinished cereal.

She waves a hand at me, like she's saying, *Get on with it*, before picking up a spoon.

I don't waste any time. I head straight for the kitchen.

4

I glove up and open cabinets as Jackson stations himself on the other side of the counter, with his back facing me. He's watching Angela for the purposes of officer safety, but it helps that she's gorgeous. I make a show of it because I can't hide the gun in the first place I search. More importantly, I need to be seen searching thoroughly by Jackson so he can later write it in his report. He's my witness. What he sees and does here will help me cover my ass.

There's nothing worth finding under the sink: a box of trash bags, soaps, a bag of dried corn husks. I check the pipes. I feel behind the exposed metal basin of the sink, running my fingers between it and the wall. One time I found a guy's stash this way, tacked to the sink with magnets. Here, there's nothing.

I finish up by going through the mail, facing the table where Angela crunches quietly and turns a page. My eyes aren't on addresses. They're on the base of her neck, and I'm wondering what it'd be like to kiss her there: what her skin smells like, tastes like, how she'd react if I bit.

(*Okay, now,* I say to myself, *settle it down. Go slow. Be methodical.*)

I move to the living room. I toss the couch and check under it, and then put everything back as it was. She doesn't say anything, but I can tell she appreciates it. There's a chair in there I turn upside down. I check the television for loose paneling. There isn't any.

I enter the hallway where the bedrooms are, and Jackson looks to me as I'm about to go into Wizard's room.

He says, "You need anything?"

"I'm good," I say. "I'll let you know if I do."

He's twenty-two, but Wizard's room looks like it belongs to a kid: World Series Dodgers pennant (1988), a Fernando Valenzuela poster, old car photo spreads he ripped out of magazines. He has a small tape player setup and stacks of tapes (rap crap mostly, but some heavy metal and Latin stuff). The first time I ever entered, I thought it was either the room of a person you'd never have figured for prison, or that he simply never changed it when he came back home. I spend extra time in here. I toss the bed. I do the closet next, every inch of it.

I've never been able to ascertain how Wizard pays for the house he lives in, but I'd not be surprised in the least if it was propped up with drug money. I believe his mother owned it (and then she died, or just left?). It'd be good to know that. In case I need to use it at any point.

After I've spent over twenty minutes in Wizard's room, I make my way to the room Angela shares with Dreamer. Before I go in, though, I shoot a quick glance to the front of the house. Angela's still there reading. Jackson's staring at his fingers. Just walking in nauseates me. That a girl this fine wastes her feminine gifts on a scumbag is a fucking tragedy. It's hard being so close to the bed where I know she sleeps. I toss it, but I do it quick and light. I go through the sheets. Angela's pillow is the one with her long hairs on it. I check the door, then smell it. It's cinnamon. My heart goes crazy at that.

(*You can do this*, I tell myself. *Slow down. Breathe. No one can see you.*)

I check under the bed. I check the closet, but I'm done in a moment. Next to it is a poster of Princess Jasmine from *Aladdin*: brown skin, silk clothes. Seeing that? Wow. It's like she's handing me a key to her fantasies. I make a promise that I'll treat her like a princess sooner than she thinks, and I turn to the dresser.

It's old and wooden, with chipped white paint. There's plenty of room between drawers and the base, which is to say that if a revolver were to be placed underneath the bottom drawer, it would not impede the motion of the drawer above it. It could be used normally, and nobody would know it was actually there unless they looked.

I take my time with each drawer. The top one is Angela's. It's full of her underwear: beige, purple, light blue cotton. I want to touch them with my bare hands, but I don't dare remove my gloves. The second is also hers: shirts, skirts, jeans. The third is Dreamer's. The bottom one is his, too. That's the drawer I remove fully from its tracks.

When it's out, I check the door behind me to make sure Jackson's not standing there. I glance at the window. Nobody is watching me.

The drawer feels light in my hands as I transfer it to my left arm just long enough to pull the revolver Augie found from my back waistband. Since my belt is tighter than it has ever been to hide this piece, I have to wiggle the handle (extra, extra carefully) to get the bulky cylinder out from under my belt and vest. When I get it, I double-check that it has three bullets still left in it and three spent casings. I place it on the carpet with all the reverence the gift-wrapped conviction of two worthless scumbags deserves.

I raise my voice. "Jackson? You've got to see this."

Jackson enters the room with Angela in front of him and has her sit on the bed. He looks to me, and I nod at the dresser. His stare penetrates into the cavity where the last drawer used to be, and where the gun is now.

"Would you look at that?" Jackson grins. "I need to call this in."

He looks to Angela. "Can I use the house phone in the kitchen?"

She looks stunned.

"Yeah," she says.

Before he leaves the room, I tell him to also call Montero to see if he got my note.

Jackson goes out to the kitchen. I hear him report the parole violation of Omar "Wizard" Tavira, and the discovery at Wizard's residence of a .38-caliber revolver possibly employed in the shooting of Lucrecia "Scrappy" Lucero. He asks if someone will be sent to photograph and bag it. He apparently is told no, that resources are not currently available, because he says he will preserve chain of evidence himself. Beside me, on the bed, Angela looks devastated. Tears hang on her eyelashes. She looks down, and they fall on her shirt.

I want to hold her. I don't. I can't (not yet).

"I have a camera in my car," I say to Jackson when he comes back in. "I can photograph it."

"Good," he says.

Jackson keeps eyes on the weapon and Angela when I go outside and put new film in my camera. I drag the process out: a photo of the house from across the street, a close-up of the painted address on the curb, a photo of the front door, one of the living room, one of the hallway, one of Dreamer's room, a photo of the dresser with the gun clearly visible inside the hole. I do all this for documentation, but also to make absolutely certain that the gun isn't still warm from my body heat when Jackson picks it up.

Before Jackson bags it, I take close-ups with a flash. He then takes custody of the weapon. As far as the report is concerned, he'll state: *While conducting a parole search of the residence of record for Omar Tavira, Parole Agent P. Petrillo located a Rossi, nickel-plated, .38 Special with a faux-wood handle and the serial number ground down. The gun was removed from the second bedroom, which was unlocked and accessible to Tavira. The gun was concealed inside a dresser located at the southeast corner of the room which roommate Jacob Safulu shares with Tavira's cousin, Angela Alvarez.*

He'll include Angela's DOB as well. He'll also make certain to note how it was found (Petrillo, during a search of his parolee's residence), how it was documented (Petrillo, photographs), and how it was retrieved

(Jackson, using gloves). His report will state that I never touched the weapon; my report will reflect this fact, and reinforce Jackson's statement of events. Our asses will be fully covered.

When we have finished, Jackson says to Angela, "Have you ever seen this weapon before?"

"No," she says.

"Did you know it was here?"

"How could I if I've never seen it?"

That stops him. It takes a second before Jackson says, "Ma'am, would you mind coming to the station with us, so the detectives can ask you some questions?"

It's a delicate moment. If Angela pushes back and says no, he will make it clear to her that he can have her arrested for possession of an unlicensed handgun, as it was found in her room. He will then, most likely, have to cuff her. I hate the idea (it burns inside me; I want to be the first one to put her in cuffs, and only when we're alone and she has begged me to), but it isn't my show anymore. I have to stand by and see how it plays out.

She looks to Jackson, and then to me, and I've never seen any girl look so beautiful as she does right now: helpless, confused, vulnerable. Everything I've ever wanted. It's obvious how much she needs a protector, a real man, *me*. I send her a mental radio frequency that the best thing to do is come in, clear up that it isn't her gun, that she's never seen it before in her life.

We go almost a minute standing there before she says, "I'll come in voluntarily."

PART II

DOCUMENTS FORMING THE BASIS FOR ARREST OF SUSPECTS

Documents create a paper reality we call proof.

—MASON COOLEY

THIS is a taped statement of Angela Alvarez, who resides at ▮▮▮ Virginia Avenue, Lynwood, California 90262. Miss Alvarez has a date of birth of ▮▮▮▮. Statement was taken at the L.A. County Sheriff's Department, Firestone Park Station. Present is Detective Montero, who conducts the interview. Present also is Lieutenant Judith Sakamoto-Hirsch for purposes of observation. Today's date is December 7, 1993. The time is approximately 1315 hours.

MONTERO: [Inaudible] . . . starting the tape. OK. The time is 1315 hours. Present is Detective William F. Montero, Badge number ▮▮▮▮, and Lieutenant Judith Sakamoto-Hirsch, if she would please identify herself for the record?

SAKAMOTO-HIRSCH: Judith Hana Sakamoto-Hirsch, Badge number ▮▮▮▮.

MONTERO: Thank you, Lieutenant. OK. I want to state for the record that, Miss Alvarez, you are not in custody, you are free to leave at any time, and neither are you being charged or held in relation to a crime. Do you understand?

ALVAREZ: Um, I understand.

MONTERO: Good. Please state your full name for the record.

ALVAREZ: Angela Carla Alvarez.

MONTERO: Thank you. And what's your date of birth, Miss Alvarez?

ALVAREZ: ▮▮▮▮▮▮▮▮▮▮▮.

MONTERO: Do you have a current place of employment?

ALVAREZ: Tom's Burgers, but I'm studying to be a nurse too.

MONTERO: That's real good. What nursing school are you doing that through?

ALVAREZ: It's an ROP through Lynwood High.

MONTERO: And what's an ROP?

ALVAREZ: Regional occupational program. It's for geriatric care.

MONTERO: And how long have you been doing that?

ALVAREZ: Um, about a year? I think it's six months to go now. After that, I take the licensure test.

MONTERO: I see. Do you reside at ▮▮▮ Virginia Avenue in Lynwood?

ALVAREZ: Yes.

MONTERO: And how long have you lived there?

ALVAREZ: Prolly I've lived there thirteen years now, since 1980?

MONTERO: Do you currently live alone at the Virginia Avenue address?

ALVAREZ: No.

MONTERO: Since you don't live alone, who lives with you?

ALVAREZ: Um, Omar and Jacob.

MONTERO: Would that be Omar Tavira and Jacob Safulu?

ALVAREZ: Yes.

MONTERO: And do they go by the street names Wizard and Dreamer?

ALVAREZ: I don't really know if I can say about that. To me, they're just Jellybean and Jacob.

MONTERO: Jellybean?

ALVAREZ: When Omar was little, his favorite thing in the world was them. It's like a family nickname, I guess.

MONTERO: OK. Are you aware that both individuals are involved [inaudible] gang here in Lynwood?

ALVAREZ: I don't ask about that stuff. It's not really my business.

MONTERO: OK. Look, how long have you known Mr. Tavira and Mr. Safulu?

ALVAREZ: Um, I've known my cousin his whole life, since he's younger. Jacob? I've known him since prolly five years ago now.

MONTERO: And when did Jacob Safulu move into the Virginia Avenue address?

ALVAREZ: About a year ago.

MONTERO: Are you sure about that?

ALVAREZ: Yes. We got together right before I started nursing school, and he moved in pretty soon after that cuz his mom ran off.

MONTERO: When was the last time you saw Omar Tavira and Jacob Safulu?

ALVAREZ: I haven't seen Omar since Wednesday, but I've been going to work and school, so it's not all that unusual if we miss each other.

MONTERO: And when was the last time you saw Jacob Safulu?

ALVAREZ: Last night.

MONTERO: Last night, Monday, December sixth?

ALVAREZ: Yes. We were together.

MONTERO: And how long were you together last night? Did he leave your company at any time?

ALVAREZ: He left just before nine-fifty.

MONTERO: [Inaudible] at nine-fifty p.m.?

ALVAREZ: Yes.

MONTERO: And how come you know the time exactly, Miss Alvarez?

ALVAREZ: I left some food in the microwave. I meant to eat it before, but we ended up getting into this big talk, so I didn't. After he left, I went into the kitchen and got it, and I looked at the time before I opened the door of it, since it has the clock right on the front.

MONTERO: [Inaudible] talk last night. How was Mr. Safulu acting during the time he was present?

ALVAREZ: He was acting fine until I broke up with him.

MONTERO: You ended your roughly yearlong relationship with Mr. Safulu last night?

ALVAREZ: Yes.

MONTERO: And how did he react to this news?

ALVAREZ: He was real quiet. He just took it.

MONTERO: Was this unusual behavior on his part?

ALVAREZ: Um, I guess so. Yeah. I'd never broken up with him before, so I can't really say . . .

MONTERO: Are you aware that Lucrecia Lucero was shot at approximately nine-thirty last night in Lynwood?

ALVAREZ: No. I wasn't. But . . . wait. If you're trying to say what I think you're trying to say, it wasn't Jacob and it couldn't have been. We were still together then.

MONTERO: Are you certain you were together at that time, Miss Alvarez?

ALVAREZ: A hundred percent certain.

MONTERO: Is it possible you were emotionally upset and not remembering the time correctly?

ALVAREZ: No. I was hungry. I wanted my mac and cheese and I saw the time then.

MONTERO: Do you recognize this gun?

ALVAREZ: I only recognize it cuz I saw it getting carried out in a clear baggie at my house today.

MONTERO: It was collected during a search of the premises. Is that correct?

ALVAREZ: Yes.

MONTERO: And who performed that search?

ALVAREZ: My cousin's parole officer.

MONTERO: Was it unusual for this parole agent to search the house?

ALVAREZ: No. He'd searched it before. Like you said, Omar's on parole.

MONTERO: How many occasions (inaudible) did the officer search the house?

ALVAREZ: I would say five.

MONTERO: Had he ever found anything worth reporting before?

ALVAREZ: No.

MONTERO: But this time he uncovered a weapon in your bedroom. (Inaudible) at the bottom of a chest of drawers. What was it doing there?

ALVAREZ: I don't know.

MONTERO: Did you put it there?

ALVAREZ: Hell, no.

MONTERO: Do you think it's possible that this weapon belonged to Omar Tavira or Jacob Safulu?

ALVAREZ: Um. No. There's never been a gun in the house before. Not even once.

MONTERO: [Inaudible] would you lie to protect Mr. Tavira?

ALVAREZ: No. Jellybean's my cousin, but he's crazy. I don't approve of what he might have been up to, especially if (inaudible), but I just tell him, don't bring drama home, and he doesn't.

MONTERO: And would you lie to protect Jacob Safulu?

ALVAREZ: No. I don't owe him anything. But he was with me last night. What he did after, I don't know. But it wasn't shooting anybody. I know that for sure.

MONTERO: We have not established an exact time of the shooting, only an approximate one. And since he left the residence, and you were not with him after you ended your relationship, is it possible for you to say with certainty where he went?

ALVAREZ: Oh. OK. I see what you did there. No.

MONTERO: And have you seen him since?

ALVAREZ: No. I said we broke up.

MONTERO: Those are all the questions I have for now, Miss Alvarez.

AFFIDAVIT UNDER OATH

I, Augustine Patrick Clark ("Declarant"), am a resident of Lynwood, County of Los Angeles, State of California, and do hereby certify, swear or affirm, and declare that I am competent to give the following declaration based on my personal knowledge, unless otherwise stated, and that the following facts and things are true and correct to the best of my knowledge:

Last night I was on Josephine at about nine o'clock in the evening. I was feeling very sick from drug withdrawals and was just trying to get to see Scrappy. She lives down the block. I knew she could help me feel better. I knew it was a bad idea but I was feeling very ill.

I did not see anyone else on the street at that time.

I visited Scrappy and she came out of the house to meet me on the lawn. We had an altercation. She punched and kicked me because I should not have gone to her mother's house at night. I understood but I wasn't feeling good. I explained that to her. I told her I needed her help to feel better.

I got what I needed after that and I was walking back to the place where I stay. I was walking for not even a minute when I heard someone yell out "Scrap" and I turned back and looked at Scrappy's house. Scrappy was still standing in the front yard and she was looking up to where somebody called her name.

I saw Wizard on the sidewalk holding a gun and aiming it at Scrappy. Next to Wizard was another person I recognized. His name is Dreamer. Dreamer was wearing a yellow Lakers sweatshirt and I could see it even in the night because it was so bright. Wizard and Dreamer are in a gang together and Scrappy is in a different gang.

Wizard shot the gun three times at Scrappy as he walked closer to her. The first shot was from the sidewalk. Approximately twenty feet away. The second shot was from the grass. Approximately ten feet away. The third shot came when he was standing approximately four feet away from her. She was already on the ground then. So he shot down on her.

I watched Wizard hand the gun to Dreamer, and Dreamer put it in the front pouch of his sweatshirt. After that, they both ran away. They got in a car that was parked up the block and drove off slow like they hadn't done anything but they did.

I was worried Scrappy was dead and I ran to her when I could see I wasn't in danger.

I could see that Scrappy had been shot in the leg. She had also been shot in the stomach. And also near the neck.

I was in the Navy so I know what to do in emergencies.

I put Scrappy's hands on her stomach and told her to put pressure there.

I saw how there was a knife on the grass. I don't know whose it was but I thought it was Scrappy's. I opened this knife and I cut away some of her left jeans leg. I used a strip of this to create a tourniquet for her leg. I tied that on tight. She was moaning. She was in a lot of pain.

She also said "Motherfucking Wizard" because she knew he shot her too.

Her mother had heard the shots and opened the door then and I told her in Spanish to call for an ambulance. She went back into the house to do that.

After that there wasn't really anything I could do and I was really scared. I didn't want to be there when the ambulance and sheriffs came. So I ran away.

I swear that the above information I have provided is true and complete.

WITNESS my signature this 7th day of December 1993.

Augustine Clark
Signature of Declarant

SUPERIOR COURT OF THE STATE OF CALIFORNIA
FOR THE COUNTY OF LOS ANGELES

THE PEOPLE OF THE STATE OF CALIFORNIA,

Plaintiff,

v.

OMAR ARMANDO TAVIRA, AKA "WIZARD"

(D.O.B. 07/30/1972)

JACOB AARON SAFULU, AKA "DREAMER"

(D.O.B. 09/02/1976)

Defendant(s).

CASE NO. ▮▮▮▮▮▮

FELONY COMPLAINT FOR ARREST WARRANT

The undersigned, certifying upon information and belief, complains that in the County of Los Angeles, State of California, the defendants committed the following crimes:

COUNT 1 (Pen. Code § 182, Sub. (a))
CONSPIRACY TO COMMIT A CRIME

That on or about December 6, 1993, in the County of Los Angeles, State of California, OMAR TAVIRA and JACOB SAFULU did knowingly and unlawfully conspire between themselves and also with other persons whose identities are unknown to commit the crime of Murder, in violation of Penal Code Section 182, subsection (a), a felony.

The object of the conspiracy was to murder LUCRECIA LUCERO, a human being, for her participation in criminal activities, specifically the sale of illegal narcotics, for a rival street gang.

Thereafter, in the County of Los Angeles, pursuant to the above conspiracy, and in furtherance of the object thereof, the following acts were committed:

OVERT ACT NUMBER 1

On or about December 6, 1993, Omar Tavira, then on parole, did unlawfully obtain an unregistered firearm for the purposes of murdering LUCRECIA LUCERO, a human being.

OVERT ACT NUMBER 2

On or about December 6, 1993, Omar Tavira did enlist the help of Jacob Safulu to participate by driving the escape vehicle so that he could discharge said unregistered firearm with the express purpose of murdering Lucrecia Lucero, a human being.

OVERT ACT NUMBER 3

On or about December 6, 1993, Omar Tavira and Jacob Safulu went to Lucrecia Lucero's residence in the city of Lynwood for the willful, deliberate, and premeditated purpose of murder.

*****

COUNT 2 (Pen. Code § 664/187, Sub. (a))
ATTEMPTED WILLFUL, DELIBERATE, AND PREMEDITATED MURDER

On or about December 6, 1993, in the County of Los Angeles, State of California, OMAR TAVIRA and JACOB SAFULU did willfully, unlawfully, and with malice aforethought attempt to murder LUCRECIA LUCERO, a human being, in violation of Penal Code Section 664/187(a), a felony.

It is further alleged that the aforesaid offense of attempted murder was committed willfully, deliberately, and with premeditation within the meaning of Penal Code section 664(a).

It is further alleged as to count 2 that said Omar Tavira personally and intentionally discharged a firearm, a handgun, which caused great bodily injury to Lucrecia Lucero within the meaning of Penal Code Section 12022.53(d) also causing the above offense to become a violent felony within the meaning of Penal Code Sections 667.5(c)(8).

*****

COUNT 3 (Pen. Code § 245, Sub. (a)(2))
ASSAULT WITH A DEADLY WEAPON (FIREARM)

On December 6, 1993, at approximately 9:30 p.m., in the County of Los Angeles, State of California, OMAR TAVIRA and JACOB SAFULU did willfully, unlawfully, and with malice aforethought commit the crime of Assault with a Deadly Weapon, employing a handgun, in violation of Penal Code Section 245(a)(2), a felony.

It is further alleged that the aforesaid offense is a violent felony within the meaning of Penal Code Sections 667.5(c)(8) and 667.5(c)(12).

*****

COUNT 4 (Pen. Code § 206)
MAYHEM

On December 6, 1993, at approximately 9:30 p.m., in the County of Los Angeles, State of California, OMAR TAVIRA and JACOB SAFULU did willfully, knowingly, and with malice aforethought inflict cruel or extreme pain for the purposes of revenge or persuasion by discharging a firearm three times at LUCRECIA LUCERO, a human being, thereby committing the crime of Mayhem, in violation of Penal Code Section 206, a felony.

Executed this day of December 8, 1993, at Los Angeles, California.

Darrel J. Murphy

Deputy Attorney General

Based on the forgoing complaint, and the Affidavit in Support of Arrest Warrant filed by Detective William Montero on December 7, 1993, I find there is probable cause for the issuance of a warrant of arrest for the above-named defendant(s).

Wan F. Clay Jr.

Judge of the Superior Court, State of California

PART III

EVENTS LEADING TO ARREST
OF SUSPECTS

city of angels

so far removed from heaven.

—LUIS J. RODRIGUEZ, "CITY OF ANGELS"

5

I wake up at Spider's after too much weed. People are asleep all around me. Piled up on each other. On the floor. On the couch. And I get this feeling how I need something good in me, something not in this stale-ass house, cuz this whole last day has been blurred together and right now I miss being at Little Guy's. Chilling with his sister. I can't be dragging my ass over there like a failure tho. Not after I called his mamá a stupid fucking bitch that don't know shit.

Yeah . . . there's no way to be proud of that one. It was mean. I was drunk. That's no excuse tho. I feel terrible about that.

And since I can't be going back there, all I can think of is how I need to be out where the air is. How I need to be moving.

I walk my ass to the Cork N Bottle. Ricky's there. He's behind the register, looking all worn out. Everybody knows he likes to get wet. He nods when I come thru. And I nod him back.

I crack the door open to a fridge case and go in for a beer and he lets me. Doesn't even ask me to pay. I hate the taste of it. I got that cotton mouth tho, so I have another to wash the first one down. Some Miller Lite Ices. Blue cans.

I say, "Those South Gate fools come thru last week?"

If they come just over the road right in front of us, they're in enemy territory. Our territory. Basically, they can't help themselves from running little missions.

"Yup," Ricky says.

"It was on a Wednesday morning like this?"

"Yup."

"I bet they thought they could come thru early and nobody challenges them."

"Maybe," he says.

"What I been hearing is they robbed your ass."

"They did. But it wasn't me working. It was Majid."

I say, "Money's still gone tho, right?"

"Money's still gone," he says, and then, after he opens one of them little headache medicine packets and pops the pills in his mouth, "Hey, you hear Scrappy got popped last night?"

"I heard."

I didn't hear, that shit is news to me. Can't be having Ricky thinking I'm not up on it tho.

"Yup, but did you hear she lived? Word is, your boy did it."

A lot of my homeboys would want to fuck Scrappy up.

"Nah, man, everybody was at Spider's last night," I say. "Bunch of hippie gangsters going all-out on acid and spraying each other with Super Soakers. That shit was laughs."

It don't really matter if he believes me.

I walk around the store like I'm patrolling or something. The buzz is getting into my cheeks already. And I'm remembering how I didn't eat last night. And I don't even know what I'm feeling now. I'm tired of feeling it tho. It's tired but it's this *can't go to sleep* feeling. It's sad but it's *fuck this sadness* shit. It's this *I don't care anymore* shit.

I do tho. I really do.

When Angela said it was done with, that home wasn't home no more, I couldn't sleep there after that . . . It's her place and it's Wizard's. I was there cuz she wanted me, cuz he put up with me, so I went to Spider's. And there was already some kickback going on with blunts and tabs that was turning into a party cuz somebody's cousin was in town from San Diego.

I open the beer case and close it. Open it. And close it.

I like feeling them bursts of cold air making the hairs on my arms stand up.

I think about throwing one more can down. This burp creeps up on me tho. And I know I shouldn't.

Ricky's talking to me about cars, and like some new Porsche or something, I don't really want to hear that tho, so I go over to the tire spot next door and talk some shit to the paisas for no good reason other than I can and they let me. The beer's hitting me as I'm kicking the tires they got stacked in there. They make this hollow sound when I do that, like a *phwoomt-phwoomt*. And I do that for like a minute before everybody goes still around me. And I know something's in the air.

I turn and look out the front where everyone's looking and there's three South Gate fools crossing Imperial Highway, sprinting against the light when there's no cars and holding their khakis up, right on time for another round of stick-up shit on our turf.

I see a broom. In the corner. Next to a mess of tires. I take it up and kick its broom part off. It's longer than a bat, and it's heavy enough. It's wood. I swing it once and it gets tangled up in a chain I didn't see above me. I scare myself with that shit.

I even say, "Fuck!" real loud too and it kind of echoes in there, off the cars and the ceiling, as I untangle it.

The grease monkeys mug like they're about to say some shit. They don't tho. They just step back and watch me go out the garage and around the Cork N Bottle to creep in the back way. I get the door going real quiet and slip in.

6

I see two near the front of the store. One at the back. Near the coolers. He leans forward and looks in. His ass never sees me coming. I step to the side and bring the broom pole down on this fucker's hand. I bang wood off his knuckles so hard he lets go of the door and I kick it straight into his face. His nose and forehead mash the glass and wipe some frozen mist straight off it.

He goes down flat to the floor and I sock him in the neck. One. Two. And he ain't passed out or nothing but he's covering up, so I crank on his forearms. The smacking sounds are like hitting baseballs at a batting cage. Just, *phwak, phwak*. The broomstick's stinging in my hands while I do it, but it feels good too.

It feels live.

I look to Ricky. He's getting low behind the counter. Turning cameras off. Good. Ricky would never call sheriffs on some neighborhood family business. And I'm all over this payback for him. And they know it's on.

The second dude's big but he's slow coming up the aisle at me. He's trying to charge at me like he's played some football or something. I don't even wait for him to get to me tho. I sling the end of the pole into him. Maybe five feet. Or six. And he sees it coming. Tries to stop. Tries turning his face before I catch him with the blunt end.

And I must get this chubby dude flush on the bone or something cuz this line of blood opens up across his jaw. And he starts bleeding bad. Putting his hands on it to stop it.

And then his other homie is jumping over him cuz he thinks he can get to me. And he can . . .

Cuz I let him. I drop the broomstick. I say, "Take the first shot."

And he stops. In the middle of the aisle. He looks at me. And then at his homie trying to pull himself up by the freezer case. And his homie bleeding beneath him. And then his eyes show me how he's thinking, *Fuck it*, and he comes right at me, maybe thinking I'll flinch.

I don't tho.

I take that shit on the jaw. Hard. I feel spit fly out my mouth too. Was a good shot.

And I smile at him. I spit blood. I smile harder.

I been hurt before. I been punched and kicked every way you can be. I been knifed a few times. Been knocked out with a bat to the ear. Broke an arm from a tire iron. One fucker even slung a chain at me once and took one of my fingernails out with it. And I never showed any of those fools that they hurt me.

Nah. You do that? That's you letting them win twice.

And besides, that's not how this world works.

I don't care what you fucking do to me, you don't get to hurt me and then see me hurting.

To this fool standing in front of me looking scared I didn't go down, I say, "That's good, chavala. Shit. Good job."

He don't know what to do with that. He's younger than me. And smaller. And he's realizing how maybe this shit was a trap, and he's backing up. I'm already faking a punch tho. And kicking him in the stomach.

He makes a moan like something ripped inside him. And goes down. That's when I walk back to the broomstick handle and pick it up.

When I bring it down on his ribs, I shout my crew out, like, *This is our hood! Our land*. And none of these punk-asses is ever gonna take it away.

If Angela saw me right now, she'd hate this. I know it. And I'm okay with it.

Cuz if she don't want me anymore, then this is all I'm good for. Being a guard dog. A fighter. I try telling myself that. With my blood up. Banging in my ears.

I'm hearing wheezing and coughing and words like *stop* and *please* and *fuck you*. I tell them to fucking callate.

I thought Angela was my family. That shit makes me laugh now. Cuz she did me exactly how my mom did me. They both ditched out. Just like that.

And that shit's got me all fucked up. Thinking for sure something must be wrong with me. Something must be broken inside me, for people to keep leaving me. Throwing me out like some trash. Cuz you don't throw out good stuff. You only throw out things that aren't good anymore. Things that are useless.

And there's wetness all down my face. I think it must be blood, so I swipe at it.

It's not. It's tears. What the fuck, you know?

And I don't even know what to do with them, so I try to get them off. I swipe at my eyes like a motherfucker.

And when my vision clears up, I notice how the South Gaters aren't in front of me anymore. They're out the front door. Carrying each other. And sirens are coming.

And I'm hearing Ricky behind me. "You better go, man. You better bone the fuck out!"

So I do. You don't have to tell me twice.

I bounce.

I go back into the neighborhood. Down Wright Road and over Los Flores. Where it turns into Duncan. And I'm getting calmer, and my heartbeat's slowing down, and I see how I still got the bloody-ass broomstick in my hand, so I drop it behind somebody's fence. By some pink rosebushes.

And it's not till I'm passing by Borson that I start wondering who shot Scrappy. And why.

7

My new girl drops me in the alley behind Jerry's house, puts some kisses on my neck and ear, wherever she can get at me through her open window, before laughing and speeding off to her mom's house. She's crazy, that girl. I love her to death. But not because she's pretty, because she'd do whatever for me. That's the best part of her. Loyalty is the best part of anybody, and just thinking that, a line hits me. Loyalty being an afrodisiac. I take my little notepad out my back pocket and get scribbling. *Loyalty is the strongest* <u>afrodisiac</u>, *something-something, more addictive than* <u>crack</u>. Instead of writing *something-something*, I just put a long underline to fill in later, then throw my notebook in my back pocket and keep going.

I duck through the side yard of the house next door and come up onto Jerry's porch. Well, it's Jerry's and it's not. He has his name on the paper of this place, but it's all ours. Everybody knows it's clica property. A casita to stash shit. Move shit. It's Jerry's. He lives here with his dumbass dad, but it's not Jerry's for real, no matter how good he brings that money in for us. I'm about to use my key on the front door but I try the handle, and it opens, so I push in and lock it behind. The living room smells like rum. Jerry's dad's on the couch with his arm around one of Jerry's new fresas. She's got shiny shower hair, looking like a wet rag. Below that, she's skinnier than a straw. Crack will shrink you like that. She used to be heavier. That's obvious from the puckers below her short-ass running shorts that she's showing off because her feet are up on this overturned cardboard box. Jerry and his dad used to have a coffee table made of real oak. Now they got this sad shit. And it's not like I even need a reason to let Jerry's dad have it, but this'll do fine.

I tell him, "How many times I tell you to keep this door locked, huh? Thirty?"

"I heard it one time. Now." He smiles at me like he's the man around here.

This motherfucker. I swear, every time he drinks, he forgets who runs what, but he always remembers he hates me. He's got that fixed permanent in his little eyes as he pulls the girl closer like she's a shield against me taking him apart. She isn't. In fact, when he does that, he makes her my target. I point at her, and his eyes go big. He knows what's coming.

Before I even open my mouth he's already recoiling. "Hey, fat man, you really think she's all *that*? With those stretch marks, she's older than old *hat.*"

Her mouth falls open. She's new. She doesn't know I run shit and can say whatever the fuck I want. She's too busy getting all offended. She looks to him, like, *What are you gonna do about this situation here?* And she's about to find out that answer is nothing. He's gonna turn red, is what he's gonna do. He's gonna wait for my next line to hit, so I give it to him. "She's skinnier than a praying *mantis.* Why the hell would you wanna fuck with *this*? She'll bite your head off when she gets a *chance.* She'd rather do that than be in your *pants.*"

His cheeks go red. He's boiling mad, and she's right there with him. She'd cheer right now if he got up to sock me. He'd do it too, if he didn't already know he'd end up at the bottom of the L.A. River for trying, Jerry or no Jerry. We both know the next move is mine. It's always mine, and I can keep landing on these easy targets or I can say what's really bugging me and be done with them.

"The whole reason you're here is to take care of this place, Gordo. If you don't do that, then I'll put in someone who will." I aim my eyes at a big rain stain on the ceiling in the shape of a brain, one that leaked all down the wall in a line like a messed-up spinal cord, and tell him he needs to fix that fucking roof seepage. All I get back is a nod. He's tuned out, but the girl's looking at him now with this look that says, *Is he for real?* And if she doesn't know the answer to that yet, she's dumber than she looks.

I move toward the back of the house, but I don't get far before I have to grab my pad out. I snag what I can remember of the lines I just spit. "Older than old hat. Mantis. Fuck with this. Chance. Pants." And farther down on the same page, I write *big* rain stain *in the shape of a* brain*, spinal cord trailing off.* But is it more like *coming down?* Or *trailing down?* Shit. *Dripping off?* Fuck it. I'll hit at it later. I close my pad. I'm hungry.

The kitchen is busted up. One of the cabinet doors hangs half in the air, connected by only one hinge. I tweak it enough to reach in and grab a bowl out. I find what's left of the Froot Loops and pour. Half a bowl of o's, and half a bowl of busted-up, crayon-looking pieces is what I get. I dig for a clean spoon in the drawer, but there isn't one, so I pick my way around the edges of the sink and find a little spoon that's not too crusty. I use hand soap on that bad boy since that's all there is, wash it until it's squeaky, rinse, and dry the thing on my shirt as I open the fridge. It's empty except for a milk carton hiding at the back. I sniff it, and it's still good, so I pour until it's gone. I take my first bite of cereal, but it's stale as hell and even the milk can't save it, so I set it down on the counter and roll through the back door to go find Jerry.

8

Walking up on the detached garage, I can see through a window how there's three down-ass homeboys standing around, smoking, watching No Neck get tattooed by Jerry. No Neck got named because he doesn't have much of a fucking neck. It's straightforward like that. The audience around him is Silencio, because he always talks at the wrong time, Lil Puffer, because that fool won't ever stop smoking anything you put in front of him, and Dreamer, because he daydreams too much.

Jerry hears the door open and turns to me as some cuts of sunlight come in and run across the room, through the smoke before disappearing right back where they came from when it shuts. Jerry's smiling one of them deceiving type of smiles at me. His teeth are messed up, but that's what happens when you get clocked with a shotgun barrel in your mouth.

He says to me, "Well, if it ain't Mister Gangster-Trying-to-Be-a-Rapper."

"Shut up, fool. Don't make me write about you."

"Only foo here is you." Jerry's got a mouth on him, just like his dad.

He's looking down, dipping the needle in ink, then moving it back to skin. The little engine buzzes. I can see how that tattoo is a skull going onto No Neck's upper right shoulder, so he's got death right behind him. Or about to. And I guess that's appropriate, what with the shit we got up to the other night. The lines of it aren't as good as any of Pint's stuff, with their bug eyes and brochas and general locote natures, but don't say that shit to Jerry. Everybody's got to learn somewhere.

"You know what your problem is, Jerry?" I'm about to tell him. "The fucking roof's leaking and your dad won't fix it. Call my cousin. He'll dry that house out with a fan and re-patch that drywall too. I'm not gonna tell your dumbass dad again. Why's he even living here if he doesn't take care of it?"

"His name's on it. We own it together."

"He doesn't keep it up. You seen that kitchen?"

The tattoo machine stops and Jerry looks to me. "What kind of monster you think I am, man? He's my dad. Can't throw his ass out."

I snap back, "Can't because you never tried, homes."

"Can't cuz he's family. He's a fuckup, but I ain't putting him out on these streets. Have some respeto, fool." Jerry sets his little rig down and comes over to me slow.

I tell him, "You better step your ass back."

"Or what?"

"Fireworks." I cut my chin up at his forehead, reminding him how much taller I am. How I'd be punching down on him if he tried any-thing. "In the air. Behind your eyes. It'll be a real good show before sleepytime, fool."

"Go on and do it, then, foo."

"With them big bags under your eyes, you'd prolly thank me for laying you out. Catch some nice zees."

"You think so?" Jerry grins.

"I *know* so. You started counting sheep yet, or what?"

"I figured you could count them for me." He rolls his neck. It cracks.

Tension chews the room up. Seconds pass with us staring at each other while everyone wonders when we're about to start swinging. No Neck in particular is trying to pop his neck out for a better look. If he did it, it'd be the first fucking time.

Silencio breaks the silence at the exact wrong time. "You really think they're about to go?"

He's not saying it to anyone in particular, he's saying it to the room, and he gets shushed by like three people. But not by me. I'm still staring Jerry the fuck down as I tell him, "I'm just *fucking* with you!"

The laughs are explosive after that. It's a release. Everybody takes some breaths again when I smile and Jerry smiles right back. For real this time. Front teeth still there, but no incisor and no tooth right next to them. I can see his tongue inside, in that hole. I got my hand up after that and we're shaking before throwing it off and going into a half hug. Now's not the time to tell him that family will drag you down and sell you out. My dad's sister got him sent to Folsom and he's still there. That shit happens when you give people too much benefit of the doubt because you got blood between you.

Silencio's talking at me. "Hey, Wizard, did you hear how Dreamer threw down with some fools at the Cork N Bottle? South Gaters too. Three-on-one and he took them. Used a broom and everything. Sweeped those fuckers up!"

No Neck and Lil Puffer laugh at that as Dreamer turns the rest of his face toward me, and, man, it is fucked up and red. Damn. He looks bad. Nose is a swollen-up plum. One cheek's raised up so big, it looks like it's got half a baseball under the skin.

I tell Jerry, "You mind stepping aside real quick? I need to get up with my homeboy right here."

I nod at Dreamer to go outside with me.

9

Wizard's standing by the old wooden fence around the back of the garage. All the smiles he had before are gone. He's leaning in. Eyeing where I got hit . . .

He says, "You look bad."

I say back, "This ain't shit, Wiz. I gave a dude first shot on me and this is all he did."

He shoves me. Not hard. Just to make a point.

"You can't call me that, man. You know I ain't about to be some piss." He's smiling and he's serious at the same time.

I say, "I mean it like you're a whiz, tho. A word whiz. A whiz kid."

"Doesn't matter what you mean. Matters what people *hear*. And the first thing they think of, it ain't math, man, I'm telling you."

"Got you," I say.

He's nodding while he gets a cigarette out of his pocket. He shields the end of it from the little wind there is and lights it. He hits it once.

"Hey, so, someone I know had to step to Scrappy the other night," he says. "You hear anything?"

"From Ricky."

Wizard rolls his eyes like, *Fuck.* "What'd he say?"

"That Scrappy got caught," I say.

"Right. Well, if Ricky knows, every fool knows. He name names?"

"He's too smart to."

Wizard runs the edge of his thumb along this scar on his chin. He got it from busting his jaw up on his own bike's handlebars when he was younger. Just an accident. Now tho, when people ask what it's about, he never says how he got it, so people leap to conclusions. He's always used it as an example of the ways silence can be good for you. Good for everybody.

"The decision came from above, man. She got green-lit and that's that. I don't sit around and fucking question it." Wizard takes a puff. "That's how it is, you know it."

"I know it," I say. I done some stuff on a big homie's say-so that came down from Wizard. Not like shooting. I know how it goes tho. "Ricky was saying how she *lived*."

Wizard looks off to the back door of the house and shakes his head. "That dude runs his mouth. How's he even know?"

"Stacy's sister's a nurse over at Saint Francis, that's how."

Stacy's been Ricky's girlfriend for most of the last ten years. They got a kid.

"Okay, so, I can't run up in that hospital. Half her crew could be in there." Wizard puffs it out for a second, then he says, "You know what? Scrappy making it? I don't see that as a problem. She won't tell. She knows where that bala came from. She knows more can come. Our problem right now is the gun."

The way he says it, it sounds like it's got to do with me. And it better not! I never had a gun, not even to hold for somebody. And I'm getting a real bad feeling about this. My mouth goes dry quick and my stomach rolls sideways before I say, "What gun?"

"The one the person maybe used on Scrappy." He's staring at me, wanting me to read between some lines.

My stomach flops on me. And I get the courage up to say, "This got something to do with me? I need to alibi you or what?"

Wizard looks away. He takes a long-ass drag before spraying smoke out. "Might be nothing. But sheriffs pulled a gun out of your room yesterday."

For a second I can't breathe. And then it all comes out in this kind of cough. My face's getting hot. "Say what?"

"You heard me," Wizard says. "Does anything about that sound right to you?"

"Hell, no!"

"Well, from what I know, fucking Petrillo marched through there on one of his searches, but he brought a sheriff with him to do it this time."

I'm trying to keep my mouth closed and just breathe through my nose. Trying to calm down.

"So he was acting on some information?" I say. "From who?"

Wizard shrugs. Could have been a lot of people dropped a dime to him.

How they'd know there was a gun there when I didn't even know it, is crazy. Unless Wizard's lying to me, which is possible, I guess. He's done it before when he didn't want me to know something. I doubt it tho, cuz he looks worried too. Real worried. And that look on his face isn't making my stomach any better.

"The craziest shit is that it might actually be the gun that got used," he says. "There's a chance."

I lower my voice. "How?"

Wizard holds his hand out in front of him. Open. Palm up. "I mean, I can't see it, but if it was a .38, then maybe it was."

I'm about to say something. I can't tho. I just try to get some saliva back in my mouth.

Wizard takes one last hit. Finishes the cigarette. "That's where it's crazy, because you know whoever did that job did it how Big Fate always said and dropped that gat at the scene."

I say the first thing that makes sense to me. "Somebody's framing it up."

"Yeah," Wizard says, and he's looking at me hard, like he's trying to figure if I'm the one that put him in it.

And I didn't expect that, cuz why the fuck would I do that to both of us? That's stupid.

All I say back is, "You know it wasn't me."

"Can't ever be too sure." He looks at me sidewise before nodding like he's made his mind up. Like I'm still all right.

And when he relaxes, I relax. A little. On the outside. I'm all amped up and scared on the inside tho. This shit is no joke. It's jail. And I never done that shit before.

"Okay," he says, "Tranquilo, you Samoan motherfucker. I don't think it's you. It's somebody. Let me ask you this quick: Did you have a piece stashed there? Any type? Not just a .38? I mean, I know you'd never have one in the same room with Angela, but I got to check."

"Never. Beyond never. You know she wouldn't have been good with that. Shit. I wouldn't either!"

He's nodding cuz he feels the same way. And I know I have to tell him. "You know we're done, right? Me and Angela?"

"Angela called me at my girl's. Said she gave a statement about the gun, and then she told me." Wizard gets his arm around my neck. Grabs me in for a hug. "Fuck. I'm sorry, homes. That shit sucks even more when you might be catching a charge on top of it. Shit. I bet we both will."

He lets me go and I say, "And if that gun's connected to that thing somebody maybe did?"

Wizard frowns hard. "Well, you know how that goes down if it comes, right?"

"Just say *lawyer*," I say.

"That's right. Deal with those cuffs and give them nothing. But for now, you've got to be the hell up out of here. It's too hot. Go to Little Guy's or something. I'll find you."

Just thinking about going over there and facing Little's mother fucks me up even more. I get guilt on top of some pain. On top of all the fear already balling up in my stomach. I still say to Wizard, "I got you."

"Good," Wizard says. "That's good, man."

I got one more question before he goes. "What are we supposed to do about finding out who put this frame on you?"

Wizard has an answer to everything. Not to this one tho.

Not right yet.

10

I go by the Compton tire shop on Atlantic that Omar "Wizard" Tavira listed as his place of employment. All the boss tells me is that scumbag Omar hasn't been in since last Saturday, which figures. I buy a tire gauge on my way out and drive north on Atlantic into Lynwood. It's around Rosecrans when I realize I'm not far from Virginia Avenue, and Angela. What I want to do: go to that door, knock on it, see her face. I still have authority to do so, and even though folks in the neighborhood recognize parole vehicles, they don't mess with parole business.

When the light on Martin Luther King Boulevard is green, I take it as a sign. I turn right, go up MLK, and as I'm passing Virginia, I turn my head to see a sheriff's cruiser sitting on the curb outside Angela's house. I execute a U-turn in front of Ham Park and get some hairy eyeballs from scumbucket "homies" on the corner of Wright for doing it. My pulse is racing now, but not from those looks. It's because I know this is my lucky day.

We don't sit on a suspect's house because we think they'll just come home to get arrested. We do it to disrupt patterns. Humans take risks when they can't sleep or eat where they want to. Pattern disruptions create mistakes, and that's when scumbuckets get themselves caught. Policing presence is important too, though. It rattles certain neighborhoods. Depending on what's going on around that house (say, drug deals or gun sales), it can create pressure from other, larger criminal forces. This can prompt turn-in situations, such as when somebody calls to let authorities know where suspects are because they're sick and tired of having a marked car on the block, messing up their "business."

I don't park. I cruise down the middle of the street, stop directly across from the cruiser's driver's-side window, and roll my window down slow. The car has two uniforms in it. The driver, I don't know. He's a black. I recognize the other one, though: Mirkovich. He's a big Slav, also from Pedro, one who's probably never going to pass a sergeant's exam. I give him a nod. He narrows his eyes at me, but when he finally clicks we've played softball against each other, he nods back.

Their window comes down. I identify myself. The driver makes the connection that I was the one who was here with Jackson and documented the gun.

"Nice catch," he says. "Thorough."

"Thanks," I say. "I'm Petrillo. I've met Mirkovich. He has a mean slide coming into third."

"I bet he does, the asshole," the driver says, and Mirkovich hits him with a backhand on the shoulder. "I'm *Louie*. Spelled L-o-u-i-s. Like the crab."

"So that's French, is it?"

"Haitian," he says, and he looks me over to see if I have a problem with it. I do (we already have enough blacks in this country; we don't need to import them), but there's nothing to be gained from showing it, so I don't. We small-talk: morning weather (about to get colder), the latest in the case (arrest warrants issued for Omar Tavira and Jacob Safulu), Major League Baseball (fuck the labor talks; owners should just pay the players), but there's only so long anybody can talk about a game when it's not actually being played, so I say, "Have you knocked?"

"Yes," Louis says.

"Anybody home?"

"The girl's home. Babysitting. An older woman brought two kids by." He turns to his partner. "About what?"

Mirkovich looks at the clock and says, "Thirteen minutes ago."

"I need to make contact at the residence," I say. "I never got a statement from Miss Alvarez concerning the gun. My boss needs a follow-up."

I get two versions of the same skeptical face staring back at me: one in black, one in white.

To smooth it down, I say, "I'm still Tavira's agent for as long as that lasts. I've talked to the girl on a few occasions. We have rapport. I'm hoping she tells me where they might be, even if she doesn't mean to."

They weigh my words for angles and motives. Good law enforcement suspects everybody, all the time. It's built into their jobs to parse lies just like it's built into mine. We can't help but be cynical until the truth is proven, and since the city set itself on fire not so damn long ago, everybody's under the microscope. Everything's by the book, or else. That's just how it is.

Louis raises an eyebrow at me. "You're not just showing interest because she's one tasty treat, I take it?"

My mouth says, "Just doing the best job I can."

But the wink I add at the end says: *Absolutely.*

Mirkovich in particular finds this amusing. He smirks.

Louis laughs before he says, "Go on, then."

I park the car across the street, and get out clutching my notebook. As I near the door, the vertical shades in the front window twitch.

11

Angela Alvarez opens up before I even knock. When the door swings wide, a rush of air blows through her hair and hits me in the face. She smells like Pert Plus and Ban roll-on. There's a shine to her brown skin, like she's been roughhousing, and behind her, two small children giggle from behind the safety of chairs at the dining table.

This throws me. She took the power position by getting to the door before I did, and though I don't like it, I know I need to let her keep it (for now).

I don't have an opener for her, apart from asking where her cousin and Dreamer are, or asking about the children. (I can claim child endangerment if they are exposed to the suspects.) Both are bad moves: one too stiff, the other too much like a threat. I decide to use my silence instead. Make her speak first. I survey the place from where I'm standing. It's the same as the day I searched it. The only difference is that there's a fan behind her. It's blowing, medium speed, pushing her hair toward me.

She crosses her arms and cocks her chin. "How old are you?"

Her gesture looks confrontational, but she might just be putting on a show for the deputies or the neighbors. At that moment, it occurs to me that it is possible both suspects might be in a nearby house, hiding, watching. That's why every bit of this needs to be as professional as possible.

"Ma'am?"

"I don't know where they are! Haven't heard from them. Haven't seen them." She throws her hands up, and I'm certain she thinks somebody outside might be watching her, too. This is a performance. "So, how old are you, really? Old, or what? You look twenty-five."

She crosses her arms again, higher on her chest this time, while giving me a stony look, but there's something underneath it (attraction, and she's fighting it). It's that, or she's gathering something to tell Wizard or Dreamer later. Still, it's an invitation to deviate from protocol. I watch her watch me. Her gaze darts over my face as I tent my eyebrows and bite my lip (showing her my worry to reveal something personal about myself). She notes this, and her shoulders relax. They drop half an inch. That's why I tell her the truth. It's important to reward her walls coming down, however slow they crumble.

"I'm thirty-six," I say.

She wags her chin at me, like what I said isn't acceptable. "Yeah, right. What year did you graduate high school?"

"Seventy-four."

She does the math. "You graduated at seventeen?"

"I turned eighteen right after graduation," I say.

"Where are you from, Phillip?"

First names already? She moves fast. I want to smile. I don't.

"Phil," I say. "San Pedro. Born and raised."

She hasn't uncrossed her arms. "So, you were a Pirate? We ran against you guys once or twice in sectionals."

"San Pedro High Pirates. That's right."

She shrugs. "Yeah. Is there anything else? Cuz if not, I need to get lunch into these little ones."

I try to hand her my card. I say, "If you hear anything, please do let me know."

She looks down at it, tsks, doesn't take it. "You know I can't do that, Phil."

Angela Alvarez is a challenge, more than Renee ever was. I like that. Makes the hunt worth it.

"I had to at least try," I say.

"Did you?" Her tone is normal (almost warm) when she says it, but her look is not.

She turns and closes the door hard. I hear the kids laugh on the other side. Anyone watching would figure I am no longer welcome here again. It's what she needed to do, given the context of our meeting, and I respect it. I take a few moments to compose brief notes on my pad before going back the way I came: "hostile, unhelpful, claimed not to know where either suspect is, claimed no knowledge of the firearm found at the residence."

When I get back to the cruiser on the curb, they're ready to head out. Mirkovich's window is open this time. He turns his head as I approach.

He says, "Learn a whole lot?"

"Nope," I say. "Standoffish, negative, like she wanted the whole neighborhood to see how well she handled it."

Louis scratches his chin as he looks at the closed front door. "I'd probably do the same in her position."

"In this neighborhood? Shit. I definitely would," Mirkovich says.

I nod. "Well, I got what I need. I'm sure I'll hear when they're in custody."

Louis has no answer to that. He's looking up the street. I follow his eyeline, Mirkovich does too, to a figure standing in a yard three houses up: a child with no shirt on, only long shorts that go below his knees, no shoes. He's approximately ten years old and deep brown from the sun. He should be in school now. He's not. He's staring at us, marking us. We all know our visit is getting reported up the chain to somebody. Good. Let's see what happens to Dreamer and Wizard then.

"Thug-in-training," I say.

"I guarantee we're locking his ass up in a couple years," Mirkovich says.

Louis covers his mouth with a fist and burps before saying, "Man, don't lookouts just get younger and younger these days? What do you call it if it's not nurture?"

I'm about to say *nature*, but Mirkovich says, "Survival."

Louis grunts.

I do, too. "You guys have a good day. Stay safe."

"You too," Louis says as he puts his sunglasses on. His gaze hasn't shifted from the kid, and the kid's not moving either. "You want us to wait until you're in the car and going?"

"No," I say. "I'm good."

Louis starts the cruiser. I walk to my car and get in as they pull off. I execute a U-turn and follow their line as they pull parallel to the kid, whoop-whooping at him with the siren as they drive by. It was meant to scare him, but the kid doesn't even flinch. He stands there, hands in tight fists, as I drive by next. (He sneers when I pass; that's the gall this little fucker has.) In the rearview, I watch him watch me go, memorizing my license plate number, no doubt. When I turn on MLK, he thumbs his nose like a boxer and heads back toward the front door.

12

I take the back way to his mamá's house using the alleys and go see Little cuz Wizard said so. The whole walk there . . . it feels like I'm sick to my stomach. I don't want to go to jail. If they come for me tho, it's not like I have a choice. Worst thing is how it'd be for some shit I didn't even do. If I did it, I could at least understand. With this one tho, I'm just thrown in. It was my room, so it's on me. Almost a murder weapon, and it's on me. Some shit Wizard did, and it's on me. I want to scream to let it out. I want to throw up. Something. Anything. I can't tho.

Instead, I punch a fence I'm going by. I smash one of its boards hard too. It makes a sound like, *thok*. And nothing happens to it. Pain blasts into my hand. And it rips up my arm. And I regret that shit immediately. I feel stupid and worse for doing it, especially with the same hand I was punching fools with. And I hold it all close to me now, to my chest, and when I see Little's house, I just go from one set of worries to another. I start thinking about what Little's mom will say to me. The face she'll make. What she'll think seeing me again. If she even wants to . . .

Little opens the back patio door for me. He's got this black fluff of hair sticking straight out the side of his head. I can't help but laugh at it.

I say, "You do that on purpose? To your hair?"

Little don't even smile. He says, "You do that on purpose to your face?"

"Nah," I say. And I'd smile if it didn't hurt so much to try.

"Have you even washed it?" Little's staring.

"Not really," I say.

"You did or you didn't," he says. "Are you coming in or what?"

I want to. At the same time, I don't tho.

I say, "Your old lady home?"

"Cooking. My auntie's here too." He watches my reaction to his mom being there.

And it's me freezing, that's what it is. It's me looking toward that kitchen. Not wanting to surprise her in a bad way. Not wanting to make her feel bad again, or have an argument. So I just say, "Your aunt? The one from San Diego?"

"She lives in Orange County now."

Right when Little says that, this stew smell hits me and grabs me up. It walks me thru the door like in cartoons when the smell pulls somebody inside a place.

It's beef. Spices. Tomato sauce. Chiles. The kind she chars a little first, on the blue gas fires from the cooktop. It's so good, it's almost enough to make me forget the shit going on.

"¿Hilachas?" I'm sniffing. There's also something sweet coming to me on the air. Fried plantains, maybe. "Platanos too? Dang."

Little's looking at me sidewise. "It's good you're not forgetting about our Guate food."

He's older than me by a year, almost halfway thru his senior year in high school. He's five-foot-and-a-half. He's got some shoulders to him tho. He works out. He's smart too. Smartest person I know. And he has this quiet way about him that makes people forget he's around. We bonded back when we figured out neither one of us was Mexican. We're outsiders like that. His fam's from Guatemala. Guatemala City. The capital. Mines is from Samoa. I don't know from what city. My mom'd never talk about it even tho I asked. So I gave up. I guess that's the biggest lesson she ever taught me. How to keep my mouth shut. She was the best at that.

After the riots, she decided the whole Lynwood thing wasn't safe cuz she used to work at Clark's and it burned down. She wanted to go find her sister in Oakland even tho they hadn't gotten up with each other since I was born. She didn't ask if I wanted to go. And then one day all her stuff was gone. And she was too. I think about that a lot. How she just did her thing. She's like that. Makes decisions like snapping fingers. And then it's done. Worse than Angela. Cuz she wouldn't even tell you.

When I had nowhere to go, it was Wizard that asked Little to step up and get his family to take care of me. I guess that was smart, since Little's always been soft. He wanted to be in good with the neighborhood cuz he was never going to be a gangster. That's just not him. For a good couple months, I slept on their floor with a sleeping bag some hype stole me from Kmart. The best thing about staying was the food. Little's old lady could make dirt taste good. Ixchel, her name is. Named for the Mayan rainbow goddess.

"I should bounce. I don't wanna mess everything up."

"Please. My mom sets out a plate for you at every meal. Hoping you'll show up."

Hearing that? Man . . .

I want to cry. Cuz that's so nice. And I'm worried still about seeing her. And under that is the Wizard thing. The gun thing. And how I feel right now is good and bad at the same time. Happy and super fucking worried. Up and weighted down.

"Damn," is all I can say to that.

"Don't sweat it." Little smiles at me, and then looks across the room to the TV showing some little kid werewolf on the screen.

It looks like the kind of thing Jimena would watch. And usually this is where she's at in the house, but I don't see her on her bed. So I say, "Where's Jimena at?"

"She's right there." He points past the Electropedic they got for her. "Hiding."

"I'm *not* hiding," she says.

Jimena's sitting at the end of the adjustable bed. On the floor. I see the back of her head now. His little sister. Round face like an orange. When she smiles? Cutest one you ever seen. She never really goes out. Her mom won't let her. It's dangerous. She could get the seizures anywhere. She could fall. Little never said how he does what he does for the crew cuz of Jimena. I mean, he likes us, for sure. He wants to be like us. Having some money in his pocket to get that special bed tho? That's the real why.

Little says, "Been a bad day. Huh, Jimena?"

She looks down at the floor.

I sit down next to her. I say, "What the hell is this you're watching?"

"Don't say 'hell,'" she says. All serious.

"Sorry. What the *fuck* are you watching?"

Jimena covers her mouth. I can tell she's smiling a shocked smile behind it tho. Little hits me on the arm and I act like it hurts.

When Jimena can see I got punished, she nods and says, *"Adventures of a Two-Minute Werewolf."*

We all look at the screen. At this little white blond kid.

"Okay," I say. "I got a question tho."

"I don't like your questions," Jimena says back. She loves my questions.

"What's the point of being a werewolf if you only get to be one for two minutes? How does that work out if you're in a bad spot and you need super-strength?"

Nobody has any answer for that. And there won't be one either.

Cuz Jimena's getting one of her big deep breaths.

I know what's coming. I look to Little. Cuz I don't even know if it's okay for me to help with Jimena anymore. I only ever held her like twenty times before. When they come tho, they come. No stopping them. And living here, I had to get used to her seizures. Sometimes a hundred a day.

Little nods at me to go, so I get behind her just like he would so she don't fall backward. I don't touch her before she makes a gurgle sound and droops her head forward.

Then I lean my chest on her back. I bring my arm across the top of her collarbones to grab her far shoulder.

I hold her head up with my other hand. Thumb on one side of her jaw. Fingers on the other side.

And then she just . . .

Drops out.

It's like her whole body's getting electrocuted when it happens. She shakes. Her spine gets limp. Her arms go straight out ahead of her, zombie-style. Her hands reach at the air. It's just her brain short-circuiting for a second.

I just hold her.

"Todo está bien," I say it like how her mamá says it. "Todo está bien."

Her seizures start as these deep tremors inside her. Little told me once how he thought her body was like the earth, and her brain was a fault line. A San Andreas crack in her head. I never forgot that. The shaking don't take long. Maybe ten seconds. There's lots of them tho. All day. Every day. Some worse than others.

When it's all the way gone, she says, "I got it. Quit."

So I let go. She sits up. And she looks at me over her shoulder then. Her glasses slid way down her nose. She says, "Are you back for good?"

And I just look at Little. And Little looks at me. Cuz neither one of us has a good answer for that.

13

Little's mamá and auntie did up a feast on the dining room table. Hilachas on the far end. Next to them is a plate of rice fried up with some cut-up carrots. And peas too. There's Guatemalan chow mein noodles with more cooked carrots and raw green onions on top. Cooking in the steam. Ketchup's next to it. I never had chow mein before I came here to stay with them, so I didn't know having ketchup with them was weird till Wizard took me to this Chinese place on Imperial and I asked where the ketchup was. He said, *What are you, a chapín now? Get out of here with your fucking ketchup on noodles.* There's fried platanos too. A bread basket for bolillos. My favorite bread in history. And there's chuchitos made of super-soft masa. Chile slices on top. This is mainly for Jimena. Weekend meals are all about her.

She loves food. *Loves* it. Wants to be a chef. She thinks about it all the time. Wonders what's in stuff. Tries to just close her eyes and name ingredients. Mrs. Matta will always be putting different little things in the recipes to see if Jimena can taste it. Random stuff. It's a game they play, cuz the more Jimena's brain is locked on something, the less seizures she seems to have.

Little leans on my shoulder and says, "My mom misses you. She wants you to come back."

It feels good to hear that. And weird.

"I'm not even her kid," I say.

He nods to the kitchen's entrance. "Don't tell her that."

And there's Mrs. Matta staring at me. Smiling. I disrespected this woman in her own house. Yelled in her face. And here she is smiling. Big brown eyes behind her glasses crinkle up. And that smile tho? It turns to a frown when she sees my face all messed up. She comes over. And she's like half a foot shorter than me. It don't matter tho, cuz she gets up on her tiptoes and hugs me. Like moms should, you know? Not like how mines ever did. Like they do in commercials and movies tho. And I don't even feel like I deserve it. She doesn't let go till I hug back. And I wanna cry. I want to just say sorry for everything right there. And tell her how scared I am about this gun and . . .

I choke it down.

I say, "Lo siento mucho. For real, Señora Matta."

She slaps my shoulder. And then she's out of the room and back in it again with some rubbing alcohol and dabbing my face with a cotton ball. And that shit burns. I take it tho.

Cuz, all this? It makes me never want to leave this place. And it's scaring me how deep that feels. How I just want to be in this house with the Mattas. Don't want to go outside. Don't want to see Wizard. Don't want to hear bad news from him. And even if I could say how I'm feeling in Spanish, it wouldn't matter. Cuz Mrs. Matta isn't about conversations. She's about food. And she wants us all to sit. Eat. Now. Before it gets cold.

So Little picks up the bowl of refried black beans right when his auntie rolls into the room with a little drinks tray and shuts him down. Everybody's got to hold hands in this house first before food gets passed. Mrs. Matta puts her head down and prays in Spanish for the whole table. She's grateful for the food. And she blesses it. And she calls for Him to guide and protect our absent loved ones. Little's auntie squeezes my hand then. It's for my mom. I squeeze back for her brother, Little and Jimena's dad that got deported right after the riots cuz of some bullshit he got caught up in. And then we eat.

I start with a big bite of hilachas. All salty tanginess with the fat of the meat getting in there too. It gives me tingles all over my body. First thing I've eaten in two days that's not cereal. Eating this, it's like I'm living again.

And Little must be looking at my face while I'm thinking that. Cuz he says, "You could come back whenever, you know. Get a job. Help with rent. She'd like that."

"That'd be good." *Too good*, I'm thinking, so I whisper, "Except I'm about to get snatched up on some bullshit."

"Like questioned, or arrested?"

I shrug. "Dunno. Prolly arrested."

Jimena's ears are too damn good, cuz she says, "Who's getting arrested?"

This sets off her mom and the aunt. They wanna know what's being said and about who. Little's all over it.

"Nobody," he says, "come on, Jimenita. We're talking about this one episode of *Cops* where a dude got stuck in a bush after he tried to jump it. That was crazy."

I smile. I nod. Jimena's eyes shoot over to me like she knows we're lying. She can't prove it tho.

So I switch it up on her. "You figure out what the secret ingredient is yet, Jimena?"

She frowns. She knows what I'm doing. She's still about figuring out that ingredient. She has me pass the chow mein over. One time, Mrs. Matta did a carne guisada with pistachios in it. She ground them up and tried to hide them from Jimena. I don't know how Jimena guessed it around the heavy tomato taste of that sauce. She did tho.

When she's all busy with tasting again, Little leans over. "Arrested for what?

Under the table, I make my hand into a gun shape and show Little. He rolls his eyes up at the ceiling.

I lean back and whisper again, "Wizard might've done something. And his parole officer heard he might've did it so he came over and searched the spot. And supposedly they found it . . . you know. In my room."

I take a bite of noodles. They don't taste so good anymore tho.

Little brings his napkin up to his face and whispers behind it, "So this is what you need help with?"

I nod. "I need to know who got that gun into Angela's house. Cuz that gun got dropped way over at Scrappy's house. Wizard said so."

Little's got his jaw set now. He's taking it in. He says, "You sure it wasn't Angela's?"

I'm shaking my head at that when there's a knock at the sliding door. On the glass. It's loud too.

Mrs. Matta wants to know who it is. Little looks at the wall clock with the cat on it that he got her at a yard sale. He tells everybody it's just a friend he told to come over and forgot. He's slick like that. Always has answers.

We keep talking as we leave the living room. I say, "Angela always said never to have contraband shit in her house. She knew what type of risks there were in putting up a parolee."

"Don't stress on it," Little says. "I was just wondering. I'm not exactly sure how I'm about to figure this all out, though."

"You're crazy smart," I say. "You can find out shit other people can't."

He looks down. Says nothing.

At the door, we check who's behind it. I pull the curtain. We both look out. And what we see is Wizard. Just the sight of him so fast makes my heart sink way down. He's looking at the ground. Stepping on ants coming out of a little ant hole in a crack of the concrete. He's not looking happy. Little unlocks the door so he can slide it.

When it goes, Wizard looks up and nods his chin at me. "I'm here for you, man. We're rolling."

I think I'm gonna throw up when I hear that, so I try to look as cool as I can when I say, "Where we going?"

Wizard makes a face like he's swallowing some nasty-tasting medicine. And he says, "We're getting our asses caught. Get ready for some fucking bracelets."

I bite my lip so hard I bleed inside.

I taste it. Like metal.

All so I don't cry. Right here. For having to leave. For not having a choice.

14

I know Jacob enough to know he's dying inside. He's trying to play it cool, but I can see how pale he is. He's never got himself arrested before. He doesn't want this, but he'd never tell Wizard that. The shrug he comes up with next is also for Wizard's benefit, to make it look like he's accepting of it, like whatever. Because he'd never question Wizard. Nobody would. He's got juice.

Y ahora, Wizard's watching smoke drifting over the fence from where my neighbor's barbecuing. Wizard frames his hands up around me and Jacob, like we're in a picture. "Ha! Keep standing right there."

But then he steps to his left so it's just Jacob in the empty space between his fingers. "Looks like you got smoke coming out your hair!"

He drops his hands and takes that notebook he carries out of his back pocket. He gets to writing. When that happens, you just wait. Anything you say while he's trying to get lines down never gets heard, and might even make him mad if it distracts him. But I can't even lie, it's sexy how he's always writing.

I give Jacob a look to see what he's thinking, and I can tell something's bugging him. He angles his head at me. "If that piece they found is the same one that got used, I may not be coming back."

And I'm whispering, "You think someone could have picked it up at that spot and moved it to your place? Who could do that and not get seen?"

"Told you he's fucking smart," Jacob says to Wizard.

His words put a smile on me, but Wizard's looking at me hard. His pad's back in his pocket. And he's giving me this caveman stare like he's about to pick up a rock and bust me with it for knowing too much about shit I shouldn't.

He nods over at Jacob. "Why you telling this fool anything about anything?"

And Jacob's saying back, "Somebody needs to figure shit out for us if we can't. He's out here. He's low-pro. He's *smart*."

Wizard sniffs. He looks down on me for a few seconds before saying, "Okay, then."

And Jacob's saying, "Okay."

And they both look at me like I need to say something, be smart, so I jump in with, "Does Scrappy have people that could pick the gun up and bring it to your spot? People that could walk in the back door and hide it, before dropping a dime on you?"

They look at each other and Wizard grabs his head. "Shit. I never thought of that."

I keep rolling. "And was there a time window to do that in? Maybe when you two and Angela weren't there?"

"Almost anytime." Wizard shrugs at me. "She's always working or at Lynwood High for that night nursing thing and I been low since that thing happened. Getting some pussy. It's possible, I guess. I'm sure they got hypes fiending enough to do it."

The way Wizard says *pussy* is just indecente, man. But I don't hate the way his lips move when he says it. It's a weird mixed-up feeling, good and bad.

Jacob's adding, "And I haven't been back since she dropped my ass."

I'm nodding. "Maybe I start asking around the neighborhood if anybody saw anything, and getting up with some hypes, then?"

Wizard's saying, "Those aren't bad ideas."

That feels good coming from him. I say back, "Maybe let people know I'll be asking questions on the block? People would talk better if they knew Wizard was behind it."

He's nodding. "True. Anything else you need?"

It's the first time in my life Wizard Tavira ever asked me if I needed anything. It feels good, especially when it's coming so soon after he looked like he wanted to hit me.

I tell him, "Somebody big to go with me sometimes, so that my questions actually get answered, you know?"

Jacob nods.

And Wizard's saying, "I'll get you up with No Neck and Jerry."

I nod too, because that sounds good, and then Wizard leads us out back, past the garage, to the car he's got parked in the alley, but he stops cold. "Man, I knew I recognized this spot! This was where Payasa's brother got *got*, huh? That shit was sad as hell. I remember I got posted up down there."

He points down the alley before saying, "You could see the lights of the park and everything, but I wasn't close enough to see what was going on with it."

I don't tell him I remember that night, first night of the riots, Ernesto on his way home when me and my older brother were in the backyard because he was trying to go out and get wild and I wanted him to take me too, and then we heard the car come through screeching. And we both looked over the fence to see some dude stab Ernesto up. We didn't go out after that.

Wizard snaps his fingers in front of my face. "Pay attention, Little Thinker Guy. I hear shit about you, how you're different, how you got that sweet to you. Telling you right now, that shit don't matter to me if you don't make it matter. What's first is how you're about to be on this Find out who moved that fucking cuete. No excuses."

The way Wizard says *different* with a sick look on his face, he may as well just be saying *faggot*, or *puto*, or *maricón*, or whatever people say to somebody like me.

There's no secrets out here. People see what they want, or look away if it's easier, but everybody knows everybody. Ernesto's sister, Payasa, told me that once before she left. *The only way to stay safe in here*—she hit me in my chest—*is be your fucking self.*

So, I'm saying to Wizard, "I got you."

And I put some tone on it because this is me stepping the fuck up, like three whole levels. And how I say it means more than just, *I understand you*. It means, *I accept this crazy-ass responsibility*, and *I won't let you down*.

And Wizard feels it, because he's getting in the car and saying, "Good shit, Little Thinker. You do this one thing right and won't nobody be able to step to you ever again."

Jacob smiles at me like he's glad, but he's still stuck in his own problems, and my heart breaks just looking at his busted-up face, and I can tell how bad he's hurting.

Me and him, we never talked about the being-different thing. I know he knows, but he's always been one of those people that just looks away.

I give Jacob one of them half hugs and I want to hold him longer, but I can't, because then he needs to get in the car too, and then it's going. I watch it pass the spot where Ernesto died, next to Mr. Romero's garage and his fence with the hole in it. My neighbor used to put flowers in a little cup inside that hole. She did it every week for a year almost. I only saw her do it a couple times, but whenever I went by, they were out there and never looking wilted. It was special, her doing that. I guess that's why I kept up with it even after she married some firefighter and left. That's how Payasa found me. She saw them flowers again and asked around to see who was doing it. I became her Little Flower Guy, she said. That's how I got named. After a while I was just Little. I still think about her all the time, how she always said I had to make sure my family stayed safer than hers. That's the feeling I'm feeling right now too, that responsibilidad. Because Jacob is my family, and he's in danger of getting lost for good. He needs me doing all I can to save him, and that starts with going out and asking people questions they don't want to answer.

15

I shift around in the driver's seat. Can't quite find the right space to relax in. Since I told Dreamer we were going to Tam's Burgers because somebody's dry-snitching us out, he's been off in his head, daydreaming again. He's looking out the window at houses going by while we ride past the fire station by Platt. We go straight down MLK on nothing but green lights. My window's down. I got the radio so low it sounds like buzzing coming out the speakers. Tiny treble hits pop over the noise of the street.

For real, Dreamer looks like he's going to puke in my car. I love me some Dreamer, man, but this fool's greener than Gatorade. He's avoided so many scrapes because I've either kept him out, or No Neck and me told witnesses they didn't see shit, or I told him to stay as clean as he could. No tattoos. No locote moves. This fool hasn't even been arrested yet. Matter of fact, his cherry's getting popped today. I didn't give him a big speech, just told him keep his head down and don't talk to anybody but a lawyer. I told him he's just got to get through it and take the advice that comes, because when we wind up at County Jail, it's a whole new education. It's doing stuff you never thought you'd have to do. He'll learn.

I don't tell him I had to drop him at Little's and go pick up five balloons that I got to take inside with me to County because the big homie said so. It ain't the first time I've muled it. I make ten times inside what I do out here on that. I get a six thousand cut, all of it going to Angela, so she can put it toward the house. It's like the rent she'll be missing out on with me gone anyways. And that's good, because it's not like any judge will give me bail on shooting somebody. Not on gang shit. Not these days.

I didn't even ask what's in these blue and red little balloons. Heroin. Speed. Whatever. I just made sure they're tied up good and tight. I checked for little holes before bagging them again in condoms, and then I went to the bathroom and cleared everything out of me before I grabbed Vaseline and greased each one up. I went slow. One at a time. Breathed out, stretched, took it in. You get used to it. I learned how to pocket in Chino. Mayate motherfuckers were always looking to throw down there. You never knew when you needed a weapon. So you wrapped a shiv up in toilet paper, slid a condom over it from the state health people who were all worried about disease spreading, and got it up there. Better being uncomfortable than being dead. First few times I did it, all I could think about was how it would cut me up inside. It didn't. But the thinking about it was always the worst part. Still is. Dreamer doesn't need to know all this, man. I'll carry this weight for the both of us.

I lean over to him. "We get sheriffs on us first, that's a good thing. You get stomped? You take it. It's better than getting blasted by Scrappy's homies."

He nods, but he's staring off into space. Shit. I remember being like that too, my first time.

A homie of ours got popped in the face at Tam's. Fool was in the drive-thru. He's got shiny scars down one cheek now, because he turned, but he lived. Tam's is over the line for us. It's a big risk doing it like this, but it's worth sending a message, and besides, sheriffs love Tam's. If you're looking for them around this time and they're not at the station? Chances are a few of them are munching out at Tam's chili fries.

I turn onto Louise from Long Beach, bust a right on School, and then onto Virginia. I get a chill. These are the same streets from the other night when I got wet with No Neck, and Jerry drove us over to take care of Scrappy. We knew the mission. She needed to get hers because that's what the big homies decided, and that was it. It was her or us. The order comes down. You do it. Or else. We all felt that when we rolled through that night and saw this hype barely walking he had it so bad, and No Neck said we should follow him, because if he was going anywhere on that street at that time of night, you know he was going to Scrappy's. That shit was like prophecy. We watched the hype go right to her door, get told no, and start peeling siding off her house. I never seen anything like it, man. When she came out and beat on him, I told No Neck to grab the .38 and I gloved up while he passed it to me using his sweatshirt cuff, but she was quick with kicking him and already rolling back into the house. Fuck, man. I thought that was that. We missed our window, I was sure, but then she surprised all of us when she came back out to hook him up. That was all we needed to get close before No Neck shouted, "Scrap!" and that was it. She turned to look, I did what needed doing, and Jerry kept the car running.

I go right onto Long Beach again from Virginia and then into Tam's parking lot. We head to the back to find paramedics there. An ambulance takes up the back corner by the Dumpsters, its doors open for loading. As I pull into a spot next to it, I see an older lady on a gurney getting loaded in. Scalp all bloody. Face all white. Around her, there's four bags of food nobody picked up and two spilled drinks. I get out and check the lot. There's four other cars, but nobody in them, so we get out and go maybe five feet to the first bag of food on the ground.

"Hey." I try to get the attention of one of the dudes in uniform. "Hey, what happened to her?"

There's two paramedics. One old. One young. The young one doesn't even look at me before saying, "She fell."

A lot of people fall around here. It's about what makes you fall, though. Shit. I mean, Scrappy fell the other night after I put a few in her.

I nod at Dreamer to pick up the food bags. He does it. One or two burgers hit the ground, but that's no reason to get rid of them. They're still wrapped, so they get pushed back in bags. Inside the truck, the lady looks upset. Must be thinking Dreamer's gonna run off with them or something. Crazy.

I knock on the open back door. "Is it cool if we just put these in there for her? For later?"

The young paramedic looks up. He's white. Blue eyes. He sees the bags in Dreamer's hand, then looks to his partner, and that gray-mustache-wearing dude shrugs, so yeah, that's that. They get set inside by an oxygen tank with a FLAMMABLE sticker on it. When it's done, the mustached one moves us along. "The quicker you get out of here, the quicker we get her the medical care she needs."

"Yeah, man." I nod up at the lady in the ambulance. "Hope you feel better, ma'am."

She blinks. Nobody says shit back, but that's cool. Dreamer and me, we're already rolling. I lead. I go in the back door first with my chin up. The seating area's narrow as hell. Booths left and right. Skinny aisle between them. Black Mean Streak tags all down the metal legs of the tables anchored to the ground. Windows scribed to fuck by Scrappy's crew. I scan the room hard and quick, and my pulse's going up since there's no sheriffs here yet and I don't know how I'm liking that, but I'm checking faces for fools from Scrappy's clica that I might have to deal with, and I'm not seeing any, which is damn good. There's a family in the front corner. Mom, daughter, dad or boyfriend. There's an old man and his wife working on some fries. There's two teenagers. I put eyes on them and they stare straight down at their tabletop. Punk bitches. They don't even know that us strolling in like this is showing everybody in Lynwood that we don't run. We fucking stick.

This is like saying, *You don't own shit if I can walk right up and take it.* We're basically in Scrappy's backyard, standing the fuck up like a couple of down-ass homeboys. This sends a loud fucking message that fools will be hearing from far off. *I know where you live,* that's what this says. *I know where you eat. I ain't afraid of you, or cops, or anything.* Everybody knows I wasn't afraid of Scrappy before, but now they know I'm not scared of Scrappy's brother, or cousins, or fucking uncles either. *Fuck your whole shitty-ass crew,* this says. *I go where I want. I do what I want, where I want. I shoot anybody I want. I take what I want, and then I have some fucking chili cheese fries, nigga.*

16

Somebody is getting loaded into an ambulance as we pull into Tam's for a bite. It's not the first time I've seen a unit here. It won't be the last. They run cleanup after fights or shootings. This, though, looks like only one victim—female, mid-forties, brown hair. She's on the gurney, but my guess is five-foot-four. She looks familiar. Louis must be thinking the same thing, since he cranes his neck over the wheel as he pulls into the end spot that faces onto Long Beach.

By the time we get back there, they've loaded the gurney but haven't shut the doors, and I recognize her as Scrappy's mother, Rosalinda. Her eyes are glazed. Beside her is a young tech who looks up from his clipboard when he hears us approach. I ask him how she is.

"Stable. Concussion. Dehydration. Negative for stroke." He looks down to cross a few *t*'s. "She was murmuring to herself when we got here. Says she needs to get back to the hospital."

Louis looks to me, then asks, "She say why?"

"No," the tech replies.

My radio buzzes. It comes through in stereo on Louis. The call's not for us. It's for another patrol unit. I ignore it and tell the tech that her gangster daughter got shot the other night.

"You could throw a rock and hit the house from here," Louis adds.

"Bad luck." The tech puts his pen under the clip. He's done. "Take care out there."

"You do the same," I say.

The way it was relayed to me by Vazquez, Scrappy's mother came in and gave a statement about what happened during the night of the shooting, but it soon became obvious that she was in the house and did not see it, so we had to thank her for her time and send her on her way. Before she left, she begged us to catch the people who did it. Vazquez said she didn't even seem to know what her own daughter was into.

Louis and I watch the ambulance turn right onto Long Beach as we head to the front. He asks, "She walked all the way here from Saint Francis?"

"Must have. What a world, huh? Scrappy's mother, on a break to get some food—possibly for her daughter—faints in a parking lot. She hits her head. Now she's going back to the same hospital as her daughter. Jebiga."

"Why do you tell every story like you're writing a report, Mirk?"

"I've written so many, they've rewired me. It'll happen to you someday too, Louis."

"Gosh, I hope not," Louis replies with one of his best smirks. "At least she gets a ride back, you know? Only has to walk one way."

I laugh at that. "Always looking on the bright side."

"Can't help it. Hey, did you hear we got two calls to Saint Francis last night?"

"Nope."

"Gangster convention in the nearest waiting room to Miss Scrappy. They got loud, abused staff. We sent a car."

"We didn't have her on watch?"

"No resources. Besides, if they were gonna try shooting her again, it would've been in the ER, not upstairs."

"So what happened?"

He smiles. "A few parole violations on gang association."

"Good," I reply.

We go through the front door of Tam's to find there's no line, which is our good luck. Louis looks up at the menu. I scan it too. The polish sausage breakfast plate is a strong maybe. Breakfast burrito with machaca is always good. I'm staring at the pastrami burrito, though, when our walkie-talkies come on at the same time and tell us to be advised that the wanted suspects of the 664 the other night have been spotted. Our suspects. From the same house we've been sitting on. Tavira and Safulu.

A hot itch runs up the back of my neck as the address comes in over the radio. "One one eight one six Long Beach Boulevard."

"Isus Krist!" My heart skips a beat. They're at *this* Tam's—#9. Right where we're fucking standing. The jolt of that is like my spine getting plugged into an electrical socket.

My hand goes to my gun. I unholster and pull. I take it to forty-five degrees with my finger indexed and off the trigger as I turn and put the room in front of me, the door to my back. I study my backdrop and potential civilian casualties.

Louis takes my six, already calling dispatch, telling them we are 10-97, before dropping off and shouting, "Sheriffs! Stay where you are. Do not move!"

My listing procedure takes over: Are suspects in the room as advised? If so, where? Are suspects armed? Are their hands visible? Do suspects outwardly intend myself, my partner, or bystanders harm? I do a room count. I got a family near me, with a kid—about eight years old. I got two seniors—seventies. I got two teens—upper teens. And yeah, I fucking got eyes on Wizard in the farthest booth. He looks just like his mug shot, except now he's got a shitty, thin mustache. One of his elbows is on the table. The other hand is below. I only see the back of his companion's head. It could be Dreamer. It should be.

I say to him, "Omar Tavira. Do not move."

He replies, "Does it look like I'm moving, Officer?"

His words have tone on them. Surly. Untrustworthy.

"Do not move," I say again.

"Okay," he replies. "Don't do the thing I'm already not doing."

To his companion, I say, "Jacob Safulu. Turn. Face me."

He's slow about it, but he does.

"Hands!" I order. "Show me hands!"

I raise my weapon to stay on top of the situation. It's so Wizard knows he can't pull and shoot faster than I can. I aim at Wizard's center mass, as he puts his other hand on the table. It has a fork in it. I exhale with relief and close the distance between us. In my peripheral vision I see a dark pickup truck slow in the drive-thru lane next to the restaurant. The driver has his mouth open as he stares at me. I pass the family. I hear Louis behind me evacuate them safely. I pass the seniors. Louis attempts to do the same again.

The old man says to him, "Would you get me more ketchup? Please, young man?"

Louis tells them they have to leave. They don't want to leave. They're difficult. They're not done eating. Louis ceases trying to shift them, presses on. He moves to the teens. They need no convincing. I hear them run out the open front door. I am four feet away. I see sweat on Safulu's face. I see both his hands. I see both Tavira's hands. I see chili cheese fries, half eaten. There is nothing under the table. No bags. No backpacks.

I say to the suspects, "Hands. On the table. Flat."

Wizard smiles and waves his fork in the air. "You want me to put this down?"

I lose it a little. I tell him, "Jebo ti vrag mater."

Wizard looks to Louis. "What'd he just say to me? That's got to be assault right there!"

"Steady," Louis says behind me.

I step back. I keep an angle on the table, my pistol pointed at Tavira, the pička. Louis has Safulu stand first, place his hands behind his back, and get cuffed. The relief of metal snapping into metal and holding fast on a bad guy is one of the best feelings on earth. It's a feeling that lets me breathe deeper. Louis removes the cuffs from my belt and then does the same procedure on Tavira. I'm ready for Wizard to resist. He doesn't. He gets locked up good and tight, and I put hands on him. My arms buzz like I just put up 250 on the bar and it feels light in my hands. I feel steady, strong. I Mirandize them.

Louis calls it in clear—reports both suspects in custody, and we are en route.

As we walk them out, Louis says, "What the hell were you doing on this side anyway, Wizard? Gloating?"

Tavira has no smart answers now, only silence.

PART IV

IN CUSTODY

If you want to know who your friends are, get yourself a jail sentence.

—CHARLES BUKOWSKI

17

In the back of the cop car, I'm on the right. Dreamer's on the left. They got me good on the cuffs. The things are so tight the metal's cutting into me, but I can't show it. My left hand's going numb, but we just sit in the heat as the black one calls us in. Suspects in custody. En route. I lean my head forward onto the seat in front of me to take weight off my wrists, but it cricks my neck up bad, so I sit back. Back here, it smells like hobo armpit. It's nasty as fuck, so I breathe out my mouth. I look to Dreamer but he doesn't seem to be smelling it, or at least not showing it. He looks all right for this being his first time. He's got his chin up. That's good, but it's because I'm here and we're in this together. If he'd gotten rolled up by himself, it'd be trouble. It'd maybe be tears and talking, but I'm cool, so he's cool.

The big white one starts the car up. I wait for a second to see if he's going to put on the air, but he doesn't, so I lean forward a second time. "Hey, Officer, can we get some air, please?"

They hate it when you call them *Officer*. They're sheriffs, but they like *Deputy* best. He doesn't answer. It's a power move. He rolls his window down an inch, just for him, and that's it. The rest of us just get to cook as we roll out of the parking lot, onto Long Beach Boulevard, and then right back into the neighborhoods on Josephine. This big fucker, I know what he's doing. He's driving us by where Scrappy got hers. Trying to be all psychological. Both deputies got sunglasses on, but I know they're looking at me, so I don't give them anything they can write up in a report. I look straight ahead as we roll by Scrappy's and turn left in front of Wilson Elementary. He's driving all slow, which has me thinking this big white sheriff is driving me through Scrappy's neighborhood the long way on purpose, so I can get seen in the back, and they can seem like the big men laying down the law. I want to fucking laugh because they'd never have got us like they did if somebody didn't snitch us out on purpose, but whatever, man.

We take Lynwood Road to Bullis and go under the freeway, and I think we'll just shoot straight up to Lynwood Jail from here, but we turn again, on Fernwood, and I know for sure they're fucking with me. This is payback for how some of them had to sit out in front of Angela's house. He turns on Birch, driving like he's all proud and shit, like he's a fisherman showing everybody what he caught. There's not many people out, but there's some. Dudes walking to cars. An old lady on a porch. We pass the park and head up toward St. Francis Hospital, and that just feels wrong. I open my big mouth again. "We going to Lynwood Jail or what?"

Neither one answers me, so I trip out on time. Can't help it. I think about how many years I might get for this if they can prove it, if the gun they found really is the gun, and how many months I'll be locked up in County before I even get to trial. Time, a concept worth unpacking in a rhyme. What are some of those riddles, again? Time, it flies without wings. Time, it's harmless but it kills you. Time, it's undefeated. Against it, not even mountains can win. I want to write them down. *Flies. Kills. Undefeated. Mountains.* The worst part about being cuffed is that I can't write anything down in my pad. Shit. What if I'm in jail for six months just waiting? Man. Fuck it. I can do that time. I put in work out here to be ranked up in there. Don't even matter who the Sureño shotcaller is. When I get there, it might even be me and I'll have to take the keys over.

Hold up. We're pulling into the hospital, the entrance where the ER is at, and then stopping. The big white motherfucker smiles at me in the rearview, then opens his door and goes inside. Dreamer looks to me like he's wondering what this is about, but I give him a look to sit tight and he must get it because he puts his head down. The car is still running, and the black one doesn't seem worried at all, but he fucking should be, because being here is like sitting in a firing line and waiting for somebody to open up on your ass. If Scrappy's in there, it means her people are in there. That means they can come out this way, and see me sitting here with nowhere to go. They can pull their pieces and sling bullets. I want to say all that to the black cop, but I can't. He's either stupid as fuck and doesn't know he's sitting himself in danger, or he thinks it's worth it to fuck with me. If some of her people come out and see me they're just gonna open up, and they'll shoot his mayate ass too because he's on the same side of the car as me.

Every time the automatic doors go, my stomach jumps up. The first time, a nurse walks out. I breathe out pretty good then, trying to be as quiet as possible and not give this black cop any satisfaction. The doors go again, and it's an old man with his head all wrapped up. The doors stay open and a little girl runs out behind him, his granddaughter or something. After that, there's nothing for a minute. Only the sound of the engine as we wait. A bird flies by, low and under the concrete ceiling in here, and that little fucker goes straight through to the other side. I shift my wrists. Both are numb now, but that doesn't matter, because when the doors open again, I sit up to see who it is coming through them and it's the big-ass white cop strolling out, staring right at me. This motherfucker has a Baby Ruth from the vending machine in his hand. He even smiles at me as he takes a bite. That's the worst, man. He was fucking with me, and I gave him a reaction. He knows it worked, and that burns, man. Deep down. He won, and he knows he won, and he loves how I can't do shit but take it.

18

Wizard's all calm as hell sitting here cuffed. Me tho? I'm not good. Not even close to good. My wrists hurt. And my mind's fucking racing on how this ain't fair. It's all hitting me now. It ain't fucking fair! I didn't ride! Didn't pull a trigger! And the worst part is I can't say shit. Not to nobody. Especially not now. I'm glad my hands are behind me so Wizard can't see how bad they're shaking. My fingers tap in the plastic pocket behind me. So I make fists.

I try memorizing how we came, in case I need to know. We came thru on Alameda . . . Imperial to Alameda. Turn right. And go all the way straight till Nadeau. That's how we cruised up into the Nineties streets, then the Eighties numbers. And I know I never been up this far before, so I'm on the lookout for new stuff. For whatever. And I'm not even sure how many more outside looks I'm gonna get for a while, you know?

It hits me again. *Fuck*. I'm going to *jail*.

I knew it was coming sometime. Not like this tho. Not for something I didn't even do.

We pass this little red building on Nadeau with a hand-painted sign saying CARNICERÍA in capital letters. I wasn't even hungry after them chili cheese fries. Seeing that sign tho? I'm hungry again. And they got some Miller Lite neon going next to it. And I want one of those fuckers too. Ice-cold. In the back of this hot-ass car. Maybe that'd calm me down.

We turn left on Compton Boulevard, past this concrete building on the corner before turning right just past it. We go between two cinder-block walls about head-height that they got painted white. The big dude drives us thru a parking lot filled with cop cars. Thru a fenced gate. To the back of the building. We pull up to the curb on Wizard's side. The black sheriff takes me thru the back door into a little lobby area with white walls, a bench, and a caged-in desk with a door next to it.

That's when this feels like there's no hope now. No getting away from it. More real than in the back of a car. In a place with cages already. And bars I'm about to have to be behind. I always used to imagine the ways I'd go down too. In some gunfire in the street. Running from the cops and just barely getting caught. All heroic. This is just . . . sad.

It's like an office in here. Phones ringing in the background. Sheriffs walking around behind the cage.

Señora Matta would be so upset at me for this. So fucking disappointed at me. That's the shit that burns.

"That's the third-quickest collar we've ever had," says the dude opening the door with this metal cage on it. He's smiling at us like me and Wizard are a prize. "If only you'd driven faster."

The big white one cuffs Wizard to a wooden bench before going up to the open door.

On his way thru, he says, "Is Kelley in?"

"Nope, brass meeting. But he wants to talk to you. He voided your citation for the forty-four-fifty-seven."

None of that even makes sense. They got their own language.

"What the hell? Why?"

"Check the memo. Think he said it was a forty-four-sixty-four." The guy behind the cage laughs.

"He thinks that lady vandalized her own damn license plate?"

The dude holds his hands up. Like, *Don't shoot*. Cuz it ain't his fault.

They make me go first for photos. They do one with what I'm wearing. I stand still holding a piece of paper with my number on it. My name too. And it's in front of measuring tape they got on the wall to show how tall I am. They do one straight ahead. One to both sides. The flash is bright white. A spot stays in my eyes even when I'm blinking after.

"One more," the photographer cop says.

And they make me take my shirt off. And put on a special type of shirt before facing front again.

I do it cuz I can't *not* do it. I still say, "Why?"

I don't expect an answer. I get one tho.

The dude behind the camera says, "It's nonprejudicial. That way, you can go on a lineup card and be wearing the same thing as everybody else."

When we're done, the guy behind the desk nods at me and says, "This one have slides on him?"

He must be talking to the black sheriff, cuz that's the one that answers back.

"Nope," he says.

A slide is my fingerprints on a card. Right hand. Fingers. Thumb. I hear how it's all going into a national database for crime prevention so everybody in America can feel safe at night. Except for people in my neighborhood tho. I want to say that. I don't.

"We'll know who you are forever now," the black sheriff says. And his name tag flashes at me. LOUIS. "You get out. You do anything? We'll come right to you."

He's trying to scare me. The worst part is it works. I almost trip out. So I bite my lip again on the inside. Not so hard that I get blood. Close tho. After, they tell me they have to photograph my whole body. I have to take my shirt off. Have to take my pants down to my ankles too. It's for the gang book. My photo's going right into it. My name too.

From the bench on the other side of the room, Wizard says, "He ain't in no gang. I'd never roll with this punk motherfucker. You got the wrong dude right there."

It's good to hear that and bad at the same time. Good for how I know he's saying it cuz I'm innocent. Bad for how it hurts. The way he calls me a punk motherfucker feels real. And it cuts into me. Cuz I'm here, you know? I ain't a punk. I'm standing the fuck up for some shit I didn't even do and he's calling me out like that? Fuck. It shouldn't hurt. It does tho. It does.

ARREST BOOKING SLIP AND PROPERTY RECORD, it says on the booking form, then below it, *LOS ANGELES COUNTY JAIL*. Louis fills it out for me. He asks me my full name.

I say, "Jacob Aaron Safulu."

Weight. Height. Eye color.

"One-eighty. Five-nine. Brown," I say.

Arraignment date. He leaves that blank.

And the crazy part is Louis don't even ask for alias or nickname. He just writes *Dreamer* in there. My skin turns cold. Like, how in the *fuck* did he even know that if I'm not on their paper yet?

That's some bad shit right there.

Serious bad shit.

And that's when I know I'm not coming back. That's when I know it's done for me. I mean, them knowing my name? Shit. Somebody had to have thrown me in on purpose. Used that name. How the fuck else would they know it? The only way is if somebody framed me on purpose too. Not just Wizard. And it's like every time something goes down, I'm thinking, *Okay, this is it. It can't get worse from here.* And then it fucking does.

Louis gets down to cash and property on the form. He writes in everything they took off me. Seventeen dollars. Brown belt. No glasses. No watch. No rings. He puts his name in the little boxes of *Arrested by* and *Booked and Searched by*. Then he turns the paper around at me. He puts a finger down on the part where I have to sign. *Prisoner's Complete Signature.*

I sign it. I can't really believe it.

I'm a prisoner, I'm thinking.

I signed my name that I am. Shit. That's *real*.

It means I got to be a monster now. Got to kill my feelings. Cuz it ain't about to be me getting took advantage of in County Jail. I got to do what Wizard says. Survive. No matter what . . .

They put Wizard thru next. He goes quicker than me. Maybe cuz they already have a file on him.

After, we get taken thru a heavy door. And Wizard gets recognized by the guy turning the keys.

"Oh man," the sheriff says. "They just let you out, and you're already rolling back in? What your mother must think of you."

Wizard's back goes stiff. And he turns to the dude.

All cold, he says, "My mother's dead. She don't care about nothing now, puto."

I expect this sheriff to beat his ass.

The dude just turns and looks Wizard straight in the eyes tho. And he says, "I'm real sorry to hear that. Lost mine in February. I know how it is."

Wizard spits on the white tile floor. And says, "Fuck you, Vazquez. You don't fucking know me."

19

I come in through the door meant for the public and not on-the-clock assholes like me, because getting called in on your off-day is enough for me to justify it. I don't need to get stuck holding hands and handling shit when I should be taking Sheryl to some dinner and a hockey game. We're new, me and her. I'm trying hard not to screw it up.

I'm surprised to see Ruiz out front looking clean and sparkly for phone duty.

"Jesus," I say, "I don't see you for one week and then when I do, you're busted back to desk. What'd you do this time, Ruiz?"

He says, "It is my rep's opinion that I should keep my stupid mouth shut."

Jankowski's our rep. That's exactly how he talks.

"You know I'm just going to find out from someone else, right?"

"Better from them than me," Ruiz says.

"Good man. Is the lieutenant in?"

"Brass meeting, downtown. Her and Kelley."

"I see."

"You going to the game tonight?"

"Yup. Got a date for it."

"Nice! Panthers are gonna go crazy tonight. I can feel it. It's in the air, Sarge." This Miami-born idiot reaches up and grabs the air like it's got a Florida win in it. What an asshole.

"They better not," I say. "Gretzky doesn't lose to expansion teams. And why the hell are you Florida people so damn smiley about your terrible hockey team?"

"Terminal positivity," he says. "It'll kill us someday, but we'll be smiling when it happens."

I don't give him the satisfaction of a reaction, I just go through to the back, where I find Mirkovich and Louis sitting on their asses and shuffling papers.

"You're not back out on the street, huh? This is what happens when the Lieu's gone?"

"Paperwork's not done," Louis says.

"I bet it's not," I say. "Which one of you got who?"

Louis speaks up like he's used to being the mouthpiece for the pair. "I did Safulu."

"Which left Tavira to your big dumb Croatian ass?" I point at John Mirkovich.

"Hey." He says it like he's offended. "I'm not that big."

He smiles after that. Ruins everything.

"Tell that to your mother, Deputy. She feeds you too much, but goddammit I still love her mostaccioli. How's your sister, anyway?"

Kristina Mirkovich and me, that was never gonna work, but you couldn't have told us that to start with. She was too high-strung, and I was too loose, but that didn't stop us from trying to find the middle for two good years and one really bad one. The being civil afterward part, that's the worst kind of work, and her brother knows it all too well, but hey, I must've done all right. He hasn't put a knife in me yet.

John Mirkovich kicks the desk leg like he's testing it. "Kristina actually got a promotion. You didn't hear?"

I look at him to see if he's fucking with me. He's not.

"No," I say, "I didn't."

"She's an AHD on hardcore gang prosecutions now. You might even hear from her on this."

I don't know if it's medically possible to get an instant headache, but I get one. Right now. "You shitting me?"

"No, sir, Sergeant, sir."

"Your tone, Ivica." I give him the eye. "I don't like it."

Mirkovich makes a face then that only an ex-brother-in-law can. Tongue out, eyebrows up, and it's good nobody else sees him do that, because now I don't have to pretend I didn't see it.

I turn to Louis. "You handing me paperwork, or do I have to waste my whole day off standing here?"

I flip pages, but I'm thinking, *God, I fucking hope not. In fact, Jesus Christ, if You're listening, please do* not *give this case to my ex-wife. That'd be great. Thanks. Oh, and also, it'd be great if Gretzky had a hat trick of assists tonight and the Panthers get shithoused and pull the rug out from under every*

Panther fan on earth, all thirty-six of them. That'd be great, Lord. I'd rub that
shit right in Ruiz's stupid face next time I see him too, but, you know, God,
respectfully so.

But then Mirkovich's news is catching up to me, and I'm thinking,
Good for Kristina. Seriously. She's got the nose for HG cases, not to mention
the guts. She'll be great at it. When she has something over somebody,
she never lets go. And I know that better than anybody.

To get this conversation back on track, I say, "Good collars. Might
be worth some Attaboys. They give you anything rough?"

"They were waiting for us." There's a little heat in how Louis says
it. "I think their own people snitched them out, and I think they
knew it."

The property boxes on the form are pretty bare. Neither one had a
wallet on him. It scans that they planned to come in. Something interesting about Safulu's form is how Louis noted he has scars that look like
they were once punctures down his upper left and lower left arm, and
also on his left ribs. There's also one more thing about these forms I
don't like: two blank spaces in the *Indexed information* sections that I'd
rather not see.

I say, "Why hasn't WAD gotten back on arraignment dates yet?"

Louis shrugs. "Just waiting for the follow-through. I'll update you."

"Thanks," I say. "You got anything else? I'm sure they confessed and
we can just pass go and collect all their years of sentencing right now."

"They're hardcore, Willie." Mirkovich has his serious face back on.
"Some new branch off of Big Fate's clique. You know, the one that killed
Trouble and all them last year but we couldn't prove shit?"

Yeah, I remember. Worst crime scene evidence I ever saw, the most
unprovable clusterfuck there ever was. Homicide guys still talk about
it. And nobody's said shit, but it's pretty much the reason Erickson
got transferred too. They called it a lateral move, but it was a demotion
in all but name.

"I don't know if they're both hardcore," Louis slips in. "Tavira sure
is. But even he didn't like having to sit out front of Saint Francis if Scrappy's crew might come out at any second. I think the other one's green."

Louis is a smart one. He'll rise. The good black ones always do. If he
can keep his head down and fill out his paperwork correctly and in a
timely fashion, that is.

"And they've asked for legal representation, I take it?"

Louis says, "We put in the PD requests, but we haven't heard anything."

"Say it with me, deputies: 'It is the policy of this Department to provide the most expedient method of communications between persons in custody of this Department and their attorneys or other persons attempting to secure their release.'"

They don't say it with me. They don't have 5-03/060.00 memorized. Amateurs.

It might just be my willingness to get to my date this evening, but I still just state the obvious when I say, "We're not holding them over unless they're eager to talk, but at least tell me Vazquez scheduled transpo late."

Mirkovich winks at me. "I heard the bus had an engine issue."

Louis opens his mouth to disagree but then he catches Mirkovich's elbow with his ribs. He coughs and says, "They're on for the morning bus, but Vazquez says we'll see how that goes if their lawyers get here."

"Sounds about right," I say, and head back to the cages.

20

I have Vazquez bring them in and get planted in chairs. Tavira in Room 1. Safulu in Room 2. Separate but equal. After that, I take in the new note next to the thermostat that says, *Don't even think about it, Montero,* and I abide by the note and turn the air-conditioning on in the rooms without even thinking about it. Now, if it said, *Don't do it, Montero,* that would be different, but it doesn't, so I take it all the way down to sixty-five degrees fucking Fahrenheit, and I put on my spare blazer.

Usually the lieutenant lets me do whatever I want when it comes to suspect sit-downs, but she's been saying how she was going to take the AC out of my arsenal the past few weeks, and that it won't be coming back on again until May. Budget cuts. I tell her when the crime rate rises and the conviction rate around these parts declines, it will all be because I can't freeze some turkeys out. Since she's not here, however, and I'm technically not supposed to be, I get to work how I want to work, and she can give me an Awshit later, but that's only if she finds out.

I got a couple spare Attaboy certificates lying around, so I walk them back to Mirkovich and Louis. On the front, it says:

> For Your Outstanding Performance
> You Are Awarded
> "ONE ATTABOY"

And on the back, it says:

> One thousand Attaboys qualifies you to be a leader of men, work overtime with a smile, explain assorted problems to management, and be looked upon as a local hero.
>
> NOTE: One Awshit wipes the board clean, and you have to start all over again.

98 | Ryan Gattis

Those Awshits are tough too. Everybody's got a different way of presenting them. Kelley gave me my first one with a punch in the gut. I was doing some paperwork while hiding in the back room at Goldhammer's Liquor Store on the corner of Ninety-Fifth and Alameda, and he made me stand up to take it before sitting me right back down. It was because I went in the wrong crackhouse door with my head high and my gun out. I could've, and probably even should've, taken a bullet, at least a through-and-through. I didn't. I got who I needed to get, but I should've waited. That's what James J. Kelley was saying to me, *Good job*, and *Fuck you, don't do it again*, at the same time. That lesson got learned.

Me? I just hand them over, say, "Attaboy!" to Mirkovich and Louis, and I put on this cheesy grin when I slap both their faces like something out of *The Godfather* and then leave my palms on cheeks for two seconds too many. Ivica I hit with my left, Louis with my right. I make it real uncomfortable for the pair of them. They don't say shit. They take it. As they should.

Back by the cages, I see Vazquez puttering around and I can't let the opportunity pass. I got to ask.

"Hey, what'd Ruiz do? Why's he on phones?"

Vazquez stares at my chest. "What's with this tie? Is it a fish pattern?"

"Marlin," I say. "You should come out on the boat sometime."

"Pass. Kelley says it'll sink under you someday."

"Kelley doesn't know shit about boats. So, what about Ruiz?"

"Shooting."

"Where?"

"Five blocks down Nadeau."

"Which way?"

"Towards Alameda."

"The one that used to be Sonny's?"

"Fucking Sonny's."

"And?"

"And the bad guy had a knife. He had two, actually. Who needs two? This guy while he's robbing a bar."

I say, "How did I not hear about this?"

"You were out in Riverside interviewing a witness maybe. You're a busy man."

"So?"

"So, Ruiz rolls in, Jackson on his six."

"New guy Jackson? The one that documented the gun for . . ." I aim my thumb down the hall at the rooms holding Tavira and Safulu, the knuckleheads who bring home the pistol they shot somebody with just so it can be found.

"Yeah, that one."

"Uh-huh," I say.

"So, they go in, and some lady shouts that the baddie is behind the bar, hiding. Ruiz turns. Bad guy stands, makes a motion that indicates he's trying to throw one of those knives, and, you know . . . bang."

"Two bangs or one?"

"One."

"Where?"

"Center mass."

"Good," I say. "So, they couldn't save him? Aim was too clean?"

"Aim was fine, but he would've lived. The problem was he held on to those knives as he was bleeding out. Both of them. Nobody would go near him to administer."

"Shit," I say. "Well, in my professional opinion, it sounds both in policy and fully justified."

"You know Review. These things take time. Until then?" Vazquez mimes answering the phone and then puts on his best goofy voice. "Hello, Firestone Park Sheriff's Station?"

I start walking. "Your imitative phone manner is atrocious. I ought to report you to the lieutenant."

He barks a laugh that bounces down the hallway ahead of me.

Inside, Room 1 is cold. Just how I like it. And Tavira's fighting it too. He's hunched down, trying not to show weakness, but he's cold as hell sitting in that metal chair with no cushion on it. It's the little things.

Before the door is even closed behind me, Tavira's hassling me. "I asked for a lawyer, and I don't see a lawyer, so we're done."

I give him his Miranda. Just to be safe. To dot *i*'s and cross *t*'s. Things have been buttoned the hell up since the riots that we're not supposed to call riots, and my personal feeling is it's a good thing. He's under arrest, has the right not to say shit, if he does say shit we can and will use said shit against him in a court of law, if he can't afford to hire a scumbag defensive attorney an overworked public defender will be assigned to him.

I flop his file open. I tell him his charges and he doesn't flinch. I say, "How come we've never crossed paths before with you being up to so much? I mean, I know your name. I see your rap sheet. I see you in the gang book, but it's nice to see your face in color."

"Lawyer," he says.

"We are still awaiting contact from your assigned legal representation."

I'm digging a little, seeing if he contradicts me on the "assigned" part, if he tips his hand about already having somebody, but I also have Vazquez's note sitting right here that Mr. Wizard already got his three phone calls and not one was to a law office. That could just mean he called somebody to call somebody, though.

I ask him what he thinks of the Dodgers this year. Nothing.

"What about the Kings? You like Gretzky?"

Nothing.

We go around like that for fifteen minutes. Me needling. Him not saying shit. It's pointless, but I'm good with it. It takes me one step closer to cuddling with Sheryl in the upper deck but at least it's on the blue line of the attack-twice end. What are the odds of finding a woman who likes hockey, anyway? I've never been so lucky until now.

When I walk out, Louis's waiting. "WAD came back. Arraignment's December tenth."

"Stick it in before the end of the week. I like it." I nod toward Room 2. "Let me hit this one and see what happens."

21

This chair tho . . . it's the coldest thing I ever sat on. It's like they dipped it in ice. I feel coldness just trucking up thru my bones. And I'm trying not to shiver when the door opens and in comes this wide-load dude in a sport coat like football announcers wear on TV. Except it barely fits him.

He lifts. You can see how he lifts. Power stuff. Like with a belt and everything. He looks like a Mexican Hulk. If Bruce Banner went all brown-skinned when he changed up. And not green. The only thing not making the picture is he's got a big-ass black mustache.

He looks up from some papers and says, "I'm Detective Montero."

Hulktero, I say in my head. *Hulkitito.*

I can't tell yet if he's good cop or bad cop, or some crazy-ass Lynwood Viking, so I decide I'll wait and see. I'll sit here. And not complain even tho my whole ass is numb. I'll listen. I'll watch him. He's looking at me like he's sizing me up. Seeing what I'm about.

"First time getting arrested, huh?"

No point saying yes. He knows it.

He says, "Is Safulu your real name, or are we going to have to wait for your prints to come back before we know for sure?"

I don't say shit back to him on that. Little's older brother went in on his cousin's name and Social number a grip of times. Stealing some liquor. Having an itty bit of weed on him. It wasn't till somebody ratted on him for graffiti that they put a warrant out on the name. Sheriffs picked his cousin up at work and marched him right out. They booked his ass and everything too. Took them half a day to figure out that he didn't match all the mug shots they had. They had to let him go then.

The Mexican Hulk says, "You want some soda?"

Good cop. I don't say yes. He goes back to looking at the papers he's got.

He says, "What the hell is a Samoan doing with a gang of Mexicans, anyway? What's the matter, you couldn't figure out how to get down to Carson?"

It's a one-way conversation now. He's just going off my looks. Wizard says they can do that. Just read you. I'm trying to show him nothing.

"So," he says, "where did you got all those scars, those ones down your arm? They look like teeth marks."

I'll never tell him.

And he must already know that, cuz he's saying, "Is the reason they named you Dreamer because you stare off into space like this?"

I shrug to cover up a shiver.

"Never mind, I think I know the answer to that one." He taps a pen against the table we got between us. "So, let me get down to it for you. Mister Wizard over there says you pulled the trigger, that it was you earning stripes. He was only there to oversee and make sure it went down. He's saying he'll admit to being an accessory. What do you think about that?"

I almost jump straight out of my chair. Almost shout, *Man, I didn't pull no fucking trigger!*

Almost.

And I almost bite my lip.

Cuz even if this *were* true, what he's saying about Wizard saying this? Me doing it?

The gun still wouldn't be in my room after that.

Shit.

I'm getting crazy just thinking about it.

Blood's rushing fast to my face. And he's looking at me going red.

He knows he got me. He's bringing his eyebrows together all like he cares about what happens to me. He's trying to good-cop me for sure.

"You got no record. He's got a long one," Montero says. "He's probably lying, but I don't know that unless you tell me something."

I got a nervous sweat going. And I got this voice sitting up in the back of my head. Wondering if Wizard really did say that. If he really tried to do me like this. And I know for sure that even if he did, I can't do nothing about it right now.

Right now I just can't show weakness.

And I know I can't say shit . . . that I shouldn't say shit, but I can't help it.

The truth's bubbling up in me.

"I wasn't there." I say it fast. "You got the wrong guy."

It don't feel good to say it. It feels like, *Oh shit*. It feels like I was trying to do something good cuz it was true, then maybe ended up hurting myself. Cuz I see this little flicker in Hulktero's eyes then. That's when I know I made a mistake.

I got to shut the fuck up right now. *Got* to.

Can't say anything more on anything, even tho part of me wants to say what happened that night. I even think for a second how he could help me. I know that's just wishful tho. Nothing I could say gets me out of here. It only gets me deeper. You look how I look in my neighborhood, and they pick you up? You disappear. It's over, man. Cuz they throw you away.

And I know how anything else I say right now will just get twisted up. And I know that, cuz Wizard told me. He told me to be cool. Told me this is how it goes. Told me the most important word, and it's on the tip of my tongue and I'm saying it . . .

I'm saying, "Lawyer."

The Mexican Hulk makes a face at me like he's real disappointed in me. And I almost laugh. Cuz he does it like I've never seen anybody older than me make that stupid face at me before. Like I'm not some kind of expert in it. And he just gets up.

Before he leaves tho, he says, "Hey, Jacob, a lawyer isn't enough if you didn't do this. You need to save yourself on this one, because the system is the system. It always gobbles up the ones with the lowest distance to fall. Think about it."

22

Lights snap on and some new-shift sheriffs are telling us, "Up!" and "Time to move." They're looking fresh, like they're used to being up this early. It's always the young ones that get the bad shifts, but these ones are eager, ready to clear this little jail out so it can get filled back up again, and right now I'm glad as hell that I woke up and readjusted myself with the packages after midnight. There's no cameras in here, and I had to take advantage of that, so I popped out all my cargo when it was still good and dark. Fished it. Checked it. Washed it in the basin and was stupid grateful they had soap in the little wall dispenser. There was no Vaseline, so it all had to go back in with spit. Better than nothing.

Damn, but I *definitely* shouldn't have had those chili cheese fries. That was a dumbass move. I was all overconfident from being on the other side of the line, and I got so caught up in the power of it. I've been paying for eating them little greasy bastards ever since, with some cramps and gas, but no runs. *Thank you for that, God.* When I was done and buttoned up, I soaped my arms like I was a surgeon after. Twice I went all the way to my elbows. Nobody ever even came by to look in on me either. I got lucky.

I got a couple wannabe Crips in here with me. One was dead asleep, and the other was faking when I was doing what I had to. You get good at doing that when you're used to being locked up, so you don't have to talk to people, or don't have to see stuff it'd be better for you not to see. But all three of us are awake now, standing up, waiting to get cuffed. I'm worrying about Dreamer right now, because they put his ass in another cell after that bullshit questioning. I knew they were trying to play him. Shit. If I was a sheriff, that's who I would've zoomed in on and tried to crack. I would've put some lies in his ear about how, *Wizard said you did it! He's gonna testify against you!* I know he must be tripping on it, especially with how he was in there for a long-ass time, but he'll be good when we get to County and I can get back up with him.

They line us up outside the cell. Me and the tall wannabe Crip get cuffed together. We don't even look at each other. They line the other little dude up with a guy from another cell and do their wrists. After that, they do up everybody's ankles too. That's new on me. They didn't do that the last time I got scooped up at Lynwood Jail, which has me wondering if somebody tried to leg it out of here so now we've all got to be locked down. I huff some hallway air because it smells better than sharing a cell and a toilet with two other people. I'm feeling sick to my stomach right about now too, but it isn't because of the chili. It's for the journey I got ahead of me, making it all the way to County without deputies finding what I got inside me, because if they do, that's new charges. Felony possession. Felony intent to distribute. That's years of my life I'm carrying inside me right now. *Years* sitting in my guts. Double fucking digits, man. It's nothing to what would've happened to me if I disobeyed, though, so I carry this weight, and I move when the door goes.

The air outside is so nice when it hits me. I smell trees and I want to stand there and keep smelling it for a while, but the sheriffs have shotguns, and nobody can fuck with that. I go where they tell me to go, off the curb, over the asphalt, around the front of the bus so the headlights hit me in the eyes, and it's already running and its nose is pointed out at the street so they can roll straight out when it's time, and then I'm going up the steps.

The bus is this big silver sheriff's thing that looks like a Greyhound but it's only for prisoners heading to the big jails. We must not be the first stop because there's already some heads popped up over seats behind the cage door as it swings open, but I don't see anyone worth recognizing. No one from Scrappy's crew. No one from down Long Beach Boulevard, allies or otherwise. The only good news is seeing Dreamer already in the way back, sitting up straight even though he's chained to some twitchy-looking dude. I throw him a look, one that I'm hoping tells him that I'm here for him and I got him, so don't even trip. He nods up at me, and that's good. That gives me heart.

This one time, before Dreamer lived with Angela and me, we went out robbing houses because Big Fate said so. He put us onto this little crew that some hype was running, and the whole mission was to sneak into houses and try to see if we could find guns or knives to either use or frame people up with. It would've been fun times, if it wasn't being run by a dude that was high on everything, all the time. At the first house, I watched this fool eat every pill in a medicine cabinet just to see what it would do to him. Lil Creeper, his name was. That fool was fucking nuts for real, man! Shit. I even heard he got shot in the face during the riots, but you can't believe everything you hear. Anyways, Dreamer and me are out with this fucker, and we hit three more houses smooth. We got our little gloves on and we got a driver coasting along in the alleys behind, and it's all going good until Lil Creeper sees this house and says something like, "Oh, that's Dwayne's house. Fuck that dummy. We're gonna bust his shit up." And Dreamer and me don't wanna go, but we have to, and I swear to God, man, the moment we get up over this tall fence and down into that yard, we hear barking. Loud. Scary-ass barking. Coming right towards us. I hear some scrambling right behind us then and look up, and there's Creeper, already back on top of the fence like some fucking ghetto gymnast, bouncing the fuck out like no big deal. I turn back to see these eyes shining out, getting bigger and closer, and then Dreamer fucking pushes me backwards and shouts, "Go!" Then he steps up to this monster dog, man, and he swings on it! That's how I knew that Samoan fucker was all warrior, and I'll know it until the day I die. He left that fucking dog moaning and came back over the fence a few minutes later, bleeding down his arm and on his left side. He makes it to the car where Lil Creeper and me are waiting, and we slip on out of there without saying a word. Dreamer never even asks to go get stitches, never once complains how he's all bit up, not even when we go one more block and Creeper tells everybody, "Oh wait, *that wasn't* Dwayne's house. This one is."

I laugh, man, sitting right here on this bus. Can't fucking help it. Even here, now, I'm carrying it all with me.

23

Being chained up to some dude I never met before is worse than I thought it could be. Every time we pass a streetlight in this bus smelling like farts, he's jerking. That pulls my wrists out and away from me cuz we're locked together. So I keep my arms tight. It don't help. He keeps jerking. Mumbling. Spazzing out. And my cuffs just eat my wrists up. Rubbing. Ripping.

I hate the feeling of it. It makes my skin all crawly. Makes me think of how that dog wouldn't let go of me all those years ago. How it just stayed locked on. And I been trying to keep my head down. I can't tho. I can't.

This fool's pushing me way past where I'm trying to be. And I got Wizard's words inside me, about how I can't show weakness.

So I say in his ear, "You keep pulling these chains, I'll find a way to choke you with them."

He looks at me. Yellow streetlamps light his face up thru the metal mesh over the windows, crisscrossing his face with shadows.

I see his eyes. Red. Wide. I see how big his pupils are. And then we pass into more dark. Seeing those eyes tho? That gets me thinking, *Uh-oh.* This dude's about to go off. He's not all the way there. And I'm wondering if threatening wasn't the best move. If I should've just asked his name instead or tried to calm his ass down. Then the next light comes . . .

And this motherfucker screams like I'm stabbing his ass.

"Agggh!" It's all throaty and deep. "Agggggggh!"

My stomach jumps inside me.

Up front, the deputy's yelling, "What the hell is going on?"

And the only thing I can think to do is hold my hands up so they can see I didn't do nothing to him.

"Sir," I say, "this fool's crazy! He's freaking out on me."

Other people pipe up too. They say they don't need this so early. How this fool's 5150 for sure. And somebody needs to shut him up. And

I look to Wizard nodding up at me like, *Do what you got to. Nobody's about to blame you for it.*

Cuz this bus ain't slowing down. And his yelling's not stopping. And I even watch how the nearest white deputy with a shotgun looks at me then straight turns his back!

So that's that, I'm thinking.

A square of yellow streetlight rolls down the whole bus then. And I wait for it to pass. For it to get dark again. Before the monster comes out.

I take a good hard look at this dude next to me. I hunch my shoulders down before bringing my elbow up. Hard. Right to his jaw.

The first one don't work. The second one either. The third tho? I bounce his head off the window frame. Like, *pa-klank*! He goes real quiet then.

Nobody cheers. Nobody says nothing the entire time.

There are some grunts after. That's it.

My elbow hurts. And I feel bad about it. This dude didn't even protect himself.

I try to figure out if I'm in trouble. The sheriffs don't say shit tho. They must be happy he's quiet.

The mood's all changed now. Fools lay back, watch the freeway go by. I do the same. The whole way up the 110, I just look out over this dude bleeding right next to me. It don't look bad. He'll be fine.

A busted-up Camry glides alongside us for a ways. The driver's a girl. She's wearing a uniform but I can't figure out what it is. It's black. It's got a patch on the arm. It's security or something. I stare at her for a couple miles. At the back of her neck. How it's so smooth there. Soft-looking. It's depressing as fuck to think this is as close as I'll be to a woman in a long-ass time. I can't talk to her. Can't try to make her laugh. I don't even find out what her face looks like. She never looks up. Doesn't matter how bad I want her to.

And I start noticing the same thing everywhere after that. All over the road. From every car. You're invisible on this bus. No drivers bother looking at us. I can even see some of them getting low behind their wheels. Leaning forward. Hiding, almost, from the jail on wheels. They don't want to see in. And nobody wants to be seen by the bad guys inside looking out.

So I stop thinking about them. The drivers. I think about the cars instead. Like, what will they even look like when I get out? I heard of how low-totem homies go in for six months and get told by big homies to put in work. Move drugs. Stab some fools up. Whatever. That's how six months turns into ten years.

That's what happened to Wizard's cousin. He turned ten months into two years. Then two into eight. He served six and a half.

When he got out, he didn't recognize anything. He was talking about it like *Back to the Future*. How being inside, everything stays the same, then you come out and styles are different. Cars are different. Reading newspapers isn't the same as seeing it for yourself, he said. In color.

Man . . . if I do six and a half? That's me not coming out till the next century.

And I trip on that for a minute, basically till the dude I'm chained to wakes up. He opens his eyes.

I show him my elbow with his blood on it. Just in case I need to use it again. This fool puts his hands over his face.

"Don't scream," I say real quiet, "and I won't smash you again."

He nods under them hands. His braids shake. And we don't say shit between us from the 110 to the 101 to the Alameda exit. Soon as we get off, other people start talking tho.

It's how I know we're getting close. Dudes go off about this being different or that being the same. This bail bondsman that had a spot two streets over is gone. He shot his wife cuz she was running around on him. He's out at Pelican Bay now. And somebody else is going on about spreads. How he's gonna be just fine inside cuz everybody'll be coming to him for his tortilla- and tamale-making skills. And out loud, I almost say, *They let you make tortillas and tamales in there?* But I don't. I'll just ask Wizard later.

All of them talk like County's just a hotel they go to, that they're back for a little stay. Wizard's been there before. Never heard him talk it up like this tho. I guess that's a lesson too.

I get a weird feeling when we stop at this light next to Union Station. My mom took me when Metrolink first opened. She said she wanted to go someplace where she could see trees. She picked Moorpark off the map cuz it had the word *park* in it. We took the bus from Lynwood to downtown. It was a long-ass trip before even getting on a train. And we ride it. It's nice and all. Nicer than a bus. It's still almost two hours being around old white dudes wearing conductor hats and holding little binders of train pictures. When we get to Moorpark tho, there's nothing to do. We just walk up and down the one street till we go in a little restaurant. The Cactus something. She gets iced tea. I'm only allowed water with a lemon slice and two sugars. Then we get back on the next train. And go back down. Two weeks later she left. I think she took the Amtrak to Oakland. See her sister. She only took me on her test run. Then she left me behind.

The light's still red. Across from me, some bum digs in a trash can. He don't look up when we pass.

24

The bus stops in some sort of bay. The door opens. And we're up and moving. Wizard's way ahead of me. We get led into this underground area where we walk down a long hallway that trips me out cuz it's almost like a school. It's got painted murals everywhere around us, all saying cheesy stuff like County of L.A. this and that. Everybody's looking at them till they yell at us to keep our eyes front. They don't have to yell. Nobody's saying anything or acting weird, not even the dude I'm chained up with.

They take us thru a bunch more hallways. That's got me feeling dizzy somehow. Almost like somebody made the place this way just to confuse us or something. And I don't even know where we're supposed to be going till the lead deputy opens up this white door with a little window in it and tells us all to go inside.

We get our cuffs unlocked at the door before we go in. One by one.

Inside, it's not like how I pictured from movies. It's not bars or thick-ass glass. It's just a room. Off-white walls with a grayish yellow to them. The floor looks like concrete when it gets wet. Off in the corner there's a toilet with a little half block of wall next to it, for some privacy. You can still see whoever is sitting on there tho. The top half.

I see Wizard and make a move to where he's at. He's got his back to the wall. And he makes some dude move so I can do the same.

He looks happy to see me. Tells me I did good with the crazy guy I had to hit. And I guess he was worried about me more than I thought.

That makes me feel grateful and happy too. The best I felt since before the first cuffs went on. For real.

We keep it close so we can talk low and quick. Side by side. I let him know how Montero tried to play me.

"Told you, homeboy." Wizard smiles like he knows the game. "But listen, when you get in with your lawyer make sure they don't separate the cases."

I say, "What's that mean?"

"It means me and you together, homeboy. Riding."

"Same trial?"

"Same trial, same everything."

That's not sounding right to me.

Cuz if he shot Scrappy with me not even there, it seems like this kind of shit hurts me to help him.

I get it, I guess. It's a power move on his part. A way to try to get out of this.

And since I'm lower on the totem pole, that's just how it goes.

But it don't feel right.

It makes me feel . . . I don't know. *Bad.* Bad and sad at the same time.

Like, I thought he fucking cared about me, you know? I thought we were boys and he'd get me out of this if he could . . .

But maybe this is him just playing me for angles. And even tho I seen it coming, I still got to let it happen.

I got to stand up and take it.

And it's been so long with me being quiet that Wizard's looking at me to see if he has to explain it again.

"Okay," I say. "I thought that's how it was gonna be, anyways."

It's not really a choice. I know that.

If I back out on Wizard now, he won't have my back in here. And that shit's a no-brainer.

Cuz everybody in jail needs people looking out for them, even if they're really just looking out for themselves first.

"Good, homes," Wizard says as he looks over the other fools in the cell. "Real good."

He has me watch people, start trying to read who's what. From where. I also look for anybody from Scrappy's crew. I don't see anybody. There might be a few in the jail part. Wizard keeps his eye out for big dogs, if they came for a trial date down here or something. He doesn't see anybody.

Everything's too much. The smell most of all. All these dudes sweating, farting, breathing. Some of them junkies that ain't showered or even worn deodorant in forever. It's the worst smell I ever smelled. I got to act like it ain't a big deal tho.

This place is a whole different beast to the streets. You can always hole up out there. Be alone. But in here? There's nowhere to go but into people. Into their space. With your eyes. With your body.

And it feels like anything can pop off at any time. It has a wild feeling to it.

Wizard's watching my face, reading me.

"You're getting that zoo feeling, huh?" Wizard's got his shirt collar up over his nose, bandito-style. "Everybody's trying to figure which animal is which. Who's about to get eaten. Who to stay the fuck away from."

The door goes and the guards tell us to step back. More bodies come in. They don't take any out. We look at them. Three black guys. Two white. They look for space to stand in. They don't even move for the benches. There's too many of us in here now. Forty, maybe. Forty-five? Only one of them is meeting stares with some cold-ass eyes.

"Oh shit." Wizard's raising his voice next to me. "Is that Big Dev or what?"

Bodies part as Wizard moves toward the biggest of the new black ones in here, the one glaring at fools.

I follow. I watch Wizard's back all the way. I see some dudes from the bus looking at us. They're nodding at me cuz they know what I did with my elbow.

When we get up close, Big Dev recognizes Wizard. "Yo, what the fuck, Wizard? Haven't seen your ass since Chino!"

And Wizard says, "What's up, my nigga?"

They do one of them half hugs and they're all smiling.

This room tho?

Shit! It got cold as hell when Wizard dropped *nigga* in here.

And I feel eyes on me now. On us.

I swear I even feel fists getting balled up, ready to get thrown.

And I'm definitely wishing I had my back to a wall right now. Not out in the middle of the room with bodies on every side of me.

Big Dev knows it too.

"Easy, y'all," he says, and he's swinging his eyes around at everybody. "This fool's South Central, and if you mad, then you obviously ain't from where we from. It's how we fuckin talk. And anybody tryna get at this motherfucker in here has to get at me first, just so you know who to start with."

Wizard smiles at that. I can tell he's pushing buttons on purpose.

He knows what he can get away with. And this is him showing power. Big fucking power. The kind nobody wants to step to.

And I'm getting now how I made the right decision not to separate cases. Cuz there's a lot worse ways to come into County Jail than on Wizard's hip.

I'm grateful for that as I'm looking around to see if anyone's wanting to test. Nobody does tho. Mainly cuz there's a new problem . . .

One of these hype-ass junkies is on the only toilet, trying to hide himself behind that little half wall. You can still see his shoulders and his face tho. So everybody knows the dude putting out the monkey-house stink that's taking over the whole room.

And it's about to cause a riot too.

Somebody shouts, "¡Aguas, aguas, aguas!"

Cuz he wants him to add water.

Another dude says, "Courtesy flushes, fool. Drop one, flush one! Fuck!"

And it's Big Dev that's saying, "Don't you fuckin know how to do time, bitch? You ain't alone in here!"

And that one hits me. Cuz I'm thinking, *Yeah, I* definitely *ain't alone in here.*

Nobody is.

25

When they finally open up the holding door, they just take all of us. We roll down another couple corridors to one giant reception room that's got all these benches in it but you can't really sit, you got to straddle them because they're so narrow. I stand off to the side of one. I'm not about to put that pressure on my ass with what I got inside of me. They let me stand, and that's good too, because one of the deputies yells at the sitters, "I want everyone to scoot together. Nuts to ass!"

They separate the K-10s out first. That's the famous or super-dangerous ones. Four of those dudes get pulled while the rest of us all go through medical evaluations. TB tests. Making sure you don't have blood diseases. We get interviewed next. Questions like, what set you with? They don't ask me that. They already know. It's all on my paper. They got my tattoo photos on file too. We get sent through these revolving bars when that's done, and it's on the other side of those that you know you're in jail for good. I see it on Dreamer's face when we get the fish kits. Razor. Deodorant. Soap. All in a little baggie. And then we wait again. That's jail, man. Go in somewhere. Wait. Go out. Wait, then wait again. It's their clock. You just have to move to it.

A trustee brings out a big box of food with sandwiches and fruits, and everybody but me grabs something. I tell Dreamer to go on ahead with it, because we don't know when the next round of food's coming. He asks me if I'm sure I don't want anything. He's a good dude, Dreamer. He's there for his homeboys. But I ain't about to put anything else inside me right now, so I tell him I'm good. Dreamer goes away and comes back with a mashed-up PB&J and an apple that looks like somebody dropped it.

I'm relieved he didn't fight me on keeping our cases together. He sure thought about it. He's smart enough to know it wasn't good for him to do it, but he knew better than not to go along, which is exactly why I need to keep him close in here. Keep him happy. Make sure he has what he needs. They call me for the strip-down then, so I give Dreamer a little nod and I go stand next to this door where they tell me.

Last time I was through here, the door was closed when they did naked evaluations on you, but this time it's open, and I think maybe it's open because the trustee left it open when he went to go grab the blues and the deputy inside didn't notice. I don't know. They are damn busy right now. There's at least a hundred other fools in that giant room right now all waiting to be processed. Standing here, I make sure my feet are solid under me, because this is where it could all go wrong. I'm puckering myself up down there. I imagine all the balloons rising up higher inside me. Helium. I imagine they're rising up, getting up to my ribs, and bonking up against bones. I pray they stay.

Nobody's looking at me, so I lean and look in the room that I'm next for, just so I can see what I'm dealing with. What type of deputy. The wannabe Crip I was chained with earlier is in there, facing the wall. He's a skinny six-foot black man with a shaved head and a hanging ass like somebody let the air out of it, but I couldn't give a fuck about that. It's his feet that get me. They're pink, like completely fucking pink, like a white dude's feet got slapped on a black dude's body. Never seen that before. There's these splotches up his shin bones too, looking like thrown pink paint on his blackness, and that's it. No other splotches or pink parts on his whole body except three little ones on his back. It's mostly just his feet. Crazy.

"Step up." The deputy aims a finger at the floor.

I notice how he's not wearing gloves and that's when I figure he must be new at this, like it's his first day or something, which explains the open door.

Wannabe Crip dude steps up. He stands on the patch of tile that got pointed at. I pull my head out as the deputy tells the dude, "Catcher squat. Cough and give me three."

He must go on with it and give the deputy the County smile, because I hear the click of the flashlight in the officer's hand. One cough, then two, but before he gets to three, the deputy's announcing, "Contraband," like it's no big deal, like he sees it all day.

I sneak a peek and all I see is some metal poking out of dude's pocket. I don't even really know what it is at first, but then I turn my head a little and see, yeah, wow. It's the top of a lighter! Crazy. It's not even wrapped up in anything! That's amateur, man. You can get it stuck inside you like that and get all infected, and I don't even *know* how he got through Firestone with that up in him. That's what I'm thinking when the deputy turns around and looks to the door, *sees* me, and orders, "Inmate, grab that lighter."

I look back at it, and it's sticking out more now. The bottom part of it is red, all looking like some Wile E. Coyote shit. A cartoon stick of dynamite right there. Like his ass is a mouth, trying to smoke it. I try not to laugh. I swear. I try so fucking hard because I need these balloons up in me. I need them staying stuck. *Helium*, I tell myself. *Helium*. And, man, deputies hate nothing in the world more than repeating themselves, but he does it. "Inmate, grab that lighter!"

I sputter out with, "Uh, no disrespect, sir. I'm not grabbing that butt lighter."

Crip dude is shaking now. He's been in that squat so long, his legs are buckling. He whines, "Can I stand up now?" just as the trustee comes rolling in past me, and I don't even know where he came from because I didn't see him before, but he's got the blues in his hands and one of them little baggies for evidence. He's a veterano. He knows the drill with this as he closes the door behind him, so after that, all I can really do is lean closer to hear.

"Remove it from yourself." This is the trustee's voice. "Deposit it in this bag."

Crip dude gets asked if there's more in him and he says no, that's all he had time to do, and then he gets let up and it's done with. The door opens and dude comes out behind the trustee wearing his blues and there's another deputy walking up holstering his walkie-talkie to go write this fool up a new charge.

It's my turn then, and I'm sweating fear-sweat. I strip like he tells me, and when I step up on that same spot for getting inspected, it's all hitting me. I feel so full inside. I face the wall feeling like I want to cry, but fuck that. I'm tucking my stomach up and in before I go down in that catcher squat. I swear I feel the balloons up near my ribs, and I know the only way they're coming out is through my mouth. There's no exit down low, I tell myself. None.

The key is don't do it too fast. Don't do three quick coughs like you're obviously trying to get it done with. You do one, then two, then three. The coughs aren't for making you shit anyway. They're for anything you got hiding in your throat. When the flashlight clicks on, I cough the first cough, and it's good, not too deep. I feel everything holding up, but the fear of letting go is creeping into my brain, and I start worrying about instinct taking over and not being able to beat it, so I pretend there's string inside me tied to the back of my tongue. It goes all down through my guts, and it's tied to everything, every single balloon, and they're all strung together like a whole bunch of chorizo, not going nowhere. I cough again.

"Hurry up," the guard tells me.

I pray. *La Virgencita, hear me. Keep this all inside me. Don't let me drop this right here on this floor. Don't let me drop these years straight out of my body, because they'll bag it, Virgencita. It'll be evidence and I'll be gone a real long time. Don't let me let go of these years. Please. Please-please-please. Let me hold them inside. Let me hold them.*

I cough a third time. Inside, I feel something slip because gravity's coming at me, and I want to stand up but I got to give it that one last split second until his flashlight clicks off, and it does, and I stand up quick and pucker so hard that I tuck everything that was slipping back up, and I just tell myself, *Helium, helium, helium!* And it's working, so I'm thanking La Virgencita with all I got. I'm naming off saints in my head too, the ones I can remember, but thanking La Virgencita the most, because she just saved my ass today, like, for *real* for real.

26

I'm not on an even keel, but I'm good. I can walk. I can talk. The dope I got last night saw to that. I don't love how I got it. But you can get shit in here if you really have to. And I *had* to. So there's no earthquakes today. Not yet. And I'm even up for breakfast.

Fifteen minutes is all you get for it. I had oatmeal that tasted like dust and water stirred and warmed up, and it's after that when I'm trying to figure out if I should try reading the copy of *Villette* that's missing the first ten pages that I got off Desi One-Ear, or check on Ralph's pruno, when a deputy calls my name for visits, and I'm saying to myself that there's no way I've got a visit, but I go up to him. You can't not.

Picking my way through the dorm, I'm wishing it's Irma. With her damn bony hips.

Irma wouldn't be through here, putting her name on a visitation log, and she doesn't even have a driver's license card to show at the front. I miss her. Irma. I even miss saying her name to her. Nobody could score like she could score. Nobody else I ever met could play you so good that when you caught her hiding your dope from you, you weren't even mad, just impressed that she could even figure out how to pry off the back of a mirror in a motel medicine cabinet and get some powder wrapped and ironed out so flat that she could stick it up in there.

Goddamn. Irma. And that woman sure had a pocket. Could hide anything up there. A whole kit. Two baggies. Shit was magic.

When I line up where they want us to line up to go out to visiting, a few other folks are kind of bouncing in the line like happy dogs, and I've got Irma in my head now, how her hair used to smell after she cooked up, how she used to like it when I choked her, just a little, when the big beautiful wave of a hit was coming on, and my brain's getting itself fired into all kind of crazy scenarios and my heart's going with it. That is, until I get told I'm meeting with a lawyer, and that's a new one on me.

I'm not trying to sound rude, but I can't help saying it. "Boss, I didn't even know I needed one, being back in here. I thought that was it. Do the time out."

Behind me, somebody laughs.

"That time's doing you." It's Ralph that's saying it. The dick.

We all get checked and say our last four numbers on our wrist things, and then the names get crossed off. While we're standing there, I ask why I might be having to see a lawyer.

"Inmate," the guard says, "I hold the list and tell you what's on it. I don't make it."

He's always like this. We call him BBQ behind his back, because he's so red all the time it looks like he's roasting under his uniform.

BBQ doesn't say anything back to me, just gives me my pass for the attorney room, so I get to walking with the other three from my block in our light blues. It's a ways following that line on the floor and saying, "Walking," every time we get to a doorway or to a hall or need to turn a corner, and we go to wait to get a nod from a deputy before we keep on. Only jail I ever been to where they let you walk on your own.

We cluster up tight because gen pop dark blues look at us different, like the worst of the worst, like we're all snitches or kiddie fiddlers in the PC dorm, and that's cool so long as they don't come near us or try earning some stripes. Pretty much all of us are trying to avoid the reds, the SVPs that got to walk escorted with a sergeant, cuffed the whole time.

It goes good. Quick. Following those lines so you don't got to think. Going down the escalator to the western hallway with its murals that are always good to look at, but it's drafty as hell in here. Ralph took a towel with him and wrapped it around his neck and down into his top because he's smart. It's like a scarf.

The group leaves me on my yellow line to check in and they keep going on orange for visiting. Only Ralph gives me a nod, so I give him one. I check and give my numbers to the deputy at the desk. He marks me down and takes me past the stools toward the usual zigzag of glass that goes up and down through the room, where I've always sat before, one hand cuffed up and one hand on the phone, but he's got me going to the little green lockbox rooms at the back, and that's got me thinking, what the hell's so important for an attorney to come at me here?

I'm the first one inside this little law room, so I get to sit here for a minute trying to find peace. I try to take a couple breaths and I think about expanding my body to all the air in the room so I can take it for myself, just me.

"All this air is mine," I say to my empty half of the room.

And it is.

Until the door opens on the other side and I swivel from looking back at the main room to look at a deputy ushering in this black guy in a brown suit with a brown tie that's got diagonal yellow stripes all over it and then closing the door again. This guy must be the new lawyer, because he sits down in the chair next to me. He's in his forties. But his face looks hangdog, like it belongs to a much older man. That's what my daddy would call it when your cheeks droop down.

He picks the phone up, so I do too.

"I'm Manfred. Your new PD." He smiles before he talks, and after.

He's big but he doesn't take care of himself. I could roll him if I had to. Go for the throat and then run. You can't help thinking on stuff like that in here, even though there's this thick-as-hell glass between us.

I say, "Why do I need a public defender here? I'm in for violating parole on an existing judgment."

"I don't know any more than you do. I got a call on this earlier, and now, here I am."

"Huh," is all I say. "What's the weather out there like today? Sunny? Who're the Dodgers playing?"

When the door opens again, a woman sweeps in, and I mean *sweeps*. She's got a rush to every inch of her, her long hair flowing back, quick little heel clicks on the floor, not even shaking Manfred's hand as he gets up and puts it out. White woman. Five-foot-eight. Skinny. Black blazer. Black skirt. Black pantyhose. Black shoes. None of it so much expensive, but picked well. Out on the street, if I had to, I'd still rob her fine ass, but I'd appreciate her first.

Manfred sits back down as she sits right next to him. She brushes her hair out of her eyes, showing me she's got a kind of cat face. Blue-green eyes like cats have. The outer shape of them. And they're sharp inside. Cold too.

My lawyer, he says, "Why are we here, Kristina?"

And they're on a first-name basis, so I'm saying to myself that that's good.

Kristina puts a card up to the glass for me to see. It's got her name on it, and her first is spelled different from how I thought, but then the last name is like this mess of *r*'s and *k*'s and a *v*, and I don't even catch it, really. *Mrrrkrrvv*. Or something. But here's what I do catch.

County of Los Angeles, it says. Everything neat and lined up with a little seal and everything.

Office of the District Attorney.

Her name, and then the kicker. Her title. *AHD Hardcore Gang Prosecution.*

She says, "That's my name, so you know who I am and that I'm real. I'll do what I say I'll do."

The words *Hardcore Gang* don't fill me with happy thoughts. The second I see them I know this is about Wizard. That they got him. And then I start getting real worried. If he's caught, where is he? Is he here? In County? Where in County? Thunder Dorm? Gang unit? Gen pop? My stomach's sure going, but I'm trying to keep it cool. Hold it together. At least they housed me protective custody straight off. That's what my light blues are for.

I say, "What's AHD stand for?"

"Assistant head deputy." She flips papers. My papers. Already on to what she's here for. "Mr. Clark, you're currently serving out the rest of your sentence for violating your terms of release on yet another possession charge, are you not? Another five months."

My lawyer looks at me. I don't even know if he's checked my file.

"Yeah," I say, but I'm almost scared to, because maybe they're pulling a trick on me with an easy question. "It's four months and three weeks now, though."

She squints at me a little.

"My mistake," she says, but the look on her face says that it doesn't really matter. Not to her, it doesn't. "There's something I need to bring to your attention: there are changes afoot in the criminal justice system here in the state of California, in particular how we look at and prosecute criminal drugs cases. Are you with me?"

I nod. She talks like hard books read.

"Good," she says. "Are you familiar with the term *drug court*?"

I say, "I'm familiar with going to court for drugs."

She squints at me again. "Indeed."

The way she says it sure makes a man feel small.

She's about to say something else, but I cut in. "You ever read *Villette*? I'm trying to figure out if I should read it. I guess I got time, huh?"

I don't even know why I say it, I just do. I guess I just want her knowing I read. I can at least do that. I'm not nothing.

She turns to Manfred and says, "Counselor, please instruct your client to listen, rather than talk."

Manfred puts his hand up like I'm a kid and he's showing me a stop sign.

"I ain't no fucking kid," I say to him.

This Kristina lady, she smiles at that.

"What I need to hear from you is that you will stand by your affidavit, that you will sit reputably on the stand in court and identify Wizard Tavira as the man who shot Lucrecia Lucero in an attempted assassination, and that Dreamer Safulu stood by while it happened. In short, Mr. Clark, I need to hear from you that you are solid."

I guess I kind of knew she was gonna say that. I knew how I'd have to do that eventually. But I don't say I will. Not yet.

"That solidity comes with a price," my lawyer says.

And it's such an interesting choice of words that I got to turn and look at Manfred in a whole new way. He's smiling at her. Maybe I didn't give him enough credit.

"Indeed, it does, Carlos. Drug court is a program that will begin early next year. I can't say for certain when it's starting, I'm not a Sacramento bureaucrat, but I assure you that it is happening. The entire focus of this particular judicial revolution is rehabilitation, not incarceration. From your pattern of offenses, Mr. Clark, it is obvious that you need help more than you need to be locked up with violent criminals, even in a protective custody capacity. Would you agree?"

I like how this is turning for me. "I would."

"So, here is what I can do for you today, Mr. Clark. Pending review by a judge—and if you accept, I can get us in tomorrow with Judge Olney to sign off—I can get you ahead of the game with drug court. First on deck, so to speak. One, you will be back out on parole as soon as possible, abiding by your terms. Two, you will be in a halfway house, *not* residing in a hotel frequented by known drug offenders, as you were before. Three, you will be attending mandated NA meetings, so that when I bring you in front of drug court next year, you will look like a model citizen succeeding at getting his life back together so that you will get the best possible sentence we can manage."

Nobody's asking, but I ain't exactly interested in doing all those hoops. I'm more worried about who looks for me once I go out, and if I can keep breathing.

I say, "If you put me back out there, Wizard's people are just gonna find me. You got witness protection or anything?"

She squints the hardest I've seen her yet. "We can get you into a halfway house somewhere other than Lynwood, so that the likelihood of running into any of Wizard Tavira's associates is greatly reduced. We can't do more than that. We don't have the resources of the federal government, and believe me, although we are using a new method for fast-tracking cold-blooded gang cases, it is by no means a priority in the way you might like it to be."

"Maybe I just stay in here. Maybe it's safer."

She darts her eyes at my lawyer before she says, "Mr. Clark, what I'm about to share with you is not public knowledge, but I believe it is in your best interest to know it: Wizard Tavira and Dreamer Safulu were transferred to this very institution last night. They are here now, and I don't think any of us are naïve enough to presume they cannot reach you in here, even in your protective dorm, by some extraordinary and nefarious means. Once we charge them tomorrow and their lawyers are furnished with our supporting documentation—including your redacted affidavit."

She sees me blink and stops.

"*Redacted* means your name is taken off it, but we've seen many cases where that doesn't matter. Somebody gets sloppy with the black ink or a scumbag lawyer tells them. Either way, they will find your name and know what you said. As such, I think it's best to assume that you are safer out there than you are in here."

I don't know how to argue against all that. And she knows I know it.

"Talk it over with your attorney. I'll be back in ten minutes," she says, and sweeps to the door.

27

I come back out through the sally port to sit on an empty bench in the lobby. I rummage through my briefcase for my cell. I call the office. I tell my assistant the offer is on the table and I'll call back when it's done. That was a quick one—easy. The second call won't be. There's a thrumming in my lungs as I dial. It rings three times before my ex-husband answers.

"Montero." He's terse, must not recognize my new number.

"It's Kristina."

"Counselor." He's surprised, but not shocked. My brother must've told him about my promotion.

"Detective." I thought I was over his voice. I'm not. I miss the bass of it. His laugh can still turn me inside out. I'm not proud of that. "You're not thinking about Catalina, are you?"

"Not until you mentioned it."

"Good." I pivot to the reason I'm calling. "I got your case, the Tavira conspiracy with attempted."

"I was afraid you might. Congrats on the promotion, by the way. Ivica ratted you out."

"He never could keep his mouth shut around you." I switch the phone to my other ear. "Listen, I just sat with our star witness, Augie Clark. He's shaky, Willie."

"So, you're trying to shape him up, then?"

"Spoken like someone who knows what that feels like."

"Spoken like someone who *benefited*, and who got out the other side a better man."

"That's low, Willie."

"Why is it low? Because I said I got out? I *also* said you made me better. Shit. What do you even need, Kristina?"

I like it when he ties himself in knots. "I need you to know that, pending approval, I'll be sending Clark back out on his original parole before shifting him to drug court in the new year."

"Hell of a perk. Which judge?"

"Olney."

"A slam dunk, then."

It is. On the other side, I can feel Willie studying the ceiling the way he always does when he's waiting for the other shoe to drop.

"You still haven't said what you need, Counselor."

"I'm having him sent to a halfway house. Ideally, one near Firestone—"

"Stop right there. I got a job, and it's not looking after witnesses. That's what parole's for, but I'm sure not much on this case rates. Hell, the vic didn't even die."

"Sadly, that's true."

"Shit. You hear yourself?"

"It's a joke, Willie—a tasteless, unfunny one—but a joke all the same."

"Look, I know you want to start with a conviction and get those stats going, but I can't babysit for you."

"And I'd never suggest it, but if your department were simply aware of a witness's whereabouts, perhaps they could check in from time to time and see that he's all right."

He heaves a sigh at me. "Listen, and I mean this with all due respect, you don't fucking want me for that. You want *parole*. That's their damn literal job description: checking the fuck up. I'll put you in touch with the parole agent that found the gun. Petrillo. I'm sure he'll happily do legwork for you."

"Who." I can't help myself. "The parole agent *who* found the gun."

"Right. We done?"

His neck always goes red when I correct his grammar. It might even be creeping around to his ears by now.

I can tell I'm losing him, so I pivot again. "What are the chances of Lucrecia Lucero testifying against Tavira and Safulu in open court?"

His response is a bitter laugh.

"That bad?"

"It's never happening, Kris. If you're lucky, we get her for an interview. One percent chance she says who did it on the tape, but I'll guarantee she doesn't. Even if she does, and you call her, she'd deny it. That's how their code works. We don't matter to them. They only matter to each other.

And her pointing fingers? No way. Court is a far-off fantasyland that they only visit from time to time. The streets are what's real. And what's behind bars runs the streets. They do something and get locked up, but they're in good with the big homies? They got *nothing* to fear. Shit, they got it *made* in there."

"Interesting to hear you say that, because I've got my investigator chasing rumors that somebody up the chain ordered the hit on Scrappy from inside. Would that change her mind?"

"Jesus, are you even listening to me? *Of course* it came from up the chain. All the more reason for Scrappy to take what came her way, stay alive, and earn points for not talking. Scrappy doesn't care about Wizard. She cares about the people *above* him. That's what keeps her mouth shut, and always will. And as far as why, let me solve that mystery for you: *drugs.* She was selling in the wrong places, or to the wrong people, or she wasn't paying her tax to the big dogs in the Bay or at Quentin. You're fucking welcome. I'll get you Petrillo's information."

He always has to get the last word. The growl of it sticks to me. It makes me excited and sad at the same time, and then more than mad at myself for feeling anything at all on account of William Montero, but, God, I already miss his voice—the certainty of it, the strength.

I could've done that better, made him happy to hear my voice again somehow, but I botched it. I tried to add something to his plate that he didn't need, and he's all out of favors. I'm putting my phone back in my bag when I see someone I haven't seen in a long time, Nick Park, turning the corner with his head in a file.

"You keep walking like that, Nick, and you'll bump your head. What is it, anyway?"

He looks up, sees me, and tries not to frown. "Gang case. I don't see many of these anymore."

Nick and I worked together in the DA's office until last year, when he defected to the criminal defense side.

He flips pages. "There's nothing on this kid. No record. Nothing."

I get a feeling then. "Is it Safulu?"

Nick looks at his paperwork. "How did—"

"He's a bad guy, Nick. Come on. I've got gang cops ready to testify that he *is* in a gang. You don't share a domicile with Wizard Tavira because he likes you. You do it because you're doing his bidding, and if you're present when the crime is committed, that makes you just as guilty."

Now Nick smiles. He shuts the file. We share a look. I already know his case and how he's arguing, and he already knows mine.

Mine: the fucking gun was found in *his client's* goddamn bedroom in a house he shared with one of the most notorious little gangsters in Lynwood; my victim *IDed the shooter*, his client's roommate, with a dying declaration, and you know what? My eyewitness may be a junkie, but he's white and an ex-serviceman, and both of those things still mean something in this country—especially with the right jury. He'll also look a lot better clean and ready for drug court. I guarantee that.

His: his client wasn't there; he has an alibi; he's a wayward lamb, unjustly accused.

Nick rocks back on his heels. "The ex-girlfriend's statement confirms he wasn't at the scene."

Bingo. Lame defense strategy confirmed. Nailed it. I *need* this case in the win column. One, it justifies my promotion. Two, it mollifies the barking assholes on the city side who convinced themselves that I only got this bump because I'm female. The fact that I'm standing across from one of the assholes who low-bridged me in the office for years when we worked together is too damn sweet. It's justice, is what it is. This morning, when I woke up, I didn't think it was possible to want it more, but then I run into Nick Park like fate is handing me the opportunity to stomp his fucking guts.

I smile. "That's hearsay. There's no way to track what the girlfriend said to the exact time of the shooting, and by the way, why wouldn't she lie for him?"

"Because she's his *ex*?"

"Because up until that very night she resided with two known gang members and might as well be classed a gang associate living in that house." I laugh. "Besides, I've done a lot of things for exes."

Hell, I'd lie for William Montero any day of the week and like doing it.

However, despite his newfound willingness to believe every pity story he hears, Nick Park is a worthy opponent, and he proves it by spouting some good sense. "I'm going to try to get him to separate the cases."

It's a smart play. Wizard going away is a slam dunk, especially when the ballistics on that gun come back. Dreamer is less so, but if he sticks with Wizard in that courtroom, the taint of association won't come off any time soon. I also know if the cases stay tied together the likelihood of a plea deal down the road is much higher. I'm banking on these cases staying locked. And they will. They always do.

"My conviction rate would rather you didn't, but good luck with that. You know that's not how things happen down there—to do that would be going against the code." I sound like Willie, and I can't decide if I like that or not.

Nick opens his mouth to say something, but I step up to the window to check back inside. "Got to go, Nick. It's nice to know I'll be seeing you later."

"It is."

I don't look back to see if he's smiling or scowling.

28

Seeing Kristina Mirkovich makes me feel like I am twenty-six again and still fighting with her for the privilege of doing pretrial motions. I asked her out once, like an idiot, and got shot down with a line about how she didn't date—and this stuck with me—*within the office gene pool*. It was nothing personal. I always thought it was a slimy way of saying she didn't date Asians. To this day, I still don't know if she thinks it's one of the reasons I left the DA for the state's PD office last year—as if making sure we were no longer colleagues were some misguided attempt to woo her.

During Sa-I-Gu last year, my cousin got arrested in front of a burning building in Koreatown for possessing a gun that wasn't his. Everything was a mess post–King riots—God knows I never did so much paperwork in my life—and yet no one at the office was surprised when I left. They knew about John and how closely I followed his case. Kristina, on the other hand, never asked and never cared. In her world, the answer was simple. I quit prosecuting because: (1) I couldn't hack it, or (2) I liked her, was rebuffed and yet still interested in her enough to risk my career, or (3) both. Which is precisely why nothing on earth would make me happier than beating her in her first case in her fancy new job, and if that did happen, well, it wouldn't be fucking personal.

When the deputy at the window tells me my client is being brought down, I head for the door and wait for it to buzz.

Jacob Safulu is seventeen, but looks fifteen. He has light brown eyes, big shoulders, and no visible tattoos. His hair is jet-black, and it's all there, which is good. He isn't shaving it bald yet, like Wizard Tavira in his intake photo, and I'd prefer he didn't. Doing so would only confirm him as a gang member in the jury's minds, and Tavira and Safulu sitting next to each other in court, looking exactly the same—a virtual illustration of guilt by association—is precisely what I hope to avoid.

When he picks up the receiver, I introduce myself and ask him what time he got transported.

"I don't know," he says. "Early bus."

He rubs the knuckles on his cuffed left hand. They're going purple.

"Did they house you yet?"

"Yeah. In forty-seven hundred."

I would rather he be in a dorm than a cell, because it would suggest a lower security priority, but at least he's in the dark blue uniform of the general population, which means they haven't escalated him simply by association with Wizard Tavira—who, allegedly, has links to the Mexican Mafia. "Where is Mr. Tavira housed, do you know?"

"Why?"

I stop taking notes. I look him in the eyes. "I'd like to know because I want you to consider separating your case from Mr. Tavira's, and I think the likelihood of that happening is better if you're both housed in different units."

Safulu smirks. "Where I'm from, man, we don't separate cases. That's not how it goes down. Besides, he's up the row from me. He's in forty-seven hundred too."

"On the night in question"—as I say it, his smirk melts to a wince—"were you there when Mr. Tavira fired the weapon at Miss Lucero?"

"I wasn't. I was with my girlfriend." He catches himself. "I was with my *ex*. She was breaking up with me when Scrappy got it."

"That would be Angela Alvarez?"

He waves a hand like he's trying to swipe her name away. "Yo, man, yes. Can we quit talking about her, please?"

"In her statement, she corroborates what you just said."

He stares at me.

"*Corroborates* means she agrees with you."

His brow wrinkles. "So, how then, are the sheriffs saying I did it?"

"A witness claims you were there."

"Claims Wizard was there too?"

"Claims he was the shooter, yes."

Safulu laughs. "Man, that Hulk detective down at Firestone had me sweating! Talking about how Wizard said I was the shooter, but the whole time he had a witness and he was just trying to mess with me? That's fucked up!"

"That's how the game is played, Mr. Safulu. Law enforcement use every means they can to get people to talk, including lying. There's nothing illegal about it."

He smiles a sarcastic smile before sinking in his seat. "Was the gun they found in my room the same one that got used on Scrappy, or what?"

"We don't know yet. We're awaiting ballistics tests."

He nods.

"Mr. Safulu, separating your case is the best, and possibly *only*, way to get you out of a lengthy prison term. In all likelihood, Mr. Tavira perpetrated this crime—"

"For real, Mr. Park, I'm not trying to be a jerk or nothing, but there's no home to go back to if I bail on Wizard like that." He hangs his head. "Wizard's big enough to take that away, no matter where he is. Pelican Bay? Lompoc? It don't matter."

"The DA has an eyewitness."

"Scrappy won't say shit."

"It isn't Lucrecia Lucero, Mr. Safulu. It's a bystander who bought drugs from Miss Lucero that night, and who, it seems, saved her life."

"A hype paramedic?" He sniffs at the thought of it. "Well, let me ask you, what if Wizard didn't do it? What if somebody was just trying to frame us up? I mean, I got no idea how the gun showed up in my dresser."

"The likeliest scenario here is that Mr. Tavira shot Scrappy, brought the gun home, hid it in your dresser in your room, which was not locked and he did have access to. If anything, Wizard was trying to frame you in order to get away with this crime."

At that moment, Safulu makes one of the purest, most incredulous faces I've ever seen. You could put it in commercials. It could sell breakfast cereal and toys. It's that good.

He says, "You playing me right now?"

"I am not. I thoroughly believe it is in your interest to, at best, separate your case, and at worst, be very careful around Mr. Tavira."

He actually nods at that. For the first time, I am making progress. He must have some misgiving about Wizard Tavira, or he wouldn't react this way.

He says, "So when am I seeing you again?"

"At the arraignment tomorrow. Your charges will be read, you'll plead—and it's my strong feeling that you should plead not guilty—and we proceed from there. I should tell you this has been classified as a hardcore gang case and handed off to a specialist prosecutor. I am sure you'll meet people here who have been waiting months for trial, which is normal with the system overload. However, your case will be up as early as next month. These types of crimes—gang-related walk-ups and drive-by shootings—are precisely what the district attorney's office intends to hit as hard as they can for the foreseeable future in an effort to deter gang violence. Do you understand?"

He nods.

"Good. We need to discuss penalties."

Penalties. He recoils at that word.

"You are on trial with the remainder of your life at stake, Mr. Safulu." I show him the charge sheet. "Do you see this, assault with a deadly weapon? Charged as a felony, it brings two, three, or four years with it, but that's just the appetizer. Attempted murder? Charged the same as murder. If you're found guilty, it's life in prison with the possibility of parole. Conspiracy to commit murder? If it's a violent felony—which yours is—it's an additional ten years as an enhancement on top of everything else. If it all goes poorly, you could be looking at life plus fourteen years, Mr. Safulu, even without the mayhem charge. It could be your entire life. You could very well die in a California state prison."

"Fuck!" he says. His eyes well up, and he looks down at his hands before swiping fiercely at tears.

I already know the answer, but I ask anyway. "Did Mr. Tavira specifically ask you *not* to separate your cases?"

He looks up at me, then left and right, as if he's worried that Tavira can hear us, even here, alone, before saying, "Yeah."

"Do you think he had your best interests at heart when he asked you to commit to that?"

He sighs hard, straight into the receiver in a gust. "No."

"Are you *certain* you don't wish to separate your case from his?"

He twitches. Of course he's not certain. Here he is, in the scariest place a human could ever end up in—outside of war—and he's jailed with someone he thought he could trust. Part of Safulu wants to separate now, badly. I almost watch that notion win within him, but then he takes a deep breath and says, "I can't, man. I *can't.*"

"Why not?"

"How long you been doing this?"

"Practicing? Seven years. I clerked before that."

"Then you know why not."

I do. If he separates, he'll get no protection from Wizard, and can likely expect retribution, which—with no one to watch his back—could be grievous at best, and deadly at worst.

I tell him, "The idea is for you to do it now, so that you do not end up in prison. Separate the cases, tell the deputies you fear for your life, and they'll put you in a protective custody dorm for the duration of your time here."

I can't tell if he laughs or sobs next. It sounds like both. I've known hardcore gang members, I've represented them, I'm acutely aware of their mannerisms, and I can say without a single doubt that Jacob Safulu is no hardcore gang member—at least, not yet.

When he's together enough to talk, he's made up his mind. "I can't. I'm sorry. It's more than just me on the line here, okay? And besides, they found that gun in my fucking room, man. My fucking dresser. I couldn't be framed up any better! There's no way I'm getting out of this. *No way.* This is just what they do to people where I'm from. I mean, I already know I'm not coming back any time soon. Life plus fourteen, you said. Okay. That's happening. It don't matter if I did it."

The worst part is, he's not wrong. It is indeed what the DA does to people where he's from, to people who look like him, and to people without money. The Kristina Mirkoviches of the world make cases on them, the wheels grind, and their bodies get locked away.

29

That shit my lawyer said still fucks with me. It fucked with me when I walked the line. It fucked with me up in my cell. And worse yet, I had that sheriff detective's words bubbling up in my head too. *The system is the system.*

That was hardcore, the way my lawyer offered me an out if I just abandoned Wizard. I wanted to. For a second. I wanted to real bad. And I wasn't so much worried about what would happen to me in here. I was more worried for what would happen to the people I care about out there. Little. Mrs. Matta. Jimena.

Separating my case hangs them all out to dry. Their lives could turn into hell at the drop of a hat. Mrs. Matta could get dry-snitched to INS, get deported back to Guatemala City. Never see her kids again. And the family that's left? They could get moved out of their house to some shitty gang apartment that's running drugs thru there. And how do you take care of Jimena then? Little could live his day-to-day with no protection from anybody. And it'd be open season on him for being how he is . . .

Nah. I can't do that. Not to Mrs. Matta. I can't do anything bad to her ever again.

I refuse that shit.

So that's my choice right there.

Pick myself or pick others.

That's easy. It's others, all day.

And I don't even need to cry on that.

Cuz monsters don't fucking cry. Monsters got no feelings.

Except rage. Rage blocks everything else out.

And I don't even need to try to find mine.

It finds *me.*

Getting locked up on some shit I didn't even do? Rage.

Wizard using me like a shield for himself when it might not even fucking work? Rage.

Thinking I could trust Wizard's ass? Rage.

The thought of anything bad happening to the Mattas? Rage.

It's getting me going now. It's energy. And when it's time, it'll be more than enough to explode on anybody I need to. Make a name.

Be a dude never to be fucked with.

Here or anywhere.

That's what I got bouncing around in my head when we get told it's time for yard.

All of 4700 that's allowed for roof time has to line up. You line up, you go. Single file. Stop where they tell you to stop. Go when they tell you to go. I don't stare anybody in the face when we group-walk, passing bodies from other units. I don't spend time looking at my shoes either. I keep my head up like Wizard says. Just walk and carry it. Cuz it's another day that my body belongs to the county and not myself.

When the green door to the yard opens, we shuffle in for our three hours. I'm really only looking ahead of me. Ahead of me and up. Somewhere nearby there's a speaker going that sounds like it's made out of tinfoil. It's playing that song about some guy walking 500 miles and showing up at your door.

This yard is big like what a warehouse would be, like half a football field. Longer than it is wide. It's got sections too. Right side. Middle. Left side. Between each one are these metal pillars in rows. And no ceiling above them. Only chain-link and sky. And the sun's not above us in that space right now. It's passed us. Some other unit got that today.

There's pay phones on one wall in the back. And dudes moving to them. Some weights off to the side as we came in. There's spots on the far right where people figure out some handball matchups. And basketball's starting up in the middle. Half-court-style cuz there's two hoops, both facing the same way. It must be so two games don't end up on top of each other, cuz there'd be fights that way. Actually, that's smart how they did it like that. Off to the left is high-powered cages. Rectangular cells with what look like black bars. Inside is just a dip bar for working out and a pay phone. The dudes in those can't be with the rest of us. There's a red uniform in there now. All the other ones are empty.

It ain't bad up here. I'm pretty sure it's the highest I ever been in the air. I hear the city all around us. It's far away tho. There's cars. Not whooshing, just humming. A long, mad train horn from Union Station that fades off as it goes. I feel like it's going north. Or maybe I just want it to . . .

I spot Wizard not far from the basketball with six homies I don't recognize.

I first feel that rage just looking at him, that *fuck you* surge of blood going to my head, and then it's not so simple. Cuz it's good to see him too.

I'm getting used to feeling two opposite things pulling me different directions.

He looks at me and nods, so I head his way.

When I get to where he's at, he tells me to turn my back to the metal, then looks at me in my dark blues and says, "I guess that's your cherry gone, huh?"

He introduces me around as his homeboy from the neighborhood. I don't remember names so much as places. City Terrace. Lincoln Heights. One fool was from Chula Vista, down by San Diego. He got caught up in L.A. doing some shit for his brother-in-law. Wizard tells them he's got to catch up with me, so we step off.

He says, "You see them guard towers yet?"

There's one above, I saw that. Wizard's pointing toward another in the corner, saying, "Yeah, they'll shoot you quick too."

On the half-court ball, it's black against white. Blacks are winning. They're better player for player. There's a bad-ass white boy tho. Hitting fades outside the key.

The dude goes four-for-five before Wizard says, "See how everybody's to their own?"

"Yeah," I say.

"That's just how it is in here. Race stays to race."

I been seeing that, so I just nod.

"You're doing good," he says. "You're watching, learning. Not feeling sorry or anything."

That gets me. Cuz I'm looking at him and thinking, *Fuck you, motherfucker. I'm in here cuz of you! I feel sorry for myself all the fucking time. I'm just not about to let you see it.*

I swallow that rage for later and say, "I figure I'm here so I better get on with it."

"Smart," he says.

I follow where's he's looking. It's at the high-power cage with the dude in it. The guy in there, he finishes up some dips, then turns at us to throw this quick little nod at Wizard. That could've been nothing anywhere else. In here tho? It's something.

Wizard sees me see it. He says, "We're good in here now. We're good wherever. I got some stuff in for that dude."

I don't ask what that means. Seems better not to.

"You got questions?"

I think for a second. I got a million for him. There's no use asking them tho. Wouldn't change anything. So instead I'm remembering back to the bus.

And I say, "What's a spread?"

"Man, so check this out! Fools take their sandwich bread from when we get those, right? And they mash them up and then . . ."

Wizard stops. A little Mexican with long hair is coming toward us with a serious look. Turns out some dude sat on his bunk. When Wizard gets the name of who did it, he turns to look at a group of white boys sitting near the basketball game. And this white dude that looks like a skinny Rowdy Roddy Piper nods back at Wizard before meeting him in the middle to talk. It's not even thirty seconds before Wizard's back over to me. And Roddy goes back to his crew. And three white dudes are standing up, and going over by the basketballers.

"That's some Wood business now, homeboy," Wizard says. "Okay, there's prolly not much time, so tell me about that lawyer. I heard you got called up."

I tell him everything that don't involve separating the cases. Like how they don't know if the gun found at the house is the one used in the shooting. They're waiting on a test. There's another witness too. Some dude that saved Scrappy. Wizard says he knows about that. It's just some hype. He'll find out a name. We'll get at him. He won't testify for shit. I tell him about the sentencing we're staring at. How hearing about it fucked me up. He puts a hand on my shoulder then. Like he cares about how I feel or something. And I'd shrug that shit off if it wasn't disrespectful. If I didn't know he'd take it wrong.

By the time I've said all there is to say, the white-boy basketball team is switching out. And the three dudes already standing over by the court drop a beatdown on their best player. The motherfucker that was hitting fades.

People whoop. And shout.

And Wizard don't even watch.

I do tho. They kick him in his knees. Bad.

And when he goes down? Head. Ribs.

The siren screams out. And we all got to get down. Hands above our heads.

Wizard says, "Politics, homeboy. There's ways to do things. Same as outside. Don't ever sit on anybody else's fucking bunk. You do that, and even I can't save you from a brown-ass beatdown."

When the deputies break it up, the white boy is bloody like some paint got dropped on him. And he's cuffed up. The other three are too. They're all getting marched out.

And then we're getting told to line up.

That's it for us. No more sky.

As we move to the sign that says LINE UP HERE, Wizard says, "Hey, so, what the fuck is up with that faggot friend of yours? Is he finding anything out or what?"

I shrug again, cuz I don't know. I really fucking hope so tho.

PART V

STONY PLACES

Prisons are built with stones of Law . . .

—WILLIAM BLAKE, "PROVERBS OF HELL"

Jeovanni Matta, a.k.a. Little, a.k.a. Little Guy

30

I got this confession I need to get out. I really don't like people. If it was up to me, I'd be in my room playing *Link's Awakening* on my Game Boy all day till the weekends, when I can go down to Long Beach, and walk into the Silver Fox, and watch the videos, and dance, but always with my back to the wall, so no one can get behind me without me deciding if I'm okay with it first. And if he's cute, and if I've seen him around before, we might go to the bathroom, into a stall without locking it, and I'll lean with my back to it, and say I'm not about kissing, but he can stroke me, but I don't want a blow job, and if he's not okay with that, that's fine, I'll touch him, but if he wants more, I don't do that with boys I first meet, and if he gets mad, I leave, and if he tries to stop me from leaving, I tell him I have a knife, but I don't say it's in my back right pocket, I just say I'm not going to hurt him unless he tries hurting me.

I got another confession. Some people can tell what I'm like just by meeting me, seeing me quiet, seeing me waiting or hanging back. And I've been forced to do things before. The older ex-cons, they come back from Lompoc, or Chino, or wherever, but they got a taste, or they're just used to it, or it's who they are and what they like already but prison made it real for them. I was fourteen when it first happened. It started with an OG. Four times it happened that year. I never told anybody, not even my brother. I just wanted to be alone. But I carried a knife ever since. I still do. Always.

People are mierda. People are low, and mean, and stupid. People don't see what's in front of them. But I'm not out here asking questions for people. I'm doing it for Jacob, so he can have a life. But, you know what? I'm doing this for me too. Can't lie about that. I'm doing this so I can hold my head up on my block and go wherever the hell I want, so my brother can, so my sister can, so they don't have to be ashamed of what people say about me. And if people got bad things to say about me, se pueden callar sus pinche bocas and keep it to themselves! That's how life should be when people respect you.

Me and No Neck, we've gone two days and got nowhere talking to every junkie we could find. All of them wanting ten or twenty bucks, or a hit if we got it. And they look No Neck up and down like they know he's got it but he's holding out. Frustrating days. Upsetting days. Going nowhere, until I have this idea to get up with the lookout on Wizard's block, and it's so good, I'm mad at myself for not thinking of it sooner.

He's in his yard when we get there, this kid. He's got no shirt on and some Chivas soccer shorts. He's running around the lawn with a ball that he's no good with.

As we walk up, he stops and looks. "Sup, Mister No Neck?"

He's bouncing like a puppy around No Neck. He won't even look at me, so I'm saying, "Who all has been by Wizard's place since that night Scrappy got shot?"

This little fucker makes a face like he can't even believe I spoke to him. I see on his face how he thinks I'm less of a man than him. And he ain't even one yet.

Y ahora, he smiles and spits on the ground. "I don't got to talk to you, punk-ass buttfucker. Hey, no offense, but, why don't you go fuck some butts till your dick falls off and you die?"

He laughs like he just made the funniest joke ever. Props to No Neck beside me for having a blank face.

This little kid, he's ten years old, Adalberto's youngest. I don't need to break his whole world by telling him what his uncle gets up to on the low, that Ramón from Guadalajara is sometimes Sirena in Long Beach when it makes her happy, so I speak to him in a language that he'll understand, and I step to him like I'm gonna whisper something in his ear, but then I hook my foot behind his and push him hard at the same time. He trips and tumbles backwards, goes flat on his ass in the grass.

"Don't ever talk to me like that again, little boy." I'm saying it as I pull my knife out. I flip the blade up out of its body, so it's naked and sharp. I hold it close and low along the seam of my jeans, so he can see it and think about what it can do when he's on the ground like that. His eyes bug out. I want to be good. I do. Lo prefiero. I want to be nice to everyone, and I want everyone to be nice to me. But that's not how it is in this world. It broke me up and put me back together this way. And this is what it gets now.

He hasn't even stood himself up before he's running his mouth again. "What word? *Buttfucker*? Or was it *punk-ass*? *Maricón*, then!"

He smiles this horrible smile people do when they think the world agrees with them and they can get away with their nastiness.

I look to No Neck like I'm about to handle it then and he just needs to be okay with it, but he steps up.

And he's saying, "Here it is, lil homie. You talk to this dude like you're talkin to Wizard. This is on that llavero business. We ain't messin around."

There aren't really words for how much more bug this little kid's eyes go, and how far his mouth falls open, before No Neck's saying, "Apologize."

That's when the horror sets in, and this kid gets how none of this is a joke anymore, and he handled it all the wrong way.

"Lo siento," he's saying, but No Neck's not having that either, because the kid ain't looking at me.

No Neck barks at him. "Look him in his eyes!"

And he does. He apologizes, big time, and it doesn't even matter that it's coming from this place of wanting to be in good with Wizard and No Neck, or that he'll run right into that house and cry about it and hate me all the more afterwards. What matters is he says it. I put my knife away, quick like I practiced. It's good, this power. The way having muscle behind me makes people act like actual fucking human beings. I could get high on this shit. And that worries me, but it doesn't, at the same time. People should always act right around others. They should be polite and respectful, even if you have to force them to.

I ask again, "So, who'd you see go in and out?"

"Angela. This parole officer came twice. One time with a deputy, and the other time he drove up when a sheriff car was babysitting the house."

Me and No Neck kick a look back and forth.

And I'm saying, "What parole officer?"

"The same one Wizard's always had. Petrillo."

I turn to No Neck. "You think Angela's home right now?"

He shrugs. It means, *Only one way to find out.*

31

We walk down to Angela's house and I knock. She opens the door wearing the top half of her work uniform and some faded jeans going white down the seams. They're pretty fly. Deeper in the house, Boyz II Men's finishing up and Shanice's coming on. I figured Angela for an oldies-type girl, not R&B, but I guess people can surprise you.

"Got to be at school by four-thirty. What's up, Jeo?" She smiles at me in a way that makes my chest warm up, but she turns a cold-ass death stare on No Neck. "Hernán."

The way she says it, I'm wondering if she's blaming him for how Wizard is locked up right now, but I trip on how she called him his baby name. I never even thought to ask No Neck what his mom named him. He was just always No Neck to me, but now he's Hernán too.

"Hey, Angela." It sounds awkward me saying it, because I haven't seen her much since she and Jacob were getting serious. "Can we come in?"

She points at No Neck. "Him too?"

I take one look at her look and know for sure she'll be more open to talking to me if he's not there, so I'm saying to him, "Can you go get that thing from the car?"

"What thing?" No Neck doesn't get it.

Angela smirks and does this thing where she dips and puts a hand on her hip. It's so easy how she moves.

I kind of scrunch my face up, hoping he'll just figure out that I don't need muscle to talk to Angela. I need some silk, but it's not getting through, so I have to be like, "Can you just wait in the car, please, Hernán?"

He gives me a stare that means, *You don't get to call me that.* It also means, *We'll talk about this shit later.* But he goes.

Angela waves me in with a hand to follow her back to her bedroom, the one she used to share with Jacob.

I'm saying, "I know you've already been asked a million questions, but Wizard asked me to do some looking around for him."

I almost say for Jacob too, but I leave that out just in case there's bad blood from them breaking up. Shit, I know my brother didn't talk to Jacob for a good month when he heard how he was moving in with Angela. I think he still thought back then that he might be able to get back with her even though there was no way.

"That's new for Jellybean, sending someone like you. All respect-ful." She throws them words at me over her shoulder as she's shrugging her shirt off. "Is he getting smarter or what? He usually has Hernán or Jerry out there talking, and not exactly with words."

It takes me a moment to realize when she says Jellybean she means Omar, but as far as what she's saying, I definitely get it. I bite my tongue on telling her it was Jacob's idea, because that'd shut her down for sure. I like her. I like him. I liked them together, but that's done with and now I got a job to do.

She turns the corner into her room, and by then her shirt's off and she's got this black lace bra that she's undoing away from me. Man, she'd never be doing this if No Neck were still here. Es obvio. And I can see how she trusts me, and doesn't think I'm any threat, and I'm grateful for that. She still runs, does push-ups. I see it in the shape of her back. It makes me feel like I should do more. Shanice finishes up with singing how she wants to be together forever and ever as Angela gets herself into a more comfortable bra, a blue one with wider straps.

She looks to me. "I thought you had questions."

I point to the dresser. "Is this where they found the gun?"

"Under the bottom drawer." She pulls a white Dodgers T-shirt over her head and fluffs her hair up after. The white looks good on her skin. It brightens her up.

"Can I check it?"

"Go for it."

Angela digs in a backpack to make sure she's got everything. I pull the last drawer as far out as I can get it. It doesn't take much to figure how to pull it out. But it's sad how when I get it, it still has Jacob's stuff in it. My heart sinks seeing his T-shirts and all. I guess he never had time to come back and get them.

"Did you ever know, uh . . ." I try not to say *Jacob* or *Wizard*. "Any-body to hide anything under there?"

"I didn't even know you *could*. I thought it was solid at the bottom. I found a missing sock down there after they pulled every drawer out and left it that way."

"When did that happen?"

"Sheriffs came back after they found the gun and searched again. They didn't find anything else I know of."

Naughty by Nature's "Hip Hop Hooray" comes on.

I'm saying, "Is this like a hits mix or what?"

I always liked how *O.P.P.* was flexible. How it could mean everything. Property. Pussy. Penis. It's open like that. I got time for Naughty. And Treach. With those lips and those tank tops? Forget it.

"I guess so. One of these guys at work gave it to me."

"He likes you, then."

"Ugh, really?" She tilts her head at me like she never even considered that, but that's a lie. Everybody that ever saw Angela and goes that way likes her, and she knows it.

I laugh, then she does.

"I missed you, Jeo." She puts a hand on my arm before letting it slide off. "Your brother? No. But you? Yeah."

Y ahora, I should probably confess how I don't have a lot of friends, or any friends besides Jacob, and my brother and sister, so that catches me off guard. There's so many things I'd want to say to Angela and ask her about, this young woman with experiences, but I can't. Maybe someday.

"I guess I did too," I'm saying back.

She smiles and zips her bag up. "Another time, then. Just come over. I'd like that. It's empty here now. C'mon. I got to go."

I follow her out. "So, nobody's been here in the house but you, Wizard, Jacob, the parole officer, and the deputy since? No signs of a break-in or anything?"

"Breaking in? Uh, no. Jellybean rigged up these windows himself. You'd have to smash some glass to get in."

We're to the front door. She's about to open it.

I'm scrambling. "And has there been anything weird you noticed?"

She stops. "I think Jellybean's parole guy likes me. He showed up looking for him the other day when there were already sheriffs out front. That was a little weird. He didn't need to, you know? It was obvious Jellybean wasn't gonna be here."

There it is. Like the pendejito up the street said.

"How many times have you seen him before?"

"Maybe four or five since Jellybean got back from Chino. He's just doing his job, checking up."

"Did you ever know him to look in your dresser before?"

"No, but he could have. I don't always lock the door, and if it was unlocked and he thought Omar could have access, he checked it. They have to."

"He have a name?"

"Petrillo. Spelled like you'd pronounce it *Petriyo*. He's kind of fine. You'd like him."

I get a feeling in my stomach like pilots must get before they have to eject. "You know you can't go at him, right?"

"I would never," she's saying, but I see in her eyes how she might.

It's like, what do you call it? A glimmer. A small one. But it's there. And then she opens the door.

32

Jellybean and Jacob are on the afternoon slots for hearings and I'm at the registers ringing up breakfasts at Tom's. I been feeling this ache in my left side ribs. I noticed it the night I had to end it with Jacob. It's not like a stitch from doing distance running. I'm used to those. I run through them. This one is deeper. And I'm mad at myself for how it's only been days, but I miss his stupid laugh, and it sucks not having him around trying every damn thing to cheer me up now that I really need cheering up, which is stupid, cuz I made him go.

I ring up a coffee only. I ring up an omelet, the signature, no onions, no peppers.

It hits me how that's like me, I guess. I mean, I want the meal, but I don't want it how it comes. I want things taken out. I want Jacob, but I don't want the standard-menu Jacob. I want him, I don't know, *different*.

I ring up a bacon-and-egg breakfast burrito. I ring up a plate of pork chops and eggs.

And I'm about to ring up chorizo and eggs when the weirdest thing happens. Phil Petrillo walks in the door and stands in my line with a newspaper in his hands. My stomach jumps up like it does before a race then. All nervous and scared. He's tall. He's a *man*, you know? Thirty-six? Not like anybody I ever been with. He could be in movies if his nose didn't look so broke. He's fine, though, with that slicked-back hair. The type you look at and wonder where his people are from, like, is he white? He don't look it, not all the way. Already there's other women eyeing him up and down, thinking things about him, I can tell.

Damn. He's got me in my head! And all this feels wrong, but I'm curious. I don't wanna be, but I am. Cuz what's it even *like* being with somebody with a job and his shit together? I hate myself for thinking it, like how I'm betraying both Jacob and Jellybean just by my thoughts.

I mean, there's neighborhood folks all through here getting their breakfasts and if I talk to him a certain way, it'll get back to No Neck, and maybe even Jeo, since he's like the dude on this now, which is crazy, but whatever. Ugh! I been kicking myself for saying what I said to Jeo. I know I shouldn't have said anything about Phil to him.

My line's moving. An old woman with wrinkled eyebrows orders in some huevos rancheros, extra sauce, extra tortillas, cuz she's obviously splitting it with her little granddaughter that's too young to be in school even though she's walking and trying to run her ass off to somebody else's table, and I ring it up without charging this abuelita for the extras.

After, Phil is one person closer, and he's still looking down at that newspaper like it's more interesting than me. I can't help thinking he's helping me out by not looking at me, though. Shit. If I'm this weird now, how am I about to be when he looks at me? And what would I even say to him? I can't say anything. I won't.

The construction worker stepping up to my counter wants steak and eggs, but hard-scrambled eggs and a medium-well steak, and potatoes a little underdone, but I don't talk back. I turn and ask my cook in Spanish if he can do all that, and he can, so we're good.

Phil hasn't looked at me yet, not even once. I'm not his type? Too young? He's married? I never seen a ring, though. Maybe a girlfriend. I stare at the top of his head as he's looking down reading.

The construction worker pays to the penny out of this little coin purse, and moves off to go get napkins.

It's Phil's turn next, and he's stepping up. And my stomach's still nervous, still scared.

33

It's called Tom's Burgers, but this morning it only smells like bacon and eggs. Preparation is the key to success, and I've planned this encounter with Angela for some time (because she's worth more than Renee ever will be). I've visited this establishment on mornings she does not work so that I could be known here, seen as a regular. This is why I have come eighteen times in the last ten weeks. No one could possibly know that I saw her in her uniform once on a homecall and knew she worked here. After that, simple surveillance revealed her schedule. So, to any interested parties, this is simply a Lynwood coincidence.

I surveyed the place through the plate-glass windows before I came in (only after I was certain none of my parolees or their known associates were present). I knew which line was Angela's, which made it easier to play hard-to-get. In line, I don't look up once.

It takes effort, feeling so drawn to her, being so close and not, at the same time. It's worth it. It gets to her. She recognized me immediately, and someone like her, she's not used to being ignored. She wonders why. She panics a little, maybe even thinks there's something wrong with her. This is very good. I want to unsettle her, and I didn't think it'd be so easy.

All eyes in the place are on me. I see her quick looks in my peripheral vision, over my newspaper. I force myself to read something other than her. Patrick J. Morris, a judge in San Bernardino, wants to ban the manufacture, sale, and possession of all handguns. (Good luck, you liberal whacko.) He also wants to institute drug courts for treatment rather than incarceration. Sure. It'd also be a great idea for us to feed and clothe everyone while we are at it, and hold their hands when they're scared.

I turn the page. The person in front of me moves up. I shuffle forward as forks scrape plates all around me. I hate the sound, but I remain perfectly calm. I focus on news. Apparently Lyle Menendez's attorney choked up during closing arguments and that murdering defendant of hers cried for the benefit of the jury. Plenty of people have been through tough stuff with their parents, and not everybody kills them because of it. Nobody's responsible for anything anymore. I'm fed up with it.

When I hear Angela engage in conversation with a fellow cashier, my gaze drifts over her neck, lower. I don't linger, but I wonder: What underwear is she wearing? This is the problem with having seen and committed her underwear drawer to memory. (Is it purple, light blue?) No man could help picturing it. It's normal, natural.

Before I can decide purple (definitely the purple), Angela spins around to scoop up a plate of food from the kitchen and transfer it to the side counter. She calls the number. A little girl runs for it, only to have an old woman get there first and bat her hands away. It's then I decide: when she says yes to a date, the first place I'll take her is somewhere she can be waited on.

The person in front of me moves, so I step to the counter. She turns.

"Welcome to Tom's," Angela says, "what would you like?"

There it is: the crucial moment. I have to play it right. I don't look at her. Instead, I skim my gaze above her head and squint at the menu board behind her.

"Take your time," she says back. "There's not a line or anything."

There's irritation in her tone. It's perfect, exactly what I needed. It's how I know it's working.

I stretch the decision out before telling her I want a #1 with two pancakes: two eggs (scrambled), three bacon (crispy).

She writes my order down in shorthand, stabs numbers into the register.

I drop my eyes back to my newspaper. An L.A. County employee (juvenile detention officer) by the name of Michael Cornell Bullard, thirty-nine, was arraigned on charges of trying to sell twenty-two pounds of cocaine to Orange County undercover drug agents. Bail set at $1 million.

She clears her throat (practically begging for attention). "Anything to drink? Juice?"

I look at her for the first time then, finally. She looks for my acknowledgment, and when she doesn't see it, she blinks.

I want to tell her I'm not going to the arraignment today. Although it wouldn't be unusual for a member of parole oversight staff to attend, it's an unnecessary risk, and I certainly don't want her to feel uncomfortable with me being there should she choose to go.

"No," I say, "I don't need a drink."

She taps two buttons on the register and charges me for a soda before ringing up the total. I hand her $10 and she takes it. I don't say anything. I want to see how this plays out.

She looks at the ticket, grimaces, and says, "Uh-oh!"

Something is off about her exclamation. It's not genuine. It doesn't match her face. At her house, when I told her how old I was, her jaw twitched. I've thought about that face she pulled every day since, and she's not making it right now, which leads me to believe she isn't surprised at all, merely pretending to be.

"Is it cool if I don't give you a new receipt?" She tears the paper off where it unspools from the register, and strikes through the soda purchase, but she writes something on the old one. "We're trying to save paper."

"Sure," I say.

Angela pings her register open and goes back into the cash drawer to refund the difference. When she hands me the money and receipt is when I catch her off guard. I smile. I give her the best one I have: impressed, interested, curious to know more. I show warmth.

It lands because she didn't expect it. She blushes red, but before it overtakes her cheeks, she spins to face the kitchen so no one else can see.

Over her shoulder, she says, "Thanks. It should be up in a few minutes."

I step to the side of the counter, out of the way. It's only later (after I've eaten and left) that I retrieve the receipt from my right front pocket, open it on its hasty crease, and look: there, under the crossed-out price of a Coke, is her unlisted phone number.

34

Me and Jerry get back to his house and explain to Little how everythin
went down. He just listens like he's already a boss. That trips me out
cuz it's like he's a natural at it. I tell him how we followed the parole
guy from his office to the back parkin lot of Tom's and watch him go
up to the side window and look in before goin in and pickin Angela's
line. So Jerry goes over to the window and turns his back. He starts
smokin but what he's really doin is blockin people's view so I can look
inside and not get spotted. Everythin goes good after that. Nuthin
strange. Dude reads the paper. Angela rings shit up for a minute but
then he gets to the front and she screws his order up. Little leans closer
when I tell that. I been to Tom's a lot when she's there and never seen
her do it before. She knows that menu and what people ask for. I seen
her handle lines like crazy, so her messin up made me think how Little
was right to be askin questions about her in the first place. Jerry hits
me then and says to tell about the receipt. I say I saw her print up his
receipt and cross sumthin out on it but then she *wrote* sumthin too. We
all wonder what. Little thinks it's a place to meet up later. Jerry thinks
a phone number. That's when Little puts his head into his hands and
says fuck. Jerry wants to know if he thinks Angela had sumthin to do
with Dreamer gettin framed up. Little's shakin his head at that. He says
she hasn't tried it on with this parole guy yet. He says he sat with her
and heard how she talked about him. Me and Jerry look at each other
and agree to take Little's word on it. Little says we don't even know if
he likes her for real yet or if he's even schemin on her. I tell him how
the parole guy looked at her. Little shakes it off. He tells me a look ain't
proof. When he says it like that I remember how Little's still that nerd
that used to do all our homework comin up. We'd be skippin school
and he'd pick up our makeup work. He kept us all from failin out till
we straight up quit. He was always good like that and he still is cuz he's
sayin we need more information. What we got right now isn't enough

to tell Wizard. We get that. We all agree. Nobody wants to worry Wizard till we know for real.

Little looks at his watch. He says we keep followin her. Maybe Angela meets up with parole guy and we see it happen. Little wants to know if Jerry can drive him up to Wizard's hearin or what. He says afterward he needs to get up with Dreamer if that fool is allowed visits. But Jerry can't do it. His dad's truck broke down and he's got to take him to work and pick him up so he tells Little how to bus it there. I'm startin to feel like the dude left behind so I ask what I'm supposed to do. Little nods real low at me and gives me a mission. He says I need to find the fool that saved Scrappy's life.

35

I'm gonna find this fuckin fool. I'm gonna find this fuckin fool. Those words run all thru my head on repeat. I owe Dreamer bad for steppin up so I don't have to sit there and get hit with them charges for poppin Scrap. I'm gonna find this fuckin fool. There's only one person could've saved Scrappy. It had to be the hype that was tryna mess up her house. He had a hood on him but it fell down when he was snatchin Scrappy's shutters off her casa. He had a patchy-ass bald head too. He was a gabacho and skinny like a teenager but old. That's the dude I got to find. And I'm solo on it cuz Jerry's off with his dad and Little's catchin buses. Silencio's got an appearance for child support and Lil Puffer fucked up his ankle at a party last night so I decide to do like Wizard always says and train a lil fool up. I take my wheels and roll to Adalberto's where the kid is playin out front with a soccer ball. I push him for his name and he says Johnny so I tell him he's rollin with me today as soon as he puts a shirt on. He gets a face like I just bought him all the candy at the Cork N Bottle and I tell his ass to chill. He runs to the house and comes back with a Chivas jersey on that has the name Galindo on the back. We roll by all the spots me and Little hit before but we do it again and we go slower. The park by the swimmin pool. Nuthin and nobody. The swap meet. Nuthin. The Chucky Queso's behind the swap meet where hypes sumtimes sell the shit they stole. It's all nuthin but it takes us to the time that hypes wake up and start needin fixes and food.

I cruise us to Tacos El Unico. I buy Johnny two tacos and the kid goes in so hard on them that I ask him if he's had his breakfast today and he tells me he found crackers in the couch but that's about it and hearin that shit made me wanna find Adalberto and beat his punk ass for not lookin after this kid. I buy Johnny another taco and watch him go ape on a plate of marinated carrots he swooped from that salsa bar while he's waitin for it. I'm standin by the counter when my homie Fat walks in the door. Fat goes by a lot of names. Gordo. Gordy. Fatty T. Even Juan John Silver. He's got a lot of fuckin nombres. Anyways so I get Johnny his other taco and me and Fat get to talkin. He just got back from Arizona and seein his sick aunt. I say that shit sucks and then I tell him the type of hype motherfucker I'm lookin for and what he looks like. He knows who it is straight off the fuckin bat. Augie is the dude's name. I ask him how to spell it and he writes it down for me to give to Little. This dude Augie got so crazy with his speedballs that Fat wouldn't even deal to him anymore. A lot of fools wouldn't. But Fat says Scrappy never met a dollar she didn't like so she kept on sellin to him and this other bitch that Augie used to run with. Irma's her name and Fat knows where she stays at so I grab Johnny and we go.

All kinds of bad shit goes down at the Islands Motel. This fool Gancho got killed in the parkin lot a couple years ago. Growin up around here I hear it called by another name too and that's La Ciudad del Fresas, like City of Strawberries. That's cuz it's where all the hype bitches go when they need to sell pussy or scheme or just get buckled up when they get up off their backs. Fat takes us to Room 14 in the back corner and knocks. The door opens and Fat introduces us to Irma. I see she's got a bruise goin black on her forehead and her eyes are like animal eyes the way they move fast and don't look at anythin for too long. So anyways Fat asks her where Augie's at. She says she don't know and that's when Fat points at me and says this dude right here needs you to find him but only if you're quiet about that shit. She's listenin then. She says she wants to know what she's gettin for it. I don't beat around no bushes. I tell her it's worth all the shit she can shoot. Her eyes open real wide and she says she'll find him. This bitch is cold-blooded. I tell Irma that's good for her and I take a breath and I smile and think about how I'm for real gonna *find* this fuckin fool.

36

The Criminal Courts Building is where I go. I come down the concrete steps from Temple and walk to the end of the building marked EN-TRANCE. They got a metal detector in there, and an X-ray machine, so I do like other people are doing and take my wallet out, and my keys, my bus pass too. I put them in a white plastic bowl that's all dirty and gray at the bottom. I hold my breath when I go through, and the guard on the other side just looks at me and waits for me to grab my bowl. I ask him where to go from there and he just nods behind him.

In the main lobby, there's another desk that says INFORMATION above it, so I ask the deputy sitting there for Safulu.

She goes through some papers. "Floor Nine, Department One-oh-two, turn right once you're out the elevators."

At Department 102, I put my face down by the low window next to the door handles, I see there's two more doors to the left where the court is, so I go through both sets of doors and sit in the back. The courtroom's barely full. It's wood everywhere. The walls. Where the judge is sitting. Where the lawyers are sitting. It looks real classic. Above, there's this whole ceiling that looks like rows and rows of lights. A deputy bailiff in his brown uniform comes over to me and asks what my business here is. He makes me nervous with how he looms over me and I'm just sitting in this wooden bench with my knees tight together.

"I'm here for the arraignment," I'm saying. Por supuesto. Why else would I be here?

He wants to know which one.

"Uh, my best friend's." This takes me off guard, saying those words out loud like that. *My best friend.* I've never said it before, but I know it's true. It makes me feel weird, like my skin's getting tight on me all of a sudden.

He wants the name.

"Uh, Safulu. Jacob."

He looks at a list, and it must be there, because he turns and leaves me alone after that. Pretty soon after, the judge comes in, and it surprises me how it's a lady named Susan Ayers. She's got silver hair, a black robe, and those half-glasses things for if you can see far away, but need help seeing up close.

They do another case first. A black guy with a scar on his scalp that looks like a wave pleads guilty because he already reached a deal with prosecutors. He gets three years in prison. His mom cries at that. She's two rows over. I make a promise to myself right then not to do this shit to mi mamá ever.

Y ahora, I feel a hand on my arm. It's Angela's. She's sitting down next to me. "They haven't been up yet, right?"

I shake my head like, *No.*

"How'd you get here?"

"Took the buses," I'm saying. The 60 to the 81. No Neck told me how.

"You want a ride back?"

"I need to try visiting Jacob at the jail."

"I'm going to see Omar. I'll drive you."

"Oh. Right on. Thanks!"

"You're welcome." And her hand goes back on my arm again. "Don't worry. The first one of these is always scary. They get easier after."

I nod at her. I'm sitting here on this bench feeling nervous and strange, wanting to ask Angela every question under the sun about what she wrote on that receipt for Petrillo, but I won't. The guy with the scar goes into custody, that's what the judge called it, and disappears behind a door by the bailiff. His lawyer grabs his briefcase and escorts the mom out while the lady judge drinks from a cup of water, nods at the guy sitting at the desk by hers, and they call the next case.

The People of the State of California versus Omar Armando Tavira and Jacob Safulu. They say the case number.

Angela slips her hand into mine. It's warm. I'm cold. She squeezes. She knows I'm hurting for him. I hate that it makes me like her more.

Wizard stands first in his dark blues and moves to the table in the middle of the court part. Jacob goes after. His head's shaved. He looks like a dog worried about getting hit. I want to grab him and run. He doesn't turn and look back. But Wizard does. He looks at Angela first, and when he sees me next to her, he nods. He looks happy to see me too, like I got his back. Then the charges get read, and they're bad. Conspiracy to commit murder. Attempted murder, because it failed. Assault with a deadly weapon. Mayhem, which I don't get what that is.

The Judge Lady checks that the defendants are in the courtroom and asks how they plead. They both plead not guilty, and the judge turns to her clerk, a skinny black man in a tan suit and glasses, his hair cut very short, almost bald. "Are we separating these?"

He raises his hands like he doesn't know.

The lawyer sitting next to Jacob stands up. He's saying, "Nick Park, Your Honor, representing Mr. Jacob Safulu. It's my client's wish at this time not to separate the cases."

"*Not* to?" The Judge Lady looks confused.

"Yes, Your Honor."

"Well, it's his funeral."

It hurts hearing that. It seems like such a bad and unfair thing to say with the person sitting right there.

"I'd also like to challenge the conspiracy charge, Your Honor. It's too vague as it's laid out in the complaint for a warrant."

The Judge Lady holds up a hand like she really doesn't care what he's about to say. "Miss Mirkovich, is Mr. Tavira a documented member of a known street gang?"

"Yes, Your Honor."

"And is the victim"—she stops, looks down at her desk—"a Lucrecia Lucero, also a documented member of a street gang known to be its local rival, with a history of violent incidents?"

"Yes, Your Honor," the lady lawyer's saying back.

"I find that factual basis to be good enough for me, Mr. Park. Call me old-fashioned, but I trust our law enforcement to know these things. If you want to punch holes in it, you may do so at the preliminary hearing. Speaking of, how does a week sound to all parties?"

The lady lawyer jumps in with, "Your Honor, I have motions set for the sixteenth and seventeenth, can we do the fifteenth?"

The Judge Lady looks to the clerk. He nods at her.

"We certainly can. Any objections, Mr. Park?"

"No, Your Honor."

"Good. I'm glad that's settled." The Judge Lady clears her throat. "Now, is there a bail number the People are looking for here?"

"Your Honor, the People request that the defendants be denied bail at this time."

Jacob's lawyer isn't having that. "Your Honor, my client has never before been arrested, to say nothing of convicted—"

"Mr. Park, if your client wanted to be treated differently in the eyes of this courtroom, he would have separated his case from Mr. Tavira's. Since he has not, I'm left with no choice but to treat them equally." The Judge Lady turns back to the lawyer lady. "Why are we seeking to deny bail today, counselor?"

"We believe the risk to be too great, Your Honor. Mr. Tavira is a high-ranking gang member and career criminal. The State believes the possibility of witness tampering and violent reprisals to be extremely high in this case."

The Judge Lady goes into the papers and doesn't find what she wants. She turns to her clerk. "Do we have his background?"

I guess she must mean Wizard's rap sheet, all the bad shit he's ever done.

"Yes, Your Honor," the clerk says. He's cute, but I think he knows it.

I study him walking over to the judge's desk and handing a folder up to her.

"Thank you." She flips pages, makes a face, and flips a few more pages. "You're a real class act, Mr. Tavira."

Wizard's saying, "Thank you, Your Honor."

Judge Lady looks down over her glasses, mean-auntie-style. "I assure you, it wasn't a compliment."

She sets the files aside. "I agree with you, Miss Mirkovich. Bail will be denied for both defendants in this case. Let's spare any more spilled blood, shall we? Defendants are remanded back into custody."

The gavel comes down with that bang sound I've only ever heard before in movies.

37

Court closes at four-thirty and then everybody in holding needs to be loaded and bused back over, so I rush us over to Men's Central Jail visiting as soon as it's done. Me and Jeo been sitting since the walk-ins opened up for the five-to-seven visiting. The lobby's packed with people and we could be waiting for nothing, but we do it anyway. At least there are soda machines. I've already had two Diet Pepsis and used the joke they call a bathroom three times. Most people here already have appointments, so we have to wait.

We start slow, cuz there's nothing that could make me feel guilty for giving my number to Petrillo more than sitting next to Jeo, but we warm up quick. He doesn't like the Raiders. I love their stupid asses. We agree Long Beach is the bomb. We're both all about *In Living Color*. James Carrey is a straight-up fool. I ask Jeo about the "Men on Film" stuff they do. Jeo says they're all right, says sometimes it's funny how it points out all the little things in society that sound gay without saying the word, like, gives a different look at them, but he said it also makes him feel uneasy seeing them be all over-the-top cuz not everybody on his side of the fence's like that, and maybe people will think they are. He says there's lots of different ways of being how he is, and shuts down about it after that, and I guess it's cuz we're out in public, and it's not something he talks about, but I want him to know I know and that's okay, but I think maybe I didn't do that right.

I can't really get him talking again after that, and I think it's prolly cuz me and him haven't cleared stuff up about Jacob, or why we broke up, but I guess part of me still feels like he doesn't really need to know that. It's my business. But also, I don't want to tell him how bad I feel, or that I miss Jacob, and how that's confusing, and sad, and stupid.

So I tell him, "Jacob was with me that night, at the time it happened. I told the cops and everything."

He's looking at me like he knows but he's glad to hear it. Glad I went out and said something.

And we're about to talk more about it, but they call my name, and I go up, and when I'm up there, they call his, but they don't call him like *Hey-o*. They say *Gee-oh-vanny*.

At the counter, I tell him I'll see him outside after, and he nods at me.

The deputy at the desk takes my driver's license, and sends me through into visiting with a clip-on pass.

I get to the little booth right as Jellybean does. He likes how I know the drill with all this. The lines are monitored, so if he wants to talk about something, he has to talk around it, make it seem natural. And he knows I'm not about to be up in the streets doing anything for him, so we have an understanding. He takes the receiver up on the other side, so I take mine.

"Hey, hey," he says. His voice sounds good, like he's hanging in.

I'm like, "Sup, Jellybeaner?"

And that gets him smiling and nodding. "Oh man, if I'd known you'd get all racist with me, I'd've declined my visit!"

He laughs. I do too.

"What're you doing, coming all the way out here? Don't you got school tonight? It's Friday."

"It's just one day, you know? I cleared it with my teachers already."

"So how's that going?"

"It's school. Lots of reading, tests. I'm getting there. Just a little more till I go for certification."

"You'll get it." He's nodding. "You never failed at anything in your life, Ang. You always get what you want."

He's a little distracted, keeping tabs. He's watching people, turning around, checking his back. "So, hey, can you drop some money on my books, or what?"

"Just got paid," I tell him, "so you know I already did."

"Thanks, Ang. I been needing paper *bad*. Not writing is killing me."

After that's out the way, Jellybean wants to know what's going on with the neighborhood. I tell him I been looking after our cousin Elisa's kids more at the house cuz their mommy likes the fact that he's not around anymore, makes her feel safer. He scoffs at that, but he tells me that it's good so long as it doesn't get in the way of my studying or working. I talk about how the rapper Snoop Dogg was also getting arraigned today, how there were cameras and shit in the hallways following him.

He blinks at me and says, "How's Jerry doing? Is his dad fucking up still?"

"He's trying to marry that tramp he runs with."

"Man, of course he is. He knows I'm not out there to check him so he's doing whatever he wants now."

I just shrug at that. None of my business.

"Oh, so tell me you heard from Jose, then." Jellybean nods up at the end of it, like, just to make sure I know it's *that* Jose, but even when he first said it, I knew it was Big Fate. It feels like this was the question he really cared about the whole time, but he felt like he had to work up to it.

"No, I haven't." And I don't even know why I would, personally, but it seems important to him that I do.

"Okay," he says, but he looks a little worried. "You will."

I say, "Why?"

"I was just paying some bills, trying to contribute to all that rent you're missing out on."

"Don't sweat it. I'm making it through with extra morning shifts." I'm like, "Worry on you. Keeping that long-ass nose of yours clean."

He gives me a smile and a look with that. It's like he's saying to me he wouldn't even if he could. He *likes* being stirred up in it. And he's never said anything, but I've always kind of known that he goes as wild as he does on the streets so that when he gets locked up again, and there's always an again, he's nobody's punk. He's got some juice.

We change over to talking about the arraignment, and for sure Jellybean definitely has no good words to say for that lawyer of his.

"And did you see how Dreamer's was all up in it? Questioning this and that? I mean, sure, he got slapped down, but that fool was trying! Man, they gave me a bad one on purpose. He didn't say shit the whole time. Just sat there. How the fuck did Dreamer end up with a state

lawyer and I got some learn-on-the-job motherfucker? That's on purpose. They're trying to send me up north on the back of him being
incompetent as fuck." He stares off for a second on that, before smiling
and saying, "He's sloppy, though, and maybe that's good too."

Jellybean doesn't tell me what he means by that.

38

Y ahora, seeing Jacob in front of me, he doesn't look so bad, and I didn't really know how much a relief it would be to see his face and know he's doing okay. It lifts the weight that I've been carrying around, the one that's so tight around my ribs, the one that presses down on my shoulders. It's been like wearing a heavy jacket. My arms are free and everything else is locked up tight. I smile, and I try to breathe like everything's normal and good and fine and I'm not staring at Jacob behind glass in a jumpsuit, and that makes me want to cry my eyes out right here, but I'd never do that in a million years. I can't do that to him. I have to be strong.

Angela warned me going in how I shouldn't talk about anything in the case because people will be listening in.

I say, "How you doing?"

"Good as I can, I guess."

"You holding up all right?"

He looks down and taps the tabletop in front of him a couple times, like he's touching wood for luck. "It'd be a lot worse if I didn't have friends, you know? I'm getting looked after. People keep an eye out for me. It's good."

I have to confess: I want to keep asking him questions about how he's doing, but also, I don't. He's talking himself out, I can tell. It feels like it's been a long day for me, and I can't even imagine how it's hitting him right about now.

I say, "My mom was mad when she heard."

"Yeah? Shit." The skin between his eyebrows wrinkles up. "Tell her I'm sorry, man. That I didn't even do it. Not like it matters."

"Why wouldn't it matter?"

"They got me tagged for it, hermano."

I kind of shudder with how he calls me *brother*.

"When's the last time you ever heard of anybody beating a case? Not like pleading down, not going on probation, but actually beating something?"

No. I never heard of that.

"That reminds me," he says. "You remember the thing that happened on Augustine Avenue and Clark Street? The corner house? It was a long-ass time ago, not like it was last week."

I must be making a face because I damn sure don't remember anything like that.

"It's cool if you don't remember," he says.

Last week. The way he said it, I can't help thinking about how that's important, how maybe it has something to do with what happened to him, but Clark Street's tiny. It only goes between Atlantic and Edgebrook. Or Phillips if you go north instead of south. It crosses through Wright. There's an old church on it, I know that. And there's Abbott Elementary too. It doesn't hit an Augustine that I know about, but I could go back through there with No Neck, or I'd have to hit up a map. As I'm thinking that, I don't even know if there's an Augustine anything in Lynwood, not even a restaurant. En serio.

And that's when it gets me. He's clueing me up to something.

It's a name. Has to be.

Augustine Clark, or Clark Augustine. One or the other.

And I don't know where he got it, or how, and if I wanted to know, I couldn't ask, so I try to put it together with what I already know.

Scrappy had somebody save her life that night. We know that. It's why Jacob's sitting here on an attempted charge and not a murder one. But that's also probably the witness they got to put a finger on Jacob.

I say, "Was that the one spot where, uh, the dude did CPR on the old grandma that got hit by that drive-by a while back and saved her life?"

"Yeah," Jacob says, and he smiles at me.

It's good seeing him smile. It's good being responsible for it. That moves the weight even more, makes it lighter. But then he says, "That's the one. You know if he's still around? My mom wanted me to write to him."

The second he mentions his deadbeat mom, I know that shit is serious, like life-or-death serious.

So I say, "I guess I can ask about it."

But what I mean is, *Yes. Te lo prometo. I'll find him if it's the last thing I do.*

"Yeah, do that," he says.

39

My work cell rings when I'm on a date that my mother set me up. It's with Marina Sedlak's grandson, Peter, whom I've miraculously managed not to meet despite the fact that we've lived two miles away from each other almost our whole lives, and now he's sitting across from me at Ante's, with its stained-glass windows and tall-backed booths. He's five years older than me, a plumber, and about as attractive as the dad from *Rose-anne*. Actually, he's exactly as attractive, except he's not funny. It's honestly the kind of setup where I have to wonder if my mother still loves me. To wit: he's allergic to mushrooms, and doesn't like pizza. When I tell him how preposterous that is, because pizza can effectively be *anything you want it to be*, and if you don't like it, you are a human being devoid of imagination because it's you who picks the ingredients, he makes a face like I pinched him, and tells me that maybe it's because he doesn't like bread. Isus Krist. I've known Peter for thirty-seven tortuous minutes and already I'm thinking how convenient it is that the harbor is only two blocks away so I can go drown myself in it. The chances of this working out are effectively zero, so, yes, I answer the phone call, at the table, and then I walk outside. He makes that same pinched face, of course, because he's already casually mentioned how he doesn't like women working. He's a real man, that Peter. I honestly can't figure out why he's single.

"Mirkovich."

"Kristina Mirkovich, DA's office?"

"The same. What's this regarding?"

I'm out the big wooden door and looking across South Palos Verdes Street. It's quiet in downtown Pedro for a Friday night. Nothing doing on Seventh Street, no drunks out yet, but it's only seven. Give it time.

"Ma'am, I'm calling from Central Jail, and I've been told to inform you that one of your defendants just mentioned Augustine and Clark as street names on a monitored line during a visit. We believe it was a coded attempt to convey the name of one of your witnesses."

"Do we have a recording?"

"I would love to say yes, ma'am, but we don't have budget for that. I'd recommend just being happy we caught it."

"I need the visitor's name."

"Jeovanni Matta, ma'am." He spells it for me to be clear. "You have a good night."

I don't say *have a good night* back, because mine just went to shit. I call the office. Margaret isn't there.

I call her at home. When she picks up, I can hear the TV going in the background. It's *Jeopardy!* I hear the daily double sound.

"Margaret, I need Nick Park's home number."

She says she'll have to call me back.

I click the phone shut. I have a brief flash that I could lose a witness to another Scrappy-style walk-up attempt at any moment.

Margaret calls back with the number. I scratch it down on the back of a dry-cleaning receipt I find in my purse, hang up, and call Park's house.

A woman answers. In Korean. I apologize for disturbing and ask if Nick Park is available.

She switches to English. "One moment, please."

When he gets on the phone, I punch below the belt. "She sounds pretty, Nick. And *young*."

He recognizes my voice immediately, and sighs a sigh that tells me to mind my own damn business. "What do you want, Kristina?"

I switch gears and accelerate. "Nick, if you pulled this shit, I swear to God—"

"Whoa, what happened?"

"A few moments ago, your client just said my witness's name in a coded way to a visitor at MCJ."

"Coded how?"

"Coded like street names, Augustine and Clark." I wait for it to hit him. "I'll take this right to the judge, Nick. I'll push her for contempt if you did this."

"I have no idea how he knows, but I will find out."

It's a good lawyer answer, always put off to tomorrow what you don't want to do today.

"How else would Safulu know? Did you show him the affidavit? Was it not redacted?"

"It was, but I didn't show it to him."

"No responsibility. I got it. So how would your client know?"

"Tavira's lawyer must have shown him, or had the papers out so he could see? I don't know. I'm not comfortable speculating."

But he just did speculate. For me, he speculated.

"Still doesn't explain how Safulu knew it."

"It seems pretty obvious, Kristina. If Tavira knew, that's all that's needed. They went right back into lockup together. There's nothing else to do but talk back there."

Of course. I could find Tavira's PD and pressure him to recuse, but the damage is already done. Clark's name is out.

"I gotta go. Enjoy your dinner."

He starts to say something, but I hang up and dial Montero.

"One moment." He answers and then puts one of his clumsy bear paws all over the phone.

I hear him excuse himself from a table. There are whispers, and glasses clinking. I surmise that he's on a date too, and he just did exactly what I did; he walked out the door. When he gets to the street, a car honks.

"Talk to me." Willie Montero, always to the point.

"Jeovanni Matta."

"Should I know him?"

"Is he a gang member? Is he dangerous?"

"I'm not at the office, but you're in luck. I have all gang members' names memorized, Kristina. I'm a human computer that way." Willie Montero, mayor of Sarcasm Town.

"Great! So, tell me."

"I'm not really—dammit, Kris. Are you saying he's in Tavira's crew?"

"I'm asking you *if* he is!"

"Okay, let's climb down off the top rope, huh?" He blows into the phone, not on purpose, but because he's trying to get his composure back. "There's no Mattas I know of, but shit changes every day. There's a lot of churn. I got a buddy in OSS that might know better. I'll call him tomorrow. Why are you even asking?"

"Safulu took a visit from Matta at MCJ today and said the words *Augustine* and *Clark*."

He gets it. "Ah, good old Augie."

"Do you know where my witness is?"

"As it turns out, we're having dinner now, me and him. It's magical. He's having the soup, and—"

"Great. Where are you? I'll come right over."

I almost mean that. I want to see him. But I don't. But I *almost* want to see her, this new woman.

"Jesus, Kristina! Didn't you hear me before?" Willie Montero, about to boil over. "Just call Petrillo!"

"Right. I will."

"Good!"

He hangs up as Peter pokes his head out of the restaurant. "Are you coming back in?"

I look at him, this guy who would never eat chicken marsala, or a double mushroom pizza from Niccolo's, and I shake my head. "Oh, no, I'm sorry, but thank you."

40

I'm on my way home when I get paged, so I go to the nearest pay phone (a 7-Eleven on the Wilmington side of PCH) and use my state-issued calling card. I get a dial tone as a long-haired, chubby guy in a Giants cap turns and looks at me. He's smoking a menthol cigarette about fifteen feet from the gas pumps, the unbelievable dickwad. I toss him a nod, so he knows I see him. He doesn't acknowledge me, but he takes another drag: a long one. It pulls an orange ring of fire down the wrapper. He's a good ten feet from me, but I can hear the sucking sound.

I used to smoke. I miss it. I'm not mad at him for doing it, but there's a right way and a wrong way.

"You're a little close to the gas," I say to the guy. "You need to smoke that farther back."

I jut my chin at a rainbow stain of oil at his feet, and nod toward the pumps to indicate them, too. He blinks at me, goes back to smoking. What is he, deaf? I keep a hard eye on him, letting him know that if he tries throwing that butt when he's done, so help me.

I dial the number. It rings twice.

A woman answers. "Mirkovich."

She sounds haughty, the way pretty girls can get after years of being told they are.

"Phil Petrillo. You paged me."

"Thanks for calling me back. Kristina Mirkovich, AHD hardcore gangs with the DA."

"Who can I help with, Counselor?"

"I need to locate a witness."

What she means is she needs me to. I pull the Tom's Burgers receipt out of my pocket. It still has Angela's phone number on it. I wrestle a pen out of my pocket, too.

I say, "CDC number?"

"Sorry, I don't have that in front of me."

"You mean you don't carry around all the CDC numbers you might need at seven at night? I'm appalled, Miss Mirkovich."

This is the point where she can tell me she is a Mrs., or that I should call her by her title, but she just laughs. It's a good laugh: almost flirty.

"You have a name?"

"Clark, Augustine."

I smile at that. Must be my lucky day.

"Okay," I say, "was he released from jail or prison, and when?"

"Men's Central," she says. "Today."

"Listed address?"

"Halfway house." She gives me an address. I know the place. It's in Huntington Park.

I've got another question, but it dies on my tongue when the chubby guy looks right at me and flicks his still-lit cigarette to the ground. As it lands, it spits orange, sparking ash.

"I need you to hang on, Miss Mirkovich," I say. "I have a situation here."

"Um, sure, I—"

I put the receiver down on top of the phone box, snatch the flung cigarette butt up off the ground, and catch Chubby on the other side of the 7-Eleven as he's about to get into a car. I pin him against the driver's-side door before he can open it, breaking his key off in the door.

He struggles, goes nowhere. He's about to shout but I hold the butt up close to his face. His eyes cross staring at it.

"Eat it," I say, and push the butt at his mouth. He shakes his head.

"Eat it, or you're eating this." I put a lock on his wrist and turn him so he can see my holstered service weapon. It spooks him. He bucks, tries to run, but I torque his wrist so hard he falls to his knees.

"Okay," he says. "Okay!"

He opens his mouth. I drop it on his tongue. He makes a face like he'll puke, but he chews it three times.

"More," I say. "Count to twenty."

He does, getting greener and greener.

"Swallow," I say.

His eyes plead with me not to. I lean on his wrist. He gulps. He coughs, dry-heaves. Serves him right.

"Don't you *ever* do that shit again!" I let his wrist go. I walk back to the phone and pick it up like nothing ever happened.

"Sorry," I say, "where were we?"

She huffs. I like the way she does it, like she's not used to being asked to wait like that. "Everything okay?"

"Is now," I say. "Has anything happened that makes Clark high priority?"

"His name may have been given to gang associates who wish to discourage his testimony."

Well, that's a wrinkle, not an unexpected one for Augie, but a wrinkle all the same.

"He's required to report within twenty-four hours, at which point I'd normally detain him and notify you, but seeing as this is high priority, I'll run by that halfway house now."

"Thank you." She means it.

"Happy to help." I can feel she's about to hang up, so I say, "Can I ask you something, Counselor?"

"What's that?"

"Are you related to a deputy sheriff?"

"John? Yes. He's my older brother."

"That's the one. You're not twins, right?"

She laughs again. "No. Thank God. Three years apart. How do you know him?"

"We played softball together a few times."

"Oh? Where?"

"Peck Park," I say.

"You're not from Pedro, are you?"

"Guilty," I say. "Went to Pedro High, moved away, and then came back not too long ago."

"Shut up. What year?"

I tell her. We figure out that she was a senior when I was a sophomore. I don't remember her, though, and she doesn't remember me. It was a big school.

"Still, we must have seen each other at some point. Passed in the hall or something."

"Two teenage ships," I say.

"Well, Agent Petrillo, how about this? If you find my witness and make sure he's squared away, I'll buy you a drink in Pedro sometime."

"Deal," I say.

"Call me when you've found him."

"Will do."

She doesn't say goodbye after that. She hangs up. She's that type.

I get back in my car, and I open up the still-warm bag of King Taco (chicken burrito, all meat, extra onions) I was saving for dinner on the back patio, because I'm not going home after all.

The fencing on the Spanish-style halfway house on East Fifty-Eighth Street is the giveaway. The driveway has a street gate, and behind it, the strip of concrete ends at an arch with another gate, as tall as a man, not necessarily to keep people out, but to keep the right ones in.

I called ahead. Augie Clark is already out on the weedy lawn waiting, wearing short shirtsleeves and rubbing his bare arms. His sleeves were long last time I saw him. Otherwise I would've noticed his telltale doper tattoo: the peacock down his left arm. Faded blue tail feathers make a nice pattern on the interior elbow crease. They trick the eye away from needle marks. It's also how you can tell he's right-handed. He shoots into his left arm.

I don't put out my hand to shake. "Welcome back, Augie."

"Agent Petrillo." His tone is wary.

"I just got off the phone with Kristina Mirkovich at the DA's office. Ever meet her?"

"Yeah. She says I can get something called drug court."

"Sure," I say, in a way that means: *That remains to be seen.* "You clean?"

"I'm good." He stares at the ground, kicks a dirt patch.

"Don't shit me, Augie."

"They got me on methadone."

"You sprinkling a little H on top, to help with withdrawals?"

He blinks at me. "I-I don't chip."

Liar. I ask him where he goes for it.

"Six blocks over."

Seems sketchy. I say, "Which way?"

"Towards Vernon."

"You're lying, Augie."

"No, I-I'm not. It's a mobile med for homeless. They take halfwayers too. They said they'll sign my card if you call them."

He pulls a flyer out of his pocket. It's for a mobile medical unit, which is really just a van with a barely qualified doctor manning it. The card says it's a pilot program called "Clean Streets," an initiative from Cedars-Sinai Medical Center.

"Pilot program means it can disappear any day."

"Right, I-I mean, it's this or take the sixty bus down to Saint Francis."

"Straight back to Lynwood? Sounds great. Should I call Wizard's crew, tell them you're coming?"

He flinches. He's scared. Sure, he's scared. He's not stupid.

"Where are your meetings?"

What that means is: Narcotics Anonymous.

"Cedars," he says.

"Why such a hard-on for Cedars? It's too far. You won't stick. Do Koreatown. Saint James Episcopal on Wilshire."

"But don't anybody know me over there," he whines.

"Exactly," I say. "Listen, Augie, you did great. You held up your end, and here I am holding up my end, too. You think Mirkovich came up with springing you on her own? The hell she did. It's her signature on everything, and her in the room playing the big dog, but it was *my suggestion* to her that has you out now."

Kristina Mirkovich did in fact come up with this little deal on her own, but he doesn't need to know that. Right now it's better for everybody if he thinks all this good luck isn't really good luck at all: he needs to think it's coming from me pulling strings and keeping him safe. That way he'll keep doing what he needs to do.

I say, "Are you on a thirty-in-thirty?"

It could be ninety meetings in ninety days, but that's unlikely if he has to testify soon. He nods, confirms the lower number.

"Good," I say. "Do your month. Get your court card signed, and when the time comes, you get up on that stand and back your statement. You say, *Yes, ma'am, those are my words. Yes, ma'am, those are the shooters,* and that's that."

I hear him gulp.

"Hey, are you staring at gun charges and intent to distribute right now? Are you booked for double digits in Pelican Bay? No. You're half-way free." I see that sink into him. "I've got you this far, haven't I?"

He's staring at the dead grass part of the lawn, not looking up.

"I need you to answer me, Augie."

"Yeah," he says.

"And I'm going to get you all the way, too. That's what happens when you work with the system."

I leave him there, standing where he's standing, and get back to the car on a high. This is working. Wizard and Dreamer are going away, and that's not only good for me, it's good for anyone they might some-day rob, stab, or shoot. It's justice, and I can't wait to call Angela.

I put my hand over the receipt in my pocket. It's warm, almost like a lighter I clicked on too long and then put away hot.

41

The phone rings, so I put my book up quick cuz I'm thinking maybe Phil's calling. My heart's going when I dash to the kitchen and then get mad at myself for doing it cuz I don't want to seem all flustered, and then I'm feeling disloyal to Jacob, and then feeling stupid for feeling that way. Ugh. My throat's been hurting since this afternoon, and I been scared it's from being in the jail and breathing all the dirty air they just keep recycling back through those vents, so I take a cherry Sucrets before I answer cuz I got a little packet by the phone, suck on it for a couple rings, and then I pick up and can't help smiling when I say, "Hello?"

The response is the machine message telling me this is a call from County Jail, and my heart just sinks, and I remember Jellybean told me how he's on 4700 in a four-man with six bodies. They got a phone in the back of the cell on the wall. They can call out with prepaid cards, but can't get calls in. When my cousin comes on, I ask him what's up.

"Hey, uh, the reason I was calling is cuz I really just wanted to say thanks for coming through today. And for the commissary. That's already coming in handy."

"No problem. I'm here for you."

And I *am* here for him. I showed up, didn't I? Put money on his books, didn't I?

But then I think about Phil, and feel guilty all over again for even thinking I could get with him, but it's not like anything's happening, and besides, it's not like Jellybean's done much for me. All he ever does is get me into messes. But then something clicks and I'm thinking there's no way he could have picked up phone cards by now. It'd be tomorrow at the earliest.

I say, "Did you get phone cards already?"

"Nah. A cellie let me borrow off his stack, cuz he had one that's almost cashed," he says, and then he's throwing a few words at someone else in the cell. "Yeah, thanks, Peeper, man. Thanks, homeboy."

I hear a hand go over the receiver real quick, and there's talking noises behind it, but I can't hear the words.

Jellybean comes back on. "Hey, he wants to talk to you."

"Who does?"

"Peeper. The dude that gave me the card. Don't worry. He knows who you are to me. No sex talk or none of that."

Peeper? How did he get *that* name? Lurking in the night, skeeving on some girls?

"I don't want to," I say, but it's too late, the phone is already getting handed over.

"Hey." The voice on the other end sounds like he's got some sort of throat problem. Jellybean's mom sounded a little like it before she passed from the cancer. "Hey."

A lady's voice comes on the line and says, "You have one minute remaining."

Peeper hears it on his end too. He speeds up. "Can you tell me what the weather's been like today where you are?"

This fool. "Uh, the weather? It's been nice, I guess."

"Can't picture nuthin with nice." Peeper sounds pretty let-down. "Was it sunny, or what? Warm? What'd it feel like?"

I got to think about it a little. "It was actually pretty cold."

"Cold like what?"

"I don't know, like, sixties? I wore a jacket."

"Was there sun?"

I say, "Hold up, did you not get up for yard time today or something? Did you not see sun or clouds or whatever?"

"I did," he says, "I just wanted to know what it was like away from here." He's serious. And that's making me a little sad.

"Oh," I say. "Well, it was all-over gray this morning, but it burned off by the time I got off work. A little bit windy in the afternoon, like the kind where it feels like it might rain but it doesn't. You know that kind?"

"Yeah. Thanks," he says. "I'ma get your cousin back."

There's a rustle, and then Jellybean comes on. "Hey, you good?"

"Yeah, but there's like a couple seconds left on this."

"Okay, cool, so you know Jose's coming through at some point, so, you know, just be there."

"I will," I say.

"And good luck studying. You'll be a nurse before I get out of here, for real."

That one sticks with me. He's prolly not wrong.

I try getting the last word in, saying something stupid like *keep your head up*, but the line just goes dead, so I put the receiver up on the wall in its little house. My aunt always called it that and so I do too.

God, I *miss* her. I hate being the grown-up on my own. I even miss how she'd make the worst coffee you ever had in your life. Burnt-tasting and with too much milk, so it got cold fast. That was her. One time she came home with her arms full of peoples' fruit she picked off their trees sometimes, tangerines, apricots, and she'd never ask if she could. It was always because she knew it'd go bad, and nobody else was doing it, so she was gonna do it. After, she'd go back by those houses where she picked and bring them jams and jellies she learned to make from her Betty Crocker's. She was always putting things in bottles. She tried to do that with Jellybean too, always telling him he couldn't go out, but he *hated* being cooped up like that, so he broke out. He doesn't know I still got some of her plum jams that I hid. I been saving them for me, in the back of one low cabinet behind the pans. CIRUELA, it says on the labels. Her very favorite. She did that batch a week before she died. She was still working right up to it. Got everything in order too, putting the house down to me, and not her own son. I was the good kid. I was going places. I was running. And Jellybean knew all about how people had houses in other peoples' names, so it was never a problem with us.

The phone rings again, rattling its little house. Someday it's just gonna fall off the wall.

I don't even want to answer it. Jellybean said Peeper had a stack of phone cards. If he liked my voice enough, and still wanted to go on about the weather, I guess I'm in for one more so I can at least say I don't want to talk no more.

I pick up and say, "This is my phone. What?" cuz I figure it's gonna be the recording.

But, at first, there's nothing on the other end, and then this voice comes through, deep, like, sexy, without trying to be, "Hi, it's Phil. You gave me this number so I could reach you."

"Yeah" is all I can say, cuz my heart is up and doing jumping jacks even though I'm standing still.

And then he's like, "Do you want to go out with me on Sunday?"

This feels wrong, but his voice is honey, and it's so, so stupid, but all I can think about right then is how I never been with somebody taller than me. And he is. By a lot.

And then I'm saying to him, "Depends on where," before I can even stop and think.

He pauses, and it's like I can hear him smiling on the other end even though he's quiet.

"A ways," he finally says, and I can tell how he means out of the neighborhood, and I'd like that. I'd *need* it.

He picks Long Beach, and I'm not sure if it's far enough, but maybe it is. And this all feels wrong, but Jellybean isn't on parole anymore, so he's not Phil's to deal with, and that's what I tell myself, that these two things aren't connected anymore.

And I want to say no to him, and I should say no, but I don't.

42

I walk into the Potholder on Broadway twenty minutes early to secure a table, only to see Angela already sitting in a padded booth: bent over a textbook with a ballpoint pen in hand, hair up in a loose ponytail. She beat me. This is a good sign. Perhaps she's eager. I watch her underline a long passage. She's wearing a black top with a high collar and long sleeves, but the solidness of it stops beneath her rib cage, and it becomes a sheer piece of silk that hangs over her bare stomach. Her belly button sits just above the line of the table. From where I'm standing, I can comfortably see under the table, and she's wearing a black skirt that meets her knees. I think of her underwear (the black lace, must be). Her calves flex, she kicks the heel of her right shoe against the toe of the left, bopping to the radio playing in the kitchen. It's that Meatloaf song nobody can get away from lately, how he'd do anything for love, but he won't do that. Frankly, it makes no sense to me. You either do anything, or you don't.

I don't walk straight to her. I take a longer route. She never sees me coming. "Didn't we say one o'clock?"

She looks up, appraises me, and says, "I got us a table. You're welcome."

Not what I expected. I sit. "I was trying to beat the lunch rush."

She looks at her watch. "By coming *during* the lunch rush? That's amateur. You show at eleven-fifty if you want that. You'd know it if you worked in a restaurant."

Her hair bounces as she says it. Something I'll never tell her: I bought a travel bottle of Pert Plus—I don't use it, but I smell it to remind me of her wet hair that day. It's in my car now, the glove compartment. Smells are important for forming intimate bonds.

She closes her textbook. Her lips: deep burgundy, lined in black.

"Thank you," I say, "for the table."

She waves a hand at me like I didn't need to, but I did. Gratitude is clearly important to her.

"Are we splitting this?" She means the meal.

"No," I say. "It's on me."

She smiles down at her menu before bringing her eyes back up to mine. "You must really like breakfast."

"I understand how you'd get that impression."

She snorts, makes a face: all big eyes, jutting chin. I've never seen her this animated before, this free. She's so open now that I almost wonder if she's playing me, but I remember where we are (Long Beach), and I must concede that maybe this is what happens when she leaves Lynwood. She can be herself. She can breathe.

I say, "Did I say something funny?"

She draws herself up into the straightest possible pose and mimics me. "'I understand how you'd get that impression.'" She breaks into a laugh. "You talk funny. You know that, right? Tell me you know that."

"I know that," I say. "Is it bad?"

She squints. "It's different. I like how proper you talk. It's just not what I'm used to."

A list of the things Angela Alvarez is used to: spic gangsters, neighborhood gunshots, and periodic property searches. I look to the kitchen, the ceiling. I let the silence work, and it does, because she blurts into it.

"It's so bad of me being here. Some people would be real mad if I was, you know? But you're *fine*, though, and you've got a real job, even if it's one I'm supposed to hate." She covers her eyes with a hand, peeks at me between fingers. "Sorry! I didn't mean to say that out loud."

I lean forward. I say, "I wouldn't be here if I didn't think you were worth taking risks for, and to answer your earlier question: I'm not a big breakfast person, more of a burrito person, you know? Solid. Reliable. A whole meal in one go, that's me."

This shift surprises her. She laughs. "What?"

"I don't know." I put my head in my hands. I haven't put my head in my hands like that since I was a child, but I know it's important to mirror how she touches her face, so she can see we're the same. "It sounded okay in my head and then it came out as probably the stupidest thing I've ever said. Sorry."

"I like it," she says.

"Like what? The burrito comment or me sounding stupid?"

"Um, both?" She laughs again. She leans over the table and touches my arm. "I like how I only ever seen you as this take-charge guy but now that it's us sitting here I can see how you were as a kid too. Like, you're this little dude worried about how he's going to come off."

The waitress comes by, takes our order. I don't even look at her. I order the special. Angela wants pancakes, orange juice. She also wants a side of eggs, scrambled. She then tells the waitress I'm paying. She points at me as she says it (reveling in it), and when the waitress is gone, Angela says, "So, what do you even do for fun?"

"I plot and scheme."

She laughs loudly, without pretense. It's a laugh not used to being out in the world. "Shut up! Stop lying!"

She touches my arm again, but it stays this time. It sweeps my arm hair up with it: goose bumps.

"I play softball," I say. I pair it with an earnest look (making her wonder what I'll say next). "And I cook."

"Shut up!"

"I can shut up if you want me to." I say.

She puts her finger up to me, her right index finger. It means: *Tell me more; don't hold out on me now.*

"I grill, mostly, but I do pastas, lasagnas. Italian food. My grandmother taught me. She didn't have granddaughters, so it fell to me."

"Where was she from, your grandmother? Not L.A."

"New York, but her parents were from Abruzzo, which is hilly and the best wheat grows there, so they make the best pasta."

"I hate pasta," she says.

I know she's kidding. I mug for her anyway. I supply the surprised and devastated reaction she wants. It thrills her. She throws her head back. Her throat bare, flushing: no necklace on it. I want to give her one in that instant (silver, maybe, something that will impress her without being too expensive).

Finally, she says, "I'm messing with you! It's prolly my favorite. I ate so much of it when I was running. My aunt would always cook it, but she'd do it her way. I'd ask for spaghetti and meatballs but I'd get spaghetti and chorizo! Or I'd get marinara with chiles!"

"That doesn't sound bad, actually."

"It wasn't! Mexican-Italian food." She puts that index finger back in the air between us. "It could be the next big fad."

Angela blinks, looks down, frowns: obviously caught in a memory.

I say, "Was she a good lady, your aunt?"

"She was the best. Nobody had a bad thing to say about her when she was around, or after. And that's rare. Usually somebody's always looking to gossip or snitch you out, or put your secrets out there when you're gone."

"That's humans," I say. "That's everywhere."

She smooths down her hair, checks her ponytail. "You're a wise old man, you know that?"

I smile. "What do you do for fun?"

She doesn't bite on this. She rolls her neck. It pops. "I go to work for fun. I go to school for fun."

"Neither sounds fun."

She blinks at me, narrows her eyes. "I got no time for fun. I inherited a mortgage, old man."

I press. "That's twice you've said that. Does my age bother you?"

Her shoulders drop. "No."

I say, "How old are you?"

She stares at me, uncertainty there, as if she's wondering if this is a deal-breaker. "I turn nineteen next year."

It's the perfect age (unspoiled). I betray nothing. I don't move a muscle. "So, eighteen, then."

She blushes when she says, "You know, you don't look scared away yet."

"Oh," I say, "*that* comes later."

She laughs that laugh again: surprised, happy, happy at being surprised. It's my new favorite sound, the thing I most want to hear, the thing I'm starting to need.

She lowers her voice. "Did you think I was being crazy when I gave you my number? You know no one can know about this, right?"

"I know. I've never done this before." It's not a lie, if Renee doesn't count (and she doesn't, the whore). "I don't know what to do here, exactly. I only know I want to talk to you more."

"I want to talk to you more too."

The food arrives, steams in front of us. She picks up her fork, but before going after her pancakes, she says, "Do you have a gun on you right now?"

"Always."

"Good," she says.

"Why?"

"Just so you could protect me, you know, if you ever needed to."

"I'll always protect you," I say, and I hold her stare.

She doesn't look away.

43

She's in there over an hour. She touches his arm. She makes eyes at him. She laughs more than I ever seen her laugh, but what hits me is how she's so bold with it, all throwing her head back, touching her hair. At the end, she comes in with a hug. It lasts. They both want it.

It's me sitting shotgun, No Neck in the driver's seat. Jerry in the back.

To the car I say, "Dios fucking mio, man."

Her own cousin's parole officer. It makes me so fucking sick, but that feeling's mixed up with something else, and I'd never tell anybody, but I'm amazed at how brave she is. Trying to love who she wants, even when she knows it's dangerous. Man. I don't really even have words for that.

Petrillo walks her to her car, opens the door for her, waves as she drives back to Lynwood. I bet she stops on the way and changes out of them clothes too. Wipes her lipstick off. Acts like none of this happened. L.A. is a crazy-big place when you know how to escape in it. Y ahora, I got this crazy-ass feeling.

No Neck's putting a trim on a thumbnail with a knife he picked up from somewhere when he sees me looking sick. "Sup, Little?"

"He did it."

"Did what, homes?"

"Petrillo moved that gun from where Scrappy got hit."

"And why, even?"

"The why's right in front of you, No Neck! He wanted everybody out of the way so he could get at Angela. He's the one winning, with them locked up. Going on dates and shit."

In the backseat, Jerry pipes up. "Damn, foo. That's cold. That's ice."

No Neck's still not getting it. "But, like, how?"

"I don't know yet," I'm saying, "but I know that gun got dropped. We find Augie Clark and we find how it got moved."

No Neck finishes with his nail. "Irma said she heard he was in County, but when she called up there, he wasn't there anymore, so either they moved his ass, or he's out."

Jerry's saying, "She's a dog on the hunt, that Irma."

Y ahora, Angela's smiles keep sticking to me. They got me thinking how people are so messed up and *selfish*. Even the ones you like will betray you and people you love. The only way to deal with those people is to make them fear you. No other way. I get that now. I see that power and want to use it.

"And there's something else," I'm saying. "If this fool planted that gun, I bet Angela doesn't even know about it, so when we find out what we need to find out, that's something we can use against both of them."

"Chingón." That's No Neck.

Jerry hits No Neck on the shoulder. "I *know*, huh?"

And then he hits mine. "You're turning gangster quick, foo! I didn't think you had that shit in you, but man, you *do*."

"For real." No Neck's staring at me like he's weighing me up, then starts the car. "Oh hey, did anybody hear Scrappy rolled the hell out of the hospital today?"

That confuses me. "Rolled, like walked?"

"Rolled like *rolled*, homes. Wheelchair wheels." Jerry pumps in his arms at me like he's sitting in a wheelchair in the backseat and he's really getting somewhere.

44

It's the first time I ever visited the Long Beach courthouse, or any court-house for anything, really, that didn't involve me being in cuffs. First time in the Family Law Clerk's Office too, and it's a sad fucking scene, people. It's a fucking epidemical wave of ass-whoopings that women catch. My mom's messed up, man. Couple fingers broke. Scraped-up head. It's fucking stupid, is what it is. They told me not to walk out of that hospital. But my homeboy stole a wheelchair and here I am, writing out fucking forms. Application for temporary restraining order for reasons of domestic violence, that's what.

Do things the right way, that's been my mom's whole thing since it happened. I told her that something could happen to that dude that hit her. I didn't even say my dad. I took that connection out of the equation. I kept it foggy, but I made it clear, you know? Like, something could happen to that dude, you know? That boyfriend you had that never married you, the one that left to go scam on some younger pussy? The one that don't send you money or anything. The one that stole money from you too, on top of everything. Maybe that dude can have an accident. He can be touched, you know?

But that was when my mom really got crying. All of that was what brought bullets to my door, she said, being like that, making decisions like that. Doing evil brings you evil, she said, but not with that *e*-word. She said la maldad, actually.

A mal nudo, mal cuño, that's what I fucking said back. You got to meet rough with rough.

And I'm thinking of that now, what with seeing this amount of women in this little office with this sad long line and clerks behind glass. There's like thirty of us standing here, and they just opened up! Two got black eyes and one even has a broke arm. That's got me feeling, like, maybe we need to fucking stand up, you know? Wives and girlfriends with guns and baseball bats. A fucking *woman* gang. Let that shit be known, if you come at us, you're getting it. Only thing I can think of to stop it, really. A certain type of weak-ass dude really only understands what hitting does when he's getting hit the fuck back. Bitch-ass cowards don't even really get pain till they're *getting* pain, you know what I'm saying?

If I had been there in the house and not up in the hospital when my dad did that to her? That punk would've *felt* it for going at her on the night she was getting back from being treated for dehydration, man! You know he waited out there? He don't have keys. He was lying in wait, like how lawyers say. Premeditation. And when she got home all feeling like shit, just wanting to get socks for me and change her clothes and take a shower, he comes at her, and he hits her? Screaming how it was her fault what happened? That she needed to protect me better? Please, fool! Since when did you ever care about me beyond that money you always asked me for? Besides, me getting popped is on me. Not her. I know what I did. And like I'm saying, if he came at her when I was there? I woulda beat his fucking ass. And I still will, next time I see him. I don't even care. People only do the shit you let them do. It's like, if I don't walk out the house that night for Augie's worthless ass, I don't catch anything. That's on me for being stupid as fuck.

Shit. I'm way up on painkillers right now, and I ain't even swallowed right since it happened. It's like I got this thing stuck in my throat and it's not about to go anywhere. I know they said it passed through me, but it don't feel like that. It feels like it's in me and not ever coming out, but that's whatever. It don't make it so I can't write. My mom watches me. She's a hawk, man, an eagle. There's a line about who the order is supposed to protect so I just put our names and my son's too.

The three nurses and the two doctors, they all said I needed weeks to get good with this. I lost a lot of blood, they said. But then I said, didn't you put new blood in me? And they were like, yeah. So I was like, okay, then! They went on about how shit missed my "vital organs" and how lucky I am for living. Please! I hit them with a listing of people I knew personally that had been up in the same hospital for catching bullets and lived. I did one for every finger, started over, and then stopped after I did three more. I coulda gone on. Getting shot around here, that ain't shit and everybody knows it. Man, in some cases, you ain't even real till you've caught one.

This detective's been calling the house, my mom's been saying. Montero, his name is. He even came by the hospital once and left me a victim's rights card. Fuck that shit. My mom says the meaning of that fool's last name is actually like a job. It's the person that goes along on hunts in the mountains and hits the bushes with sticks so birds fly up to get shot at. I take her word for it. My mom, she's a smart lady. She's always reading, and what she reads sticks to her. Wish I fucking had that. Maybe if I had, school woulda been easier. Yeah, but probably not. Getting pregnant and having Adrian was school being done for me. I ain't telling that Mountain Motherfucker shit, I know that. They'll have to compel my ass to speak on it in court. Subpoena my ass, you know? And even then I'll sit there and not say shit. I'll go on contempt, I don't give a fuck. Lock my ass up. I'll do that time.

Shit, but I crossed a big line. I crossed that race line the big homies set down in the sand and been saying not to cross. I did it. On purpose too. Cuz I was thinking we were gonna lose the house, what with my mom's headaches and her not working. And the only shit that was coming, was coming from Mexico through El Farallon, and look, I paid good tax on it, a lot of fucking tax, so everybody shoulda been good. But when the rest of the southland's in a drought and nothing's coming in for those Crips, from Louisiana, from Houston, from wherever the fuck they got theirs, and when I'm connected up to the only game in town, and some desperate Crip wants a *lot*, and is willing to pay ten times street for it? Shit! And if I see I can go to another level if I just run some shit down to Compton so Adrian's dad can get his game up and make it look like I didn't sell it directly, then that's that. I fucking did it. And the only bad part is the big homies found out I did. But, shit, I'm still breathing, so I don't regret nothing, not even with this whole black-versus-brown shit.

It wasn't always like this. War. Wasn't good, but it wasn't like this whole fuck everybody that don't look like you or your family, till way more recently.

Me and Adrian's daddy, we did middle school together. All kinds of people from everywhere in there. Thai fools. A dude from Arabia somewhere. Everybody was from everything. That's where I came up. It was the eighties, man. It wasn't good, like I'm saying, but it wasn't straight hate. Black and brown were all mixed together, and you couldn't tell me shit. Mom tried. You know she fucking tried. But coming at me with, don't hang out with that boy? Shit. That don't work on me. I was a knucklehead times ten, me. I went out and stayed out. We did ditch parties before they were even called that, man. Please! Like nobody did that before it got a cool-ass name for people? That shit was hooky, cutting out. So many young fools these days thinking they're inventing shit. News flash, dummies, you fucking didn't. The eighties was way worse with that rock coming through. Man, people lost their minds off that shit. Adrian's daddy's daddy went to Chino for murder behind selling that high. That's why his family moved down the map too.

I don't regret nothing, like I been saying. I'm breathing now, but *keeping* breathing is a different thing. I been hearing whispers about how Wizard's locked up on charges behind what he did to me, and that's cool and all, it's not like he don't deserve it, but I need to get up with Wizard's people. My homies are good. They're fucking strong and they don't give a fuck, man, but they can't have my back everywhere. I know that. But Wizard's people? They need to know I won't say shit, and I need to trade my closed mouth for something real. Otherwise, I don't know what I'm about to do.

My mom's hitting my arm. She's waving at me to keep writing, keep filling that form out. She wants me to do things the right way. But I ain't really about that shit.

PART VI

AMONG THORNS

Who we are and what we do

appears to us

like a man dressed in a long black coat,

a bill collector

who offers a paper to sign

and says we have no choice

but to sign it.

—JIMMY SANTIAGO BACA, "ACCOUNTABILITY"

45

It's raining on the yard. Big drops fall through the fencing and splat concrete as me and a crew of Sureños hang out under the roof part near the handball walls, so we can appreciate the water but not get wet. That's key. If you get wet up here, you carry that shit down with you and can't get that cold out. It sinks into your bones. Makes you sick. I try to put together a rhyme about that, but I hold back. I don't have my notebook. Had to leave it in my cell, and I don't want to come up with something just to lose it.

Besides, I'm distracted with keeping an eye on the exit door, and this Counting Crows song on the fuzzy speakers. It's mostly this guitar strumming and a dude singing the words "Mister Jones and me" over and over, but there is this one moment when he mentions going through the barrio.

Beside me, somebody scoffs. "Yo, what does this fool know about barrios, anyways?"

Another homie laughs. "Strolling, right? He said *strolling*? Like, walking all loose? He should try strolling in my hood. See where that gets him."

"We can stroll his ass to the hospital, man. Fucking White Memorial." The first voice is back at it. "Who the fuck picks this music, anyways? We need to get something else playing."

I nod, but there would never be a day when some deputy lets us pick what to listen to. It's a power move. I think they also get off on making us listen to terrible shit, but I don't care. It's nice hearing music, even if I don't like it. It means the world's still spinning, and there's more going on than cells, and yard time. Dreamer steps up to the exit door with his pass. Man, all I feel is relief seeing that. He gets checked by a deputy, but then he's in. I leave the crew behind and meet him halfway. We find a spot to post up where our heads can stay dry and our backs can hug a wall.

"I thought you'd miss yard at the fucking least. They didn't throw you in the hole on the back of that Augie shit?"

He shrugs, like, *I guess not*, but he doesn't look happy. He looks like he's trying to figure me out, wondering if I set him up, and that's hard, because I did. I even told him how to code it with street names and everything. I'm sorry he got caught, but not sorry I did it. Dreamer was the only option there was. That witness's name had to get outside these walls for Jerry and No Neck to work on. Couldn't do it myself, not with Angela.

I get sincere with him. "Listen, homeboy. I'm sorry about all that. I wish it would've been me talking to Little, but it wasn't, so don't even trip."

It doesn't fix it. He's still tripping. I can tell there's not as much trust as there was before, but that's okay, because he doesn't have to trust me. He just has to do what I say if he wants to be good in here. He knows that. He nods.

"All right, good." I lean closer. "They're getting ready to move me. I can feel it."

Not without good reasons. Some fool died off the dope I came in with. They can't pin it on me, but they got suspicions. Narcotics sat me down to talk. They wanted information that I said I had no idea about, but I told them what they wanted to hear, that I'd be looking around, asking questions, doing my investigations. Your average locked-up, no-power fools look at that stuff as a respect move from the deputies, but this one OG told me how it's easier for deputies to talk to one person instead of thirty, so it turns out they need shotcallers as much as we do. The hierarchy we got going actually helps the system cut through the bullshit. They keep authority. Shotcallers keep power. It's better for everybody.

On the same damn day, I was in with the head dude on the Gang Squad, and he wanted to know how Dreamer knew the name Augustine Clark. I told him I didn't know, but the guy was smart as shit. He knew I was being fake with him. I thought I'd kept my name out of it, but they already knew it was my lawyer that showed me the paper, and that I handed the name off to Dreamer. The head dude said the DA was coming for my lawyer on the back of that shit, but there's no way for me to know for sure until I get my next pass for legal consultation.

I tell Dreamer, "It's not about keeping your head down anymore.

From now, you walk like a G. Act like a G. You need to do some shit? Go hard, like it's your business not to give a fuck. There's good eyes on you, big homies watching, and that's good because I'm not gonna be on your hip for much more."

"That sucks." The way he says it, I can't even tell if he means it or not.

But I keep going. "It does, man, but I'm not in control of housing. Be happy we had a run as long as we did. When I go, all you'll be hearing from me is on them wilas."

He squints, and I know I have to break it down. "Kites, man. Folded-up papers with tiny-ass handwriting on them. First ones I ever saw were like that paper football game, but they're smaller now. So here's the next thing, and this is important, don't ever write one. Just receive. When you're done reading, get rid of it. Eat it. Flush it. Whatever you have to do. You can't hand anybody evidence against you if it's grabbed up."

His head pops up at that. "Just against me? You're not writing them?"

"Somebody will put their number on the line, not mine."

His eyes change when I say that, and it's almost like I can see him putting it together with the Augustine Clark shit in his brain, but I don't have time for that now.

I elbow him. "There's some shit coming with the mayates. Don't know if you noticed, but their shotcaller got transferred off."

He shakes his head at me, because no. His ass didn't notice that the black shotcaller got bounced.

I let him have it. "Fucking Dreamer, man! You *have* to get better at noticing things. Information is what keeps you alive in here, homeboy. It can have you seeing trouble before trouble sees you and throws you in the mix."

"I got you, Wizard."

"You better." I stare him down and nail that in before I get back to the matter at hand. "You remember Big Dev from that holding cell? That's who's gone."

Dreamer nods. He remembers. I never told him that Dev and me were in Chino together, or how a big-ass fight popped off in the mess once, and Dev could've smashed me, but he hit the deputy coming at me instead. He did a month in the hole on the back of that and caught a charge for assaulting an officer. I asked him later why he did it and he said he wanted to hit that deputy more than he wanted to hit me. That was it. Only reason Dev wasn't wearing a red jumpsuit in here was because he did that once, years ago, and these County Jail motherfuckers are serious business. They only class people that way if they're habitual. Anyways, I took care of Dev on my commissary after that. I made sure he always had stamps, and when I heard how his girl liked art, I made somebody do up some drawings every week for him to send to his girl back home. It's a shame, but those days are gone now. Black sticking up for brown? Brown helping black? Our big homies don't want it like that no more, and I ain't about to go against that.

"Stick to Raza," I tell Dreamer. "You got my name on you. Anybody steps or talks shit, things will get bad for them, but you still got to be that same warrior I saw fight that dog, because that's all it is in here. You and some bloodthirsty-ass dogs."

Dreamer flexes his arm. His bite scars move under the hair there.

I nod toward the basketball courts. "You weren't here to notice, but none of them knew which team to be on today. Normally Dev picked teams because he loved to ball, and he wanted all the unselfish ones with him, but now that he's gone? They had to shoot free throws for it." I keep talking as Dreamer's eyes drift towards where the blacks are balling. "They're gonna do King of the Mountain to figure out who's up next for them on the block."

He squints. "Like Royal Rumble?"

"Exactly. No rules. Just a bunch of ruthless fuckers. Whoever's left standing is the king."

"Caveman shit." He doesn't sound happy about it, but it's dawning on him that he's got no choice. He doesn't. He skips out on this, and I can't protect him.

I nod. "Yup, and whoever wins that shit, I need you to crack on him, then we're all coming through because I'm going out with a bang. We need to send a message that the streets are ours because we own what's in here. We're done just taxing our people. We wanna tax the fucking black gangs too. We got the numbers in here, so we're taking over. It's our fucking time now."

I see in Dreamer's eyes how a shift happened. He made his decision. He's doing this, and I'm glad.

"This is chess, homeboy." I watch Dreamer clench up a fist, then let it go. "It's about who wins where, and nothing is more important than owning spots nobody can get out of."

We stand around until the music cuts out and we get called for lineup. Fools shuffle over with some wary eyes and pick their places. Nobody wants to show their back to anybody, but you have to in a line. Everybody's quiet about it too, and even deputies get nervous at that. If you've been locked up enough, you know what's coming, a bunch of tensed-up motherfuckers walking, just looking for a moment to jump things off.

46

I shouldn't be in here. That's what I'm thinking. *I didn't ride. Didn't pull a trigger.*

This ain't on me. I'm paying for it tho.

And now I got to walk headfirst into some shit cuz Wizard fucking says so?

Fuck, man. It ain't right.

It ain't fair how this's going down.

Me about to do something dangerous as fuck. Something that could be a whole new crime. And more time.

All cuz it's the only way to stay safe in here. And I don't even know how those two things make sense together like that.

It's true tho. For real.

And the only thing good in this right now is how I'm almost glad I get to punch somebody so soon after what Wizard said.

How he was sorry. And how I shouldn't trip.

I wanted to say, *I'm definitely fucking tripping!*

I thought this fool was my friend. I looked up to him forever.

And now he's out here setting me up, getting me in trouble so he won't be.

And that's got that rage going inside me . . .

And I guess I'm glad knowing I get to throw down and get that feeling out.

I don't got to bite my lip or shut my mouth. Don't got to wait for it to eat at me for days. I can just step up. Can just let go on somebody.

And I'm getting so hyped thinking about what a relief that's about to be that my blood's up.

I'm watching everything on the walk back down to the tier. I'm looking for dudes to be antsy or sweaty or waiting for it.

I don't see shit tho. Just people walking. Shoulders moving normal. Backs of heads.

I mark out all the fools I think got a shot at being King of the Mountain. There's Tim Muhammad. He's six guys ahead of me. Everybody's heard of him. The middle linebacker and tight end. He was this big football star at Compton High till he killed his girlfriend one night in the summer when it was crazy hot. He thought she was cheating. I don't know about that. I just know the news said he took her head off with a shotgun blast . . . just, *blau*.

Tim's six-foot-three and ready to punch down on anybody. He's up on the yard doing his bench work every day. Doesn't mean he can fight tho. Just means he's strong. And strong don't mean you can take pain. Strong don't mean you can duck. Strong don't mean smart.

Two behind Tim is this dude Sykes. Goes by Pretty Boy. That fool tells anybody that'll listen he was a pimp on the outside. And that he won the Illinois state lottery. Fuck that dude. Word is, he got caught after pulling a pawnshop robbery cuz his ass stopped for a sandwich two blocks away. That's how stupid he is.

Behind Sykes, there's this dude people call Barrel Roll for no reason I know. And hearing what Wizard had to say about me not paying attention, I'm thinking now how that was a mistake, not asking. I need to be better. Not gathering information and knowing as much as I can about who's around me? That shit's stupid.

I got to be up on everything. Got to know who could do what. And from where. Wizard's right.

Barrel Roll's like forty years old. A tough-looking forty tho. Medium height. He squats twice his weight. And he's thick with muscles all the way around.

My uncle, before he went back to Samoa to take care of Grams, always tried to make me think like a warrior, to have that spirit. He talked about how to never fight the guy with the biggest wrists cuz he'll punch your fucking brains out. Strength don't mean shit if your joints can't hold it, can't send it, my uncle said. And thick wrists mean *run*. He used to say that.

I pull my head out of line a little. I look ahead. Tim has the thickest wrists. Barrel Roll's right there with him tho. What makes me feel good is, neither of them has anything on me. I got an advantage. A natural-born one. Cuz that's just how God makes Samoans. Down to fucking pound.

I look over my shoulder at this little-ass Sureño behind me called Peeper.

I whisper back his way and say, "Hey, Peep."

"Sup, homes?"

"Why they call Barrel Roll by that?"

"Oh, cuz that fool's a liar, bro. He said he fought in Vietnam and that he's a pilot. Got a license and everything, he says. So we been callin him by Barrel Roll to fuck with him, but also cuz he kinda looks like a barrel, right? Ha!"

From behind us the deputy says, "Inmates! Shut your mouths."

Peeper says, "Yessir, boss."

We wait for the door to pop, then we go in 4700 like a bunch of mice on the sneak. Vatos going a bit slower. Mayates going that little bit faster.

That's how we separate.

By the time the deputies figure out what's going down, the walkway in front of the cells is blocked up. They can only see us from observation behind that glass in the middle that dudes are about to square off.

And they can't do shit. They just have to watch till they can get a team in to fuck us all up.

The full siren goes.

And that shit feels like it's blowing my eardrums out my ears.

I touch my face, expecting to find blood.

There's nothing.

And that's okay. Cuz right now I'm feeling free.

I'm pushing right up to the edge of the crowd where this big fucker is blocking the walkway.

I'm going where I'm not supposed to.

Doing what I'm not allowed to.

And that's good. That feels *good*.

When Pretty Boy swings first and catches Barrel Roll behind the ear, everybody roars like we at the fights.

47

Supervisory is in the control room shouting at us over the speakers to stop. That shit ain't happening tho. Hell, no.

Tim's smart, hanging back as Barrel Roll recovers. He goes into Pretty Boy hard, bullying his ass with the weight advantage.

They go right into the bars beside one of the cell doors.

And that's it for Pretty. He comes back off the bars, a flap of skin hanging off his head. And blood going down his back.

The metal opened his head right up.

Damn.

He tries holding the skin closed on his skull. It's not helping tho.

His blues go purple in a hurry.

He's slumping down the bars. Almost sitting on the floor.

And that's when Barrel turns. And Tim steps to him.

He comes in too quick tho, too rushed. He doesn't know to judge the distance to get shots off.

And my blood's all the way up now.

In my throat, my ears, my face.

I know I got this.

I know I could take them both.

Especially as these two fuckers scuffle around.

And can't punch for shit

And accidentally punch the railing.

And head-butt.

And spit.

And that's when it happens.

Tim gets up under Barrel Roll's arms. Gets into his chest.

And he's in there, just jamming fists up into Barrel's armpits . . .

Getting leverage under him.

Like what he'd do at football practice when he's blocking.

Like what he's prolly been coached to do forever.

Get them off their balance.

And he does.

Oh man, he fucking does.

Cuz Barrel's off the ground and they're turning,

And Barrel goes up over the railing

And down one tier,

Twenty fucking feet down,

And that fool goes smack on the concrete below us.

Fucking *splat.*

And when that happens,

Everybody stops for like a second.

Maybe two seconds.

Siren still going.

Nobody moving.

And then it's like the whole roof comes off.

Peeper's jumping up next to me. Waving his hand in the air like it's a concert.

Moving his mouth like, *Holy shit, fool!*

Like, *You seen that shit, fool?*

Fuckers are freaking out. Looking over the side and everything.

I don't tho.

I got my aims.

I'm seeing Tim.

Tim's the new king.

And everybody else is figuring that shit out too.

You can see how it's washing over people. How they're getting used to it thru the shock of seeing Barrel go over.

That's when I walk.

I feel a tap on my hip from Wizard. Like, *Yeah!*

Like, *Get that motherfucker, homes!*

There's only one thing between Tim and me.

The fat dude holding everybody back from the main fights so King of the Mountain can happen.

He's not facing me.

And that gives me time to line my shot up on him.

It's like slow motion how it goes down.

And I just have this thought like . . .

I'm balling every bad thing up that I got inside me.

Fucking being locked in here. Fucking being told where to go. And when. Fucking having to sleep where somebody shits a few feet away from my face, where there's no getting away from it. Fucking Wizard using me to protect his own ass.

And I get my feet under me good and bring that rage up thru me like some type of hurricane

Down my arm as

I put it in my swing

Where I'm bringing that weight in

With every pound I got,

With some perfect-ass aim,

Cuz I lined it all up,

And when that shit lands . . .

When my fist hits him like a sledgehammer coming down . . .

His ass fucking *drops*.

One pop. Right kidney.

Done with.

I hit him so hard he screams like he's shot.

And he goes down wobbling, grabbing at his back.

Swear to god I split that shit inside him.

That poor motherfucker never had a chance.

Now he's gonna be wearing his fucking hospital browns for weeks.

And I don't even feel bad about it.

Fuck this dude, that's how I feel.

I'm hitting him like I wish I could hit Wizard.

Cuz fuck Wizard. Fuck everybody.

You got to protect your own back in here! Don't show it to nobody.

And this poor fool left himself wide open.

I swing a quick look behind me to check I'm not going in alone. I'm not.

My back's good. Wizard's right behind me, smiling like a motherfucker. *Enjoying* this shit.

Peeper behind him with a paisa-made shank in his hand just as I'm wondering where the hell it even came from.

Behind Peep is some East Los cousins I met yesterday, thuggish motherfuckers running interference on some deputies, about to get fucking sprayed. They step up.

They take that pepper shit full in their faces like some fucking Gs and stay standing, stay wrestling with clear shields and billy clubs and the helmets behind them.

I turn back to see Tim. And that's when Tim's seeing me.

He's got this look on his face like he knows it's about to go down.

There's something different there tho.

His heart's gone.

You can see how it's gone.

How it went over that railing with fucking Barrel Roll.

And that's when I learn that Tim Muhammad ain't no kind of hardcore motherfucker.

I look into his eyes. And all I'm seeing is a scared-ass little kid.

And I'm not even to him yet when I'm thinking,

I'm king now.

Tim sees that shit in my eyes too.

How I'm punking his ass with a look.

And he don't even really put his hands up to me when I swing.

He just gives me that free shot.

And I'd aim for the jaw. The neck is free tho, so I swing for that.

For the throat.

I go right thru his lazy-ass guard.

Right down the fucking middle.

And prolly the only thing that saves him is how he's turning away from me.

Catching it in the side of the neck and not full-on.

That's cool tho. Cuz it's enough to send him falling backwards.

And I'm already stepping forward with the stomps.

On his chest.

On his skull.

On his ribs.

Wherever I can get that shit in.

Cuz I'm the fucking King of the Mountain now.

And everybody knows it.

And Wizard's grinning this evil-ass grin.

And I see pride shining out in his eyes. Like, *That's my fucking home-boy right there!*

And even I know he's happy cuz this is good for him,

Me doing what he said,

His orders getting followed,

And I watch how he's getting shots in on Tim.

And one in on Pretty too while he's at it.

And Peeper's stabbing that fool Pretty Boy when I see Wizard's eyes go cold cuz the mission's done.

And a soldado knows when to stop. He's got fucking discipline.

And Wizard gives me this hand motion like, *Get down.*

And for a second, I don't.

Just to show him I can stand on my own.

And he's getting flat on the concrete floor, putting hands on his head, nodding for me to do the same.

And I stare down at him.

Just for a second . . .

Before I do it too.

Just so he knows I know how he did me. And I'm doing what I got to do.

And it still don't mean I like it.

Right before the air turns white around us and I can't breathe for shit.

Right before the clubs come down.

And I'm sure I'm fucking dying . . .

48

Jacob Safulu no longer looks sixteen. Faint redness rings his eyes. His cheeks have retained a hint of puffiness from being sprayed with pepper spray. An abrasion on his left temple looks as if it came from the sole of a boot. Worst of all, he sports a long rectangular bruise on the lower half of his face that extends from his jaw to the left corner of his mouth; it is as thick as—and almost perfectly shaped like—a baton. It's rare to see bruises so solid that you immediately know what caused them. Knuckles on his left hand, the one cuffed to the table, are split raw from punching. The narrative of what happened to Jacob Safulu is practically written on him. What he dealt, and also what he paid for doing so.

I'm no doctor, but I'd imagine that he should probably be in the jail medical ward. The fact that he's not tells me he was one of the aggressors, which is certainly not good. He is now locked down twenty-three hours a day in the disciplinary unit. He got walked in here cuffed, and with an escort. That's a pretty quick transition from the kid I saw before. He has slid so fast and so far down the slippery slope that he might as well have been on a bobsled. What I see before me now is precisely what I was afraid of; if a jury saw him like this, it would not matter where he was on the night in question.

"I came yesterday," I say. "Did they tell you?"

"No. When?"

"After lunch. Forty-seven hundred was locked down. I came back two hours later, and forty-seven hundred was not locked down, but you were no longer there."

He gives me a look that tells me he knows I'm going somewhere with this and he'll just wait it out.

"All of which"—I wave my hand at his face and knuckles, so that he knows these things are included too—"begs the question, and pardon me for saying it so crassly, but what are you fucking doing in AdSeg?"

He blinks. The curse word had its impact.

"Didn't really have a choice, boss," he says.

The way he says this infuriates me.

"Here's the thing." There is no point to biting my tongue anymore. "You will *never* refer to me as 'boss' again. In fact, don't ever call me by anything you'd use for a CO or a deputy. It's a terrible habit to get into, and harder to break. It gets inside you, that kind of thing, and if and when you get out, you carry it with you on the outside. Do you understand me?"

He blinks. He gets it. He says, "Yes."

"Good. When you get out of AdSeg, you'll be rehoused. You might go to the high-powered side, or within the gang unit. Is there anything about this that *helps* your case, do you think?"

He looks down. Finally, I've landed something.

"No," he says.

"No," I echo him. "It hurts it a great deal, actually. Your behavior in this facility is something Miss Mirkovich can bring up and use against you; it will be evidence of gang ties, of your essential character, and especially your willingness, and capacity, to inflict violence."

"Shooting and punching aren't the same thing."

"Indeed, they're not, but do you want to trust a jury of people who are very much not your peers to decide that? People who do not live in the world you live in, who cannot possibly understand its pressures? Hearing these things about you will be enough for them to think you capable. Believe me."

He chews his lower lip now.

"Are you ready for the worst surprise? That stunt you pulled, talking about Augustine and Clark streets? They *heard* you. You were *monitored.*"

Safulu makes a face like he's eaten something bitter, and that tells me he's already been questioned about the whole affair by jail staff.

"I need to know where you received this information," I say. "Otherwise, I may have to recuse myself, and you will be assigned someone else, somebody a whole lot worse."

"Wizard's lawyer slid it to him. We talked about it after. He told me how I should try to get it out there. But this shit is between me and you. I can't have people knowing this."

"I understand, Mr. Safulu, but it may become impossible not to reveal how you came by this information. If the judge hasn't heard about this incident yet, you can bet she will soon. It will swiftly become part of the evidence against you. The deputy who heard you will be called to the stand. The report he or she filed here at the jail will be used as evidence. I need you to ask yourself something right now: *How does this help my case? How does using coded language to say the name of a witness against me look?*"

His head drops. He's got it.

"Not good," he says.

"Worse than *not good*, it makes you look *guilty!*" My stomach isn't what it once was. My lunch has decided to repeat on me. "It makes you look like you're attempting to cover up the role you played in the attempted murder of Lucrecia Lucero. It makes it look like Angela is *lying* in order to protect you. This was—and I trust I am giving you the full picture here—a potentially catastrophic fuckup on your part. What you did by saying those two particular words on that phone line may very well be enough to convict you of a crime you didn't commit."

Tears form on his long eyelashes as I let that sink in, and just like that, Jacob Safulu looks sixteen again. It's good to see, actually. It means I'm getting through to him, for now, and I have to keep pushing while I have the chance.

"I have gone along to this point. Against my guidance, the cases were not separated. You need to remember one thing, however: the sentences will not be the same for you both. You won't be doing the same amount of years split between you. Your role must be weighed accordingly, and with that in mind, where did you go after Angela ended your relationship?"

He sniffles. "I went to Spider's. Smoked a lot of chiba."

I ask him where Spider lives. I get his address and actual name—Melvin Dominguez. I ask who else was at this party. Safulu gives me full names and addresses, the ones he knows, at least. I write it all down for my investigator. We don't have much time before the preliminary hearing, but if he can get to them today, we can at least have interviews down on paper to present for discovery tomorrow.

"How many of these people will testify as to your whereabouts?"

"Wear a . . . ?"

"Where you were that night."

"Testify? Like, be up on that stand?"

"Yes, Mr. Safulu, exactly that."

"Maybe two or three, but it was a party, you know? Drugs, drinking, all that. Not many people are gonna want to talk. They'll be afraid it'll be used against them."

"We still have to try. The more reliable among them, the better."

He has to think about that.

"We need more witnesses like Angela Alvarez," I continue, "good student, star athlete, a young woman who works and goes to school at night. In short, we need someone trustworthy, a stand up citizen to back up your alibi."

This last part, the one I've been building to, I've not been certain how to say it until now. In fact until just this moment I didn't think myself capable, but desperate times do call for corresponding measures.

"Should Augustine be found, it is *crucial* that nothing happens to him. I need your name as far away from him as possible. This includes anything knowingly perpetrated on his person by a member of your gang. Should that happen, if law enforcement can prove harm befell Mr. Clark as a result of what you said in that visiting room, there is no going back. However"—I let the word hang between us—"if he should happen to decide he no longer saw what he saw, that his memory has become fuzzy in the intervening time—he is a drug addict, after all— well then, that might be very good for us, indeed."

And very bad, I think, for Kristina Mirkovich.

Safulu squints at me for a moment before opening his eyes wider. There is no shortage of surprised respect in his gaze now, and I think it safe to say that he's looking at me as if I'm a gangster too, which feels simultaneously exciting and horrifying.

49

Chains ring in the antechamber. It's a Santa Claus jingle with no reindeer, and it gets louder as inmates walk into the courtroom wearing jumpsuits of varying colors. One is in leg irons, some are in cuffs only, and two are chained together. All are instructed by the bailiff to sit in the empty jury box, which is always one of my favorite moments. They pick seats. They like sitting in judgment, if only for a day.

I'm sharing a prosecution table with Janet Pettibone and Raymond Weisman, both of whom have prelims as well. Janet's up first, then me, then Ray. Janet shuffles back and forth between witnesses, and on the defense side, lawyers chat with their respective clients in the jury box. Depending on how this goes, Ray might get rescheduled, but I'm hoping Nick Park allows my witnesses hearsay and narrative so we can all get out of here on time.

Willie Montero, ex-husband to the stars, sits behind me in a row of chairs set up behind the prosecution's table with Ivica, Louis, and Jackson. The rest of my witnesses are spread through the courtroom gallery, but so are everybody else's. It's a tight schedule today, and it's a packed house. The only one not here yet is Petrillo.

The judge hasn't come in, and I've got this down cold, so I size up the jury box.

I tell Willie that Safulu looks bad. He turns to look.

"Ouch. Some deputy loved doing *that*. Oh, and Kris"—he nods toward a young woman in the gallery who is the Latin twin of Vanessa Williams—"Angela Alvarez is here."

"Isus." I'd spit if I could. "That face could launch a thousand ships."

Willie smiles. "Yup."

I hate him for that. Truly, I do.

This does, however, help me formulate an instant jury plan. It won't be good for us to have her on the stand, but Nick Park will call her if I don't. A young woman that beautiful has influence, which is precisely why I need a female majority on the jury for two reasons: women to empathize with the victim, and women to feel jealous just looking at Angela Alvarez. It's harder to believe someone who makes you feel insecure.

"Miss Mirkovich."

I turn from my notes to see Willie nod to a man shaking hands with my brother. "This is Petrillo."

Petrillo is six-foot-plus, and his black hair has a southern Italian curl to it. His nose has been punched a few times, but there's no denying it, Parole Agent Phillip Petrillo is one handsome son of a bitch. I smooth my skirt, and wait to be introduced.

"Counselor." Petrillo gives me a half smile.

I don't tell him I'm a mademoiselle now, because I'm on my best behavior, but he actually does look at my left hand to see I'm not wearing a ring.

"Agent Petrillo." I put my right hand out and he shakes it; it's warm, his grip. "I appreciate you securing my witness."

"Just doing my job." He points to a nearby pew. "I'll just grab a seat!"

It takes effort not to watch him go, but the judge is coming in and we're told to rise. Beneath her bench, the sign says: THE HONORABLE SUSAN J. AYERS.

Pettibone's 187 first-degree case is a slam dunk, so they're done in forty minutes, which means I'm up. Everybody involved in the proceedings rises as the judge's clerk announces the case number and says, "Defendants Omar Armando Tavira and Jacob Safulu. Are all the parties present?"

Both defendants answer in the affirmative and then charges are read: conspiracy, attempted murder, assault with a deadly weapon, and mayhem.

Judge Ayers tilts her head. "It looks like we'll be here a moment. Please, sit."

I start with conspiracy. It's the only sticking point, since there's no direct evidence. I call Detective William Montero to the stand. Before he takes it, I state for the record that he is my ex-husband. A small hoot arises from the jury box at the revelation of my former relationship.

"That's enough!" Judge Ayers glares at the box. Every single inmate shrinks except Tavira, who returns her gaze. He *definitely* shot the Lucero girl.

We already covered my relationship to the witness in chambers with the judge and opposing counsel, but she asks them if they have any objections to the witness anyway. Both say no.

Once Willie has been sworn in, I begin. "Are you POST-certified, Detective?"

Peace Officer Standards and Training: the minimum requirement for competency in the state of California, and the best way to let the court know my witness knows what the hell he's talking about.

After he says yes, we cover the who, when, where, and what. He describes the crime step by step, then reads Augustine Clark's affidavit aloud to the court.

"Objection, Your Honor. Hearsay."

"Mr. Park, do you really mean to tie my courtroom up with spurious objections?"

"No, Your Honor, but Detective Montero was not there and cannot speak to it."

"This is true, Mr. Park, but in the interest of expediency I see no point whatsoever in calling a witness who has already signed an affidavit."

I take that as my cue. "I wish to offer Augustine Clark's affidavit into evidence as People's Exhibit A."

The bailiff takes the signed form from me.

"So marked as People's A." Judge Ayers makes a note. "Proceed."

"Detective Montero, in your professional opinion, do the overt acts—obtaining an unregistered firearm, engaging a fellow gang member to—"

"Objection. Mr. Safulu has no criminal record prior to these charges, and no tattoos on his body that prove he is a gang member."

"Overruled. Mr. Park, the same rules apply here as on trial, and I assure you that you are doing a bang-up job, but there is no jury to impress at the moment, so if you wouldn't mind us proceeding?"

In the jury box, some inmates put their hands over their mouths in response to Park getting his ass handed to him. I love this judge.

I have Willie go into detail about the plan.

"I infer from the actions of the accused that a plan was in place. They obtained a gun, drove to the house, and lay in wait for the victim."

Willie is a pro. He's been in court so many times, he almost talks like me. He lays out the timeline beautifully.

"Detective, would you describe the sequence of overt acts as malice aforethought?"

"It's textbook." His tone is unimpeachable.

I could hug the man.

"In your professional opinion, could the act have been done in self-defense?" It's a stupid question, but I have to make certain it is an unlawful killing.

"Absolutely not."

We move on to proving the element of revenge in mayhem with recent incidents of gang violence between Tavira's and Lucero's respective gang associates, and what likely motivated the murder attempt, before Willie steps down and I call Deputy Louis. He identifies Tavira and Safulu as the defendants. I have him walk me through the date and time of arrest. He describes how neither defendant seemed troubled during arrest, and he inferred guilt from this.

"Objection." Nick sounds stressed. "Speculation."

Judge Ayers blinks. "Sustained."

Jackson's up after the break, and he lays everything out regarding the physical evidence of the murder weapon. He nails down whose bedroom it was, who lived there, and who had access. He describes how it was found by Petrillo, and how the parole agent on scene took photographs to document the seizure. I offer those photographs into evidence, as well as the gun.

"Do you recognize this as the weapon from Mr. Safulu's bedroom, Deputy Jackson?"

"Yes."

"How do you recognize it?"

"I wrote the evidence slip on it." He points to the slip in the bag.

"Thank you. I have no further questions, Your Honor."

Nick takes over. He wants to know if any prints were found on the weapon. He is told it has not yet been tested. He has nothing further.

As Jackson steps down, Judge Ayers looks to me. "If you have no more witnesses, Miss Mirkovich?"

"No, Your Honor."

"Excellent. I think it safe to say the facts in this case meet a preponderance of evidence, and it will proceed to trial phase, which will be scheduled at the next available opportunity."

This is my chance to bully the date up, and I have to take it. "Your Honor, if I may, a new piece of evidence has come to light."

"Now is hardly the time, Miss Mirkovich. Must I lecture you as well?"

"The People apologize for the poor timing, Your Honor, but it is incumbent upon me to inform the court that a secret message originating inside San Quentin State Prison from a high-ranking prison gang member calling for the death of Lucrecia Lucero has been found. The People feel this furthers charges of conspiracy, and puts the victim as well as potential witnesses at greater risk—"

"Objection. Why was this not brought forward when the elements of conspiracy were—"

"Don't make me bang this gavel, Mr. Park. You know how I love to."

Nick Park turns a shade of red I've only ever seen on strawberries.

"Thank you." Judge Ayers turns back to me. "Mr. Park does have a point. Why are we only learning about this now?"

"It was confirmed yesterday by prison staff, Your Honor." This is not strictly true; we've known for a week. "The People do not yet have the evidence in hand, as it is in transit, and, as such, I did not see fit to waste the court's time when the elements of conspiracy were already amply supported."

"I see. So, in revealing this now, what is it the People wish me to do, Miss Mirkovich?"

"We request expedition of the case."

"Oh, I see, and do the People happen to have a time frame in mind?"

"January, Your Honor."

"Next month? Are the People asking me to push?"

"Your Honor, the People would never presume to do that. However, with drug court being established as soon as the new year, it is our hope that there may be some openings in your docket that can be better filled with violent felony cases such as this one."

Judge Ayers huffs, and beckons her clerk over. He brings the calendar. We wait as he checks and cross-checks, makes notations, and then looks up. "January tenth, Your Honor."

Nick Park flinches. "Your Honor, that is nowhere near enough—"

"I am not interested in your objections at this stage, Mr. Park. Did I fail to make that clear?" She looks over her glasses at me. "Does that date suit the People?"

Inside, I'm a fireworks display. "Absolutely. Thank you, Your Honor."

"Very well, we will reconvene then." The judge brings the gavel down, and looks at Nick Park when she does it.

I *love* this judge.

50

I'm not going to sit here in Room 1103 of the Hotel Miyako and tell any-body I didn't want it. I'm grown enough to admit I did, and admitting that doesn't change the fact that I'm a primate-brained idiot. I couldn't stand it when Kristina eyed Phil Petrillo as I introduced them. That's the terrible root of it.

Sheryl and I have been on two dates. The Kings game, and dinner out. Both went good. She's out of town this week, but when she's back, we'll go out again. We're not serious. We haven't talked about getting serious. But I still feel like shit.

"Shower's all yours," Kristina says. She's back in her black skirt, but with bare legs, and no thigh-high hose yet.

Her heels sit tipped on their sides by the door.

The TV's going. Menendez coverage wall-to-wall. I offer to turn it off. She says no.

I say, "What do you think of this case?"

"I only have prosecutor brain," Kristina says as she puts her face back on, "what do you think I think?"

"Guilty."

"Willie, they said they were guilty. They admitted it."

"First-degree, then."

"It's a start," she says.

"Death penalty?"

She shrugs. She doesn't emotionally invest in cases she has no hand in. It's smart. I wish I could do it.

She still has the court glow on her, the bright eyes, the extra inch of height from out of nowhere. It's a look she always gets when she gets what she wants.

Proceed to trial with all counts? Check.

Push the trial up on Judge Ayers's calendar? Check.

Fuck with Nick Park's head? Check.

It going good is how it all went wrong.

In the hallway after the other sheriffs went back to Firestone, like a fucking asshole I asked her to get a drink to celebrate being one step closer to locking her first convictions in her new position. I knew she wouldn't say no. My shift was already covered so I could be in court, and she had nothing else for the day. We went to the second-floor bar of the Hotel Miyako in Little Tokyo, close to the courthouse, but not too close. My lieutenant likes it. She knows all the great Japanese spots. She says it's good after court, no matter what the result. The clientele is mostly Japanese businessmen and tourists. Nobody bothers anybody. Two beers became three whiskeys, and those drinks became a room on Kristina's personal credit card right before the karaoke got set up.

The rest was just the rest. The familiarity of knowing each other, not always liking each other, but *knowing* each other.

Pushing the likes. Her ears. Her neck. A certain slow rhythm. Massaging her scalp. Getting a fistful of hair and tugging gently.

Avoiding the dislikes. Never, ever tickle her. Do not pinch anywhere.

Not pissing each other off with talking too much or checking in too much or wondering if she liked it.

She likes it. She likes it a certain way and I learned it a long time ago.

It's a relief how we don't get in each other's way anymore. It's a relief sometimes, being with someone that knows how shitty the world is, how bad people are to each other, how evil. It never lasts long, the relief.

After, I'm left with a reminder of why everything broke in the first place, and how bad I was at fixing it. I remember the not-getting-pregnant, the shutting down, the scolding, the questioning that never stopped. I have to sit with it while she takes over the bathroom.

"How was it?" Kristina eventually says, smiling at herself in the mirror. "Better than the new woman you're taking out for soup?"

That's Kristina Mirkovich, turning toward me, leaning away from a fire-red lipstick that she holds still in the air where her face used to be.

She's perfectly made-up. She's competitive. She's petty.

She still has keys to me, no matter how much I want them back.

51

She's coming out of Lynwood High's ROP quick like she's got somewhere to go, and that don't exactly suit me, so I have my cousin Vulture step out. I swing my door open from where I'm sitting in the backseat so it blocks her front door and she can't get in even if she wants to. But Angela? She's not paying attention. She's walking and swinging those hips. She's looking down at her calendar or something, some papers in a green binder that look all official and like she takes her shit serious.

When she gets close enough, I get her with, "You a fine one. Isn't that how that song go?"

She stops. Freezes, more like.

Girls like her? They think they're better than me. They've thought it every day of their pretty-ass lives. So it's good popping up on them every now and again. I like it. Getting that drop. Reminding them they ain't as big as they think they fucking are. Letting them know I can take their prettiness away if I want to. All it takes is a few seconds and a razor blade.

"Oh shit," Angela blurts, and you can see how she don't really mean to say it. It just kinda pops out of her mouth.

Cuz she's surprised. Cuz she's scared. Can't imagine why.

"Back from the dead." I laugh. "Three bullets ain't shit."

My wheelchair's in the trunk, and I'm not to the point where I can set it all up myself yet, or roll around for even twenty minutes without getting dizzy, but she don't need to know that. Right now she needs to see power. She needs to see my ass risen up.

I'm nodding at her. "How's this nursing school going for you? You're gonna take care of old folks so I don't have to?"

She don't want to say. She wants to stay closed up. But you don't get to stay closed up around me. Not after what I been through.

Vulture don't need me to tell him to step to her. He just does.

She gets a little shaky when he gets close and finally answers. "Y-yes. I guess."

"I appreciate that about you. You got a good heart."

"Thanks." She pretty much whispers it.

"You're welcome."

Her legs tense where she's standing in them short-ass jean shorts. I see that paper jumping in her fingers.

"Look here, Angela, all right? You need to be cool. I can see how you're thinking about running, cuz you always run. It's who you are, and it's what you fucking do. But that wouldn't be good. Not right now. Why don't you come up here in this seat with me? It's comfy as fuck."

It's not really a question. Vulture's putting that across. And she don't want to move, but she's moving.

She's closing her notebook thing up, and holding it in one hand now.

She's sliding up onto the seat next to me, and I'm not even moving.

She gets close, and uncomfortable, just so she's not hanging out the door.

I'm just staring at her, trying to figure out what she loves most, trying to figure out how to make sure she goes and gets me what I need.

I say, "How's Elisa's kids doing?"

And, man! If you thought she was frozen up before, it's crazy now.

She's like Han Solo getting turned into a brick with his mouth open and hands up!

I can't help laughing at that shit. "Rowland's what now? Five, right? He's cute as fuck, that one. Him and my Adrian would be good together. Couple of little clowns, man. Couple of little payasos doing their thing together at a birthday party. I can see it happening. That'd be real good too. And good for Marisela. A happy brother makes a happy sister, right?"

She don't respond, so I keep going. "So, listen, Angela, I don't know who's running what now with Wizard doing that County thing, but I know somebody had to step up. You tell *that* person I want to talk. It's not about nothing but figuring this out. And I'm not saying your cousin's coming back home, Angela, I'm not, cuz I'm not no judge, or lawyer, or a fucking jury all by myself, but if that guilty-verdict shit do happen, it won't be off of my mouth, cuz I sure as shit ain't about to put him away with pointing fingers. ¿Entiendes?"

She nods her head all slow.

"That's good, Angela. You can go now. Tell them I want to meet at Mariscos El Paisa tomorrow. I bring Vulture. They bring whoever. We'll grub some fish down. Talk shit out."

She starts sliding. Her shorts catch on a rip in the upholstery when she gets out and nods again.

I say, "So, what'd I say, though?"

"El Paisa," she says, "tomorrow for lunch. What time?"

I wink at her. "What time would you want it to be?"

She makes her nostrils all big. "Twelve-thirty?"

"Make it one, then. And you know what, Angela? You look real good today. You look so nice. I hope you keep looking that way."

See, I don't threaten her for nothing. I don't make threats. Never have. I'm a meek-ass kitty, me.

But it's weird how people always go around thinking I do, right?

I mean, that shit's just crazy.

52

Jerry's driving us to Mariscos El Paisa. No Neck's talking, telling me all about how nobody knows more than me about what's going on right now, so I need to step up and talk to Scrappy.

I come back with, "Hell, no. This ain't my life like it's your life."

It must've been tough for Angela to come to us how she did, all scared. She said Scrappy made it clear if we didn't show up, something might happen to her. And I must not be a good person, because the first thing I thought then was maybe it'd be justice if something happened. I almost threw that Petrillo shit in her face, but I bit my tongue.

"It's gettin to *be* your life. And it's all you on this one," Wizard said. You're on it," No Neck says as we slow to a red light and he spits out the open window.

"Yeah, foo." Jerry puts that accelerator down when the light goes green. "You want all them good things like nobody saying bad words about you, like having power to get shit done, but you don't wanna do the bad shit? That's not how this works, foo. You got to do both. Besides, if some shit does happen to you, like, as a trade-off, then nobody's gonna be that upset about it."

I guess I knew I could die, or at least get shot how Scrappy got shot. That sends some cold feelings up my back.

"That makes sense," I'm saying. "People'll say I mixed myself up in something and didn't know what I was getting into."

Jerry don't disagree. "Yeah. That's what they'll say too."

"But ain't shit about to happen at this spot. Everybody knows who owns it." No Neck rolls a blunt where he's sitting. "Scrappy picked a good one. It's neutral. So, that's me sayin, yeah, you could get blasted off of this, but it won't be today, and it won't be at El Paisa, so relax."

*   *   *

Y ahora, as we step in, I'm taking in everything. Walls painted light blue with a dark blue line on the bottom, and all around a kind of covered patio area are shiny metal tables with matching shiny benches bolted to concrete. In the ceiling there's fans for when it gets hot in the summer. And there's music, some Chalino Sánchez going loud as hell. It's "Nieves de Enero." Perfect not to get overheard over.

By the order window is a big painting with flying seagulls and an island. Next to that is Scrappy, at the table nearest the corner. There's a big fool sitting close at another table. That must be Vulture, the dude Jerry warned me about before we got out of the car. No Neck and Jerry sit at the other end of the same table and don't like it much.

I walk up to Scrappy's table once I've got my food. She has a white patch over the left side of her neck that's going a little brown. I decide never to look at it again, never mention it either. A bowl of soup's steaming in front of her.

I sit down across from her, on the other bench. I set down my tray with my taco plate on it. "Angela said to come."

Scrappy takes one look at me and decides I ain't about shit. "Get the fuck out of here. You ain't involved."

"On this, I am."

She laughs, then looks at me sideways. "You look kinda sweet to be doing this."

By saying *sweet* she's just name-calling without name-calling. This type of shit always comes at me in a way that's supposed to mean I'm less than a fucking person, like, not a real man, not man enough to handle this. Y ahora, I got the pain of everything I've ever been called jumping up inside me and that's got me looking Scrappy dead in her eyes and saying, "I *am* sweet. I like boys. You got a problem with that shit?"

The grin she cracks then? It's like a neon sign.

"Damn, look at you!" She's saying, "You know, I got the same problem. I like boys too much. Got me a kid and everything."

"He doing okay? All this must've been rough on him, worrying about you."

She eyes me down like I'm trying to play her. I'm not. I'm just putting myself in her kid's shoes because I've been through similar. And I think she figures that out because she tells me he's been crying a lot.

I look to the ceiling fans for a second. "I did that too when my daddy got shot."

"He make it?" She means my dad.

"No." As soon as I say it, she can see in my eyes how it's true and it still hurts, but I'm letting her in to see.

She sniffs at me like she figured something out. "I like you. I'm gonna call you Dulce."

"I'm going by Little."

"Nah," she's saying, "maybe you were, but that shit don't suit a little chapín like you no more. You're a sweet type of poison, you. I bet nobody gets how dangerous you really are, huh?"

It throws me how she knew I was Guatemalan. I'm saying, "Well, Wizard must've known, or he wouldn't have put me on this."

"Or he didn't have anyone else smart enough to run with it, like your boy No Neck over there. That fool's got bricks for ears and mortar in the middle."

I want to smile, but I can't disrespect my muscle like that.

She sees this and says, "It's cool. You don't got to laugh. I know you think it's funny."

No Neck explained what a green light was to me in the car. He said it was an order from high up that Scrappy needed to go. So I'm saying, "There's nothing I can do about this green light on you."

She smiles. "You can gimme a week and not shoot my ass again."

Shit. Even *I* smile at that. That's bravada right there.

"You get those dummies to fall back for a minute." She nods at Jerry and No Neck with fish soups in front of them they aren't even eating. "And you won't have to worry about nothing. I'm gonna get that green light off myself if I have to drive to Quentin to do it. That's not for you to fix. That's for me to."

I tell her, "Okay."

She nods. "And I ain't testifying unless they compel. If you need me to mess this case up, you just say how."

"Why would you do that?"

She looks at her feet. "I fucked up on some shit. Got in the bad book, so this is me coming back right, wiping it clean. Just pass that up the chain."

"Okay. I will." But something else seems worth asking too. "Maybe you also go up on the stand and say how you don't recognize the people that shot you?"

"Man!" She smirks. "If Wizard goes down, it won't be on me, but I ain't about to get him free either. I don't need that fool on the street! What else you want?"

"I want to be able to go in your neighborhood and ask questions if I need to."

I'm thinking about Augie's friend Irma and how she roams around.

"You said the whole word! *Neigh-bor-hood.*" Scrappy laughs. "Done."

"You got the power to do that?"

"I got the power to talk to the people that got that power, so yeah, that shit's done. Next?"

I take a bite and chew. "I heard the gun got dropped at the scene. Is that for real?"

She chews a shrimp meatball on one side of her mouth as she's nodding. "Always with that old-school rule. Dump the gun. He dropped it on my foot, the fucker."

She pulls her pants leg up, slips her foot out of a house slipper, and shows me a black-ass bruise on it.

"So how did it get moved from there? You didn't scoop it and get somebody to plant it later?"

She looks at me like I'm crazy. "I was shot to fuck, Dulce. How am I about to be a criminal mastermind bleeding in my front yard? That woulda been great if I'd thought of that, but right then, man, I was just trying to breathe."

"So what happened to the gun?"

"Augie. Who else? I mean, he stole all my other shit. Stupid hype. Prolly thought he could sell it."

It makes sense. Still doesn't explain how it got across Lynwood, but it's something. "If he took it, it's not like he planted it at Wizard's. There's no why there."

But Scrappy's not listening. She takes another spoonful of soup, swallows, and stops. "It was good luck, Augie being there. Him patching me up and taking what he took kept me from a monster drug charge. Saved my fucking life too. Who knew hypes could be good for something?"

Augie's a piece to this puzzle. But I get real excited for my next question because I feel like it's all slotting together.

"You ever heard of a parole officer named Phillip Petrillo?"

She looks at her soup. "Who's he?"

"He was Wizard's PO. He found the gun."

"Never heard of him." She smiles at me. "But you're all right, Dulce. I got no beef with you. But I do need you to go now, cuz we done."

That throws me. "I got half a taco left."

"Stuff it in, then, and get rolling, cuz I ain't about to let those knuckleheads see me getting in no wheelchair."

She means Jerry and No Neck.

"I get that." I wrap my taco for later and stand.

"Knew you would. That's why I got a little something for you, Dulce." She scrunches a finger up to bring me in close. "You know the other fucker there that night? Your homeboy No Neck. I looked that fool right in his fucking eyes. That motherfucker shows up to a shooting wearing a bright yellow Lakers sweatshirt. That's how smart *he* is."

I feel the blood go out of my face.

I'm saying, "How do I connect back up with you?"

"I'll hit you up." She gives me a slow-ass wink. "Keep that shit close."

"Okay." I'm turning, already feeling like Scrappy played me a little, but I'm also feeling like she just scratched an itch in my brain that I never knew I had.

53

Little's different with me and Jerry when we leave El Paisa. He wants to go straight to Irma and talk to her cuz he wants to find Augie more than ever. He says Scrappy gave us hood freedoms and he wants to test them out. Jerry says even if that's true we should give it at least a little time cuz she can't order it on her own. So we drive and we end up in this big-ass fight cuz Little's sayin how he wants to go by Dulce now. Jerry says fuck that faggot-ass name straight out the gate. Fuck that shit. I tell Little how that type of name has got bad meanings to it. Stuff Wizard can't even fix for him. And I'm not sayin my opinion but I think that buttfuckin shit is a sin and a crime against God and I ain't about to go against the Church or the Holy Father. But Little's different too. He handles business like a G. He's so fuckin smart and never puts shit in your face. And I don't really know how to put those two together.

It's Jerry that asks if Scrappy gave him that name. He says yeah. Shit. Even Jerry's got to laugh at that. We both tell Little he can't take that name if it came from her. That there's history behind how bad it's got between their click and ours. I let Jerry tell how Scrappy's older brother killed Jerry's cousin before he got his own damn self killed cuz Big Fate's homeboy Apache don't play. We both say he can't be takin no name from an enemy. She's playin him. Tryna make him pick sumthin that'll make him a target. Little thinks on that before he says he don't see it that way. He says it's time for a change anyways. Cuz he ain't Little no more. And shit. The way he says it? He's right. I just tell him not Dulce. Pick something else. And he says people know it anyway so why not just be up front with that shit? Jerry says hold up. It ain't like that. Don't tell people shit. Your business is your business. And Little says right then that he's not here to make everybody all comfy. He's here to fix some shit for Wizard and he only knows one way to do it.

He's got to be real. He says he was real with Scrappy too. She asked for a week and he gave her a week.

That makes Jerry go off. He's sayin how that week Little gave Scrappy wasn't his to give. That he's just a little-ass hood detective. He ain't runnin shit. But Little gets loud and says he started runnin shit the second we put him at that table cuz if it went bad it wasn't no big deal if he got popped. People would just say one more dead maricón, right? Nobody cries except his family. Jerry looks at me. I don't disagree. So Little says if he's livin in this then he's gonna live it honest. And Jerry says how a lotta motherfuckers out there got things against faggots and they won't even hesitate peelin caps. Little comes back with sayin Wizard would have to give the okay. Jerry shakes his head. He says anybody above Wizard could call the shot and that's it. And then you know what Little says? This fuckin dude. *If I die because of it then I die as I am.* That's what he says! Fuck. That shit hits the whole car heavy. We ride for a minute. Nobody sayin anythin. That's some fuckin ganas right there. And if he for real went out like that? Then he'd be goin out like a G. Not givin a *fuck*. Walkin his walk.

Jerry don't want to hear it but I tell him Little's right. A man gets to decide. I tell Little that if he wants to go by Dulce then we'll call him that shit. And Little looks down at his lap and he's noddin and maybe he's got tears but I don't really look. I look ahead at the road until Little says Scrappy ain't testifying for the prosecution. He knows the gun got dropped and I nod cuz I know that gun dropped. I watched it happen. But I don't say it. Little says he knows Augie must've took it and all we need now is to know how it walked across the city. He thinks parole guy did it and then he looks at me and says he found sumthin else out too. He's lookin dead at me when he says he knows I was there that night. Fuck! My mouth gets real dry. And I start wonderin if I got to do sumthin about him knowin this and what that is if he's wantin to tell somebody and try tradin me to get Dreamer free. He says I wore my yellow-ass Lakers sweatshirt and right then Jerry points out the window at somebody lookin like Irma so I stop the car.

It's her. She's out back of Tacos Mexico goin in the trash for bottles and scrap. When we roll up she says she's lookin for sumthin to eat. So Litt . . . I mean Dulce goes in with her and gets her food. Once Irma's been eatin for a minute she says she's got some people lookin. She put the word around that she misses Augie but it's cold the way she says it. Real gangster shit. She also says that Augie gets all crazy around Christmas. His parents died then. She's sure she'll see him around soon. She says she can almost guarantee it. Dulce don't like that. He puts an eyebrow up and repeats her word back to her. Almost? And she's like yeah. Almost.

54

It's most nights that I think about Scrappy, and wonder if she lived. I think back to how I tied that tourniquet off on her leg and I wonder if it was good enough. Because sometimes people can go to the hospital and be fine, or seem like they're fine, and then one day they're just gone. I liked Scrappy. I mean, we kinda had one of those Road Runner and Coyote back-and-forth relationships. I was the Coyote. I was always trying to catch her. And the one day I did, a couple wolves blew her to bits. That was kinda my fault. I hope she's doing good. That might sound stupid, but I do. Scrappy was a lot of things, but she didn't deserve getting shot in her yard off of dealing. There's way worse you can do.

I kinda got lucky with Petrillo, and I'm surprised he didn't figure me out on it quicker. It's been a couple days too. See, the clean truck don't hand out methadone. They can't. Maybe they did once or twice but they figured it out. They'd get robbed so quick out here. So now they've basically just become a way to let people know there's options nearby, almost like an advertising service for clinics. The way it works now is, they give me a ticket, and I take that ticket to whatever clinic I choose. There's a list on the back of the slip. Some of them are private. Some of them are public, like the one at Harbor UCLA. I spend most of my days daytripping out to each address on the back of the slip. Finding out which ones are good with how they treat you, and if they're loose with the dose and give more than the usual. So far none have. But there's always that hope that there will be one.

So I've been expanding out a little. I mainly go to two private clinics near the house. They're recognizing me around there now.

On the way back yesterday, I saw a HELP WANTED sign on a Jack in the Box so I went on in there and got one of those applications. They asked if I'd been convicted of anything on the form, and I had to write yes, and for what. I said I cooked in the Navy. I cooked for a big old ship and I could get burgers going quicker than anybody. They didn't call back.

I asked at the donut shop on Slauson but the manager guy said he didn't have any work that wasn't handling money and he couldn't trust me to do that. He was sorry. I told him I was too, but I didn't blame him. I told him I'd keep getting my coffee there and keep asking. He said okay.

I don't get earthquakes from withdrawing anymore. I just get headaches all day. And all-over body aches like flu.

Every day is pain, man. That's what my sponsor says. It's all in how I manage it.

And how I manage it is going to meetings and going by the clean truck to see the pretty nurse with the braces. She's thirty or so, but she's got braces from a jaw problem, and it's cute how she's like that, vulnerable and trying to fix herself. I sign for my dose ticket and she smiles at me, and says I'm doing good, when she doesn't even really know if I am or not, but it's still good to hear it. As I'm walking out, I almost run into a guy I used to know as Todd, or Terry, but I don't say anything, because he looks in a bad way, and I know it'll be worse when he finds out he heard wrong out on the street about them actually having doses here and all he gets here is a ticket.

I hear him tell Braces his name is Tommy. He musta burned somebody pretty bad, and then he just moves along, sets up at a new place and works his way into knowing folks enough to rip them off, and then he does it again. He's coming out of the truck waving a ticket in his hand, and he's looking right at me.

"What the *hell* is this, bro?"

He's black and dried up like a skinny raisin but he talks like a surfer. I don't know if it's who he is or just a character or something, but I've never known him to act another way, even when he's high as all hell, so maybe it's real. I don't know.

"You know what it is," I say. "It ain't methadone, but it could be, if you go the right way with it."

He sits on the asphalt. Flat on his ass. Smack in the middle of the street. "I've been walking like crazy, bro. I can't anymore, bro."

"Where'd you come from? Down south of here?"

"Yeah, man."

"As far as the port, or more like Compton?"

He's itchy-looking, jonesing for anything. He says, "Yeah."

It takes me a second to get up the courage to ask about her, but I do. "Hey, you remember Irma? You met her."

"Irma?"

"Yeah, like with the glasses?"

"I don't know no Irma with glasses, bro." He's bending halfway over now. It's getting bad. It's getting to be that bone-breaking feeling. I can see it on his face.

When he comes up, he says, "I need more, man. You need more too, don't you?"

I always need more. That's how it works. He knows that.

"Nah, I'm prolly good," I say. "Besides, I wouldn't know where to get up around here, anyway."

"But where would you know how to get up for sure, bro?"

"Hey, man, Tommy or whatever it is now, don't try to play me, man. You know where to get up. You been at it long enough."

"I swear I don't, bro. I swear."

I see in his eyes how he's full of shit. Those are sad, mean eyes he's got. The kind that knows things about everything and knows how to play people too.

I tell him, "Your swears aren't worth it."

He's nodding. He's closing his eyes and nodding. He's holding his hands up. "You caught me, bro. Okay? You caught me. Okay, I did know. I did. But I ran a scam and it didn't end up working out, you know? I burnt that bridge up."

I only barely know the guy, but I know how he could. I know how I did too.

"All right," I say, and I turn to go back to the halfway house to check in.

Tommy raises his voice at me. "I was messing about Irma, bro. I know her. I saw her three days ago. I tried to hook it up with her but she said she wasn't interested in me. Said she had a broken heart. She wouldn't shut up about this guy named Augie. She said she was at the same hotel, just waiting for him. Praying for him. Hoping he remembered her."

Hearing that makes me feel lighter inside, like I can jump up right now and run, but I'm cautious. I'm thinking over the source, how he's nothing worth depending on.

I turn back around to face him. "What motel did you say that was?"

"Come on, bro. You think I'm lying? It's the Island."

No, I don't think he's lying, but it did take him telling me that to believe him.

"You got wheels? A bike?"

He shakes his head at me.

"Bus tokens?"

He shakes his head again.

"Transfers?"

You'd think his head would fall off from all the shaking.

I take him with me around the corner to a 7-Eleven where a guy going by Down Damian is standing out by the pay phone like he's going to get a call any minute. He's about to give us each five bucks cash for our two methadone tickets after I get him up from four, but then I see he's got a cigarette behind his ear.

I say, "What's up with those smokes?"

"My last one," he says.

"Bullshit, man. We need six of those too."

"Aw, man. Tryna do me like that? Two. I'll give you two."

"Four and we meet in the middle."

We shake on it, but he didn't like throwing loosies in. He puts the one behind his ear back in the pack after he takes our four new ones out, so no one else pulls that on him.

I tried being good, but now I'm back on the scheme, I know how much I missed it. I go inside and get us a couple twenty-four-hour bus transfers for a quarter each. Don't need to buy full tokens when the bus driver can't tell where you got off last. That's enough to get us to Lynwood on the 60 bus. The rest of the money I spend on different-colored lighters I can sell to fuckers asking for lights and I also start hatching a plan for how to ditch Tommy.

55

As Pedro meeting places go, 22nd St. Landing is upscale. It has a bar, but the bulk of it is restaurant space with floor-to-ceiling windows with views on a marina. It's a white tablecloth place, somewhere I take my mom for her birthday, and I get the feeling as I take the stairs that this is a test, that it could be more than just business. If Kristina likes me, or at least likes what I have to say for myself, she invites me to dinner. If she doesn't, she has an appointment or a meeting she can't change. I know the drill.

That marina view at the top of the stairs is a good one: Christmas lights strung on floating boats, some red and green bulbs (but mostly just white) stretching down piers, getting doubled by the dark ocean. I'm twenty minutes early, but Kristina Mirkovich is already here with her brother. She's wearing her hair up in a tight bun, a crisp black blazer over a high-cut green blouse (silk), light jeans with high heels.

I approach, catch John's eye first. "Are you bodyguarding?"

It's a bad miscalculation. John Mirkovich stares at me. His whole adult life he has probably had to look out for his beautiful sister. He thinks it's his duty, and to an older brother (and a sheriff, at that), duty is never funny.

"Drinking," he says as he looks over to the television.

Kristina puts her hand out to me; I shake it exactly how I did at court.

"Actually," Kristina says, "we were just talking about the Clinton grant for law enforcement. L.A.'s getting four million."

John smirks. "LAPD's getting all that money. We're not getting that money. The fucking county's getting nothing. You watch."

"Ivica," she says, directing it toward him. Her tone suggests he watch his mouth in public.

I say it how it sounds to me: "Ivitza?"

"Yeah," John says, and he turns to look at me again. "My name."

"It's not John?"

"John's easier for people to say. I never have to explain it. You know, like right now?"

"Got it." I point to his quarter-full beer. "You want another?"

"No," he says, then downs it in one. "Tatiana's doing dinner."

Kristina hugs her brother, who is half a foot taller than her even in her high heels. She says, "Oh hey, what did Morgan get on her California Missions project?"

"She got an A, which is basically the same thing as you getting one, overachiever."

Their dynamic is clear: she's the star of the family, and he's the glue.

John coughs. "You got this, Kris?"

He means the tab. She nods, and he turns to shake my hand. As I take it, he immediately applies too much pressure, looks down on me as he does it. It's a guy thing. It's effective, too.

"Have a good night," I say.

"Sure," he says.

On his way out, he goes by the far end of the bar where an old guy is sitting quietly and claps him on the shoulder. "Keep it together, Chuck. You're out of control!"

The man turns, and it's Charles Bukowski, white wine still in hand, not a drop of it spilled after being jostled. He puts a hand up in a half wave and turns back to the bar. I tried to read *Ham on Rye* once. I didn't get far.

With John gone, Kristina gets closer to me and drops her voice. "What kind of Croatian names his kid Morgan?"

"What kind of dago Italian names their kid Phillip?"

She laughs. "The ones who want their kids to be American?"

I smile at that because she's smiling. I say, "Doesn't everyone?"

"Well said. And you know, you just reminded me that my grandmother used to call the A-1 Market the Dago Store. She'd walk a mile there and back with all her groceries. Where was she going? The Dago Store. Where had she come from? The Dago Store. Where was she going soon?"

I say, "The Dago Store?"

"No," she says with a dead-on Croatian accent, "*Church.*"

I laugh when she laughs. She's had a few already. She's so loose she confesses she looked me up in her senior yearbook, and we move into standard getting-to-know-you stuff. It's like being on the stand with her. She needs everything (whats, wheres, whens). I grew up on Sixth Street, off Pacific. I played baseball: Little League at Knoll Hill, high school ball at SPHS. I went to Cal State Long Beach (blew out my knee during sophomore-year tryouts), graduated with a degree in criminology and criminal justice.

She wants more. I tell her I moved to Colorado after that, because they were hiring in parole and California wasn't. Three years later, I came back. I had enough experience to apply for a county position and I missed the weather. I don't mention my dad dying, or looking after my mom, because this now feels like a date, and it's way too early to earn intimacy points with that. I shift the focus to her. She's an intelligent woman, and most intelligent women never get a chance to talk about themselves enough. They live for it, the day someone actually listens.

I order a rum-and-doctor (rum mixed with Dr Pepper). She makes fun of it, tries it, and then orders one of her own.

Her family had a house off Thirteenth Street. They moved to South Shores when she was little. She went to South Shores Elementary, did ballet until seventeen, when it became apparent her ankles just couldn't take the punishment anymore. We cheers to our shared leg problems. She always loved to read (Dickens, especially). In fact, it's that man's fault she's a lawyer. *Bleak House*, have I ever read it? I tell her I will to get her back on track: undergrad at USC (British literature), Loyola Law School, straight into clerking for the DA, never looking back.

"So," Kristina says, "what do you want from your career? What's the next step?"

"This seems like it might be a conversation for another time," I say.

"That's an excellent idea. You hungry? We could have 'another time' right now."

The tables have been filling up for the past half hour, and food has been coming out: swordfish, steaks, mashed potatoes, garlic green beans. She sees me hesitate.

"It's just dinner," she says. "We'll obviously be talking strategy for the case. We'll go on and on about how to keep Augustine Clark safe. Besides, the county's paying."

I am hungry, and the lights are twinkling, so I figure why not. There are far worse things than dinner with a beautiful woman who could help my career.

When we get to the hostess stand, I'm surprised to find Kristina Mirkovich already has a table for two reserved at one of the windows.

Of course, it's not until we've been seated, and ordered, that she leans in and says soberly, "I need to know all about the Renee Sifuentes complaint on your record."

My face goes hot. Anger overtakes me.

She thinks she's so smart, setting me up with drinks so I could fall into her trap. She needs a lesson that you can't ambush people like this when you're on the same team. I'd love to teach it to her, too.

I should control my words. I can't. "What the *fuck*, Kristina? I've been *helping* you."

Kristina smirks and pulls a notepad from her bag. "I'm not mad. Complaints happen all the time, but I need to hear it from you. Now."

I look to the exit. I want to smash her nose in, get up, and leave her here spinning her wheels while bleeding, but she's too powerful to be treated like that. She knows it, too. Kristina Mirkovich is a killer. She's been building to this, vetting me the entire time, and she's just getting started.

56

School's on break for Christmas, but I'm trying to remember the order for starting IVs that the teacher suggests. It's like, TPFTA-something.

I look at my notes. Ah! TPFTA CF. I flip them back over so I can't see them. I remind myself it should rhyme, kind of.

Tourniquet. That's easy. Tie that sucker off.

Pick a site. Be quick. Less than ten seconds, if I can.

Feel for the right vein. The good ones aren't always visible, so use my first two fingertips.

The second *T* is for *Traction*. I need to make sure the skin is supertight so the needle won't slide around. Taut. Now, that word I remember, because when she used it in class I wrote down *taught* first and had to raise my hand and look like an idiot, but it's all good cuz now I actually remember it.

A is for *Angle*. Pick a tight one. Don't go down on the skin. This ain't a record player. Go parallel *along* the skin before going in.

CF. CF, CF, CF. What's *CF* again?

I flip my notes back over.

Shit. *Catheter Forward*. The catheter goes forward, the needle does not go back. I still don't totally get this one. My teacher said I might not understand until I'm doing it with my own two hands, but the important thing is to remember the order. TPFTA-CF. TPFTA-CF.

I got to get this certification so I can get an elder care job and move out and never worry about gangsters like Scrappy rolling up on me in parking lots ever again.

I look at the phone. Jellybean hasn't called in days and I'm wondering what's up with him, if he's okay, when a knock hits my front door.

I go to the window and see it's Johnny from down the block, Adalberto's kid. The one always playing soccer in his yard. And through the glass he's saying, "Hey, Miss Angela, I got that school thing for you."

But, see, the problem is, I didn't ask for shit.

And Johnny's holding up this blue accordion folder thing to the window, moving it back and forth like it's some kind of ship sailing stormy seas.

Behind him on the curb is a car with its lights on that I don't recognize.

My breathing gets tight inside me and I don't want to open the door, even to take what he wants me to take.

My first thought is Scrappy's pulling some shit, but I can't figure why, cuz I definitely told Jerry about her wanting to see them, and my second thought is, it could be somebody hiding, wanting me to open that door for Johnny so they could come through and get at me.

Through the window, I'm saying, "That's not for me."

"It is." Johnny's nodding.

Right then, the phone rings and rattles in its little house. I jump. I leave the window. I go to it.

It's Jerry on the other end. "Open the fuckin door, Angela."

He hangs up, so I hang up and go back over. I don't want to open the door, but I do.

Outside, Johnny laughs and says, "From Jose," then hands me the blue folder and runs back to the car.

I shut the door and lock it. I have to put my hand up against it to steady myself.

I don't go in for this kind of shit at night. It's too much.

I go back to the couch, and I don't want to open the folder, but I do. There's green papers stuffed in each accordion part. And I really can't breathe then.

Cuz it's money. A lot of money.

I count it through on the table, on top of my notes.

It's six thousand dollars in tens and twenties.

Six thousand.

I count it again, and it still is.

PART VII

WAYSIDE

Let me close by paraphrasing William Blake: "Prisons are the concrete of justice." Prisons are very much about the real world. There's a tendency, particularly among people of great sensitivity, to think about justice in airy and abstract terms: the idea, for example, that in spite of crime, all people are basically good. But it is unwise to think in the abstract when it comes to crime. Most people are good. But some, let's face it, are not.

—PRESIDENT GEORGE H. W. BUSH,
DEDICATING THE NORTH COUNTY CORRECTIONAL FACILITY (NCCF)
AT WAYSIDE HONOR RANCHO ON MARCH 10, 1990

57

I come out of the hole wearing blues. And they don't even rehouse me. They send me right back to 4700 like everything's the same. It's not tho. I learn what happened pretty quick.

Peeper's gone. A deputy saw him stab Pretty Boy. He's getting new charges for assault with a deadly. Attempted murder. All that.

Pretty Boy lived just fine. He went to medical with one bad cut and a couple pokes. He was out in two days, then straight into the PC dorm.

Barrel Roll lived after he did his real live barrel roll off the tier railing. He broke his right ankle. He's in medical. Eating better food. Getting pain drugs. Talking to nurses. Living the life. Getting dumped off that tier was prolly the best thing to happen to him since he's been in here.

Tim Muhammad got sent to another facility. Everybody says how this story is gonna follow him tho. Walk thru walls. Stick to him.

I also find out Wizard ain't here anymore. He got sent up to the gang unit housing for being a ringleader. That was good for him. It was a come-up for his rep. And what I did has been good for me too. I know I'm on my own now tho. And the weird thing is, I'm relieved about it.

I mean, I'm starting to think clearer. And see things. Put them together. It reminds me of something I heard one time. How the announcer during a Raiders game said the thing with rookies is that the pro game is too fast for them.

The game will slow down for them over time, I'll never forget the announcer saying that. Cuz I thought it was so stupid. The game can't slow down. It's always at the same speed! I think I even said that to the TV. I'm only just now figuring out he meant in their brains. It will feel like the game is slower, even tho it's going the same speed. You'll see more. Anticipate, like how Wizard said it. See it coming ahead of time.

And my luck's been running too. I didn't get any new charges off what I did. I don't think I ever been so happy in my life as when they told me! That was like ten birthdays at once. I cried, I was so happy. It was just me in the hole so nobody saw or nothing. I just let go and cried. Tried to let all the bad stuff out. Everything except the rage. Cuz I still need that.

This one sergeant interviewed me plenty before they decided. He wanted to know who organized it. And I'd never give up Wizard, even tho they knew it was him anyway.

I just said how one day Tim Muhammad cut me in line for weights. Said he needed it more cuz when he got out, he was gonna be playing football again. And this fool shot his girl's head all the way off, so if he thinks he's getting out, he's crazy. So I sit back and wait. I pass it up the chain on politics. The problem was tho, Big Dev got moved. And the mayates had nobody to handle it. That's why they were kinging it up on the tier. And that's when I saw my moment to go toe-to-toe. Settle the thing about the weights like men.

It helped that there was another brawl while I was away, bigger this time. Bloods and Crips trying to come back on Raza. After he reached his determination, the sergeant told me what my discipline was. He made me sign a paper saying I understood it. It's like even tho there's never any choice to it, you still got to give them permission to send you away . . .

On my walk down, I notice how brown fools look at me different. Like they got respect. Like I'm known now.

And I'll take that shit. If it keeps me safe, if it has fools that might want to hurt me thinking twice, I'll take it.

I get nods from almost all my cellies as I walk in. There's still six. Four are different. One's spazzing the fuck out on a bottom bunk, all twitching, talking to himself. It's the one where this Wood, Moore, used to be. I'm sad he's gone.

We never had a problem, me and him. He told stories about Tennessee, about all the trees they got out there. And how he used to steal cars easy, how sometimes he accidentally drank too much and put the two things together. The trees and the cars. That's how he got caught, he said. I liked those stories. It seemed like a totally different country to where I'm from tho.

I point at the spaz.

"Sup with this fool?" I say to the one dude I still recognize in there, Carlos.

"I don't know. I'm not a doctor," he says.

A lot of people think Carlos stabbed the dude that was fucking his old lady. He didn't. He's a college-ass Mexican in on some check fraud. Went to Cal State Long Beach for a year and everything. Now that he's in here with real motherfuckers tho, all he does is skip yard to fuck his fifi. None of that matters to me. What matters is he kept my stuff from getting vultured. And when I came back from handling what I handled, I had even more. Ten new soups from property bag. And stamps to send letters. Twenty of them. And pruno too, a brownish yellow one.

Still, it's a comedown being in my cell again. Nobody needs to watch your back in the hole.

I slept like a baby in there when there wasn't screaming in the hall. I wrote lots of letters too, even some to Angela I'll never send.

Telling her all how I wished I'd never lived with her. Wished I never knew what it was like to sleep next to her cuz I miss it so bad. How she used to put her hand on my shoulder right as she fell asleep. I miss how warm her palm was. And when I got to missing her the most, I'd just go to sleep.

I slept a lot in the hole. I learned it takes a lot of energy being worried as fuck about being in here. And sad and mad and confused about Wizard. Also grateful tho. That he's mostly looking out for me. And then there's paying attention to stuff all the time, always being on high alert for shit to pop off. Being in the hole was my first time to rest up, to actually relax a little since I been in. Weird as that is to say.

I'd get up sometimes. I'd try to read a book a trustee brought me. It was boring and hard to fight thru tho. *Villette.* I couldn't get into it.

I'd eat my meals solo. I'd think about Angela again. And my eyes would get heavy. I never minded being alone.

And I'd get my one hour of yard time in the cage. And I'd just be on the phone to whoever at the Matta house. To Jimena. To Little. And when no one was around, I'd do dips till I couldn't, mostly so everybody could see me doing them.

My phone cards kept me happy. When I called Little to tell him thanks for putting money on my books, he said he didn't do it, that Angela did. That tripped me out. Still does. I had good talks with Little. Never about anything with the case. Just about how he's doing. How he's feeling better about himself. How he's working out now for the first time in his life. Doing push-ups. I tell him about my prison workout. He says he'll try it. I miss that dude like a brother I always wished I had. I miss his mom's cooking most of all.

One time, a deputy walking me back up from the yard cage said to me, "You sure kayoed that nigger."

He meant Tim Muhammad. And left it at that. A lot of the deputies hate the blacks. How they run things. A lot of the deputies are Woods.

This jail shit is a hundred times crazier than the streets. It's like all the rough blocks in every bad hood got all the bad dudes shook out of them and they landed in here. All squashed together in tiny spaces. That shit is never gonna go good. It's how I've been learning about people. Seeing them. How they really are when you bust the human part of them down to nothing and they're just about doing whatever to survive . . .

I turn my back in my cell, making sure Carlos is between me and observation before I sip that pruno. I toast it to Angela first tho. For my phone cards. For making it so I could talk to Little on my hour out from the hole. It saved me. *She* saved me. And I don't know how I feel about that.

The pruno tastes vinegary to me. Like the bread hasn't had enough time to kick thru the banana yet. It gets warm in my chest tho. And that's nice. It's not the worst thing I ever felt.

I'm toasting to Little then too. For all he's doing trying to figure shit out. It's giving me hope, how hard he tries.

Maybe it shouldn't. Cuz I know I'm as stuck in this life as any fool ever was. And the only thing I can really count on is how it's always throwing me for loops. That's why I'm not even surprised when they call my name for transport.

I mean, I'm not even back but fifteen minutes when they do it.

So I say, "Where to, boss?"

"It's Wayside Wednesday," the deputy says.

And that's it. I got to roll up.

All I can think about then is, *I hope my stories come with me where I'm going. I hope I walk in there with everybody knowing I knocked Tim Muhammad the fuck out . . .*

58

I came straight out of the hole into new housing. They're not fucking around now. They threw me straight into the gangster unit. That Thunder Dorm shit. Good news is I got only three other cellies and they're cool. All of us are Southsiders. When I saw it at first, I thought maybe the deputies were setting me up for something, so I made real sure not to talk about shit with any of them, in case they were getting ready to snitch, but after a few days I could tell all three were stand-up motherfuckers.

More good news is, I'm staying in my blues. I gave some big thanks to La Virgencita for keeping me out of that red jumpsuit. I couldn't handle not being able to walk on my own, being cuffed up outside my cell, needing two deputies and a sergeant to march my ass all over. Right now, I'm up on yard with my unit, and it feels really empty, because there's so much less of us than was on with 4700's gen pop. I guess we're easier to keep an eye on this way. They got more walking deputies too, rolling around, listening, keeping eyes up.

I go over to one of the pay phones and use a card to get on with Jerry. He knew I was calling, so he's picking up right after the first ring.

I don't say his name. I just start in. "Sup with your dad, dude? He still with that dumbass fresa of yours?"

"Yeah, foo, but she stabbed his ass."

I blow up laughing right there, and a few people turn to look, so I just nod up at them to mind their business. "What went down?"

"His story's all confused. He says he was out at El Farallon, busting out a quebradita, and some lady he knew from years ago came over and hugged him and then his bitch straight-up took a nail file to his belly. Stuck him right there on the dance floor. No hesitation. But then he also told me he was trying to get at this lady from years ago at the bar and his girl just shows up out of nowhere and puts that file in him. He's a drunk, foo. I don't think he even knows what happened, really."

I whistle low. "I only met her that one time, but it looked like she had that in her."

"Yup." Jerry switches it up on me. "You still writing raps?"

It's like that motherfucker lined me up and punched me in a bruised spot. I got some lines scribbled, unfinished stuff here and there, but all my other shit disappeared when I went in the hole. It got confiscated. *Fuck*. I can still feel that loss in my stomach right now. Nothing else made me more sad than losing all those lines.

I tell him, "You're hitting a nerve, man. I'm not really writing. It's eating me up."

When I was solitaried, I almost wrote one about what Muhammad did to Barrel Roll and what popped off after, but even I'm not dumb enough to be writing something that could be evidence for a deputy going through my shit, and that sucks, because I'm used to writing about what I'm seeing, what's real.

Jerry keeps digging. "Why not? Too much politics getting in the way?"

The answer is yes. Mad politics. They're in my brain every day. Something shifted off that little dustup we had the other day. I can feel it, but I'm not about to tell Jerry that. "Is it eight forty-five yet?"

"Nah." Jerry's chewing something. Cereal, maybe. "Couple minutes."

"Sup with Little? How's he doing out there?"

I mean, how close are we getting to knowing which motherfucker put that gun in my house after I dropped it on Scrappy? Jerry understands what I mean, even if he can't exactly answer it on a monitored phone line.

"Oh, that foo." Jerry makes a *psssh* sound. "He's going by Dulce now."

"What?"

"I don't know, homeboy. He's getting bold and shit."

"That name's trouble, man. Tell him I said to drop it."

"I hear you. I do. Me and No Neck told him pretty strong how he needs to be done with it, but he's *about* it. I don't think he can let go of it. I'm serious. But he's smart, man. That fucker is *smart*. Brave as shit too."

Brave? Jerry doesn't usually say stuff like that. There's a story behind it, but it's not one I can ask about, so I don't.

Jerry tells me it's time, and, "Cool," is all I say back.

It's starting to mess with me why Little thinks he can call himself Dulce and not get his ass killed off of it. He needs to be a fucking submarine out there, doing his thing with torpedoes, not being a loud-ass cruise ship with lights and a party drawing attention.

Jerry starts the three-way calling. He blows air into the mouthpiece to trick the phone system, and then he can be on with me in County, downtown Los Angeles, and connect us up to Quentin, an up-north state prison, through Jerry's fucking house phone. It's beautiful. It's a triangle the jails haven't figured out how to touch yet.

When the extra line clicks in, we don't say our names. I go first. "Hey, man, been a long time."

It hasn't. I never met this fool. He's just a dude Big Fate gets up with and gets directions from. A big, big homie. A general, more like.

"Too long." He's got a real rough voice. "That thing isn't ready yet."

But what that means is, it's ready. It's happening.

I ask what I'm supposed to ask. "So maybe call you when?"

There won't be another call. I've already had a wila come through saying how I should ask when to call back, and then what I get told will just be the answer.

"Maybe we could try in two weeks or something?"

So, it's not a question, and there's no "or something." It's an order. Two weeks from today. Shit jumps off.

I tell him, "That'll work," and then he hangs up.

Jerry coughs. "You take care, foo."

"I'll be calling, man." I put the phone down, and that's that.

59

There's a kiss on my cheek, and then one on my neck before my eyes really open, and then Irma says to me, she says, "I'll be back, baby. Need to get you some donuts."

And it's good being called that for maybe one second, but then I'm thinking how she's never called me that in her life, so I start blinking myself awake. It's harder than I thought.

The mud is still kinda thick in me. I didn't fix up for so, so long. I mean, I only did some weak shit twice in jail and then it was only methadone at the halfway house, so when the real stuff comes in like it did last night it's like falling in the fucking river and here's where I washed up, in my old bed, in my old room that she kept up with my same stash spots.

It's bad but the kind of bad where you knew it was good, at least for a while, and now it's gone into the old hangover phase where I know I need to get the loop going again.

She's never called me baby. She's not a pet names person. This's a little saw blade on my brain now.

But then I'm wondering if she's falling in love with me again since I came back to her.

I don't know. Maybe not. But maybe.

What I do know is, it's morning. There's that sunlight coming in through the broken-tooth blind next to the door.

My earthquakes aren't here for me yet, but they're coming. It's like I know where the seeds of it are planted in my bones. The earthquake seeds. They're in my hips, in my ribs, all down my spine. I got to get something else in me or I'm done for.

I think I want to start with the small stuff, so I go in my jeans to see if I got any loosies left, and I don't. I look on the table by the bed. Nothing there but a red lighter.

It's my last one. The others went quick. You smoke a cigarette walking up and down Long Beach, people will ask. You avoid some people, cuz you know they just want to bum a smoke. One fool just took one after I showed him. Grabbed it right out of my hand and ran. I remember yelling after him if he needed one that bad he could keep it. He stopped running after that, but he looked over his shoulder at me a few times to make sure it wasn't a trick and I wasn't chasing or anything.

Right now my legs aren't moving like I tell them to. I say, *Left and out of bed and hold me up so I can get to this baseboard and see what they're holding*, but my legs just lie there.

Irma has never called me baby. Something else's sneaking up on me now too. I was the one that always got donuts. She never did once.

The door gets knocked on then. Loud. Three times.

My first thought about it is it's Tommy cuz it's not like he didn't know where Irma was. Tommy was easy enough to ditch. I ducked into the swap meet, took two lefts, and went out the back. If anything, I'm surprised he didn't come knocking sooner, the surfer-talking piece of shit.

"Just a minute," I say at the door, and then I think that's stupid.

If it's Tommy, it's better if he thinks no one's here.

I'm up now. Up enough. One hand on the wall. Two feet on the floor.

I hear voices murmuring outside.

Not just one. A few.

And there's the sound of a key sliding into the lock.

I look to the door for the bar lock across the side of it, but it's not on. No way it could be on, Irma just walked out of it and you can't close that from the outside.

And the dead bolt slides off, and the knob's undone too and the door's opening.

And it ain't Irma behind it.

60

I don't thank the manager for unlocking the door. If that's what he would've done for Wizard, then that's what he's supposed to do for me. Simple. No Neck goes in first. I go in behind him. Jerry has my back. He shuts the door and he locks it. This motel room's just sad inside. The furniture's jacked. The closet doesn't have a door. And Augustine Clark is standing up naked right next to the bed. He's stringy, used up, with a peacock down one arm, and what look like bites all over his right foot.

I'd look him in his eyes if he were looking up. "Hi, Augie."

He jerks back like I hit him, but he just keeps standing there.

He's got the look of a guy that has been getting hit his whole life. I know that feeling. Up until real recently, I was that guy too. And that's how I know I need to be gentle with how I play this, because this is the type that can snap. The deal is I do the talking. No Neck and Jerry have been down with that since the start.

Y ahora, I step across the room to a chair and take the pair of jeans off it that Augie's staring at and hand them to him. He takes them from me, and drops back down to the bed. I watch this sad used-up dude struggle to get them on while he's lying flat. No Neck and Jerry don't even look. They stare at the walls until Augie gets his legs right and tries to sit up, almost makes it, gives up, and then lies halfway over the pillows in the middle of the bed.

"Sit up or he'll sit you up." I nod my head toward No Neck.

Augie does it. He gets his back against the wall before saying, "I know who you are. I know what you want, anyways."

"And what's that?"

He looks tired. "How the gun got to where the gun got to."

"Why would we be wondering that?"

"Is Irma okay?" He says it quick and loud, like it's just now hitting him that we might have kidnapped her.

I tell him she can be, but it's up to him.

He stares at the ceiling. "I-I was there, man. When Scrappy took fire."

"We know you were," I'm saying. "What happened after you picked up that gun and all the dope Scrappy had on her?"

"Came here."

"This motel."

"This motel, this room," he's saying.

"And what did you do?"

"I-I shot up, man. Got right."

I wait for more, but none comes. "So, when did Petrillo come?"

He shudders when I say the name. He knows there's no getting out of anything now.

"He comes in and does his search, and he's not even my normal agent, man, and he just finds the stash so goddamn quick. And that's where the gun was, right in with it."

"The gun that shot Scrappy."

"Yeah."

"Why did you take it?"

"Figured I'd sell it."

"Okay." I nod. "And when Petrillo found it, what'd he do?"

"He pressed, man! Saying I was on gun charges and drugs distribution. He fucked my head up."

"So you talked about what you saw."

"I-I had to, man."

"And you said?"

"Two guys shot Scrappy. One of them was Wizard. The other one I didn't see. And then he says, if it was Wizard, it was Dreamer too. And I said I didn't know a Dreamer."

I look to No Neck. He's just staring straight ahead.

Augie keeps going. "And Petrillo says he'll take everything I snatched and make it go away except for violating me on using and sending me back. All he needs from me is to tell this cop Montero that I saw the shooting and it was Wizard and Dreamer. That's it. He said he'd take care of the gun."

There it is. We finally got to the bottom. I look to Jerry, and Jerry looks to No Neck, and we all look at each other. We know that's the last puzzle piece. And there's this *aha* feeling between us, and I'm glad we finally know it, but I'm raging at the same time, because crooked-ass Petrillo framed Jacob, for nothing but trying to fuck, and now we know it for sure. I feel so sick at it that I almost walk myself the hell out of the room, but I stay. I have to. Because this is the type of thing that needs finishing.

Augie takes the silence as something he can bargain with. "I-I can run. I can just be gone."

Jerry looks to me, and I love him for that. Giving me that look like the boss decision is on me.

"That's not working for us, Augie," I'm saying. "There's that statement you signed. What we need is you testifying that you were wrong. You were full up on that dope the night before and you don't really remember anything anymore."

"I do that and Irma's good?"

It'd be cruel to tell him how Irma sold him out, and I don't got that in me. It's better if he thinks her safety sits on what he does from here on anyway. I tell him yes.

"And what happens to me if they get me for contempt or something?"

Jerry's saying, "It can't be contempt if you don't remember nothing."

"I'll prolly have to go straight back in for messing up my terms. And I won't get drug court." Augie frowns and nods. "And I can trust you how? I don't even know your name. I-I don't want all your names, but I do need yours."

He's looking at me, but he can tell from my face he won't get it.

No Neck opens the door. It creaks on its hinges as it swings and lets sunlight in. And the things on the floor that get lit up are enough to make my feet itch inside my shoes. A wadded-up bit of bloody and black gauze. A whole toenail. Something that looks like wet string.

I'm saying, "You ready to go or what?"

He's scared now. "Ready to go where?"

"Ready to go where you're staying. We'll drive you to Huntington Park."

Irma told us how she found out from him last night where he's been, and I watch the last light of hope die in his eyes after I say it. The one thing he was holding on to was that he could get out of here and go back to wherever he was hiding and that would be that. But that's not how this shit works.

"We got you now. You're ours. And it goes like this." I look to Jerry.

Jerry steps up. "You got a day job working something temporary cuz a dude called in sick. They paid you thirty-five for doing boxes on a loading dock for five hours, but then another truck came in late and they needed to turn that shit around, so they had you on till five in the morning. They gave you double for it, seventy on top of what they already gave you. After, they let you sleep in their back room cuz you really helped them out, and you were so tired. He wants you to come back for more part-time jobs too, maybe even full-time. That's real if you want it. He'll put you on. We got the reference name and phone number for your house and parole to confirm. He'll confirm good too. We need you eating breakfast on the way back up so you can take the receipt in too. Get some food in you. Get right. Practice this story. You'll pay the bill with the cash you got from working so you'll have the exact change if they ask to see it. And we got clean piss for your next test too cuz they'll definitely be asking you for it today to make sure you ain't lying about any of this. Which you aren't."

We take the risk they don't send him back for breaking curfew, but there's no way that happens. That prosecutor needs him.

Jerry puts $105 in mixed bills and a clear travel shampoo bottle that's wrapped up inside another clear baggie on the sad little table next to the bed. The liquid's shaking in the light while it settles, throwing gold shapes on the bed. Next to that, I put some methadone down, in a covered cup.

Y ahora, Augie stares at it like he can't even fit all this in his head yet.

"We won't let you fail, Augie." I nod at him. "But if you do this, and you end up going back inside, you won't need protecting from us ever again. You'll be good. Because *we'll* be protecting *you*."

61

I'm processed out with a green property bag in one hand, a store bag in the other. They take us back the way I first came in. Thru a hundred corridors. Lineups. Waiting.

On the bus, I'm chained with another Southsider. We sit in the back separated. Raza in the back. Woods in the middle. Mayates up front. I guess cuz they don't want issues.

I get looks from fools. They know me. Or they heard what I did. And that's good.

I ask the dude I'm locked to his name. And where he's from.

"Lil Devil," he says. He looks my age, maybe younger.

When the bus pulls onto the street, he says he's Florencia.

We don't really talk after that. Not when there's a world to see.

Lil Devil's by the window. He don't mind if I lean to look out tho.

I never get sick of seeing the cars catching sunlight. A red Cherokee. A black Fiero. Shit, I even see a Volvo I don't hate. If it's got four wheels, that's freedom to me. Going where you want. Not getting driven. Whenever I get out, I'm getting a car. Not riding the bus no more. Not borrowing. Getting one. I have to.

We slide out past the front of the Union Station. I watch ladies cross the street with their hair all high. And skirts moving. And heels. I catch a breath cuz it's been a bit since I seen that.

Lil Devil looks to me with his forehead all scrunched up. He's nodding. He feels it too.

And it's not like you forget this world exists, it's just that it feels less real the more time you spend with no windows . . .

And being inside, I got good at not wanting things. Pushing it down. Seeing the outside tho? The sun? The people? It pulls that cork inside me. And I want everything again.

I can't help it. It's here. So close.

And it's going too fast. We're on the 101 quick. And I'm trying to look down into every car, see every driver. See people out here living. I just go on to the next like I'm only allowed into a movie for a few seconds. I go from an old lady in a VW Beetle singing, to a dude smoking in his Chevy truck, to a couple of teenage girls in a beater Honda. The one sitting shotgun is leaning over, helping the driver get something out of her eye. And just as the passenger's got her finger all close . . .

They pass us. And I don't get to see how it ends.

We take the 5. The land starts rolling up the farther away from L.A. you get. Brown hills. Dots of green around them like they're wrapped in bandannas.

And the big surprise is how there's this roller-coaster park popping up on the left side. Everybody on the bus shifts then. All the eyes. All the weight. Everybody's wishing they could be there. There's a red tower, tall as hell, standing in front. At the bottom is a white roller coaster that curves down on one side. And next to it? There's a blue ride looking like what a heart monitor does. Ups and downs. And that makes me think of Tiny Gangster. And I feel bad for not having thought about him for a long time. Life's just been crazy. I say sorry to him in my head. And rest in peace.

Next to me, Lil Devil's nodding.

"That white fucker's Colossus," he says. "I rode him once. Me and my cousin did."

I ask what it is. And right as he tells me the place is Six Flags Magic Mountain, we're past it. A bunch of fools try turning, looking back, to keep seeing it for as long as they can. I don't turn tho. It's gone. It ain't for us anymore.

We get off the freeway not much later. We go over a bridge too. And the road curves around till we're at a guard shack, then passing a shooting range.

I say, "What is all this?"

"It's a ranch, fool. It's acres. Wayside Honor Rancho's three different jails. They control everything since that guardhouse."

And that's hills. Fields. Roads.

Shit. It's the most land I ever seen! *The system is the fucking system*, I think then.

We turn on a road called Dairy. And pass a power plant. That trips me out. This place has its own power plant? Damn. It's like a little city.

We keep going up by this dirt hill that's got the letters NCCF written on it with a bunch of white rocks. We curve around the side of it, then go up to a big-ass tan building with no windows.

They run us off the bus so they can get us sorted out. The IPA, they call it. There's metal tables inside. And a counter. They don't keep us race-to-race then. We all just go into holding. I'm getting to know how this goes now. Seeing how these things are set up. They got holding areas at every jail. Same with processing. It's this whole big system of moving people. Storing them. Feeding them. I mean, cells are really just big lockboxes you put people in.

When I'm up, they run my number. They TB-test me. Make me do X-rays and everything.

In my housing interview the deputy says how he sees I was mixed up in something at MCJ. I tell him I was protecting myself. And that's true. It just wasn't from mayates. Cuz if I didn't step up and do what I was told, my ass would have gotten beat by a bunch of Raza. Discipline, they call it. Not even Wizard could've saved me if I punked out. Maybe he wouldn't even have tried.

The deputy asks me if I'm gonna be a problem here if they dorm me.

And I never been in a dorm before, so I just say, "No, sir."

The *sir* is important. Wizard told me once how deputies love that respect. I told him everybody loves respect. He said that was true too.

I get new blues, bedding. Just a mat, a sheet, and a blanket.

I get a fish kit too. Toothbrush. Toothpaste. Deodorant. Soap. Shampoo. Razor. Shaving cream. All in a baggie.

I line up with the other 600s. And we walk together. We get told hands in pockets when we're walking. Not when we're carrying our stuff tho. Later. If we forget, it's spray-painted on the walls in English and in Spanish: MANOS EN TUS BOLSILLOS.

Six-seventeen is where I'm at. One of four dorm rooms sitting in a half circle behind a guard desk . . . 615, 616, 617, and 618.

They pop doors for the lower ones first, then do 617 to walk me in. Thru some luck, Lil Devil's in with me.

This place is different to the other jails I been in. It's not built in a straight line like at Firestone or downtown. It's just a big room with a high ceiling.

There's pay phones either side when you walk in. And it's two levels, with stairs along a wall that go up over a toilet area. That's got one stall for privacy. One for pissing. And a sink to wash your hands. Then there's triple-decker beds pushed up against the back wall with numbers above them, 1–11. After that is a shower area.

And I'm right by that. Bunk 11A on the bottom floor at the end. Above me, on the second floor, there's rows 12–22.

I get what a dorm is then. One room. Lots of fucking beds.

Twenty-two times three is sixty-six. That means there's sixty-six fools in this room.

With this setup, you could prolly do whatever at night here. I can see that already. And that's a problem.

Cuz it's not me and five other dudes in a cell anymore.

It's me and *sixty-five*.

Shit. I'm not liking that at all . . .

It is what it fucking is tho. Can't change it.

I'm at my new bunk maybe one minute before Nada comes up. He's as high as my chest. Shaved head. Tattoo on his neck that's the big homie number. He runs things for the brown folks here. He tells me so. He also says, "They call me Nada cuz I don't care about nothing."

I tell him I'm Dreamer. And he sizes me up. I can tell he's got questions.

He says, "What are you, like, Honduran or some shit?"

I could say Samoan. Tho I'm getting the feeling that's not the best answer for this dude. He's Raza till death.

"I'm Lynwood," I say.

"Oh, for real? I know some hitters down that way. Down-ass motherfuckers, man. You a down-ass motherfucker too?"

I keep looking him in his eyes. That's my answer to that. If he hasn't heard about me yet, he will.

He's still wondering about me tho. Like how I look fucks with my loyalty.

So I try thinking of an answer that'll sound okay to him. And I think of Little. And Mrs. Matta. And I figure I'll say I'm Samoan and Guatemalan if Nada presses.

I get lucky tho. He gets distracted.

"Hey," Nada says, pointing at the scars on my arm. "What did that to you?"

"A dog," I say.

"For real? What kind of dog?"

"A giant one."

He laughs. "I meant, like, what breed?"

He goes on about dogs for a long-ass time. This kind and that kind. Boxer dogs. Chows. Pits. I get it. He's fucking crazy about dogs.

When he's done I finally say, "I don't know. Can't tell that at night when it's trying to eat me."

He nods then, like he still don't know about me. I'm cool tho . . . for now.

He gives me race car instructions. Where we eat in mess when we go. It's two cold meals and one hot at night. Where to do yard when we're outside. How to do dayroom when we're inside. He tells me when first-thing workouts are. Right here in the dorm. Early as fuck. And it means I got to do them. No assing out. No questions.

"Cool," I say.

"Oh, I got you," he says, and he's looking at me like he finally understands me now. "You're one of them soldados. You think you're one of them?"

I don't need to say yes. He can see that just from looking at me.

He can see the fucking monster I got inside, peeking out from behind my eyes.

62

Little flutters hit my lungs when we walk up to the gate and wait in line, and I hold my ticket hard in my hand cuz it's not feeling real to me, and then I have to feed it into a little machine, it goes out the other end, and I walk through this rotating thing, like what they have at Dodger Stadium, and then I'm staring at this sign that says DISNEYLAND, and POPULATION: 300,000,000, and ELEVATION: 138 FEET on either side of it.

"I'm learning there are things I should prolly never tell you," I say to Phil when he's through too.

"Why not?"

"Because then stuff like this happens, and you get a girl's hopes up."

He smiles. And I'm not about to tell him I'm feeling weird cuz I'm not used to people doing nice things for me. I'm always the one that has to do them for other people.

So, *this*? Being at the most magical place on earth for the first time ever is just crazy.

I should've known something was up when he wanted me to meet him in Long Beach again, but by the airport. When I got there, he had me park my car and get into his, which I almost didn't do cuz I don't know him all the way. And I get stubborn to the point that he even has to give me a hint before I'll even sit in there with him. And he asks me where all the Super Bowl winners go when they win. And I tell him Disneyland, and he just nods, and I tell him he better not be messing with me and he says he's not. He knows I've never been, cuz he asked me my favorite movie when we were eating at Potholder and I said *Sleeping Beauty*, and he asked why it wasn't *Aladdin*, and I said I liked that one fine, but the older one was more special cuz I saw it a lot with my aunt when I was little. He wanted to know if I'd ever been to the big castle at Disneyland cuz that's from the movie. And I said no. I had school and bills to pay.

On the whole ride down, he stayed quiet, so I babbled about how

Elisa saw a beauty salon was going out of business up in South Gate. They tried real hard to hang in there after the riots, but now they're just giving up and selling their hair-drying chairs for cheap, and even a barber chair, and now she's wondering if there's power in my garage and if she can open a salon for the neighborhood in there and start cutting hair. I stopped after a while, cuz I got so worried he'd think I was stupid.

But he said he liked hearing me talk, and being here now, he's the same, quiet, watching me take in how it really is as clean as it looks. And standing here, smelling flowers in the air, I'm feeling how it's not like where I'm from. Everything shiny. So many white people it makes me nervous. White people with hip packs in every color and white shoes, and me in my black Cortezes and a jacket and jeans and a half shirt cuz I thought we were getting lunch. But you pay your ticket, or, like me, somebody pays it for you, and you can be here with everybody else. Just like America.

And I don't even know where to go first, but he knows it so well he doesn't need a map. And he leads, shows me dioramas in Main Street windows. Peter Pan high above a house. Cinderella twirling with the prince. We peek into the dark movie theater where they got old Mickey cartoons playing. We walk close together, but not touching. And I want to, but I don't. We go the long way around the *Sleeping Beauty* castle. We look at ducks and statues of Snow White and a wishing well. He throws a penny in and won't tell me his wish. I got a nickel in my pocket so I figure it's worth five of his. I close my eyes and before I toss it, I wish to be treated this good forever. And then I throw it, and it's gone.

In the castle, we walk through the story. There's darkness and stairs, and storybook pages, and more dioramas. There's one where you have to look down at a pile of spinning wheels burning, but it's really just red and yellow cloth fluttering like flames. There's this one of Maleficent that gives me shivers. She's yelling at her demon minions and all you can see are their spiky shadows moving. But then things work out, cuz they always work out in Disney, and Aurora's on the bed sleeping and Prince Phillip is above her and about to kiss her when I realize how stupid I am.

This whole thing is a setup and I walked right into it. I turn to him and I'm saying, "So, what? This is you trying to be my Prince Phillip?"

But that's when he's leaning over and kissing me in that dark hall, in front of the storybook page of Phillip kissing Aurora.

And this feels wrong, but *right*. It's warm. Soft.

And he came in quick to take it, but right after I kiss him back, he pulls away before anyone can come in or ruin it.

It's just ours, quick and secret, just like in the story.

63

On the carousel, he's on the outside and I'm on the inside. I hold the leather strap as we go around, and the castle goes by four times before it's done, and each time I pass it I think that's the first place I ever kissed him, and how it'll always be that place. And when my feet are on the ground again, I'm appreciating what kind of player he is, using my favorite movie to get at me. And I want to hate that. I do. But it feels good. Him paying attention and trying.

We try to go to the new Toon Town, but it's so packed with people that we just go look at it, the funky buildings and the hills behind, like cartoon drawings. We come back through and under the bridge before deciding to try "It's a Small World." The line's not too bad. We talk the whole time and I'm getting how maybe this isn't a bad place for dates, cuz sure there's so much stuff to do, but you got to wait for it, so you have to be patient. You have to take your time. You got to talk to each other.

I squeal a little when it's time to get into the little boat, so he gets in first and guides me. And being next to him, close enough that I can feel how much bigger he is than me, how much stronger, makes me feel safe and warm, and like this might be something, me and him. Something good. We round a little bend in this fake river and I'm not even looking up. I'm looking at his hand on his knee, how it hasn't moved this whole time, and I just take it in mine. And hold it, and he doesn't ruin anything with talking, he just looks at me, this purple light sliding over his face, and then it's blue, and the music's still going about how small the world is. It's like being in a movie.

Walking through the gift shop after to get out, we're still holding hands. I haven't let go. He hasn't let go. And I'm not even trying to look at the figurines but I kind of want a Mexican one for my aunt, to sit by the phone and remember her by. I pick one and it's a child, of course, not like an older lady, but I like that. She's in a pink dress and she has a ponytail on the side of her head. There's a ruffle around her throat.

Phil asks if he can get it for me, and I say no, this is something I need to get for me.

I got cash in my purse that came from the folder. I was gonna pay for lunch cuz he paid last time. It's cash I prolly shouldn't spend but it's there in my wallet, and it's waiting for me.

And I tell myself it's okay as I go to the registers and I freeze, cuz the person standing there? Her name tag says GLORIANA, and beneath that, LYNWOOD, CA.

Every good feeling I had all day drains out of me.

"Hello! Can I help take care of that for you?" Right after that, she recognizes me and her whole face changes. "Oh! Hi, Angela! It's so good to see you."

I recognize her too. She's a band geek. One year behind me at Lynwood High, and if you would've asked me to bet on anybody I ever met driving their asses all the way down to Disneyland to work when it's already costing them an hour in gas, it'd be her. No doubts. She's into it that much. And seeing her here? It's like I was speeding in a car and I ran into a wall and part of the bricks came through the windshield and hit me too.

There was this life I could've had before I saw her. Maybe a good one, I don't know. But a different life. One with a grown man. A man who had a job and could pay bills and listened to me when I said what I liked, and cared about me enough to try to take me away from anything I didn't like.

And seeing Gloriana? That's gone now. It's dead for me, cuz she recognizes Phil too. Gloriana's uncle, he's been in the system a bunch. He's a thief like none other, but the problem is, he's always good at getting caught. And he's been on parole, and he's had a parole officer that was also my cousin's parole officer and that's how it all falls down.

That look on Gloriana's face, the one telling me how I'm betraying the neighborhood, is how I know it's done.

And the worst of it is I deserve it. I earned that look of hers. I got it from being selfish. For thinking this could be something.

There was never any way to be honest with this. There's only one wrong side, and I'm on it. Muy pequeño el mundo es.

I need to tell Jeo quick before Gloriana spreads the word and somebody else does. I think he'd be best to tell first, and he can tell Jerry and then maybe there won't be bad things coming for me on the back of it.

I take one last look at the little Mexican girl doll behind her plastic, and I set her down on the counter and walk away from her.

Phil's behind me. He catches up quick. He tries to touch my shoulder, but I move before he can.

I cross my arms hard and tell him, "I need you to take me back to my car, please."

The whole way back, I don't talk, and he lets me not talk, and when I get out, I tell him, "Thank you. I had a nice time."

And then I shut the door behind me and I go. That's it. That's all it ever can be.

One castle. One kiss. One hand-holding.

The End.

64

I have Jerry drive me to a little bus stop area outside Wayside and check in as a walk-in visitor. Jerry's not coming in, not going on record like that. There's about thirty of us, mostly families and some kids, that wait for a bus to come take us in to the visiting area. There's vending there, for candies and sodas. That's where I have to wait for Jacob to get pulled and come through. When he's ready, they let me go back. I get assigned slot thirty-five, and I pick up the phone as he comes from the other side.

Jacob looks good to me, bigger, but older too. It's around his eyes. He's got new wrinkles and he looks at me in a new way. He's trying to figure out what I've been through and what I'm going through just by looking at me. He sees me in my new black Calvin Klein 100 percent cotton sweatshirt with the crew neck. He doesn't dislike it, but he's wondering where I got it. He never used to look at me like this before, at anyone. And I'm wondering if this is how the inside's changing him. Making him pay more attention.

I'm saying, "It's hard as hell to get up here, Jacob. This place is *far*."

"Yeah. Not a lot of dudes get visits. How'd you get up?"

"Got a ride."

Jacob gives me this look like he knows it was with Jerry or No Neck, and I think it's coming from a place of him wanting me to back off with those guys somehow, but that almost makes me laugh because we're past that. We've been past that for a long-ass time.

"You seem different." He nods at me.

"Different good or bad?"

"I don't know yet. You doing okay? Like, really doing okay?"

I look him dead in his eyes. "Never been better."

Y ahora, he gets a sad look when I say it, and that makes me sad, because I want him to know how grateful I am, because I'd never be part of this without him vouching for me with Wizard. And I wouldn't know what it feels like to walk in a room and see people see me, and then have to look at their shoes on the floor. If they ever had anything bad to say about me, they sure as hell don't now. They say it in their heads. Never to me. And I get off on that power that makes people keep their poison and hate to themselves. Nothing makes me feel stronger. Nothing. But there's more to it too.

I got invited to a party. I didn't go, but, I mean, I got *invited*. And one time I was out just doing a run with Jerry because he had to pick something up, and we went by this dude Danny's house in Carson. He's older, like twenty-three or something, and he got near me and put his hip on my hip real close and slow and he wanted to know if I was single or what. And I felt a little shudder go through me. Danny's got old acne scars like Edward James Olmos, but his body's good, and in that moment I wanted him. And he came at me and made a pass in front of Jerry and everything, and then Jerry said he'd wait in the car. I wanted to do something. I *would've* done something if there weren't rules to this, to always knowing who you're dealing with. I never met Danny before, and this was on his turf and he had all the advantages, and it's just not good business out of the gate doing something with somebody I didn't know and hadn't asked around about. And I couldn't have him hanging something over my head that I can't get out from under later. So I was out like a minute later without having done anything, and after, Jerry didn't say shit. It was just this thing that happened that we didn't need to talk over. And that made it clear, like, if there was another time, and I needed more than a minute to decide what I wanted, it was all good. It was my business. *That's* freedom.

I'm looking Jacob in his eyes and I'm trying to put it across to him without words that I wish I could share all this with him, how good it feels to be actually treated good, like a man for once. But this just isn't the time or place. It's already hurting him seeing I'm growing into it, and that I'm liking it. I can't change his reaction, not without more room to talk, so I just try to show him how I got armor over my heart now. I don't flip at any little thing. I know who I am now. Where I'm going.

And I try to mash it all down and put it together for him by saying, "Nobody ever talks shit on me. I can't go back to how things were before. The taunts and shit? I can't, Jacob. I'm serious."

"Don't let it suck you in. You wanna end up on this side of the glass, or what?"

That feels low coming from him. After all the people I talked to and all the shit I found out? Man! I'm even seeing his lawyer tomorrow to make sure he knows some shit that could help in the case. Already I'm doing more than he ever did on the street, carrying more power. When he gets back out, if he gets back out, he might even be working for me. And then he'll be grateful.

He asks me how Angela's doing. And he must see my look like I don't really want to tell him if he's just gonna use that information to be sad about it, so tells me, "I don't mean like that. I just mean is she okay?"

"She's okay. The most okay she's been in a while."

Y ahora, I'm dying to tell him Angela came to me and spilled about everything. The dates with Petrillo. Liking him. Feeling awful and stupid and like she was betraying Wizard and Jacob. Going to Disneyland, getting seen by fucking flute-playing Gloriana Nuñez while she was working at some small world gift shop. Leaving after that, and how the whole ride back they didn't talk, and how she left that car and shut the door and hasn't looked back since. And how he's called twice, and she never called back, and never will, and I was so glad she did that. Made that choice and kept it. I put it over to Jerry and No Neck and they weren't good with it, but they let me make a call on it, and my call was to do nothing. We keep watching her. Maybe put Silencio or Lil Puffer on it. We keep making sure she really ended things with Petrillo, and then we see how the trial goes.

Jacob's lost in his memories of Angela, so I flip the subject. "You remember that thing?"

I nod on it. He narrows his eyes, so I put the receiver down. I put my mouth up to the glass, cover my mouth with my hand so only he can see, and mouth the words. *Augustine. Clark.* His eyes get bigger when it clicks how this is about Augie.

I pick the receiver back up. "It's all fixed now."

"Shit," he's saying. "That's real good."

And he finally looks at me good now, like he's happy for the first time since I sat down, so I bring out what I've been saving just for him. A handmade Feliz Navidad card my little sister made special. I hold it up to show how it's on red construction paper, and it's folded on the long side. There's a cut-out green tree in the middle, and above it there's the Virgin Mary looking down, on all of us family around the tree. Me,

Jimena, Mamá, Tia, my brother, and right next to the tree is Jacob. Jacob in the family. Jacob above the table with the food on it. He's smiling. I'm looking down at the card when I hear him sniffle and I look up.

It's the first time in my life I've ever seen tears in Jacob's eyes. It makes me want to hug him. Knowing he didn't do what they put him here for, it makes me want to break this fucking glass. And I promise myself again how we're getting him out of this. How anything I have to do is worth it to make him free someday. *Anything*.

65

Jeovanni Matta is exactly on time. He has his henchman wait in the small lobby outside my office, and when he sits across from me, he is polite. He asks how my day is going, and if I had a good Christmas. He says I remind him of a history teacher he once had, and he likes how I dress in court. He's not how I pictured a young gangster who accepted coded information from an inmate at Men's Central Jail and dispersed it on the street would look. He does wish to discuss the case, however, which forces me to tell him I can only discuss it with family.

"I'm as much family as he's got," Matta says.

"Be that as it may—"

He puts a hand up, like he's in class. "Do you still do private cases?"

"Almost never," I say. I did some paperwork for a family friend last month, but it hardly counts.

"How much to have you be my lawyer?" He fans $500 across the desk I share with four other PDs.

"How old are you, Mr. Matta?"

"Eighteen."

"That means you're old enough to know better." I point at the cash. "You need to put that away and forget you ever did it."

He leaves it.

"I cannot take what is tantamount to a bribe to speak about this case with you, a known gang associate."

He puts the money back where it came from. I should kick him out, but I know he wouldn't risk being here unless he had something worth telling, and that temptation is too hard to resist, because I remain certain of two things: (1) Safulu is not guilty, and (2) Kristina Mirkovich needs to lose. Reaching that outcome is one I can cut a few corners to live with.

"Here's what happened this afternoon," I tell him. "You came in and asked if you could talk about the case. I said I can only speak with family and you left. If anyone related to this case asks you, that's what you say. If anyone asks me, that's what I'll say. Beyond that, we both keep our mouths shut. Got it?"

He smiles like I'm speaking his language, and says, "I do."

I signal him to go on.

"Augie Clark said how the other shooter that night, Dreamer, was wearing a yellow Lakers sweatshirt, right? Well, Jacob never owned one. Angela can speak to that."

I say, "How did you get that information?"

Matta leans forward. "If there's a way to put a list of evidence together or something, one for all of Jacob's clothes, to show he never had a yellow sweatshirt, that'd be good."

At this point it's just an idea. I don't have to disclose an idea to the judge or to the prosecution. If there were proof, I would. Yet, no such inventory exists. We have photographs of the contents of drawers, which I can say led me to this thought—because I have to make these things sound, plausibly and defensibly, like my own ideas before I send my investigator out—but if we had that list, we could attempt to match an inventory to those evidential photos. The problem remains, however, that I won't know if it is accurate. Matta and his associates may have already tampered with it. Angela Alvarez may not even know if the list is 100 percent accurate. She may say no one has been in the room since Jacob left but she might not even know. They could have been in there without her knowledge, but if that is the case, and it could not be proven, it would not be an impediment.

"The prosecution will say he got rid of it," I say.

"How? Angela kicked him out that night. He never went back for clothes. And I know she hasn't gotten rid of anything. I asked her."

He *asked* her. Oh God. I can add witness tampering to Matta's résumé now.

"We're stopping," I say.

He pays no attention. "So if Jacob gets dumped, leaves the house, goes straight to Spider's where people see him, can they say for sure what they saw him in? I know you talked to Spider. He said your investigator dude did. He ask them what Jacob was wearing?"

It's not a bad point, and I can't stop myself from blurting, "I'd have to check. Though, again, the People will just say he ditched it."

I watch him make some internal calculations before saying, "What if Augie were to say he doesn't remember anything happening from that night? All he did was run up when he heard loud noises and see somebody running away in a yellow sweatshirt. And he definitely didn't see anybody shoot anybody. Maybe he just ran up when Scrappy was bleeding."

The hair on the back of my neck stands up. "We're stopping *now*."

If Augie recants on the stand, Kristina will just say he was coerced; she'll trot out the deputy who heard Safulu tell Matta about Augustine and Clark Streets. She'll claim interference. She'll walk the jury right to it.

But Matta won't stop. He goes on, "I'm just saying, if Augie and the sweatshirt are the only things tying Jacob to this, then maybe it's no kind of case with those two out!"

"Mr. Matta, let me be the first to tell you that your little investigation is over. You must not do anything else, not talk to anyone, not see anyone." I stress every word. "Let us take it from here. Do not be seen with *any* witnesses. Do not, under any circumstances, make another jail visit. That's how you screwed up once. Don't make that mistake again."

He smiles at me as if I've taught him something, and he says, "Okay, Mr. Park. You're the boss."

"Don't call me that," I snap. "Look, it's not just the sweatshirt and the witness tying him to the crime, it's also the gun in the dresser."

"Jacob's prints won't be on that. Never even touched it."

"How did the weapon get there, then?"

He smirks at me. "You and I both know Wizard is too slick to ever keep a gun. He dropped that thing at the scene. Scrappy has a bruise on her foot to prove it."

I remember the hospital photo of the leg wound. She did have a bruise on her foot.

"Would she actually testify to that?"

He gives me a look that says I'm the biggest idiot around if I don't think so, and that alone almost makes this whole sordid scenario worth it. "If she gets compelled, you can ask her."

"Okay, so, if it was dropped at the scene, how did the gun get back to the residence?"

"A girl called Gloriana Nuñez can help you put two and two together." Matta sets a folded scrap of paper on my desk. "This's her phone number. She's expecting a call."

I stare at the thing for a long time after he leaves, and then I pick up the phone.

66

I look at Jimena's card she made every day. I got it in my property bag. I take it out sometimes.

I'm learning here how life starts up even before the overhead lights come on. Nada has us all up and doing burpees and push-ups by our bunks while it's still dark.

There's twenty-four of us in 617. We're the most. We almost have the whole bottom row.

Blacks are up top with some Woods. And a couple others.

Time's different here . . .

Time is habits, so I count those. I count days by workouts.

And by meals.

This one time with Lil Devil, I watched him make a spread by mashing up all this bread from sandwiches he saved. He needs three to do something good. And he used the little baggies from each one to help with that. He just punched them and squeezed till he could shape it into what looked like a thick-ass tortilla. On top of that he put the bologna, which definitely don't got a first name around here. And he put some hot sauce too. The kind they let us buy from the store.

That shit hit my mouth like a touchdown pass. I mean, it's not asada, but damn . . . it was *good*.

Best thing I've had since Mrs. Matta tried to make me a fat kid.

67

I'm on bunk status at first. All I do is wait. When I'm done waiting, I wait some more.

I watch. I listen too.

This one deputy called me out. He needed to know if I wanted to do voc shop. When I asked what that was, he told me how they had sewing here. And printing. Big workshops for it. The printing one does all the official newsletters for the county of Los Angeles.

I said I'd try printing.

So I do that Monday thru Friday now. Move paper. Pick up ink. Nobody lets me touch the machines yet. They say I can't for a while. I got to pay dues first, put my time in.

I hear how some guys been here or at Central Jail five months waiting for their trials. Some are six months, or even seven.

That makes me feel bad, but not too bad. I'm glad I'll be knowing sooner.

There's so many Sureños up here it's crazy. It's like a little army. Guess that's why the mayates don't start shit unless it's over something real.

Tim Muhammad's here now. I don't know where they had him stashed before. He's in the 700s.

He sees me at mess. I see him. We don't make a thing about it.

People been talking about what I did to him tho . . .

68

This dude with a tattoo all down his arm that looks like thick black knives comes up to me in the dayroom when I'm waiting to jump in on some handball to ask me if I'm Uso.

I know he's 617, topside, bunking by the stairs. I seen him.

He looks like he don't believe me when I say Sureño. I tell him I don't know what Uso is. He says it's Islanders. He says it's a race car. And he knows I'm Samoan. He sees me. He wants to know why I'm with Sureños anyways. I tell him cuz it's where I'm from. He comes back by saying my blood is where I'm from. We leave it at that.

Later, I think on how what he said about the blood is true. And not true at the same time . . .

It's that same night before lights-out that I see something I don't like seeing.

Tim Muhammad gets moved to the top row of my fucking dorm.

And it's for no good reason I can think of. Except maybe the deputies want us to fight again or some shit.

The next morning I see him talking to the black shotcaller we got in here too, then they turn. And they both look at me.

I tell Nada about it like I'm supposed to. I don't sleep so good after that tho.

69

Man, New Year's ain't nothing.

70

I see the black knives dude. He's got a book for me, he says. A beat-up one about learning Samoan. He says I need to know the language my blood speaks. He says that it's magic. *Gagana Sāmoa*, it's called. I take it. I say thanks.

Later that day, or maybe the next, I forget . . . Nada sees it. He asks me what the fuck. I say part of me is Samoan. He really wants to know which part after that, like he's talking about dogs and breeds again. I tell him it's my fucking warrior part, homes. He says that's cool.

I know he's thinking about it tho. I know he'll keep that information in his back pocket till he wants to test me.

Man, I fucking hate being in here. I'm always wondering what the worst shit is that could happen, then trying to prepare for it at any fucking time.

71

I been reading how the word *tinā* means *mother* in Samoan. I had to think about that for a while. I wonder if I ever knew that, or called her that, would she have stayed? Or at least took me with her . . .

And I wonder why she never taught me that word. Did she just not want me to call her that? I got so many questions for her. Questions I know won't get answered.

It'll be like that time on the bus up here when I saw those girls.

When one was trying to get something out of the other's eye. It must've worked out. They must've kept driving. They must've been fine. I'll never know tho. I feel like that's how it is with my mom. She's in her own car, prolly with somebody else. And she's way past me.

72

Nada comes at me in the dayroom. He's been thinking . . . He wants me to throw that borrowed book out. Or I can catch a soft 39 before joining with the Usos on the top row, the four of them. I tell him, Todo está bien. I'll throw the book out.

He makes me do it in front of the Usos tho, just for laughs. I don't like doing it that way. It feels bad seeing their faces. And I want to keep reading.

That shit is that tho.

And I think the dude with the tattoos gets it. He don't talk to me after or ever again, not after that disrespect.

He's also backing off, keeping me safe by not asking more stuff of me. I'm glad of that.

For real tho, fuck this place.

Fuck this place and why I got to be in here when I didn't even do shit.

Fuck this place and what it's a part of.

Fuck the system.

Fuck it till it fucking dies.

73

Nada wants something else. He wants me to punk Tim Muhammad.

I don't want to. Not cuz I can't. More like I don't see the purpose to it. I can see how Nada sees this as some kind of power play tho, so I got to go along.

I'm up the stairs and walking at Tim when he's by his bunk. I ask for some soups.

Nah, I don't ask. I tell him. "Gimme one of your soups."

Tim's got a bunch of blacks around him tho. And he stands up strong. He's still got that look in his eye like he knows what I can do to him. His back is covered tho, so that's that. Me against seven for the soup or walk away.

I don't get the soup. And I just pushed them hard by going toward their space like that. It ain't good. There's all kinds of flexing after that.

And Nada thinks it's funny. He's glad I did it. And maybe he's glad nothing happened before the deputies came in.

It's a little extra follow-on from the Samoa book shit. He sees I did it. He gets his answers to if I'm brave enough. If I'd be loyal.

I sure as shit ain't a dog tho. And his ass can't train me like one.

74

Lil Devil lost his case. Nine months he jailed before going down for murder in the second degree.

Sentenced for twenty years straight. No parole. No good behavior. No time served.

And when he clears up his bunk to process out to San Quentin to do that time, he leaves me a book he got that he really likes.

It's got no covers on it. Just pages.

The Witches, it's called.

It's about these evil witches turning a little boy into a littler mouse. And he thinks he's got to stay that way forever, so he's like, Fuck it. If I'm gonna live short, then I'm gonna go hard . . .

That shit *hits* me. I feel his pain. I totally get how he feels about being turned into something else. Even my monster gets quiet when I'm reading. It's crazy.

I read that book three times already.

It has this one line in there, it sticks with me. I think about it every day . . .

It doesn't matter who you are or what you look like so long as somebody loves you.

That shit creeps up on me when it's quiet.

I stare at Jimena's card a lot after, till I can see the lines of it behind my eyelids when I close them. I think of Mrs. Matta. I think of Little and all he's doing out there for me.

And I never really been the type to pray. I fucking pray tho. More than I ever thought I could about anything. And I beg to just get out of here.

Cuz if God can't do that for me, then I'm hoping maybe He can fix it so I can die quick in my sleep.

So I don't have to keep on going.

75

Nada's been having us getting up earlier and doing more workouts. Mixing in sit-ups on these hard concrete floors that go so cold they make red marks on your ass where you sat.

This new book I got, *Treasure Island*? It's got pirates and all that? And sailing? And it's about tricking some fuckers trying to hurt you?

Damn! That's all I can say. It's got me hooked like a motherfucker.

And I never been much of a reader before. Never liked school.

In here tho, there's time to just sit with stuff. Time you got to deal with and move around and figure out how to chop up. Time to reread something if I have to. Three times, even. And no tests. Just what I can get out of something.

And when I'm reading, if it's going good, it's like time don't exist . . .

I do like four chapters after breakfast with some rereads mixed in, or flipping back. Then it's lunch. And I didn't even go to dayroom.

Reading's my time machine.

76

I dropped out of print shop cuz nobody'd let me do anything with the machines. Besides, I'd rather just be reading more.

I like Stevenson. He was tough at first, the language of it. I kept rolling with it tho.

And I'm deep in that Dr. Jekyll shit when a wila comes thru saying how I need to call Jerry after breakfast tomorrow at nine-thirty in the morning. It even has the number on it too, in case I forgot.

I didn't forget. I stare at it for a minute before I chew it up and swallow it. It's just paper.

It's like the first thing calling me back to the outside world tho . . .

The first reminder in a while that nobody forgot me.

77

I can see the time on the clock right above the guard station so I go over to the phones at 9:30. I call from the closest phone by my bunk. I put my back to the wall. And I call Jerry right when I'm told to. The line rings thru only once. He picks up like he was waiting by the phone.

I start off cautious. "Sup? You good?"

"I'm real good, man. How you doing?"

So this is how we're doing it, I'm thinking. No names.

"I'm getting by," I say. "You know, I been better."

"I know it. I know."

"Anything crazy been going on while I been cooling out?"

"It's always something," he says.

And that's how I know there's plenty of things he'd love to tell me. He just can't tell me on this line.

That's when my bad feeling starts. And I know I'm not getting a call cuz he wants to talk or something. I'm getting a call cuz I'm about to be put on something that just might fuck my life up all over again. And I want to hang up right then. I want to delay it somehow. Duck out. Make it so whatever the thing is, it gets given to somebody else.

That's not how this shit goes. I do that? There's consequences. And they'd be Nada consequences too. And I sure as fuck don't want that, so I just say, "How's Little doing, man? For real. I saw him up here a while back."

I don't know if that's enough information to lead Jerry where I want him to go. It's me trying tho. I want to know what's been going on out there to make this call happen.

"He's going by a new name now," Jerry says.

"Okay, what's that?"

"Can't tell you that, homeboy. I'm sorry."

"Cool. Can you tell me why he changed it?"

"I can tell you later. I need you to blow into the phone for me."

"What?"

"Blow into the phone till you hear talking again."

So I do. And it's staticky before I think I hear a click, so I just keep going till I hear somebody say, "Hello?"

And it's a voice I recognize. One that makes my stomach fall out from under me . . .

Wizard's voice.

One I been missing. And kicking myself every day for feeling it. A voice I thought I'd be better off without.

Now that I'm hearing it again tho? It makes me happy somehow. And I don't even know what to do with that feeling. It's confusing as fuck.

"Sup?" I say. I want to ask if he's still down at County. They monitor these lines tho, so I know it's best just to shut up till he says what he wants.

"Not much."

"You hear from anybody at all?"

"Yeah, I heard from some people. Everybody's doing okay."

They're being so guarded in how they're talking, not mentioning names, acting like we're maybe getting listened to. Makes me glad I started it off how I did.

Wizard says, "Hey, so, there might be this thing today around lunch."

Right in Inmate Dining 2, I'm thinking. I don't ask what kind of thing. I *know* what kind of thing from how he says it. He's saying it the same way he said I needed to go at the King of the Mountain. He means something's popping off in NCCF.

Fuck. I feel my blood go up into my face and I get hot there. This is me getting asked to get wild again.

Nah. Not asked. Told.

And I don't know if this has anything to do with Tim Muhammad being up here or what. It don't matter tho. When it's time, it's time. Do or fucking die.

"Okay," I say.

"If it happens, it happens," he says. "Just protect your own."

There's so much he's saying with how he's saying this. It's definitely happening. That's for real. And the way he's saying it, it sounds like I don't need to start nothing.

And that's some relief right there. The part about protecting my own tho? That's definitely him talking about Sureños. Nothing else. He for sure heard how those Uso dudes came at me with the book. And how I started reading it. And how I had to get rid of it in front of their faces. This is him just making real sure I don't get anything twisted in the heat of anything.

My hood is what I need to be repping. Nothing else. That's what this call's about. A stone-cold reminder.

"Okay," I say. "I got you."

"That's good, homeboy. Real good. Hey, I'll see you soon, all right?"

"Right," I say. "Sure."

And I just hang up, cuz I can't keep talking, not with my monster inside me getting ready to go. Talking in the back of my head. Yapping. Telling me how if I'm gonna live short I got to go fucking hard.

PART VIII

THE TRIAL

We must reject the idea that every time a law's broken, society is guilty rather than the lawbreaker. It is time to restore the American precept that each individual is accountable for his actions.

—RONALD REAGAN

78

I get to the lockup at the Criminal Courts Building before Dreamer because I'm coming from close and he's coming from far off. There's eighteen of us in here, but nobody worth wasting my time talking to except this one white dude. He's a pacer. Back and forth. I don't know how anybody's been letting him get away with that in jail, so I tell him to sit his ass down, and he does, but then he starts in with the leg shakes. Man. I give him a look to stop that shit too. He does, but he looks back at me like we might have a problem.

It's lucky that Dreamer gets led through and uncuffed then. He looks skinnier, but stronger, like he does his burpees all day every day.

I come out with, "There's my fucking homeboy!" and right away the deputy next to Dreamer tells me not to curse.

"Can't help it, boss. I haven't seen this dude since forever!"

"Keep it buttoned," he tells me.

"Sure, boss, you got it."

The deputy gives me a tough-guy look and leaves, so I get up off the bench where I'm sitting, and I meet Dreamer halfway. I can see how something's wrong with him when I go in for a hug and he turns his body to give me one of those half ones instead. I'm not playing that shit. I drag him into a full one, and he's just got to fucking deal with it. When we break and fall back, he's not really meeting my looks. He's looking down at the floor, or in corners. I'm wondering what the fuck has been going on up there for him to be like this. It's like he's here but not here, or doesn't want to be, like he's got two minds about me. I see that, and I don't like it. I want the old Dreamer back. But man, I'm telling you, I've seen dudes do this before, get all internal, and they don't always come back. Still, I'm relieved as fuck to see he doesn't look messed up from that thing that went down. His face is clean, not like when he caught that club in 4700 after busting up Tim Muhammad. Damn. It's so good to see this fool, man! I slap his shoulder. He's all muscle now.

I make a face at him. "What you been doing? The thousand push-ups a day?"

He's quiet when he says back, "Nada's got us doing twelve hundred now."

"That fool runs a tight ship, I heard."

Dreamer nods, and his eyes go far away for a second. There's some stress between Nada and him.

"You doing okay, though? You eating good? Shit. It looks like you are."

"Ramen mostly. Angela got my store up."

I think about saying something about that, but I don't. I'm just glad she did that for him with some of that six grand I earned the hard way. "That's the good shit right there. What's your favorite?"

"Con pescado. That one."

I ask what's in that and he's got his eyes on the floor again before he says, "Just any flavor ramen, some mayo, chili, carrots if they're around, and whatever seafood you got going. I had one with some canned sardines."

He'd say more, but we get interrupted. The same deputy that hates curse words comes back through to take us both up to the court level. I've had it done before where they don't cuff me again, but this deputy isn't about that. He gets us by our wrists, and him and a partner lead us up to the elevator for the ninth floor, where we get our own little room to change, just like from the preliminary, and when Dreamer sees the fresh-folded clothes sitting out for us he almost can't believe it. He nods at them. "Angela bring these?"

He can see they're different from what we wore at the hearing. She put some of that Big Fate money to good use getting me black pants, socks, and shoes. Got me a good shirt too. This pale yellow silk one with a collar you don't put a tie under, because it's just this little circle that goes all the way around your neck. For Dreamer, she mixed it up. Gray pants. Brown shoes. Brown belt. Blue silk shirt that's like an ocean-blue. I get my stuff on quick and sit down while Dreamer's still working on his shirt buttons. We look like dudes out of a music video, him and me.

"I hear it went down big up there." I don't need to say the riot.

He gets it. He tells me, "Yeah."

I tell him to go on. I can tell he doesn't really want to. Too bad.

"Maybe a couple hundred of us in the mess, I think they said. Pepper-gas canisters. All that."

"They get you swept up in any of their investigations?"

He shakes his head at me. "I think there was just too many to try. I got questioned, but then I got sent right back. Nada got sent to nine hundred on discipline tho."

I nod. That sounds right. "Anybody get some mayates?"

"A few. Nobody big. But Tim Muhammad took out like twelve dudes like he was making up for lost time."

"Did you get at him?"

"Couldn't. He wasn't anywhere near me when it went up."

"You didn't go in packing, did you?"

"Yeah. Nada said I had to carry."

"Fucking don't do that shit next time! Throw it out right as it's kicking off. I'd be pissed about you catching new charges, especially as all this is about to happen."

By *this* I mean the trial. I mean sitting here in real clothes, talking, and for the first time since he got here, Dreamer's looking at me and staying looking at me. He's got a bunch of emotions in there, I can tell. It's how I was for my first trial. Big ones and little ones. All on top of each other. Fighting.

His forehead mashes up. "You really think I got any chance here?"

I can't sugarcoat it. "I think we're fucked, man. But better fucked on one thing than on two things if you get caught stabbing somebody up."

He nods so heavy then, it looks like his whole head would fall off if it could. It makes me want to talk about something else. Anything. Dreamer must be feeling the same way too, because he says to me, "You been writing at all?"

"Not unless telling fools what to write in wilas counts."

He makes this face where he looks like a funny-ass frog. "Yeah, but are they rhyming wilas?"

I laugh. "Nah, homeboy."

He tells me, "You can write about other things, you know? Doesn't have to be from life. It can be stuff you make up. I been reading."

I punch his arm. He tenses up before I get there. It's solid where my hand lands. Crazy solid. "Oh, you been *reading*? Good for you, man. What's your favorite?"

He looks down. He stares at his hands for a while, long enough that I'm thinking he's just not going to say shit, but then he comes out with, "*Treasure Island* took me some places."

I laugh at that, not for what he says, but for how he said it all flat. I got to call it out. "Yeah. For real? Because you seem so excited."

He shrugs and leans down to tie his shoelaces. They're thin brown spaghetti in his fingers. I've never seen him like this before, so fucking sad at everything. It's weird to me. I don't really know what to say or do to fix him.

"You should write more," he tells me, still tying his shoes like kids do, with the bunny ears. "Write a story. Write a book. I'd read it. You can rhyme it if you want to."

I tell him maybe, but I never really thought about writing something other than raps. It feels weird thinking about it, since I'm not even doing that these days. I watch him finish his laces, and give him that head roll that tells him to stand up and turn his ass around. The shirt looks good tucked. I stick down Dreamer's collar. It was all messed up in the back. He doesn't have a tie or anything, but he buttoned it all the way to the top button, so I undo it and tell him, "Makes you look less gangster."

Dreamer nods at me as the deputy bailiff comes in, the same one from before, and he says how "It's time" before taking us, without cuffs on, through the door marked with a black-painted 9, and little signs for D102 and 9-305 for the courtroom.

79

We're back in Department 102 to choose a jury and I've got Ken Gibson assisting. I asked for Lisa Maroelli; she's excellent at crosses and jury make-ups. I was denied because she's needed on a Russian restaurant triple murder. That rates. So it's three-drink-lunch Ken Gibson running second chair. He does have twenty-two years' experience, and I know that because he's told me twice already. This is precisely why I was paired with him in the first place. Ken Gibson is my training wheels.

I'm organizing my papers and manila folder for sticky notes on each potential juror when in walks Nick Park with Michael Bertelsmann. We all shake before we sit. Michael has been assigned as Tavira's new counsel. I can work with Bertelsmann. He'd do a plea deal in a heartbeat.

When Judge Ayers comes in, we stand.

"Douglas"—she looks to her clerk—"bring in the potential jurors, please."

The procession comes in every shade and body type on the planet, and the first group takes their seats behind the first two rows generally reserved for family and press. That's Los Angeles for you. We'll definitely run into difficulties with law enforcement bias. Since the King tape, everybody thinks they're experts on the LAPD. My job is to find the problem children and excuse them. I'll reject anyone eighteen to thirty-three. I need an older, upper-income female majority. White women are the holy grail. They're afraid of everything. I'll also take Persians, Armenians, and recent Eastern European immigrants who can speak English. Asian women are generally solid, but the riots did change some Korean sentiment. Give me a Hispanic woman wearing a cross any day of the week in a gang case; they generally look at defendants as if it's their job to punish when the parents never did. Black women are a toss-up. By and large, the riots poisoned the pool. Men are men, the older the better.

With them, it's about education level, employment, and making sure they have zero understanding of South Central Los Angeles.

"Let's get this on the record. All counsel present. Defendants are present. Prospective jurors are present." Judge Ayers signals her clerk. "Go ahead, Douglas."

The clerk calls numbers. Those called are filtered through to numbered seats in the jury box.

The judge spiels them. "Within the confines of this case, you are not allowed to consider bias, sympathy or sentiment, public prejudice, or possible penalty when making determinations. This means you must not make decisions based on feeling negatively toward a defendant—if, say, you don't like the race, religion, or area where the defendants live. Conversely, you must not decide anything based on sympathy for the defendants. They're young, but they're here for a reason. You mustn't allow what the public thinks to affect you, and you cannot factor in possible punishment. There will be a penalty phase, should we progress to it, but it should not affect your finding of the facts."

Some prospective jurors nod. Others study the lights in the ceiling.

"Let's begin. Juror Number One, please answer the questions on the brown placard." The judge indicates a sign posted on the wall next to the jury box.

JURORS PLEASE STATE:

1. Name
2. Area of Residence
3. Occupation
4. Marital Status
5. Occupation of Spouse and Adult Children
6. Prior Jury Experience
    A. Was it Civil or Criminal?
    B. Includes (Traffic)

The judge handles preliminary questioning. We mow through twelve prospects and keep three. I'm especially happy with an older Hispanic lady who works at a community center in early education. Following up on occupation, the judge asks if she has to deal with situations when she must try to figure out if the children are telling you the truth.

The woman smiles. "Every day."

I want her so bad. I mark the corner of her Post-it. Ken Gibson agrees.

Judge Ayers asks potential jurors if they've had any negative or positive experiences with law enforcement. Most say no. Some say they've received help on the highway as a positive. As a negative, a number bring up the King tape. Isus Krist. The judge cautions them to rely only on their direct experience. She also asks if anyone is leaning to one side or the other as we start the case. Everyone says no, which makes sense. This hasn't been in the press. The press doesn't care. The last question is the big one: Have gangs impacted your life in any way? All say no.

By the time the morning break arrives, we have four decent prospects occupying chairs: a male Glendale cabdriver, a female Burbank schoolteacher, the aforementioned mid-city Los Angeles early education specialist, and a white male retired machine operator from Whittier. I like the last one, but there's no way he lasts. The rest are thanked for their service and sent down to the first floor for checking out.

The challenges fly with the second group. We only agree on two: a white female postal worker in Downey, and a forty-four-year-old black female housewife from Gardena with no previous work experience. At that point, Bertelsmann cedes jury selection to Nick Park because he's too new to the case. Nick is efficient. He works the room well. He's gotten better since last I saw him. That's when it sinks in that nothing is a given here. The only thing I can't understand about his strategy is how many women he's allowing me to stack. I already have four.

In the third group, we get through a black male airport worker, a white male electrical worker, two female students, and a host of people with issues regarding the LAPD. They ran the gamut from the ludicrous—a potential juror accusing a patrol officer of stealing her mail—to the legitimately worrying—a man states that he won a civil case against the city of Los Angeles for being harmed by police in the Seventy-Seventh while in custody. The judgment that came in for him was in the low six figures. The judge informs all potential jurors that this case does not involve testimony from LAPD officers, only from those officers within the L.A. Sheriff's Department. All of those potentials are excused anyway.

In the fourth group, we run into a fluency problem with a fifty-two-year-old dry cleaner from Chinatown who is Vietnamese. The judge wants to know if the lady understands the difference between direct and circumstantial evidence.

"Direct evidence would be that it is raining outside and you are standing outside while it is happening. You see it, and you feel it; therefore, it is raining."

"But it is sunny today," the dry cleaner says.

Laughter breaks out in the courtroom.

The judge laughs as well. "No, I understand that. This is something I need you to imagine. Pretend it is raining outside."

"Okay." The dry cleaner closes her eyes.

The judge gives an example: "You are standing downstairs in the lobby of this building, near the elevators. You cannot see windows where you are standing, but you see people come in who are wet. Their shoes are wet. They're carrying umbrellas, which are also wet. You can conclude it is raining from the circumstances surrounding you, even though you did not directly see it raining. Do you understand this difference?"

The woman does not. The judge asks if everyone else in the box understands. They do.

We run it down. Four are excused for cause, including the dry cleaner.

The prosecution then excuses a Hispanic male from Carson, because he's too likely to empathize with the defense.

The defense jointly excuses a white male, ex-Navy and now an insurance salesman. No way they wanted him anywhere near their little hoodlums.

The prosecution excuses an Asian female nurse, age thirty-seven, because I didn't like the way she swayed in her chair when Nick Park spoke.

The defense jointly excuses a forty-four-year-old black male warehouse manager whom I was hoping would be sufficiently upset by the racial motive for shooting Scrappy. That one hurts.

The prosecution declines to excuse. The defense does the same.

We break for lunch.

Even Judge Ayers is surprised when we lock the jury by 4:18 p.m. She tells the remaining potential jurors to head downstairs, and thanks the People and defense for such a speedy selection process before adjourning. Ken must've had four drinks at lunch because he's upbeat about the overall selection. Of the twelve, seven are female, as are two of three alternates. I also got my two favorites. I'm not certain why Nick Park allowed it. Perhaps he's thinking the defense will get the sympathy vote, because even though the judge cautioned against it, it can and does work. However, this heinous gang crime was committed against a woman, and I'm banking on driving that home emotionally.

Our jury is as follows:

#1: Black male security guard, Los Angeles. Name of Bundridge.

#2: White (Armenian) male cabdriver, Glendale. Name of Barsamian.

#3: Asian male medical sales, Los Angeles. Name of Murayama.

#4: White female postal worker, Downey. Name of Vincent.

#5: White female retired elementary school teacher, Burbank. Name of Francis-Stuckey.

#6: White (Middle Eastern) male nurse, Glendale. Name of Ghazali.

#7: Hispanic female, early education specialist, Los Angeles. Name of Ramos.

#8: Asian female telephone salesperson, Alhambra. Name of Wu.

#9: White female retired librarian, Lincoln Heights. Name of Coretti.

#10: Hispanic male restaurant chain owner, Los Angeles. Name of Maldonado.

#11: White female civil engineer, West Los Angeles. Name of Leitner.

#12: Black female housewife, Gardena. Name of Sharp.

#13: Hispanic male computer engineer, Los Angeles. Name of
      Duran.

#14: Black female graduate student, Los Angeles. Name of Hall.

#15: White female dental technician, West Los Angeles. Name of
      Campbell.

80

Shit. For a day I got to be a person again! I got to be in the light for a while. Got to see sunrise hitting Magic Mountain. The whole sky turned to purples. And oranges. And it spread out like a blanket. I couldn't take my eyes off those shining curves of the roller-coaster tracks tho. I wanted to be on them loops so bad. To feel the wind when it goes fast.

And getting to the courthouse was new. The jails and deputies everywhere else all treat you like you're guilty as fuck. Not there tho. They let you dress normal. Let you walk from courtroom holding to the defense table without cuffs.

Damn. Even seeing Wizard wasn't so bad. Him telling me not to carry anymore, that tripped me out.

Getting to wear real clothes tho? That was the best. Fresh clothes. Clothes Angela picked out. Cuz she cared enough to do that.

And sitting down next to Mr. Park and getting to talk to him about what I was noticing with the jurors as he made notes. And sometimes he even wrote down what I said. I watched the jury people the whole time. I sat straight like how Mr. Park told me. Hands in my lap. I smiled whenever anybody looked at me. And they looked surprised at that! I wasn't sure what to think when Mr. Park first told me to do it.

He said it was about first impressions. About the very first moment somebody looked at you being a good one. It sets a psychological template, he said. You want that first time to be good, so you smile. A real one tho.

And that was easier than I thought. The smiling. I was happy to be here. Happy not to be behind bars and glass. Happy not to have to watch my back for whatever craziness is about to pop off. So I watched and smiled. And my face got to hurting quick, cuz I haven't been doing much of it in a long-ass time.

I was so awake in court. With all those lights going on in the ceiling. All those people that got a responsibility to me to make sure I get my rights and my fair trial. Being in that court felt the same to me as when I read books. My brain's working cuz it's being challenged. I don't know what everything is with the words they're using and nobody's stopping to explain it to me so I had to figure that shit out from what was going on around me.

And I did pretty good. Some stuff made sense if I just thought about it. I loved that. And I guess I never really thought I was all that smart before. Little was always the smart one. Now I'm recognizing how I need to work that shit out too tho. Work my brain out like how I'm doing burpees for my body. Make it think on hard stuff. Do that shit every day. Write words down I don't know and ask Mr. Park about them. Keep watching. Keep reading people like they're books till I get better and better.

I did that for jury selection. I told Mr. Park how the EMT guy's got a twitch. He might be missing his speed cuz he works nights, you know? Or I told him how I like that restaurant dude. I been to one of his places once. And everybody talks about how he gives out leftovers to homeless people after a long day so he don't have to throw food out. And maybe that makes him kind. Mr. Park writes that. A short version. Or that teacher lady that says she knows all about lies? She looked at me a lot. Not in a bad way. Like she's trying to figure me out tho. And I'm thinking how good that is, cuz I didn't do shit. I hope more than anything she can see it in me, that honesty.

The only thing messing with me when everything got done with the jury was there was nobody from where we're from. No South Gate. No Paramount. Definitely no Lynwood. Nobody from South Central, even. How's anybody gonna understand if there's not one person on their side to talk about some shit being normal where we're from, and other shit not?

That had me tripping right up until the day's done. After, I had to take the new nice clothes off. I can wear a different shirt tomorrow, the bailiff said. He's cool.

I got back into my blues. And Wizard did too. We said goodbye. And we didn't hug or nothing. I looked him in his eyes tho.

And then it was cuffs. Into lockup. Onto the bus . . .

On the drive back up, I'm going over the whole day in my head. Again. And again.

When it's real dark out, we get processed back in. And I ain't even mad when they have me strip all down again to do their checks for every hiding spot a human body can have.

It's just, like, routine. They get you used to it. So you do it without thinking.

The worst thing tho, is how they won't let me shower. It's right next to my bunk and everything. It's too late, they say. They're not about to supervise me after getting back from court. Reasonable showers from six till ten, they say. So we get walked to bunks when it's already lights-out. And I don't even know how much sleep I'm about to get cuz tomorrow's like Christmas again. Up early. Some TV in the morning. A dawn ride. Some new clothes . . .

When the deputy that walked me thru is gone, my middle bunkie, Slow Poke, says what's up to me. He's from Bell Gardens. We shared some spreads when he first came in. He don't talk unless he has to. I like that.

"Sup?" I say back. I look behind me to make sure nobody's doing a sweep on my row, then stand up. I put my ear close so nobody else can hear what he's about to say.

"Nada's getting wilas saying we need to hit back hard. To just wait for the time. Paisas are already making shanks like nonstop."

And that shit? It takes my breath out.

That shit is a big fucking deal.

My face don't change tho.

I look at Poke. And I'm nodding at him like, *I got you*. Like, *Todo está bien*.

When I'm back down on my bunk tho, every good feeling I had all day is just going out of me like air out of a slashed-up tire.

And I'm knowing now how I was all gassed up before, thinking like how I was a person, and now I'm just . . .

I'm a fucking fist for somebody else to punch with.

And if I get broken when I'm up in the mix, there'll be another fist coming up. And another one.

So really I'm just like the razors they give us in here. They only work for so long.

They wear out when you use them. And you have to throw them away after.

And looking at it like that, it's like, I'm only good for a little while and then,

I guess I'm worth nothing.

81

Safulu tells me the deputies at Wayside have not been allowing him to take showers, because they say he gets up too early in the morning, and he gets back too late in the evening. This is unacceptable. I petition the judge first thing for my client to be allowed the ability to clean himself and be presentable for court. Prior to the jury being brought in, Judge Ayers grants the petition. After that, the clerk brings the jury in. They take their seats next to their numbers, and I settle in to take notes as Kristina stands.

Her opening argument goes as I expect. She attempts to dazzle the jury with her far-reaching conspiracy theory about someone in prison ordering a gang hit on Lucrecia Lucero without offering a motive, but she hints at one, and I am certain it will be coming down the pike with her first witness.

The actual piece of evidence presented during discovery, however, is a piece of paper twice the size of a fortune from a fortune cookie. It is covered with micro-script writing on front and back detailing: (1) that Scrappy, a.k.a. Lucrecia Lucero, has done something against the code of the gang, although what that something is, is not explicitly stated, and (2) that Scrappy now has a "green light" on her.

Judge Ayers looks to me when Kristina has finished. "Mr. Park, in your own time."

"Yes, Your Honor," I say, "thank you."

I bring my statement to the podium with me. "The People speak of prison conspiracies in the hopes of distracting you from the fact that the conspiracy my client is actually charged with is so flimsy that it could blow away in the wind. Judge Ayers has told you multiple times not to be swayed by sentiment or bias, but to instead consider the facts of the case. Here are the facts concerning these conspiracy charges." It's not warm in the courtroom, but I'm already sweating. "There is zero *audio* evidence linking my client, Jacob Safulu, to the planning of this crime.

There is zero *video* evidence. There are zero *witnesses* to anyone directly conspiring. In lieu of such important, provable facts, the prosecution has taken a leap of logic and fallen off a cliff. I urge you not to follow them."

Three jurors smile when I say that.

"There is *absolutely zero evidence* of conspiracy against my client."

I step away from the podium, only taking two note cards. I am in the flow now.

"The prosecution would have you believe that the crux of this conspiracy lies in a confiscated prison note that happens to mention the victim, Lucrecia Lucero. However, the individual who sent this note that you will see as a piece of evidence is neither on trial here, nor will he be a witness in order to explain what he meant by his words. More importantly, my client's name does not, in fact, appear on that note, and neither does Mr. Tavira's. In fact, their alleged gang monikers do not appear on this note either.

"Now, the People will ask you to take that leap and believe that the defendants somehow heard about this note—as it was *not confiscated* in their possession—and took it upon themselves to execute its order. Once again, there will be *zero evidence* of this. In fact, the only things linking my client to these crimes at all are the signed affidavit of a convicted felon, Augustine Clark, and a weapon found in his clothes dresser, in his unlocked bedroom, that Mr. Tavira himself had access to."

I shake my head. "There is something troubling about the location in which the weapon was found, however, because, you will see photos of Miss Lucero's wounds at the hospital, and they will show a bruise on her left foot that is consistent with this explanation: the handgun was dropped on her foot after the commission of the criminal act. So how, then, did it travel across the city of Lynwood to magically appear in a house some twenty blocks away the next day?"

I know I am on thin ice. I feel Kristina itching to object, but I cannot lose my momentum now.

"You will be asked to weigh if indeed someone else had sufficient motive, means, and opportunity for planting that weapon in the home of Jacob Safulu in an attempt to frame him for the crime with which he is charged."

Behind me, Kristina's pen scribbles furiously. *Good.*

"As we move forward, you will find this case is simpler than the prosecution would have you believe. My client *did not* participate in anything resembling a conspiracy and the prosecution cannot prove that he did; instead they will ask you to trust opinions, not facts. My client *did not* participate in the attempt on the life of Lucrecia Lucero. In fact, he was at home with his girlfriend that evening, and at the approximate time of the attempt on Miss Lucero's life, Mr. Safulu's girlfriend of nearly one year was breaking up with him."

The sympathy bomb finds its targets in the jury box. At least half the jury—no, more; seven, maybe eight—visibly shifted when I said it. I like that.

"This much is true: Angela Alvarez ended her relationship with Jacob Safulu that night at almost the exact time Miss Lucero was shot nearly two miles away. We have Miss Alvarez's statement to that effect. She was an honor student and a star athlete in high school; she is now an elder care nursing student."

I watch that fact land on the nurse in the jury. I can already see how predisposed he is to believe Angela Alvarez.

"And you will be asked to weigh whether or not her testimony"—as I say that I hold out my right hand, palm up—"is more believable than that of a convicted felon."

To represent Augustine Clark, I use my left hand, also palm up. I tip my hands like scales then, and I show them that this is hardly a choice at all. The correct decision, the real weight in matters of truth, is obviously going to be with Miss Alvarez. I stare at my right hand for a moment to let that sink in.

"All of these facts will lead you to one simple truth." I sweep my eyes over the jury box, meeting the gaze of every single juror and alternate. "There is zero evidence that my client participated in planning the attempt on the life of Miss Lucero. It is not possible to prove that Jacob Safulu obtained the weapon. There is no registration, no receipt. It is not possible to prove he used the weapon. His fingerprints were not found upon it. The simple explanation is the truth in this case: there is no evidence of Jacob Safulu committing any crime on Josephine Street on December sixth, nineteen-ninety-three, at approximately nine in the evening, because Jacob Safulu simply *was not there*."

I collect my notes. I turn to see Kristina's controlled stare and stroll right past it, drinking in the feeling of it. If she didn't know she was in a fight before, she knows it now, and it's exactly what she gets not only for charging the wrong man, but for overcharging him.

Judge Ayers says, "Mr. Bertelsmann?"

As I sit, Michael rises to provide the opening argument on Mr. Tavira's behalf.

82

Once I get called and sworn in, Kristina starts with questions about my background and experience, and then we lay out the facts of the kite and the gun—specifically, the ballistics report confirming that the bullets that went through Scrappy and into her front yard match the weapon—before proceeding to People's Two.

Kristina motions to the screen. "Detective Montero, do you recognize this?"

"Yes," I say.

"What is it?"

"It is an eyewitness affidavit."

"Thank you, and why do you recognize it?"

"I interviewed Mr. Clark. I was in the room when he wrote this and signed it."

"Do you have any reason to disbelieve Mr. Clark's statement?"

"No."

"And why not?"

"It was consistent with our findings at the scene."

"That would be on Josephine Street, on the evening of December sixth of last year?"

"Yes."

"And what was consistent?"

"All the major elements. Miss Lucero had been shot three times. She had a tourniquet on her leg that saved her life."

"Detective, can you please read the underlined portion?"

"'She also said "Motherfucking Wizard" because she knew he shot her too.'"

"Detective, what does that represent to you?"

I say what Kristina wants me to say, exactly as we discussed. "I believe it represents a dying declaration."

"So, she identified the person she thought had killed her?"

"Yes."

"Detective, based on your training and experience, how would she recognize him in order to make such a declaration?"

"Objection," Park says. "Calls for speculation."

The judge looks at Kristina. "Do we need a sidebar, or do you have something on this, Counsel?"

"Your Honor, as we have established, Detective Montero is an expert witness on the types of crimes perpetrated by these gangs. He used to work out of the Lynwood Sheriff's Station. He has served on numerous gang task forces with OSS, and even led one. Few people within the L.A. Sheriff's Department are as qualified as he is to provide the background of criminal gang cases in this area."

"Very well. I'll allow it," Judge Ayers says.

Park doesn't look happy with that, but there's nothing he can do.

Kristina turns back to me. "How would the victim know Mr. Tavira in order to identify him as her assailant, Detective?"

"Miss Lucero is a known gang member and Mr. Tavira is a member of their closest and most immediate rival gang. Both have documented case histories and identifiable gang tattoos. Their gangs share a border in Lynwood. Clashes are inevitable, and their code calls for violent retribution."

Kristina enters photographs of their gang tattoos into evidence before saying, "Detective, based on your experience of these gangs—their historic enmity and propensity for violence—would you say that, given the opportunity, Omar Tavira and Jacob Safulu would seek to murder Lucrecia Lucero because of their affiliations?"

"I'd say it was only a matter of time."

"Nothing further."

Nick Park stands for the cross-examination. I liked him when he was on our side, prosecuting. I like him a lot less now that he's a state PD.

He says, "Your Honor, may I approach the witness with People's Two?"

"You may."

"Thank you, Your Honor."

Park hands me a copy of Augie Clark's affidavit. "Can you please reread the line Miss Mirkovich had you read?"

I say, "'She also said "Motherfucking Wizard" because she knew he shot her too.'"

"Detective, only one gun, and only one shooter, is mentioned in this affidavit. Omar 'Wizard' Tavira. So why would Mr. Clark use the word *too* at the end of that sentence?"

"I don't know."

"Is this an oversight on your part? Allowing language that implies there were two shooters, when the affidavit itself only claims one?"

"No."

"And why not?"

"Because they are the signer's own words, not mine."

"Detective, can you please read the other lines I have marked on my copy?"

I read it out. "'Dreamer was wearing a yellow Lakers sweatshirt and I could see it even in the night because it was so bright.'"

"Detective, who is Dreamer?"

"Dreamer is the gang alias of Jacob Safulu."

"So you say, but can you prove my client has a gang affiliation?"

"Not prior to this crime, no."

"Detective, does the L.A. Sheriff's Department photograph gang members' tattoos? Is that your policy?"

"Yes."

"Has Jacob Safulu been photographed?"

"Yes."

"Did he have *any* tattoos related to Omar Tavira's alleged gang?"

I shift. I don't mean to shift, but I do. "No. Mr. Safulu had no gang-related tattoos."

"You stumbled in your use of tense, Detective. Correct or incorrect, Jacob Safulu *has* zero alleged gang tattoos?"

"Correct."

"I see. And has Jacob Safulu been convicted of any crimes in the furtherance of this alleged gang's known activity?"

"No."

"Prior to these charges, he had *no criminal record whatsoever*; is that correct?"

"That's correct, but—"

"Your Honor!" Park throws his hands up and turns to the judge as I'm trying to say we know he is an active younger member who is trying to rank up because of chatter we have been hearing that places him as a key figure in a number of disturbances.

"Detective Montero," the judge says, "I must direct you to answer the question only. The record does not require your extraneous commentary. I'm sure the People can provide you proper latitude to express your thoughts on rebuttal. Go ahead, Mr. Park."

"Detective, when you searched the domicile Mr. Safulu shared with Angela Alvarez and Omar Tavira, did you catalogue his clothing?"

"No."

"And why not?"

"I did not deem it necessary."

"Why?"

"Upon searching the premises, we did not find any clothing likely used during the commission of the crime."

"I see, so you did look for a yellow Lakers sweatshirt?"

"Yes."

"And did you find it?"

"No."

"Detective, since you're an expert witness, can you tell us the colors of the alleged gang Mr. Tavira belongs to?"

"They favor black and gray, or sometimes silver."

"I see. So, not yellow?"

"No."

"Did that detail strike you as strange, then, when you read it in Mr. Clark's affidavit?"

"No."

"I see." Park stares me down before pivoting back to the defense table. "Your Honor, at this time I'd like to introduce Defense Exhibits A and B. The first is a detailed list of all Mr. Safulu's clothing remaining at the house, none of which he took with him when he vacated, and the second is a multipage photographic record of those same items."

He projects the list up on the wall for all to see.

"If I may publish these to the jury, Your Honor?"

"You may."

Park hands a stack of copies of the list to the closest juror, who passes them around.

"Detective Montero, do you see a yellow sweatshirt on that list?"

I look to Kristina. She looks calm, so this list must not be a surprise. I say, "No."

"Detective, do you see any Lakers-branded clothing on this list?"

I scan it. Everything is color-coded. Brands and team names are mentioned. "No."

"Do you understand the color coding scheme used on this list?"

"Yes."

"And do you see any yellow clothing on this list?"

"No."

"So you're telling me that a rabid Lakers fan in Los Angeles has no other items of Lakers clothing and *nothing yellow* in his entire wardrobe? That seems unbelievable."

Kristina's head snaps up. "Object—"

"Withdrawn." Park's a slick one. "Your Honor, I'd like to introduce Defense Exhibit next-in-order, the transcript of Detective Montero's interview with Angela Alvarez."

The judge makes a note. "Exhibit is marked Defense Exhibit C."

"Do you recognize this, Detective Montero?"

"Yes."

"And how do you recognize it?"

"It's the transcript of the interview I conducted with Angela Alvarez at Firestone Park Sheriff's Station."

"Detective Montero, when you interviewed Miss Alvarez, did she provide an alibi for Jacob Safulu at the time of the attempt?"

I have no choice but to say, "Yes."

Park smiles. "Nothing further."

During Kristina's rebuttal examination, I expand on the fact that street gangs are changing in the wake of the King riots; they're getting smarter and more sophisticated. Avoiding detection is now a crucial part of their criminal strategy. Younger members like Safulu are often specifically asked *not* to get tattooed, so that they may be able to deny gang association when convenient, such as in a court of law.

She asks me why didn't we find the yellow sweatshirt in our sweeps of the area surrounding the crime scene, as well as the house Tavira and Safulu shared with Alvarez. I respond that if indeed Safulu had just committed a crime, getting rid of it would aid in concealing the part he played.

Kristina wants to know if I believe Miss Alvarez's alibi for Mr. Safulu. I do not. And why not? Because of her close personal relationship with the defendant, and logistically, it's not entirely possible to pinpoint the time of the shooting, only a time frame. It could have been possible for Safulu to participate in the crime. What's more, considering the difficult nature of their discussion, I think it likely that he may have left that house angry and in the frame of mind to do something reckless.

Nick Park jumps in. "Objection. Calls for speculation on mental state."

"Sustained."

"Your Honor, I ask that that be struck from the record."

"I agree, Mr. Park. I will also direct the members of the jury to disregard Detective Montero's last statement on the prospective mental state of the defendant on the night in question."

Kristina says, "Detective, do you have any doubt whatsoever that Jacob Safulu is a gang member?"

"None whatsoever. I feel that his involvement in revealing the name of Augustine Clark to a potential associate using coded language at Men's Central Jail clearly proves his gang ties."

"Objection."

The judge looks to Park. She's waiting for a basis but it doesn't come. "On what grounds?"

He's floundering. "Speculation."

And she hits him quick. "No, Mr. Park. It is not. Overruled."

Score one for the good guys.

83

I've been in court before, but not on the ninth floor of the CCB. I do parole violation hearings. I sit next to my parolee in front of a commissioner representing CDC working for the Board of Prison Terms. This is the first criminal trial where I have to take the stand. It's a relief to see Angela isn't present in the courtroom gallery. The little scumbucket I've seen her sit with before is present, however, as is an older woman (his mother, maybe). Wizard and Dreamer have no other people.

Kristina prepped me yesterday. After the ambush at 22nd St. Landing, she made it clear we had to address the Renee situation head-on, get the facts into the jury's heads before the defense uses it against me. She was right.

She opens with questions about my background and experience (how long I've been working, where, my commendation), before she says, "Has there ever been an official agency investigation into a complaint against you?"

"Yes. A preliminary one."

"Were you formally charged with official misconduct?"

"No.

"Why was that?"

"The claim was investigated and found to be baseless."

It was a he said, she said. I wasn't a doper, so they believed me when I told them Renee pursued me, attempted to seduce me. I stood firm and said when she couldn't have me, she set me up.

Kristina says, "How many complaints, would you say, have been filed against you in your career here in Los Angeles County?"

"Fifteen."

"How many of those proceeded past preliminary investigations?"

"None."

"And why, in your professional opinion, is that?"

"Specious complaints are part of the job. We have a training module on how to handle them because we supervise and manage the release of convicted felons. Generally speaking, these folks have been gravely dishonest in the past and still might be. In my experience, most will say and do anything in an attempt to tar someone they view as too hard on them during their supervision."

Kristina looks serene, happy with my answers. She moves on, walks me through how I came to be involved: being assigned Augustine Clark while Martinez was on maternity, upon my first unscheduled check-in with the doper I find him intoxicated, I search the premises (which is not the recommended halfway house), I find drugs, Mr. Clark becomes terrified and confesses that he witnessed a shooting involving one of my then-current parolees, Omar "Wizard" Tavira.

"And what did you do then, Agent Petrillo?"

"I took Mr. Clark into my custody and transported him to Firestone Sheriff's Station."

"Why didn't you take him to the Lynwood station? It's closer."

"I know Detective Montero at Firestone. He used to work in Lynwood. I knew he had prior experience with the gangs in question. I had asked him about advice regarding how to handle Mr. Tavira previously and he was generous with his insight."

"What was Detective Montero's opinion regarding—"

"Objection." It's the Oriental lawyer. "If the People wanted the detective's opinion concerning Mr. Tavira on the record, they should have asked him that on the stand."

"Sustained," the judge says, "but I'll brook no more talking objections, Mr. Park. You must state the designation."

"I'll rephrase," Kristina says. "What did Detective Montero personally recommend to you regarding Mr. Tavira's terms of release?"

"He recommended very close supervision."

"And did you do so?"

"Yes."

"Was it this vigilance of close supervision that led you to check up on your parolee immediately after conveying the witness, Mr. Clark, to Firestone?"

"Yes."

"Did you go alone?"

"No."

"Why not?"

"Because there was a possible serious crime involved, I thought it best to bring a unit with me, not simply for matters of safety, but to potentially arrest the suspect if he should be home."

Wizard smirks down at the table when I say that.

"Who accompanied you to the residence on Virginia Avenue?"

"Deputy Jackson accompanied me."

"Deputy William Jackson, Junior?"

"Yes."

We wrap up with me discussing in great detail how I found the weapon and how I witnessed it being documented by Deputy Jackson. After that, she asks me about my considered opinion on Omar Tavira. I tell her it has always been my understanding that he is a criminal capable of great violence, given his past convictions (robbery, assault), and my own direct experience.

"Do you happen to know how Omar Tavira received his gang moniker, Wizard?"

"Yes."

"And why is he called that?"

"They call him Wizard because he makes things disappear."

Wizard's lawyer opens his mouth to object, but before he can, Kristina says, "No further questions, Your Honor."

The Oriental lawyer stands and makes his way over to me. He says, "Agent Petrillo, were you alone in the room when you found the weapon?"

"Yes."

"How many times had you searched the residence previously as part of your normal duties?"

"Five occasions."

"Did you find any contraband on any of the previous searches?"

"No."

"Did that lead you to believe that Mr. Tavira was conscientious with his personal living space?"

"Yes."

He pivots where he's standing and faces the jury. "Do you know my client, Jacob Safulu?"

"Yes."

"And where did you meet him?"

"At the residence on Virginia Avenue on numerous occasions."

"Did anyone ever introduce him as Dreamer?"

"No."

"Did he ever introduce himself as Dreamer?"

"No."

"So how precisely would you know who Dreamer was when Mr. Clark mentioned the name?"

"I had heard it previously at the residence. Mr. Tavira referred to him by that name."

At the table, next to his lawyer, Wizard shakes his head.

The Oriental lawyer keeps going. "Agent Petrillo, what happened on April thirteenth, nineteen-ninety-two, while you were on duty?"

"The relative of a parolee I was supervising filed a complaint against me."

"And when did that complaint allege the incident occurred?"

"The previous day."

"What were those claims, Agent Petrillo?"

"That I had acted inappropriately."

"In what way acted inappropriately?"

"The claim stated that I had forcibly kissed the parolee." I don't smile when I say it. I want to, but I don't. The truth is, I did so much more. I had every bit of her floppy pussy whenever I wanted, every scrap left that was worth anything. She loved it. She always begged for more, and I gave that little hoodrat the best she ever had. That's a fact.

"And did you, Agent Petrillo, kiss her forcibly?"

I say, "No."

She betrayed me. When she wanted out, she kissed me in front of her mother, who immediately screamed about making a complaint. That was how Renee showed me who she really was: a whore, and a liar. I'd even bought her a silver necklace. It was nice but not too expensive. I could have been her way out of the shithole she inhabited, but she was just too dumb to get it.

"Nevertheless," the Oriental lawyer says, "the young woman's mother filed a complaint against you."

"Yes."

"And how old was this young woman at the time of the complaint?"

"I do not recall."

He flips papers. "The complaint states she was twenty-two years old. How old is Miss Angela Alvarez?"

"Objection," Kristina says. "Relevance?"

"Withdrawn." The Oriental lawyer moves back to his table. "Your Honor, we wish to submit Defense Exhibit F."

Kristina says, "Objection. Relevance?"

"Your Honor, if I may, this speaks to the fundamental trustworthiness of Agent Petrillo in a professional capacity, particularly in regard to his treatment of women."

"Miss Mirkovich, the People saw this during discovery and still put him on the stand. I'm allowing it."

The lawyer puts it on the screen to my left. It's giant, for the whole courtroom to see.

"It says here the charge is misconduct." He circles the word on the overhead. "It says here that you made inappropriate contact of a sexual nature with the parolee in your charge. Agent Petrillo, can you confirm that this document is indeed a charge of official misconduct against you?"

It also has quotes from Renee in it, but he doesn't ask me about those. Her saying I gave her gifts and made her feel uncomfortable, that she didn't know what to do. She knew what to do at the time. She took them!

I say, "Yes. It is a charge, not a finding."

He doesn't take it down. He leaves it up, glowing. It's an unfair thing having your past for a jury to see when you're not even the one on trial.

Kristina says, "May the People have a sidebar, Your Honor?"

"Yes, Miss Mirkovich."

The judge and all attorneys huddle by the clerk's desk. Somewhere in the jury box, a man coughs. When the lawyers break and move back to their seats, the Oriental one stays standing. He has a look on his face like he's about to surprise me with something.

"Is it true, Agent Petrillo, that you were observed holding hands with Angela Alvarez, cousin to defendant Omar Tavira, ex-girlfriend to defendant Jacob Safulu, and resident at the Virginia Avenue address, at Disneyland on December twenty-third of last year?"

There's a stir. Kristina's objection cuts through it: facts not in evidence.

The Oriental lawyer speaks before the judge can. "Your Honor, the defense will present a witness who will testify to these facts, a Disneyland employee by the name of Gloriana Nuñez who is acquainted with Miss Alvarez due to their time spent in high school together. Her name appears on page two of our submitted witness list."

The judge directs me to answer.

Rage: cold, hard; ice in my stomach. I keep my face calm. I focus on Kristina, whose mouth is a tight line.

"Not to my knowledge," I say.

The Oriental smiles. "Agent Petrillo, given your history of blurring lines with females in your line of work, is it unreasonable to assume you would have gone to the extraordinary lengths of planting a weapon to create such an opportunity with Angela Alvarez?"

Kristina shoots out of her chair. "Objection, Your Honor! Argumentative and verging on slander."

Her eyes tell me: *Don't you say another fucking word.*

The Oriental lawyer smirks. "Sidebar, Your Honor?"

"An excellent idea," the judge says.

I don't hear what they're going over, but I see Safulu's lawyer put his head down like he's being chastised before he fights back, and it looks like he says something that makes the judge think for a moment. Everyone returns to their chairs.

"The People's objection is sustained," the judge says before turning to the court reporter. "I'm also ordering it struck from the record, and am directing the jury to ignore Mr. Park's previous question."

But he's right back on it. "Let me approach this differently. Agent Petrillo, prior to finding the weapon, you were alone in the room, correct?"

"Objection," Kristina says, "asked and answered."

"Sustained."

"I'll move on. Agent Petrillo, if you had put something under that drawer, would anyone have seen you do it?"

I look to Kristina. She's red when she says, "Objection, Your Honor! Assumes facts not in evidence."

"Okay, Mr. Park, you have exhausted my patience," the judge says. "There is no evidence of that. The jury will note they are not to consider this during their deliberations, and I order this to be stricken from the record. Do you have anything further?"

"No, Your Honor," he says. "I have nothing further."

Judge Ayers says, "Any questions, Mr. Bertelsmann?"

"No, Your Honor."

The judge says, "Redirect, Miss Mirkovich?"

Kristina looks ill. "No, Your Honor."

"May this witness be excused?"

"Yes, Your Honor," the Oriental lawyer says, "but the defense would like to reserve the right to recall this witness if necessary."

"Understood. Agent Petrillo, you may step down. We're going to hold you over for four days. If you are not recalled in that time, I will dismiss you."

I step down. Kristina won't look at me. Her knuckles, gripping a pen, are white. Behind her, Montero stares at me from his little blue chair next to the wall separating the court from the gallery. A look passes between us: he doesn't give a fuck what I did with Angela, he only cares I got caught, that there was a witness, that it could fuck up his case (and if it does, it's my goddamn fault).

84

Instead of putting me through processing when I get back to the jail, they put me in holding with fourteen other fools and they won't say why. It could be a lockdown on my block, or quarantine, but whatever it is, it's waiting. After a while, a deputy comes in and says they're running a special bus. To where, he won't say. That gets me thinking that if they're sending me anywhere, it's up to Wayside, because it's too crowded down here. My ears on the blocks have been telling me how fools have been sleeping in sleeping bags on the walkways now. It's straight-up like some deputies went to a camping store and bought a bunch of shit so inmates could sleep on the concrete floor in here. That's definitely how it's going down on 4700. Head to toes. Some dude's nasty-ass feet right near the top of your head while you're trying to sleep, and he accidentally kicks you? Fucking sucks to be you.

Man, Dreamer's lawyer is out there getting it. I replay some of those crazy moments in my head. Got nothing else to do. He's not always winning stuff, his challenges and whatnot, and I can see how the judge doesn't always like his objections, but he's out there fighting every down. And what he did to Petrillo up there? Damn. That shit was *real*. But my lawyer? Bartlesmann or whatever? He gets in late because of the recusal off that Augustine Clark name getting out, and the first thing he says to me is that he has four other concurrent cases. One more downtown in CCB in addition to mine, but in Department 34 with Judge Firenze. One in Torrance. One in Pomona. He finished up by saying thank God he didn't have to drive to Lancaster. Man, I don't care about all that! Do your job. Today, he told me he was getting sick like I was supposed to feel sorry for him. It's like he's already apologizing for losing, telling me that, and it sucks having to put up with that kind of representation when Park is in the same fucking courtroom, bullying up on the fucking bullies. It's Park that's giving my ass hope. He has me thinking how, if the jury doesn't believe Petrillo at all about the gun, then I got a shot of having a jury that can't decide on me and ends up hung.

I'm glad I heard about the Angela shit ahead of time. Lil Puffer rolled through on a visit and broke it down because Little told him to. I'm not calling that fool Dulce. Not ever. But he's a good motherfucker out there. Loyal. I'm lucky for that. I like hearing shit ahead of time, especially about family. I would've lost it if I had to hear about Angela going to Disneyland in court for the first time. She hasn't visited me since. I don't blame her. I was super-angry at first. I wanted to see her and figure out how she let it go down like that, but then I watched Mr. Park cross-examine Petrillo, and it got me thinking how her going out with him was the best thing that could have happened. It made Petrillo's ass impeachable. It was perfect how it blew up in his face like that. Shit. Seeing him squirm up there was so good, I almost wish I'd masterminded the whole thing and asked Angela to go out with him.

The door to our holding room opens, and the deputy tells us to line up. He says we're going back to the buses and another deputy comes in with the cuffs.

A dude with a pink-ass face can't help asking, "What about my shit, Deputy?"

We all get this explanation about how there's been a pipe burst and a flood that caused relocations. It's an old-ass building. Shit breaks and goes bad all the time. They're already short mattresses and sheets from it because they're trying to dry it all. That gets me wondering how you would even dry fifty if you had that many wet ones. They take up so much space. Do you put them in front of some giant carpet fans, or take them to the yard and flop them out on the fenced-in yard roof so they can dry top and bottom? That thought makes me smile. It gives me a picture in my head of a ceiling full of mattresses, almost like clouds that fell down and got caught.

I won't know if this reason is real, if there actually was a flood, until I get up with some homies on it. All I know now is if my soups and any of my store goodies survived, they'll just get chopped up among my cellies with some left over for new Raza coming in. It ain't so bad thinking of it that way. I mean, at least it would get used then. I don't exactly like walking off without my court paperwork, but the deputy tells us we can apply for that to be replaced. He doesn't say when that's happening, because that's not on him. What *is* on him is cuffing us up by twos and moving us into the hall, where I can see there's three other holding rooms coming out at the same time. We all get on the same bus and fill it up. We go north on the 101, and I know it's Wayside for sure, and all I'm thinking then is how, if they house me right, I'll get to see Dreamer again, and how good that will be.

85

It's the pretty lawyer lady up first with me. Miss Mirkovich. The clerk does me with the swearing in. I have to say I'll say the whole truth and nothing but it, so help me, God. And there's this thing about that. I think God would understand what I'm about to do. How I have to. How if I said no I might have ended up dumped in the river or something.

She approaches and she smells like a kind of perfume where two flowers are fighting, and one is winning while one is dying. Smells come back last for me. And they're so strong when they do. It's weird. I haven't been clean a month just yet, but I've been doing my methadone every day, and I'm not even chipping anymore. I been working at the shipping company spot they got for me. There's this guy there, Jesse. He's the vice president of the company or something. He had some trouble with drinking and with getting in trouble too, and he understands. He don't understand five spoons a day, but he knows about something being on top of you and making you do stuff. He says how as long as I do meetings and go in and do drug court and see what happens, that if for whatever reason I get sent back in, he'll sponsor a work furlough where I can work days and be out making good money and at night I'll report in to sleep behind bars. He's a good man, that Jesse. I don't know what the little gangsters have over on him, but I never asked. And I never will.

She wants me to state my name for the record, please.

"Augustine Patrick Clark," I say. "My mom is from Wales. The country. Not like the animals."

A couple people in the jury laugh and I like how that sounds.

The judge reminds me to only answer the question and not add commentary.

I say, "Yes, Judge."

And she says, "Your Honor."

So I say, "Your Honor."

She nods to Miss Mirkovich, and then we go. I say where I was on the night in question, on the 3500 block of Josephine Street. I say what brought me there, being on a mission for drugs. What kind of drugs? Heroin drugs. Am I an addict? Yes, but I am currently in recovery and have been clean for about one month. I don't have shakes anymore. And do I know Lucrecia Lucero? Yes, I know her well. She sold me drugs a lot, but not anymore. All of this stuff has been straight out of what Miss Mirkovich was helping me with, and you can tell from the look on her face how she thinks it's going good, so I almost feel bad when I know it's not going to anymore when she gets ready to ask if I'm in recovery and how that's going. It's all planned to be about making me a more believable witness, but now it's about to be something else.

"Yes, ma'am. I attend meetings."

"And are you finding it useful?"

"Yes, ma'am."

"Now I wish to speak to you about the evening of December sixth of last year and your recollection of the events. Did you see, with your own eyes, the victim, Lucrecia Lucero, shot three times from increasingly close range on Josephine Street?"

I never been on the stand before. I lean too far forward and get my mouth too close to the microphone when I say, "No, I did not," and it booms all around the room.

I sit back and look up at the judge as she's looking down on me with wide eyes. In front of me, Miss Mirkovich is going strawberry-red in her cheeks.

She says, "Your Honor, I need a moment."

And then she marks a bunch of stuff up on the table with a pen. Papers and stuff.

"Your Honor, may I project People's One on the screen, please?"

"You may, Miss Mirkovich."

The bailiff pulls the screen down and the projector goes on and there's this little fan sound, and then my words are all big on the wall above the door to the back, where the defendants go to wait in between appearing in open court. I know that room pretty good.

She's saying, "And may I approach the witness with a copy of the same?"

"You may."

She brings me a paper. She says, "Can you read for the court the lines I have marked, please?"

I read the lines. It's the ones about me seeing Dreamer and Wizard and Wizard shooting Scrappy and taking the gun away with them and then me going to Scrappy and her saying motherfucking Wizard cuz she knew he shot her.

"And can you also read the final line at the bottom of your affidavit, Mr. Clark?"

I say, "'I swear that the above information I have provided is true and complete.'"

"Are you now saying that it is no longer true and complete?"

"That's what I'm saying."

"Why has your story changed, Mr. Clark?"

"It's just that I been studying the good book since I been in treatment and I think it's important to make amends for God and myself."

She crosses her arms at me. "And what is this new truth about the night that you have discovered in the intervening time?"

She sounds crazy sarcastic when she says it, like she thinks I'm totally full of shit, and I don't even know if you're allowed to do that in court but the judge doesn't say anything so I tell her how I didn't see it at all. I just heard shots and then I ran up, and as I was running, I saw two people's backs as they were running away and then I got there and I knew it was Scrappy's house, sorry, Miss Lucero, and she was hurt bad, so I tried to help her and then everything else is the same. The tourniquet and her being in pain and all that stuff but this time I didn't remember her saying anything. She was too hurt.

I'm not sure how possible it is, but Miss Mirkovich is even redder than before. Her whole face looks on fire. "You swore when you wrote it in your own words that the affidavit, People's One, was true and complete, did you not?"

She puts a lot of stress on that part about it being *in your own words*.

"But—"

"No buts, Mr. Clark. Did you swear it?"

"Yes."

"Did you then sign your full name to the statement in further evidence of this truth?"

"Yes."

"So that is your signature on the affidavit there?" She points to my name how I wrote it, and where it is on the wall now.

I say, "Yes."

She says, "I have nothing further."

"Good morning." It's Dreamer's lawyer saying good morning to me cuz it's his turn to come at me.

"Good morning," I say back.

"You stated in your affidavit marked People's One that 'Dreamer was wearing a yellow Lakers sweatshirt and I could see it even in the night because it was so bright.' Was that also untrue?"

"Well, that Dreamer was wearing it, cuz I don't know if it was him. I just saw a back. I saw a yellow sweatshirt, though."

"You also stated that you recognized my client. Mr. Clark, have you ever met my client?"

"No."

"I see. Have you ever seen my client in Lynwood?"

"I-I'm sure I have around. It's not such a big place. You bump into people."

"Can you be absolutely certain you knew my client to look at before the night in question, and—and this part is important, Mr. Clark— could recognize him? That means you knew what he looked like by sight and could identify him readily and without hesitation."

"No. Not certain-certain."

"You have answered no to my question, and yet you positively iden- tified my client in your affidavit by a moniker that few, if any, people actually knew. Is that correct?"

"I-I did say Dreamer in that. I don't know if other people knew it."

He walks over to the jury. He looks super-confused while he's doing it. "I'm wondering if you can help me, then, sir, because I am entirely confused. How is it possible for you to identify a young man whom you have never even met, and would not know by sight?"

"I-I must have heard about him."

"I see. Did this person telling you about him also physically describe my client?"

"I'm sorry. What?"

"You said you heard about him. You said you must have. The judge can have the court reporter read it back if you need your memory refreshed."

"No. I'm okay. I remember what I said."

"I'm afraid this leads me to a dreadfully important question, Mr. Clark, and I'd like you to think about it before answering. Did someone tell you to identify my client?"

"No."

"Did anyone approach you and ask you to identify my client?"

Miss Mirkovich doesn't like that. "Objection, Your Honor. Asked and answered."

Park keeps rolling with it. "I'll restate. Did someone tell you my client's moniker and either suggest, or perhaps even demand, that you identify my client alongside Mr. Tavira?"

"No." I say it pretty quick. I feel good about how I said it.

"I have nothing further, Your Honor."

The other lawyer is up. He coughs first. He coughs for a little while and the judge asks if he needs some time to collect himself and he says no. He walks over to where there's Kleenex and things on the clerk's desk and he gets one and he blows his nose loud and throws his used one in the little trash can by the bailiff's desk and he comes back to me.

He says, "Thank you, Your Honor. My apologies."

He wants to know about how I know Wizard. I say everybody knows Wizard. I say I know the name and I know the face. "He's Lynwood-famous."

"Lynwood-famous?"

"Yes, sir. It's when everybody knows you around the way, but if you were to maybe go somewhere else, nobody would know you."

"And what makes someone Lynwood-famous?"

"I don't really know if I should say."

"It's okay, Mr. Clark. You can say."

"I guess if you're tough and your name gets around."

"Mr. Clark, if someone were to be Lynwood-famous, do you think it's possible that some individuals might be jealous about this local fame?"

"Maybe."

"Enough to make up stories about the person?"

"I don't know about that."

"In your new account of the events, Mr. Clark, you say you saw no shooting. Is that correct?"

"Yes."

"You say you came upon the scene when Lucrecia Lucero was already wounded. Correct?"

"Yes."

"When you did that, Mr. Clark, did you see a gun on the ground?"

"No."

"You did not see the weapon alleged to have done the deed?"

"No."

"Now, you spent quite a bit of time on the ground. You put a tourniquet on the victim's leg. Are you sure you didn't see a gun?"

"Yes, sir. If anybody knew it I would know it, but it was very dark too and I was busy. But I didn't see a gun."

Never was it told to me by that crew that I should've said I saw the gun, so I figured it was just good to say I didn't and then that way nobody would worry about me being connected up with Petrillo to hand it over. I'd be in the clear. And then Petrillo would not have a reason to come after me somehow too. I was just some Good Samaritan who took a couple drugs off the ground and went and used them after he saved somebody's life. A hero almost.

"If you did not see it on the ground, did you see the two people, that you say were walking away, take it with them?"

"No. Things happened fast. There was lots of blood."

"Mr. Clark, can you please explain to me why you would lie about your account?"

"Why I would lie?"

"Yes. Why would you lie on your affidavit that formed the strongest possible basis for the arrest of my client?"

"I-I lied because, I think I probably got confused. I had been using again that night before and I was at the police station a long time. I wasn't feeling good at all when I wrote that."

"And were you also lying when stated that Miss Lucero identified Mr. Tavira with the words, and I quote, 'Motherfucking Wizard'?"

"Yes. I didn't hear that."

"So, you did not see Mr. Tavira fire a handgun at Miss Lucero?"

"No."

"You did not see Mr. Tavira hand said weapon to Mr. Safulu after allegedly firing it?"

"No."

He says, "No further questions," and then he coughs really hard again.

Miss Mirkovich really does not look happy with me when she stands, but that's underneath. On the top is this look of concern for me, almost like she's worried about me, and that's the kind of tone she's taking too.

"Mr. Clark, as you are aware, this is a gang case, so I must ask you, is it possible you have been intimidated into giving testimony today that is at odds with your affidavit?"

"No."

"Mr. Clark, you are aware that you can be held in contempt of court if you are found to have made false claims?"

"No."

"You can be. What's more, you can be charged with making false statements or even perjury. Either of which is enough to violate your current parole. Are you aware of that fact?"

"I didn't know that."

"Well, now that you do know that, do you wish to stand by your earlier comments today?"

"Yes."

She arches one of those sharp eyebrows she's got at me. "Mr. Clark, did you mention earlier that you wanted to get right with God?"

"Something like that. Yes, ma'am."

"Do you think you did that today?"

"I tried."

She sighs loud enough for the jury to hear it and tells the judge she has no more for me but she does want the right to recall me, and then the judge checks with the defense lawyers and asks if they want anything more with me, and they both say no, so the judge asks if it's all right that I be excused, and all the lawyers say yes, so the judge tells me I am dismissed but I should remain in court for the next two days. I get to step down onto the carpet and go around the lawyer reporter lady that looks like an older Christie Brinkley but with glasses and past the lawyer table and out the little swinging door where I go down the middle past the audience and I make sure not to look at the little dude from the motel room cuz he sure as hell's not looking at me.

86

Oh, Mr. Clark, I knew it was possible, but I still didn't see it coming. Petrillo says Clark has done every check-in. His court card is signed every time. He hasn't failed a single drug test. He goes to meetings. The job is legitimate and his supervisor reports have been excellent. So, how in the great blue fuck did they get to him?

Obviously, he's terrified, and that's understandable and very sad. The thornier issue, however, is what to do about him perjuring himself six ways to Sunday. If I charge him, I have to consider how it will look to the judge after I pushed her to use a drug court opening to get this trial bumped up, especially when Clark already has a drug court date himself. Ayers would hate that hypocrisy, especially when Clark is doing everything else right, and it's worth taking into account that she's got another decade on the bench. I'll be in her court again. So, do I risk taking a future hit on this, or just throw my hands up and say he did his best but he was scared and he cracked? The latter is the only thing that makes political sense.

Judge Ayers looks to me. "Are we going in order, Miss Mirkovich?"

"Yes, Your Honor. The People wish to call Lucrecia Lucero."

"Very well. I understand she's in the hall. Can you get her, Deputy?"

The deputy leaves and comes back pushing a wheelchair with Lucrecia Lucero in it, her dark hair in twin braids on either side of her head, falling onto a dark sweatshirt.

When she is situated on the witness stand, I ask her if she lives at the Josephine Street address where the crime occurred. She does. We establish she was shot three times on December sixth of last year, and I submit images of Miss Lucero's injuries as the People's next-in-order.

Judge Ayers makes a note. "Those will be marked People's seventeen, eighteen, and nineteen."

I inquire as to Miss Lucero's gang affiliation. She says she isn't in one, so I bring up her criminal record: an accessory to robbery guilty plea reduced to time served after she did thirteen months, and current drug possession charges yet to be resolved. She recalls neither, says she'd have to look at paperwork. Willie squeaks in his chair behind me. It's his way of telling me it's time to change tack.

"Your Honor, the People wish to treat this witness as hostile."

"Proceed."

"Is it true your brother, also a gang member, murdered a member of Mr. Tavira's gang on June twelfth, nineteen ninety-two?"

"My big bro was arrested for that. He's fighting it now."

"Is it true that a code exists in your neighborhood calling for violent retribution to perceived wrongs?"

"No."

"Do you know Omar Tavira?"

"I recognize him."

"Is he in the courtroom now?"

"Yeah."

"Miss Lucero, has anyone made threats of violence to influence your testimony?"

"No."

"Do you know of any reason why the defendants would want to hurt you?"

"No, cuz they didn't."

There it is. The direct contradiction I've been aiming her toward. "Do you contend that neither defendant fired the weapon at you on the evening of December sixth, striking you and almost taking your life?"

"Yeah. I contend to that."

I signal to Ken to turn on the projector. "Your Honor, if I may?"

"You may, Miss Mirkovich."

Ken puts a copy of People's twelve on the screen. It has been enlarged to make reading it easier. I briefly summarize how wilas and kites are used, in order to jog the jury's memory.

"This is a so-called kite confiscated from a prisoner in San Quentin. It has your gang moniker on it." I underline the word *Scrappy* on the transparency. "Miss Lucero, why would your name be on this piece of paper?"

"Don't know. I ain't the only Scrappy there ever was."

I press on. "And what does the term *green light* mean to you, Miss Lucero?"

"Nothing."

"We heard Detective Montero testify that a green light is code for murder; use of the word is effectively a go signal to would-be killers. In the way that a red light would be to stop, a green light is to go. This evidence confirms you were marked for death, is that correct?"

"I wouldn't know."

"We have heard evidence from further kites, marked People's thirteen and fourteen, that make it explicitly clear the motive for shooting you was related to you selling drugs to a rival gang, one full of, and I quote, 'mayates.' Miss Lucero, what is the translation of *mayate* into English?"

"It's like a bug."

"What color is it?"

"Some are black."

"Is it a common Spanish derogatory slang term for African American people?"

"No."

"Detective Montero testified earlier to that effect, and Deputy Jackson, when he was on the stand, confirmed the same. Would you care to revise your answer?"

"No."

"Miss Lucero, is your child half black?"

"Objection, Your Honor. Relevance?" Nick knows I have something, and he's worried.

I face the judge. "Your Honor, if race played a significant role in the green-lighting of Miss Lucero, it's worth exploring why."

"I'll allow it, but be quick, Miss Mirkovich. Please answer the question, Miss Lucero."

"My child is blaxican, yeah."

"Would that word be a combination of *black* and *Mexican*?"

"Yeah."

"Have you found this to be a stigma in your neighborhood, for both yourself and your child?"

She shifts on the stand. "No."

"Detective Montero testified earlier that the man who wrote this kite is known to control the portion of Lynwood where Misters Tavira and Safulu reside with a complex scheme of racketeering known as 'taxation' or 'cariño.' In short, they benefit from his patronage. In other kites seized from this inmate's correspondence, he has declared war on the streets against black gangs. War on mayates."

Nick Park rises. "Objection. This is a statement, Your Honor, and one meant purely to inflame, might I add."

"You may not add it, Mr. Park, but I will sustain your objection. Are we getting to a question, Miss Mirkovich?"

"Yes, Your Honor. Miss Lucero, are you afraid for your life being here today?"

"No."

"Two gunmen approached you on the night in question. Did you recognize them?"

"No."

"Your Honor, I'd like to refer the witness to People's One."

"Go ahead."

I nod to Ken, who replaces the kite with Augie's affidavit. "Miss Lucero, can you please read the underlined portion?"

"I'm not reading that."

I lean in. "If I may, Your Honor? 'She was moaning. She was in a lot of pain. She also said "Motherfucking Wizard" because she knew he shot her too.' Do you recall saying that, Miss Lucero? 'Motherfucking Wizard'?"

"No."

"That is what is known as a dying declaration. Did you think you were dying in that moment?"

"You ever been shot, miss?"

"Your Honor, I'd ask that you please direct the witness to answer the question."

She's staring right at me, leaning forward in the box. "Miss, I said you ever been shot before?"

"That's enough, Miss Lucero." Judge Ayers gives her a look. "I know this is difficult, but you must answer the question."

Lucero never takes her eyes from mine. "I wasn't thinking anything. Wasn't talking. I was just bleeding, that's what I was fucking doing."

The judge bangs her gavel for order, and I let quiet take over the room. I watch the jury watch Lucero's face, the pain on it. I look at my notes so I can drag it out, so the jury can keep looking at her, and then at the wall where Clark's affidavit is projected, giving the jury the truest narrative breakdown they're ever likely to see.

"I have nothing further at this time, Your Honor."

Ken and I have lunch at Smeraldi's. We take a cab. There's a table already waiting for us in the back.

Ken scowls over his Tom Collins. "This whole thing is a shit-show, but it was never going to be cut-and-dried. This is rapidly becoming a case of what you can salvage. You might lose Safulu to a hung jury, but can you nail something to Tavira?"

"I don't know. Nearly every witness contradicts every other witness. There's no coherent narrative."

"It's your job to know. Seriously, now, what the fuck was that with Petrillo? He pursued the Alvarez girl romantically? Jesus."

What a nightmare. On a personal level, I'm disgusted at the thought of Phillip Petrillo habitually going after young barrio women. On a professional level, I think Park linking the previous complaint against Petrillo to a seriously unethical pattern of behavior that now includes Angela Alvarez looked like the fucking *Hindenburg* bursting into flames.

"What do you want me to say, Ken? I interviewed him. He never said anything. Why would he?"

Ken looks deep into his drink. "And this girl who saw them at Disneyland, she was buried on page two. We should've asked about her."

"I *did* ask about Gloriana Nuñez. She was visiting a sick relative. Hadn't given a statement yet. That was Park's line a week ago and the judge let it go, so this is what we get."

"It stinks."

"It does, indeed. But is it now worth pursuing Petrillo for witness tampering on Alvarez? Go for a mistrial?"

He sighs. "It's your first case as AHD, Kris. Do you want to gamble that Garcetti will commit resources to another trial? Somehow walking out of this with a conviction nailed on Tavira, despite this hellacious shit-show, might still earn you some credit upstairs."

Ken's an old drunk, but my gut says he's right.

"We knew they were going to make Petrillo look like he had been inappropriate on the job, but we weren't worried about it then, and I'm not now. Nobody believes junkies and convicts when they make those complaints against custody and parole, and the jury won't either. The bigger issue is Park taking the Alvarez information and making the leap of logic to Petrillo planting the gun in order to remove any impediments to him dating the girl. It doesn't matter if that was stricken. He still got the question in about no one being able to see him."

Ken's drink is down to just ice. "And now the jury's heard it. You can't take that out of their brains."

"Nope."

"During first and second closing we'll have to nail in the fact *again* that Petrillo has never been formally reprimanded."

"Are you still taking first and I'm doing second?"

"Yep." Ken swirls the ice. "We'll also have to further nail in his commendation for his work with that capture task force. When was that, eighty-nine?"

It's only occurring to me now that Ken says the word *nail* a lot.

"It was eighty-eight."

"Right. Well, the jury is going to need to believe something. That's why, Petrillo aside, you nail the fact that we've got the most reliable witnesses. Shit. Even Clark and Lucero are reliably *not* telling the truth. Maybe there's more we can spin from that. Yes, they're lying, but why? What do they have to gain?"

"Their lives?" I sip my iced tea. "But it's not what they actually have to gain; it's what will the jury find believable?"

87

Throughout the lunch break, I find myself having to guard against overconfidence. Petrillo blew up in fairly spectacular fashion, Clark fell to pieces, and now Luccro—the actual victim—has given Kristina nothing and refused to identify anyone, though she obviously knows who did it. I am beginning to think a hung jury is the worst-case scenario, and an acquittal for my client is looking likely. I'm mulling this over at the canteen on Floor 5 when a young man I've never seen before walks up to me as I am about to take a bite of sandwich. He's well dressed in a polo shirt, jeans, and leather shoes. He's Hispanic, but he doesn't look like a gang member.

"From your office," he says, and hands me a folded note before exiting.

"Thanks." I keep my voice calm. This is not standard procedure.

There's a sheriff beside me on a stool. He's working on a form while nursing a cup of coffee. He doesn't even look up when I walk past him and head to the restroom.

I open it in a stall. The note is not signed, but it is clearly from Matta. It says: *Ask LL what happened on 12/6. She'll say.*

LL is Lucrecia Lucero. It's clear I'm being directed to ask her to describe the incident on the night in question. This is not something she would do for the prosecution, and if she did it for me, it could be a coup. The problem, however, is twofold: (1) I have no idea what Miss Lucero will say, and (2) this is clear, physical evidence of witness tampering.

For the briefest of moments, I entertain turning it in to the judge. It is potentially grounds for a mistrial and new charges, but I will be asked why the note has come to me. Did I have prior contact with Matta, who is clearly running point for Tavira's gang on this? If they choose to investigate, his name will be in my calendar from our meeting last month. The judge will want to know why I met with the potential criminal associate who was given the Augustine Clark information by Mr. Safulu—a matter she thought closed after the recusal of Tavira's previous attorney—and she will need to know what was discussed in that meeting. There will be an investigation. I might be censured if I don't go along with it. Any way you slice it, it will be very messy.

To avoid all that unpleasantness, I drop the note in the toilet and flush. I double-check the bowl to make sure it is gone, and then I flush it again.

When Lucrecia Lucero is back on the stand, I figure I can win points here simply by not badgering the recent victim of three gunshots the way Kristina did. Besides, it's obvious Scrappy is a star. She has charisma and natural talent for turning a phrase. When she's not coiled too tight, when she lets herself go a little, no one in the whole courtroom can look away—not even the bailiffs, and that's how you know what she's doing is working. Bailiffs see everything and are impressed by nothing, but they're paying attention to her, even when she's quiet.

"Good afternoon, Miss Lucero."

"Good afternoon."

"You indicated you knew Mr. Tavira in your previous testimony, but do you know Jacob Safulu?"

"No."

"Have you ever seen him before?"

"No."

"Miss Lucero, can you explain in your own words what happened to you that night?"

Kristina is roughly ten feet from me, sitting down at the prosecution table, but I swear she tenses up.

"I don't remember everything. I was pretty high."

"What do you remember?"

"Somebody banging on my house and waking me up."

"Banging on the front door, you mean?"

"Yeah. I went to the door and looked through and saw a man out there, and I told him to leave."

"Who was it?"

"It was Augie."

"For the record, the witness has indicated Augustine Clark. What did Mr. Clark want?"

"He wanted drugs."

"Why was he at your door for this particular purpose?"

"My brother sold sometimes."

"And what happened next?"

"I told Augie to go away, but he wouldn't. He damn near tore the gutter off my mom's house trying to get me out there."

"And did you go?"

"Yes."

"To do what?"

"To whoop his ass for messing with my mom's house."

Jurors Ramos and Bundridge cover their mouths to keep from smiling when Ms. Lucero says that, and she's on a roll. "That boy can't fight. I mean, you must've seen him up here, how skinny he is."

The male jurors find this funny. The females—particularly Hall—not so much.

I need to reframe this. "After you defended your property, what happened?"

"He left. I watched him walk that skinny ass down the block."

"At that point, did you return to your home?"

"I tried to. But somebody yelled out my name, I turned, and the shots came."

"The first bullet struck you?"

"Man, they all struck me. You seen the photos. I hit the ground like somebody threw me there."

The jury hangs on her every word.

"Do you recall anything else?"

"When it was done with, no more flashes and booms, I felt something hard hit my foot. It was heavy and hot. Really hot."

Wow. I try not to lose it there. The gun was hot? What a detail! "I'm sorry, Miss Lucero. Are you saying the weapon was *dropped*, that it hit your foot, and that it was hot from being fired?"

"Must've been. I wasn't wearing shoes, so I felt it."

"Your Honor, if I may show the People's image of the witness's leg wound?"

"You may, Mr. Park. That would be People's nineteen."

I put it up on the screen. I draw everyone's attention to the darkening mark on her foot, the beginning of a deep bruise.

"What caused that discoloration, Miss Lucero?"

"A gun. Must've been. They're heavy, you know?"

"Do you know what happened to the gun after that?"

"I don't know. Somebody took it and moved it?"

"Objection," Kristina says. "Speculation."

"Sustained."

"Just one more thing, Miss Lucero. Are you afraid of the defendants?"

"No."

"Do you fear violence from them?"

"Absolutely not."

She looks me square in the eye when she says it, and I believe her. If she actually does fear violence, she is the best actress in the world.

The redirect goes more easily for Lucrecia Lucero than I anticipate. Ken Gibson only sees fit to impeach her ability to tell whether or not it was a gun that struck her foot. In doing so, he plants a few more seeds for the People's closings; they are definitely going to lean hard on explaining why witnesses have changed their stories. This is fine. I'm going to counter by keeping Petrillo's predatory antics squarely in my sights.

After Miss Lucero steps down, Judge Ayers does some housekeeping. One of the jurors has a business trip tomorrow morning that he cannot shake, so the judge excuses him in order to switch in an alternate, chosen randomly. So, Juror #3, my Asian compatriot, leaves, and is replaced by Alternate #3, the white female dental tech from the suburbs. Kristina can't contain her joy about that one. I had a two-in-three chance of getting a Hispanic male or a black woman, but instead I got the prosecution's wet dream: white, female, decent income. It's a bad break.

When we finally adjourn, I tell Bertelsmann to see a doctor, and I visit Safulu in the holding room. I bring a white plastic grocery bag full of clothes. Generally, the bailiff would bring it, but I offer to take it today since I need to see him anyway. Wizard is already farther back, beyond the green sally port, so Safulu sits alone.

"More clothes," I say, and hand them over.

"From Angela?"

I nod.

He says, "What's that about?"

"She cares?"

"I guess."

"The judge's orders are being followed concerning showers, yes?"

"We get them in the evenings now."

"How do you feel today went?"

He shrugs. "I don't know. I'm not a lawyer."

"Then take my word for it. It went well. How well, I don't know yet, but if Mirkovich comes in with a plea offer soon, we need to consider it."

He says, "Okay," but his mind is elsewhere, so I leave him, and feel slightly unfulfilled at not being able to celebrate—even a little—a very good day for his defense.

88

The way it goes down in here is, if you got a court order to take a shower after you come back late from court, they let you. If you don't, you can't. That's just not how it goes. It's me and it's Wizard. That's it. And since it's only two of us, we get taken through to 900 block, Discipline. I get all stressed about it at first and think how we're in trouble, but then I find out they got showers in there and it's late so nobody's in there. A little room shaped like a T. You walk in, and there's one to the left and one to the right. The showers face away from each other and there's little metal benches.

Really, there's no order for Wizard to take one but he just got here and I think whoever runs the deputies knows our cases are tied up together and he just doesn't want to make Judge Ayers mad, cuz if he don't let Wizard take showers, he already knows he'll be hearing about it.

"Man, how can I even be in here one day and I already got whatever athlete's foot they got in Wayside? I'm wearing sandals and everything!"

Wizard's pitching his voice over his shoulder at me. I'm hearing it around the hot water. It's not really a hiss cuz the water pressure's weak here. Weak at Central Jail too. I think they do it on purpose. Make you work harder to get clean. Like, maybe it's a psychological thing, or maybe they're just trying to save money. I don't know.

"Hey, Deputy," Wizard says, louder this time.

It's an older dude. White. Shaved head. He's doing paperwork on the little metal bench while we do our thing. "Yes, inmate?"

"What's the craziest shit you ever seen inside?"

He looks up from his papers to stare at Wizard, and then he puts his head back down.

But Wizard keeps going, and if anything, he's feeling puffed up cuz he didn't get corrected for using foul language. "Craziest thing I ever saw was this one time, and it wasn't here, but down in Central Jail, there were three dudes doing some fucking Ringling Brothers shit and got on each other's shoulders to pull something out of the ceiling, and I don't know what it was, some metal or what that they wanted to make into contraband, but they were just up there digging in the ceiling. Three little wet dudes, all naked, and I guess maybe the top one gets too greedy or goes too long, cuz they get seen!"

I look back at the deputy and he's paying attention now. He's not working on his papers anymore.

"And the deputy shouts at them like, 'What the fuck are you doing, inmates? Getting metal to make a shank?' And the bottom one, man! The bottom one? I think he gets scared or something and he slips! Because he's in the showers and a bunch of them are still going and spitting water everywhere. And when that bottom part of the totem pole goes, man, it all goes. The top dude comes tumbling right the fuck down, maybe fifteen feet, and he hits the floor so fucking hard! It's loud like a belly flop. You know that sound that just makes you double over sort of? Like in a way that you can almost feel it too? Yeah. *That* sound. And when the top fool goes splat like that, it just sends water everywhere. Yeah, man. Shit. The bottom one was fine, just cracked his head on the floor a little. The middle fool twisted his ankle up bad but he got a punctured lung from when the top fool fell with half his body on him. And the top one was in medical for like a month after that. Broken arm. Broken jaw. I remember them all flopping around on the ground super-messed-up, with the water still going, and some blood gushing out too and going in the drains. Shit. I guess that just goes to show you, if you got to fall, fall from low. Don't fall from high. That shit will fuck you up!"

Wizard laughs and the deputy laughs too. The laughs echo together, bouncing off walls.

When I don't laugh too, Wizard pops in with, "Hey, Dreamer, I tell this story to cheer your ass up, man. You look down all day every day, and now you're still down? Why? Today went good for you."

I say, "You think so?"

"Yeah, homeboy. I do."

He wants me to explain why I look down but he's gonna leave it for me to pick up. I feel some rage in me then. Getting warm, but I swallow it. Cuz I don't have the right words to even say how I'm feeling around him now and I maybe never will. He's the one with the words. I'm just the one that has to be around him cuz we're tied together on this, and I'm fucking innocent as fuck, and he's never done anything to make sure I get out of this, and how is it that he don't get that? Is he just fucking with me? It's a game or something to him?

"Two minutes," the deputy says.

"Aww, man," Wizard says. "C'mon, sir! My story didn't even buy us extra?"

"Nope."

"That's rough, man. You got this badass story to tell your buddies now and we didn't even get an extra few minutes off it."

I'm finishing with my soap. Going fast so my water don't time out.

I'm never explaining shit to Wizard about me anymore. Better to just be quiet and not get into it. I mean, if he knew me, if he was my homie for real, he'd know what was up. He wouldn't need to ask. And he's been locked up before, so he should know that what's dragging on me isn't just him and his behavior, but that all this custody shit is starting to seem normal to me. Being locked up, it's starting to sink in. It's changing me on the inside. And if I don't get certain things, like not being able to read on a certain day or whatever, not being able to escape with my mind, my chest just gets heavy. My shoulders too. I can't breathe as good. It's tight. And I feel like I'm trapped. And I'm not really explaining it good, cuz I *am* trapped. That shit's obvious. That's what the fuck jail is.

And I been trapped long enough that I got the feeling inside me now. I carry it around. Like, all the time. And it's one thing to feel trapped in a jail. With some bars. With some cuffs. With some deputies following you. Hall and central command guard areas watching you. With bunk checks. With deputies walking two up, two down. With lights up and lights out. Now I'm finding that I feel that same way even when I'm in court tho. When I'm wearing nice clothes. When I'm not cuffed anymore, and I should feel more like a normal person up in that courtroom, I don't. It's not feeling like moments of freedom, moments of being a fucking person again. I'm starting to feel the same way there that I do on the bus, that I do in here. It's all just dragging me down . . . Cuz the system's inside me now. And it's like some concrete that hardens the longer it sits. And it's becoming this giant weight now, one that's so heavy I just want to be on my bunk all day. I don't wanna get up and do homeboy workouts no more. I just wanna sleep and not wake up. Just dream forever, you know?

What's crazy is, right then it's like Wizard can hear me thinking, cuz he says, "You're not about the dreaming shit again, are you?"

"Nah," I say.

But yeah. Cuz he got me. He saw thru to me without even looking at me. And I ain't about to tell him he did. Cuz I ain't good with that. Not when we're still not cool.

I was just Jacob before in the neighborhood, and since nobody knew no Jacobs, that was fine, but when my moms up and left, I went down hard. And Wizard knew what was up but he'd never say it. He knew how sad I was. He knew why I basically stopped showing up to school. He knew I flat-out slept all day. And whenever he came by the old apartment before I got kicked out for failure to pay, he'd ask me what I'd been busy dreaming about. I must have some big dreams, being able to sleep like that, he would say that every day. That's how he named me Dreamer. Fuck. To remind me I needed to be doing more than sleeping, that's why he named me that. And to try to keep me from falling back to that, to try to make it a good thing. After, he took me under his wing a bit and asked the Mattas to take me, and he had me over to his spot a lot too, cuz he knew all about what it was to be missing a mom. He could see it in me cuz he lived it too. And Angela would cook and I'd get to know her better every dinner. Every time I was over there watching movies and smoking out. And it would just be good like that. The three of us.

Over my shoulder I say, "This Angela thing is fucking with me."

And it's true, but it's not true. I mean, it's not everything. But it's something.

"It was hearing about her going on that date with Petrillo, huh? That shit's messed up."

I don't need to say anything to that. Wizard said it all. And the thing about Angela is, she ain't mine anymore. I don't get to say what she can do. Do I like her doing that? Hell, no. But it's just not for me to say. And that's life. I went past that already. I don't wanna look back, but I had to right there. It was right in front of me in court.

The water shuts off. We get dry and into our blues. We get walked together cuz we're dormed up together like they actually want us to make something go down with Tim Muhammad so they can throw us away for good. Maybe it's cuz Wizard behaved himself and didn't have any incidents at CJ, and also maybe cuz everywhere is full, the 700s, the 800s, but that's just guessing. And I feel guilty about it feeling good walking thru the door to 617 with him. You feel the nervousness in the air. It's like it's heavy before a rain. And even from half-asleep dudes he's getting nods. And already it's been better with him here, cuz Nada had to fall back a little, but he's still in charge cuz his cousin has the keys over in Calipatria.

Wizard's three bunks over from me, in the middle-middle, 8B. And I look up to the second floor as we're coming in, at some Bloods, and I feel my guts clench up and I get ready to throw if I have to. One of them has his eyes open and he's staring some hate at me. Hate and promises. Forty dudes went to medical from that throw-down in the mess the last time. More than half black. They gonna come back on us. I know that. Wizard knows that. Nada knows that. Any opportunity, they're gonna be all over that shit. And I don't know what I'm going to have to do when that time comes, but I know the monster in me will have to fucking do it.

89

It was Mr. Park that first told me what Phil, I mean, Agent Petrillo, did. That he targeted women he had power over somehow. He told me about the complaint from Renee Sifuentes, how she was older than me and his parolee. He showed me a picture, though, and it was mad creepy how much we look alike. Seeing that changed *everything*. It bruised me up inside, felt like. It meant I wasn't special, just part of a pattern. I was so fucking mad at myself after hearing it, for getting tricked like that. Cuz it felt so wrong from the start but I ignored it! I had all these buts in my head. And I still kept giving him benefits of the doubt.

And then anger came. Not just at myself, but at him. I felt invaded when I remembered how many times he'd been up in my room searching it. That he prolly knew so much about me just from that, before we even started talking. And when Mr. Park told me that Agent Petrillo might have planted that gun just to get Jacob and Omar out the house so he could be alone with me, I dropped my coffee cup and everything spilled.

I been going to a therapist. And she said what I had then was a panic episode. All I knew at the time was I felt sick, like, as deep as you can. In my soul. It made me feel a kind of guilt that I couldn't get away from. That it was my fault Jacob was where he was and not free. I mean, I knew it wasn't, but it felt like it. Still does. And it might always, if he doesn't get free.

I'm pacing nervous in the hallway outside the courtroom, waiting to be called in by the bailiff. The only good thing about today is the judge wouldn't allow Agent Petrillo being present for my testimony. Mrs. Matta and Jeo pass me going in. Jeo won't look at me. But Mrs. Matta has bags under her eyes when she tells me in Spanish how she didn't sleep all night. She been praying to Saint Leonard. Saint of prisoners. Not praying for miracles, she says, but for truth.

The jury passes me going in too, and I wait a couple minutes before the deputy comes out and takes me up to the stand, but I don't understand why it's called that because I just sit down in a little wooden chair there, in the box next to the judge's desk. The clerk swears me in, and I tell him that I promise to tell the truth. And I kind of make the mistake then of looking out to where Mrs. Matta's smiling at me like how my aunt used to. And Jellybean's nodding at me. And I know I shouldn't, but I look to Jacob then too. I've been looking at the back of his head so much, and the side, that it's so strange seeing him from the front like this. He looks older. More muscular. Like he's carrying a weight inside him. And I get sad all over again, so I look down. I focus on my hands. On my aunt's ring on my right ring finger, where she used to wear it too, and I promise her in heaven right then that I will make her proud.

Mr. Park said it'd start easy enough. Slow. Measured. I'm a defense witness, so Mr. Park gets to ask me questions first. He and Mr. Bertelsmann already decided that Mr. B. won't ask me any questions. There's nothing really I can do to help Jellybean as a character witness, he said, so the plan is to focus on helping Jacob and confirming Agent Petrillo's being alone at the residence and his behavior.

"Good morning, Miss Alvarez," Mr. Park says to me.

"Good morning, sir."

We do a bunch of simple yes/no questions after that. Am I attending nursing school? Yes. Do I live at this address? Yes. Was I there on December seventh when the weapon was discovered? Yes. Was Agent Phillip Petrillo also present? Yes. Was Deputy Jackson present? Yes. Then we get into it.

"How long would you estimate that Agent Petrillo was searching prior to the gun being found?"

"I would say about seventeen minutes."

"And how would you know that?"

"I looked at the clock when he got there. It was nine-oh-one."

"Why would you look at the clock when he arrived?"

"Because Omar always said it was a good idea to keep track of what time official people show up and when they leave. I got in the habit."

"So how would you know how much time elapsed?"

"When Deputy Jackson brought me into the bedroom I saw my digital clock on the dresser said nine eighteen."

"And was Agent Petrillo alone the entire time?"

"Not when he was in the kitchen or living room, but after that, yes."

"Can you estimate how long Agent Petrillo was alone?"

"About six or seven minutes."

"I see. Miss Alvarez, would you say you're very good with time?"

"Yes."

We cover the timing of the night when Scrappy got shot. I have to say Jacob wasn't a Lakers fan, never owned a yellow sweatshirt. I go into detail about what I said to Jacob and why I said it, and it feels *awful* putting that out in court, on record, to have witnesses to how I dumped him. But I stick to my timing. I get it exactly right. Just like in my interview with Detective Montero, the same one Mr. Park puts up on the screen.

He asks, "Do you recognize this? Is this the statement you gave?"

I have to take a moment to read through before I can say, "Yes."

"Can you please read the highlighted portion?"

I read the part where he tells me Lucrecia Lucero was shot at 9:30 p.m., and I say that it couldn't have been Jacob cuz he was with me. He asks me if I'm certain, and I tell him 100 percent. He switches it up after that.

"Miss Alvarez, when did Agent Petrillo approach you to ask you for a date?"

"It wasn't that simple."

I break it down then. I tell the court how it started with him knocking on my door, and then me being bored and trying to mess with him by asking him how old he is, only to find him different and kind of interesting. I push through my shame that Omar and Jacob have to hear it like this. But the truth has to be out. I admit I gave Phil my number. I admit to going to the Potholder with him. I admit to going to Disneyland with him on the twenty-third of December. I admit to kissing him back when he kissed me in Sleeping Beauty's castle, and the look on Jacob's face when I say *that* is just heartbreaking.

When it's Miss Mirkovich's turn, I sit up a little straighter. Mr. Park told me to be as polite as I possibly could. He said that politeness is like a superpower you can use against white people because they think it's so important. They don't see it coming, and they don't always know what to do about it when it's used on them, especially in court.

"Miss Alvarez, good morning."

"Good morning, ma'am."

She makes a little wince face before saying, "You gave Agent Petrillo your unlisted phone number at Tom's Burgers on December tenth. Is that correct?"

"I don't know the exact date, but I think so, ma'am."

"Is it safe to say you pursued him for a relationship?"

"I wouldn't say I pursued him, ma'am, but I did encourage him."

"And had you met Agent Petrillo before the day the weapon was found on your premises?"

"Yes, ma'am."

"When was that?"

"When he came by to check on Omar and make sure he was doing his parole right."

"Did he search the house on those occasions?"

"Yes, ma'am."

"And did you interact on those occasions?"

"Only for him to confirm who I was in the beginning, and that I was the legal house owner since my aunt passed away."

"So you had no previous conversations?"

"No, ma'am."

"You asserted that things changed the day Agent Petrillo came to your door on December eighth, correct?"

"Yes, ma'am."

"Why did you pursue a personal line of questioning?"

"Objection," Mr. Park says. "Asked and answered."

Miss Mirkovich huffs right by me. "I'll restate. After you pursued a personal line of questioning were Agent Petrillo's actions toward you different?"

"Yes, ma'am."

"Do you think it possible that you encouraging him changed his behavior?"

"It's possible, ma'am."

"And on December tenth, when you gave him your unlisted phone number, he did not ask for it first, correct?"

"Yes, ma'am."

"You did it of your own free will?"

"Yes, ma'am."

"Nothing further."

90

Kristina failed to offer my client a plea deal. She didn't even ask to talk after Angela's testimony went down favorably. I believe she already knew there was no point in offering, because I would have recommended Jacob's rejection of any offer on principle. She would've been right. She never should have charged my client in the first place. There was never enough evidence, and I relish the opportunity to tell the jury that one last time.

As Mr. Gibson gave his closing before lunch, the judge asks me if I'm ready to begin mine.

"Yes, Your Honor," I say, "thank you."

I step forward and take my position to the right of the podium.

"For the sake of argument, let's consider some common pieces of physical evidence you *might have seen* in this case—if indeed they existed. Perhaps a shoe print found in the front yard outside Miss Lucero's home on Josephine Street?"

I look to Juror #1.

"We did not have that, Mr. Bundridge."

He looks shocked that I remembered his name from selection, and that is excellent, because this is my knockout blow. I remember all their names. I will use every last one. It's an old trick from my prosecuting days.

"And not only are we short shoe prints, but we are short actual shoes to match those nonexistent prints.

"Why, Miss Vincent? Because *the evidence does not exist*.

"No physical evidence of that type exists against my client.

"His fingerprints were not on the weapon that was found, Mrs. Francis-Stuckey. None. Zero.

"No fingerprints, despite the fact that it was found inside the clothes dresser that Mr. Safulu and Miss Alvarez shared.

"Now, if a criminal was sophisticated enough to either wear gloves or clean, or wipe, fingerprints from the weapon, why would that person then keep it?

"Lucrecia Lucero, the victim herself, testified in open court that the handgun was dropped at the scene of the crime.

"She said it *landed on her*."

Bertelsmann puts up the photo of her leg on the projector. I point to the mark on People's Exhibit nineteen.

"That bruise, she claims, comes from that very action.

"Miss Coretti, we may not know how that gun arrived at the house on Virginia Street. I certainly have heard no reasonable explanation; nothing that fits with the fact that the victim herself says it was dropped.

"It simply does not make sense, Miss Sharp.

"Unless, of course, you consider one important fact, ladies and gentlemen: Mr. Tavira and Mr. Clark shared a parole agent, Phillip Petrillo, and that may very well—"

"Mr. Park," the judge cuts in, "must I remind you to stick only to the facts of the case?"

"Your Honor, I am sticking purely to the facts in evidence in this case," I say.

She gives me a look. "Proceed carefully."

"Thank you, Your Honor. The morning of December seventh was the very first day that Agent Petrillo took over Mr. Clark's case from his colleague.

"The victim says the gun was dropped on her foot, and yet the witness who bandaged her leg, Mr. Clark, says it was not on the ground.

"You've heard the facts of the prosecution's timeline, ladies and gentlemen.

"We know Petrillo took Clark to be interviewed by Detective Montero at Firestone Park Sheriff's Station. He then immediately took Deputy Jackson with him to the Virginia Avenue address and what do you know, Mr. Barsamian? He finds a gun.

"This allows for a felony complaint for the arrest of Misters Tavira and Safulu to be filed, but more importantly what does that create on Virginia Street?

"It creates an empty house for Agent Petrillo to pursue Angela Alvarez. We heard Miss Nuñez testify to their hand-holding at Disneyland.

"It is the only possible explanation that sounds plausible to me, Miss Leitner.

"Every other story we have heard in court about what happened on Josephine Street on December sixth might as well be a golf course. They all have eighteen holes."

That gets a small chuckle, even a few smiles.

"And yet, here is what we do know: apart from this handgun, discovered under suspicious circumstances by a less-than-admirable parole agent, there is *no physical evidence whatsoever* tying my client to this crime, Mrs. Ramos. None."

I sweep my eyes over the jury.

"So, what *do* they have?

"Do they have audiotapes, or videotapes, or handwritten notes sent back and forth between Misters Safulu and Tavira confirming this alleged conspiracy?

"*They do not.* Therefore, you must conclude that it is not a conspiracy. The facts tell you as much.

"Was my client there that night? No, he was not, Mr. Maldonado.

"Angela Alvarez got up on that stand and said so, and I, for one, believe her wholeheartedly.

"Because what's the alternative, Mr. Ghazali?

"Are you to believe the word of a parole agent who has received, by his own admission, *fifteen complaints* against him for his behavior while on duty?

"Fifteen, ladies and gentlemen. Two, maybe. Three, why not? But fifteen? That's a *pattern*.

"Agent Petrillo is a man with an allegation against him by a young woman in his charge, a man who pursued Miss Alvarez, the family member of someone he'd just sent to jail.

"Those are facts. Both of them.

"Or are you also to believe the word of a convicted felon, Mr. Clark, a man who, by his own admission, is a heavy user of illegal narcotics—and not just any narcotic, but heroin, the most addictive, the most dangerous, of all Schedule One substances? The prosecution wants you to believe *him*, Mrs. Campbell?

"They want you to believe Mr. Clark's version of the events that place my client there, when he said under oath that *he did not know Mr. Safulu to look at?"*

I make a face, one that communicates very clearly to the jury that that's the craziest thing I've ever heard in my life.

"They want you to believe him, over a nursing student? An honor student in high school, a decorated athlete, never even accused of a crime in her entire life despite living in a gang neighborhood and sharing her home with an allegedly active gang member?

"Does that make any earthly sense to you, ladies and gentlemen?

"It doesn't to me, and I can tell you right now that in my seven years of practicing criminal law, Angela Alvarez is one of the bravest people I've ever seen on that stand.

"She told a painful truth that made her look less than good.

"She did so in front of her ex-boyfriend, knowing it would hurt him all over again, but she did it because it was the truth.

"*It was the truth.* You know it and I know it.

"Jacob Safulu was not on Josephine Street that night. He was on Virginia Avenue, nearly two miles away—a fact confirmed by Miss Alvarez's statement and her testimony before you.

"Ladies and gentlemen, you've heard it time and again throughout this case, the judge has said it, and I've said it. The prosecution must prove their case beyond a reasonable doubt.

"What that means, Mrs. Wu, is that you must have a high degree of certainty regarding where my client was that night, and given the evidence provided, that simply is not possible.

"The prosecution failed to prove their case against my client, and that is why you must find Jacob Safulu not guilty of all charges.

"Not guilty of conspiracy to commit murder.

"Not guilty of attempted murder.

"Not guilty of assault with a deadly weapon.

"Not guilty of mayhem.

"You must give credence to your very reasonable doubts when you weigh the very slim facts of this case against the law.

"Then, and only then, must you set an innocent man free."

Jacob Safulu, a.k.a. Dreamer

91

I open my eyes to shaking. My whole bunk's skidding over the floor.

I'm thinking it must be Slow Poke doing it.

It's not.

I see Poke's hand above me, grabbing the side of the bed frame to keep steady. The top, top bunk is empty.

That right then is when I know this can only be one thing.

A fucking earthquake.

And I'm saying to myself, *Just ride it out.*

I'm saying to myself, *This isn't the first one you ever felt.*

It doesn't stop tho. Six seconds. Seven.

It gets stronger. I stop counting when the floor rolls.

It just does this ocean action. Up and down and sideways.

And that's fucking scary as shit.

Other people must be feeling that too, cuz voices in the dorm shoot up.

"Yo, this here's a quake!" and "It's the Big One, fuckers!" and just straight-up screaming.

I'm gripping hard on the metal of the bunk bed rail by my head.

I say, "You good, Poke?"

Poke jumps down to the floor, hits it with a smack. And he groans.

I say, "Poke, you good?"

"I fucked my ankle up good," he says. "Broke it, maybe."

It's not stopping, I'm thinking.

It keeps going, getting stronger.

Very long. Very rolling.

Not like any quake I ever felt before.

And there's just this sound to it. A grind beneath us. *Kriiiiik.*

Like the earth's grinding on its teeth.

And there's other sounds around us too.

Beds creak and pull.

Lights in their cages rattle.

Shower spouts rat-a-tat their pipes in the walls.

More motherfuckers fall out of bed and splat on the floor.

And screaming.

It's two different types tho . . .

One for the dudes that hurt themselves or are freaking out.

And one for the dudes trying to freak people out.

And the ground's still moving. And I'm wondering if it ever will stop. That's how this all turns.

That's when it's sinking in that this is about to be some shit.

Bigger than the riot a week ago.

It's about to be chaos. Some fucking blood getting spilled.

Cuz it's all about opportunity in here.

You get a moment?

You take it.

And this shit is gonna give us lots of moments.

I don't even know how long this shaking's been going.

One minute? Two? No way to tell.

It does one big bump under us then tho.

And Poke goes down again.

"Fuck, man," he says.

And that's when it stops.

And that's when I know if we don't move, we'll get caught up in the mix.

I say to Poke, "Put your fucking shoes on. Now."

I'm slipping mines on.

And he gets one on. I got to help him with the other.

The siren finally goes then.

Over it, I shout, "Poke, you good to walk?"

"I'm good," he says.

He ain't tho. He's fucking cripping next to me. So I just pull his ass along.

I keep low and move toward Wizard's bunk.

My adrenaline's up. It makes me want to run. Makes me need to.

And right now I'm actually grateful for Nada's crazy-ass training.

Cuz I'm moving Poke like he's a feather.

I got to get to Wizard. That's my only thought.

Shit comes at me in little catches from the corners of my eyes as I move.

A dude staring at his ripped-up hand. A bloody pinkie damn near hanging off.

A dude dropping elbows to his bunkie's head.

A dude up to his elbow in the toilet under the stairs.

A dude looting some motherfucker's food that he's got stashed under his bottom bunk.

A dude wearing his blanket like a cape, standing up on his top bunk like he's a surfer or some shit.

And when I finally get to where Wizard's bunk should be . . .

He ain't there.

His pillow's just lying there without a case to it.

Fuck!

I look left. Right.

On the stairs, some poor Uso fucker's getting a shank in him from a big-ass Wood.

And I blink.

And it's the dude that gave me that book. That language book.

And I can't stop myself then.

I leave Poke on Wizard's bunk.

And I shoot up them stairs, straight at that Wood.

I kick that Nazi piece of shit so hard in the knee I swear I break it.

He goes down awkward. Mouth wide open as he slips down the stairs.

I follow him down.

And kick as I go by to grab a sheet off the nearest bottom bunk.

And I use that shit to wrap the Uso up tight around his waist as two other Usos run up.

They take him from me, move him down the stairs to the wall by the pay phones.

They're trying to stay out of this shit. And I don't even blame them.

The stabbed one tho, before he goes, he gives me this look that says a ton of shit.

Mostly it says, *Thank you.*

That's the biggest. *Thank you.*

I'm going tho. No time for anything else.

I run my ass back to Poke. He's still there by Wizard's bed. No Wizard tho.

Emergency lights come on then. Finally.

Little circles of yellow high on the walls.

We decide to break out.

And we don't make twenty feet before we run into a little crew of Raza getting led by Wizard.

With a white bandito mask on his face.

Made with a pillowcase.

He gives me one of them half hugs, cuz I'm still carrying Poke.

Fuck, I'm thinking. *It's good to see this fool!*

Sting grenades come thru the bars then. Thrown by deputies.

And they pop.

Something burns in my side like fireworks exploding.

Don't stop me tho.

I roll with the others. We grab the triple-decker bunks. We run them toward the bars so the deputies can't come in.

We take them right up to the bars to block the entrance. And the others hold them there.

They push the mattresses up flat to them so more grenades can't come in.

That's when I turn and Wizard's there with a pillowcase for me.

He's wrapping it around my head for me. It's too tight.

It's cutting into my nose.

Can't do shit about it tho.

Wizard shouts, "Where the fuck is some shanks?"

I nod for him to follow me. We got eight with us now.

A good little crew nobody wants to fuck with.

I show Wizard we got shanks hidden down the shower drain, hanging from the grating by one of them clear plastic bag ropes that's twined together by some paisa weavers.

They're good too. If it's not some razor-blade-on-a-melted-toothbrush shit, it's a chunk of a saw blade that a worker threw out. And a trustee snagged when emptying trash.

Wizard gets them up, keeps one. And gives one to a sitting Poke.

His ankle's done. He's going nowhere. This is to defend himself.

I put my hand out.

Wizard's look back to me is solid.

Not to be fucked with.

He shouts into my ear, "I don't want you with no fucking blade!"

And I hear it. I hear it good.

And as it's messing with me,

like, *Is this him finally giving a fuck about me?*

Like, *Is this him trying to protect me or what?*

The ground goes again.

Sidewise.

An aftershock.

And everybody grabs something.

Floor. Bed frame. Each other. Whatever.

We ride that shit out.

When it's done, Nada's right next to us.

Like he up and appeared out of the air.

He's got six more cholos with him. Some bad fuckers too. Some ask-no-questions fuckers.

So we're thirteen now without Poke.

And I'm seeing how Wizard and Nada look at each other,

And I know . . .

We're going hunting.

92

I know where we're going. Up them stairs. At some mayates.

Bloods. Crips. Don't matter.

If it's black, it's getting fucked up.

I feel it in my stomach. I feel the cold wiggling of it inside me.

Getting closer to the back corner, the stinging in my side's getting worse.

More grenades come thru the tops of the bars.

Like the motherfuckers throwing them are on ladders.

The air's going gray with the smoke from it.

They shut our air off.

Gas comes next.

And the air goes white with it.

Deputies are happy to just do that right now. And nothing else.

They ain't coming in.

Shit, I wouldn't either.

They'd rather we tore each other up first. Got tired. Then they clean up.

My eyes go blurry. Tears come.

At least we got pillowcases over our mouths.

At least we got something between our lungs and that sting.

We take it.

We go right thru it toward the back right corner.

We go up the stairs. Wet stairs. And I'm thinking, *Why the hell is this wet?*

We watch each other's backs.

Nada cleans some dude out halfway up.

Just kicks him in the stomach. And dude bends forward. Then Nada swings for the fences with this hook that sends him over the rail. For a smaller dude, he's got power.

We get to the top floor. It's even wetter.

Makes moving slow. Trying not to slip.

In the back, back corner is where we find them. By the 20s bunks.

They got that animal look to them.

Wide eyes. Puffed up. Backs protected. Ready to fucking die.

I see the shotcaller standing by one of the upstairs toilets that they filled up with anything that would block it.

And he's just flushing it. And flushing it.

And I get it then. This flood.

The way water's flooding the stairs. Dripping over the metal floor. Dripping down thru it.

And I'm thinking how smart that is. Changing the game.

Making it harder for anybody to come at them cuz they already know they don't got the numbers.

We're already up here tho.

Nada's throwing his hands up, taunting. Getting crazy with it.

Nobody black cares.

They ain't moving. They got the good ground.

There's one thing bothering me tho . . .

They're too still.

It's like they're waiting.

And something else fucks with me too. I don't see Tim Muhammad.

I'm blinking. I'm looking. And this pillowcase that's too tight on me is getting all wet and sinking.

I look behind to make sure they don't got another crew trying to squeeze us.

I look up . . .

And see a crouching-ass Muhammad jump off the top of the nearest bunk!

That fool bodies me.

I go straight into the railing, then smack to the metal floor. Getting wet instantly.

And that's when those fuckers rush us. Right then.

Element of surprise.

Nada goes headfirst into a fucker.

And then it's just legs around me.

Water getting kicked.

I'm trying to get to my feet . . .

Muhammad's already swinging down on me tho.

The first hook he lands makes the siren go away.

My ears ring.

I try scrambling my ass up.

I can't get my hands to anything with him on top of me.

Nada tries shanking his ass. And misses.

So then Tim gets him good with a punch that makes his knees go out from under him.

Nada smashes to the floor.

And Tim's swinging at me again.

Getting me good in the ribs. So good I lose my breath.

I see him smile.

I see him think revenge is his.

And that's when I see Wizard.

Behind him.

Blood dots on his bandito mask.

Coming in with his shank to get Muhammad good in the back. The sides. Up near the throat as he's feeling the pain of it and turning.

Just *bap, bap, bap* . . .

Muhammad don't want to fight after that.

He wants to grab his neck.

Cover up.

Run.

And he does.

He bounces up. Jets off into a crowd of mayates that's throwing over bunk beds at the back of the floor.

Castling them up.

And I ain't going anywhere near that.

I'm dragging myself up by the railing. And slipping.

And Wizard's grabbing me by the back of my shirt.

Pulling me.

Saving me.

As we're falling back.

93

After all that ruckus, court's not even canceled for one day. We only know that when the deputies come in loud and heavy early in the morning, still wearing their riot gear, to wake us up to go down to IPA for processing and transport. We got beat on yesterday when the deputies came back in, and we got separated, race-to-race. They pulled all the blacks out of 617. I don't know if anybody died, but I know fools went to the hospital, and medical is so full up that they have beds in the hall. None of us know more than that. Phone calls were off-limits. No newspapers by the barbershop. It was a punishment. All of us worried about our families and our hoods with no way of finding out, so that means it's the only thing anybody talks about. It was like a nine Richter, is what people say, but I don't know where fools are getting that information. All I can think is that everything is fine because if it wasn't, our asses wouldn't be going straight back to court.

We get rolled up still in the dark-ass morning, and the only water they'll let us drink has been boiled. There's a giant pot of it sitting on a table with some cups for us to dip in, because I guess they're not allowed to keep us from having water. If they could, they would. We don't get TV in the holding room either. Some people complain about that, but none of these deputies will listen, and I wouldn't either if I just had to bust up a riot. But there is one interesting thing. For the first time ever, they throw us in a holding room with only Raza. That means they got blacks-only in a separate room. There's a feeling of peace about that too, and even the deputies seem surprised with how quiet we sit. Most just sleep or try to, because it'd be the first time since it popped off that it's completely safe enough to, in a little room like that, with all your own race car around you and so much less to sweat.

Dreamer and me sit side by side but we don't need to talk. I mean, he just says thanks to me, and gives me this look like I know what he's thanking me for, but I tell him to shut the fuck up. I don't need him telling anybody I didn't want him with a blade, or that I did what I did so he wouldn't have to. That shit is for no one to know but us, but man, I feel good knowing that he knows I got his back when it counted. When it all went down, I did something without asking him to do it, or making him. There was no other choice. I mean, with how good his side of the trial's been going? Shit. I would've had to be a dark-hearted motherfucker to let him catch new charges off some riot shit, because he could be out, you know? He could fucking make it and be useful out there on the streets, and if that means I don't? Then fuck it, man. Maybe it just means we're even. They got me up on DRB investigations for stabbing that Muhammad motherfucker. Nada's up for it too, but not Dreamer, which is good. I already interviewed. I said it was chaos, and I was trying to protect myself, but if one of those black fuckers that saw me do it says shit to the deputies, I'm cooling out for a long time. If they get me, they get me, that's how I look at it. They can bring those charges. I don't give a fuck.

We get moving pretty quick from holding. We do some squat-and-coughs and cuff up and check out for the bus. Blacks at the front, Raza at the back, a buffer of whatever Woods and Asians in the middle. We load in first to fill from the back and Dreamer's behind me. I give him a little nod that's like, *See you when we're through this*, and this dude, the one that's been so cold to me for the longest time, he actually nods back. Finally, you know? It's about fucking time I got some respect. Usually, the bus would just hop on the 5 freeway, but this time we don't. We go only on surface streets, and everybody presses faces up to windows. It's dark as hell, some streetlights on, but not all of them, and I can make some stuff out, but we don't really see much until we go by this one mall and someone yells out, "Oh shit!"

The roof of the Bullock's store fell down, and it got its whole face torn off too. You can see inside the building on two floors. Mannequins just standing there. Air-conditioning ducts hang out like a giant reached in there and grabbed them out to play with and then he just got bored and threw that shit down. Outside, there's white letters of the sign where it just says BULLO and then nothing else because it's gone. Crazy. It all looks like something out of a movie.

It keeps being like that too. We see parking lots with multiple floors gone and crime scene yellow tape up so people won't just wander in. On this one street, we drive through a puddle as big as the road. Everybody sits up and wonders if we'll make it through or just stall out trying, but we do. The dude I'm chained up to, his uncle works for the city, and he says this shit happens with earthquakes. Pipes break. Flood everything in places you don't expect. We go by this spot called the Wherehouse with all the CDs, and the whole top lip of that roof and ceiling is flat to the parking lot on one side and the rest of the building leans like it's about to go over at any second. We go near the freeway on a side road, like, close enough, and you can see how a whole chunk of it fell down. A section bigger than a football field fell like forty feet! It's all in bits at the bottom too, just fucking masses of rock and concrete now. We go by another bridge and see it busted in half. It's got all these steel cords hanging out the end of it, and that's new to me. I didn't know there was so much metal in there, under the bridges and roads, inside them like guts. I thought it was just solid concrete, but it reminds me of what happens when you get cut and find out how much there really is underneath, holding everything up and keeping it going. I guess it takes something bad happening before you can see the reality of some things.

After we get through all that, it's pretty normal, at least normal where we're driving. Streetlamps work, roads are fine, and the rest of the world moves on like nothing's different because they didn't get touched the same way up north did, and I'm tripping on it when I feel something I haven't felt in a long time. Words. They twist up into half lines about going through hell and seeing empty shells. I'm rusty. It's not good yet. It might never be, but it's something. It means I'm still here. Alive. In chains, but thinking. It's not big, but it's *something*.

94

The verdict is in. The jury was only out morning through lunch, and now I'm running through my main points from our second closing as the door beside their box opens, and Juror Number 1 shuffles in with his head down. I pray some of my words stuck with them, directed them.

Fact: Lucrecia Lucero was shot outside her mother's house. The photos prove this. Therefore, someone committed this crime.

Number 2 fiddles with his watch. My interpretation: the Glendale cabdriver looks anxious to finally get back to work.

A kite from an incarcerated, high-powered gang member called for her death by name. This gang was directly linked to Wizard Tavira's crew by Detective Montero.

Number 3 is the alternate that got switched in. She looks like she hasn't slept. Why? Guilt? Worry? It hits me then. No. She was the closest juror to the earthquake. We're lucky she's still here.

Fact: A deputy stated that Mr. Safulu revealed the coded names of Augustine and Clark to a possible gang associate.

Number 4 gives me hope. Her face is set. With her being a postal worker, I figured shootings and violence wouldn't be far from her mind, especially in the workplace.

When the gang got ahold of Mr. Clark's name, we saw the fruit of it.

Number 5 has no expression, at least, no expression I can read. Damn elementary school teachers. They can be brick walls when they want to be.

Clark changed his story because he was scared, and because he witnessed everything he said he did in his affidavit, he knows exactly what this gang is capable of in terms of retribution.

Number 6 is our male nurse, who also looks as if he hasn't slept great.

Fact: We have a dying declaration, reported by Mr. Clark as he saved Ms. Lucero's life.

Number 7 is the jury foreperson, the Hispanic early education specialist. The selection still surprises me, and worries me, and she will be who I blame if they get off.

Fact: We know that Wizard Tavira was there. No alibi was provided for him.

Number 8 pulls her black hair back, takes a pin from her teeth, and places it in her hair.

You heard from Agent Petrillo how Mr. Tavira got his ominous-sounding nickname of Wizard: because he makes things disappear; he certainly tried to make Ms. Lucero do the same.

Number 9 sits very, very straight with her hands in her lap, a slight frown on her face, almost as if she's worried they've made the right decision at all.

Fact: The weapon used to commit the crime was found in the house Wizard Tavira and Dreamer Safulu occupied, hidden at the bottom of a chest of drawers. The bullets removed from the bloody ground where Lucrecia Lucero was shot match this weapon; Detective Montero testified to that.

Number 10 stares directly at Safulu, and Safulu doesn't notice. The gaze is not unkind, which I find worrying.

This is a simple case made complicated by witness tampering. It makes the facts harder to see, but it does not make them invisible.

Number 11 places her hands on the low railing in front of her. Not once has she done this throughout the entire trial.

Now you must weigh those facts, and find that shooting someone in a premeditated fashion to satisfy your gang's nefarious purposes, and then tampering with an eyewitness from within the confines of County Jail, is not what a civilized society can tolerate.

I watch the last juror, Number 12, take her seat; the housewife gathers her black purse in front of her as she does so, as if she's already ready to walk out the door.

Ladies and gentlemen of the jury, there is only one verdict you can return: guilty on all counts.

Judge Ayers looks to the jury. "Ladies and gentlemen, I understand you've reached a verdict."

The deputy brings the paperwork to her. She looks it over. The clerk arrives at her side to take it and look it over as well.

I look behind me, to where Willie is standing. He sends me a tight smile. It doesn't look hopeful.

95

I've been doing this long enough to know you can't trust a jury to get things right. What the judge said about not considering bias, or sympathy, or the sentence these bad guys are going to get when you're weighing the facts against the law is just not how it goes down. It's one thing to say that in the hope that it will guide some of them, but it's another thing to watch a group of adults, nearly all of them with below-average intelligence or suspect language skills, revert to their opinions and whether or not they *like* the defendant on trial.

I've seen it play out wrong an awful lot over the past thirteen years. When it comes down to it, juries are a bunch of human beings who are nearly always exhausted by the end of the argument phase because they've been overloaded with a sophisticated level of legal information that many of them have never been asked to deal with in their entire lives. I have reservations with this bunch. I saw them jump at the Angela Alvarez drama that Safulu's attorney cooked up, and at Lucrecia Lucero too. Either might be enough to tip things.

All the same, it's out of my hands. Now I can only stand when I'm directed to, button my blazer on the top button, and hope like hell to hear some guilties come down. Mostly, I hope Kristina gets her win, for selfish reasons, because if she doesn't, she'll be insufferable. It'd be one more failure we'd be tied to, her and I, one more thing she can't forgive me for.

96

I look at every single juror as they sit in the box. I feel we have #1, the security guard. He seemed most impressed by Angela's testimony. His body language particularly his nodding was positive. The civil engineer and the housewife reacted similarly, as did the retired elementary school teacher. The foreperson to whom the judge asked how often she dealt with children telling lies was always the most important. She was the one seemingly most affected by Angela Alvarez's appearance on the stand, and then she went into that room and led the jury. If Jacob Safulu is set free today, it will be because she was the key. This is my hope, but there is only one way to know, and that is to wait. To wait, and not look at Kristina Mirkovich, standing so stiffly in her perfectly tailored blue suit jacket and skirt, because I absolutely could not stand the look on her face if she wins.

97

Y ahora, I'm holding my mom's hand as she's praying for Jacob. But for Wizard, I'm really only wondering one thing. If he goes away for a long time, who gets the keys? It might be me. I don't know who else it would be. Not Jerry. Not No Neck. Maybe somebody else Big Fate wants, but I proved myself already. I've done everything that needed doing, and then more. I got the lawyer pointed in the right direction. If Jacob gets free, it'll be because of me. People will know that. The right people. The ones that count.

98

It ain't the first verdict I ever got, but it's better without my mom here. I'm glad she's not seeing this shit, but Angela taking her place doesn't make it much better. I look back at her over my shoulder, and my little cousin's not looking at me. Her whole face is red, like she's gonna cry or explode. She's looking at the seal over the judge's head, the big metal state of California circle, and then she looks at the back of Dreamer's bumpy-ass head. She's more worried for him than me. Shit. I am too. I look over to the jury box side, and nobody will look at me. That's bad. That happened when I ended up getting sent to Chino too. That was the day I had to die inside to keep living, so, you know, I got practice. I could do it again. I could get rid of whatever hopes and wishes I got left. Just go into that next lockup with my chest puffed out and play the game. If they're about to call me guilty here today, I'll be good. I'll go back in and be a king of how Wayside jumped off. I'll be the one that did it right. I'll call shots, maybe even get my own block. If they find my ass guilty, it ain't no fucking thing. Mi raza own everything behind those prison walls now. It's ours.

99

My heart's going too fast. In my throat. In my head. Behind my eyes. I'm going to faint. My breathing's not mine. It's fast in and out of me. Catching, then bursting out.

I want verdicts, but I don't want verdicts. Both things bounce around in me with bad thoughts and hope.

Mrs. Matta's holding my hand too tight and I don't even care. Our palms are sweaty and too warm together, and her hair smells like black olives from a can, like the metal of it. She's got Jeo's hand in her other hand. I can't look. I just listen to Spanish flooding out of her like she's a tap and it's like this water of prayers gushing out nonstop to Saint Leonard and she's asking him for help in letting Jacob go.

She's saying it like, *Please hear me, Saint.* Like poetry.

Like, *He is a good boy,*
he will be better,
he will be more than this,
he will be so much more than this,
if only you let him.

100

The forelady opens her mouth. And on the charge of conspiracy she's saying not guilty?

I think that's what she's saying.

Not guilty for Omar Armando Tavira and Jacob Aaron Safulu.

I'm staring at her mouth. Not sure if she said what I think she said.

And then Mr. Park's grabbing me and putting his arm around me. So it must be true.

Not. Guilty.

There's a shout in the room. I don't know whose. It's high tho.

Is it Angela's? Mrs. Matta's?

I look at Wizard and Wizard looks at me.

Our eyes fucking lock.

On the count of attempted murder, they the jury find Omar Armando Tavira *guilty*.

And it feels like I got shot in my chest. I feel heavy. I feel like I'm falling when I'm standing up . . .

And they the jury find Jacob Aaron Safulu *not guilty*.

And it's like I get lifted up by somebody else's hands and can breathe again. I'm staring at Wizard tho, at where he is, and how he's looking down, and . . .

Nothing is real.

This isn't real.

On the count of assault with a deadly weapon, they the jury find Omar Armando Tavira guilty.

It's not real.

And also on the count of assault with a deadly weapon, they the jury find Jacob Aaron Safulu not guilty.

This isn't really real.

Mr. Park squeezes my shoulder harder.

I'm turning to him. Staring at his mouth when he says, "They won't find you for mayhem if they didn't for the first three."

And then they the jury are finding Omar Armando Tavira guilty of mayhem, and they, the jury, are finding me not guilty of mayhem, and they, the jury, are free to go.

And Omar Armando Tavira is remanded into custody for sentencing to a California state prison at a later date.

And me, Jacob Aaron Safulu, I am free to go if I don't have anything else binding me over.

And I don't. The clerk says so.

I don't have anything else hanging over me.

And it's fucking not real, I'm telling you!

The bailiff's holding his arm out for Wizard to show him back. So he can cuff him up.

And it hurts me to even see that, so I turn and look over that little wooden gate I was never allowed to go thru, the one the bailiff told me on the first day the jury got picked that if I tried it he would shoot me.

On the other side of it is Little. And he's crying. And Mrs. Matta is crying. And Little's older brother gives me this look like he can't fucking believe it.

And Angela's crying too. She's holding Mrs. Matta's hand. And she's pointing at me, at my face, and that's how I know I'm crying too.

So I just take my sleeve up and wipe my fucking tears cuz I got some sad ones going too . . .

Cuz I look at my homeboy going into cuffs right next to me
So close I'm even hearing them clicks
And he's looking up at me and our eyes meet up again
And we just stare at each other
No words being able to touch what we're feeling
Not even on the surface
All that happiness and sadness at once just fucking hitting us both
And I'm looking at this dude how I never looked at him before
How he saved me from carrying a shank
How he saved me from Tim Muhammad
How he saved me from more time
And my heart can't really take it with how it's beating and

Words aren't coming to my mouth, they're coming to my eyes. And I'm shooting them over to him like, *You stay up!*

I'll get you on your books. I'll put that money down once a week. Whatever you need. I got you.

And he just shrugs his shoulders like whatever

like he's got this

And it's nothing too heavy he can't carry

And he's about to be a Made Man inside them prisons

don't matter which one

And they take him out the courtroom backwards

And he says to me

He says, "You take care of everybody"

And he's thru

And it's closing

And it shuts

And behind me Judge Ayers says how I'm free to go once we do the paperwork. Once I get my CoR.

And this isn't real.

This fear sneaks up on me that they'll want me in a jumpsuit again

want me in cuffs again

want me eating when they tell me to eat

sleeping when they tell me to sleep

and where

and getting clean only when they tell me I can get clean

And this right here isn't real.

It can't be.

It isn't.

I'm not.

Free?

PART IX

SEEDS

Behold, a sower went forth to sow; And when he sowed, some seeds fell by the way side, and the fowls came and devoured them up: Some fell upon stony places, where they had not much earth: and forthwith they sprung up, because they had no deepness of earth: And when the sun was up, they were scorched; and because they had no root, they withered away. And some fell among thorns; and the thorns sprung up, and choked them: But other fell into good ground, and brought forth fruit, some an hundredfold, some sixtyfold, some thirtyfold.

—MATTHEW 13:3–8

101

I never expected to be invited to the celebration dinner, not with all the history of what's happened, but Mrs. Matta asks me herself, and when I get there, she opens the door for me and hugs me. It's a good hug too. She holds me a little too long and too hard but I love it.

"Come in," Mrs. Matta says as she lets go, "come in, come in!"

Jacob's already here. We all pack into the front hallway area to look at a copy of his Certificate of Release, his SH-AD-516. He has it folded up so he can carry it with him everywhere. He has to show it to deputies if he ever gets picked up again for anything. The original one isn't folded. It'll stay in the house of wherever he's living.

There's food already on the table. Food for days. Rice and tortillas and beans and beef and chicken. In the kitchen I meet the aunt I never met cuz she always stayed with the little girl when the rest of the family went to court. And there's a scary moment when the little girl has to sit down on the kitchen tile and have a seizure and the big brother sits behind her and holds her and Jacob gets down on his knees and smooths down her hair, like he's not worried about it at all. And I never seen that side of him before, that softness like that.

When the little girl's okay again, we go to the table. I ask if I can help, but get told I'm a guest, and to just sit. I'm on the far side of the table from Jacob. I sit with the women, next to Mrs. Matta's empty chair. He sits with the boys. I watch him with them, talking low about things that have changed in the neighborhood since he's been away. I watch how Jacob doesn't go in for some dumbass jokes anymore. He just sits still in his chair now. He doesn't bounce or shake a leg. And he can watch now, like, *really* watch. He's got this focus, this way of paying attention. Like, when he sees people's water glass getting low, he reaches for the pitcher and pours without anyone having to ask. I've never seen that before either.

Mrs. Matta comes out with the last of the dishes and it looks like some kind of noodles and right when she sits down, Jacob decides he wants to say something.

"There's this line from a book I wanted to share with everybody, cuz, uh . . ." He clears his throat. "Cuz it meant a lot to me inside there. And every time I read or I thought about it, I thought about some Mattas."

He says that and then he looks at me, and I can't tell if it's a look like he's just looking at me, or it's a look like he was thinking about me too but just didn't want to say that out loud, not in this house, and I get this little hot feeling on my throat when he looks at me, one that's not guilt anymore but something else.

He's going on about how "It's from a book called *The Witches*. It's by this author called Raoul Doll."

"Roald Dahl." Jeo elbows Jacob. "That's how you say it."

"Okay, then. Thanks, Mr. Smart Guy."

"You're welcome."

Everybody laughs then, and when it's gone there's this quiet for Jacob to talk into.

"It doesn't matter who you are or what you look like so long as somebody loves you." He's nodding then, trying to keep it together, and he's playing with something in his lap before he brings his hands up and shows everybody a handmade Christmas card. "I got your card, Jimena. I looked at it every day. It gave me strength. Thank you."

She smiles at him. And the brothers nod. And the aunt dabs at her eyes. And Mrs. Matta chokes up when she sees that, and she says she knows how Jacob lost a mom but he's got a madre now. She says part of it in English too, like, "You lost a mom, pero ahora tu tienes una madre."

And she looks at him across the table with her eyes full up and just kind of barely whispers, *"It's me.* I'm *your madre now."*

It's this thing that hits you, you know? Hits everybody. I watch it cross the table and land on Jacob. I watch him break down and cry for the second time ever in my whole life. There was court and now there's here. It's so beautiful seeing this that it gets me too, and I need to excuse myself to go use the bathroom.

I look in the mirror and redo my eyes with that L'Oréal liner I just got last weekend for court and to cheer myself up with everything that's been going on. I pull my hair back, and then I put it down again when I don't like it. And the reason I don't is cuz of Jacob. He's different now. More serious. He's seen things. Been through it. He carries that with him now. And I don't even really know how it works, but he's better for it somehow. I mean, he's reading now? He blew my mind with that. He never even *looked* at books when we were together, and now he's doing it on his own. That's making me feel things I'm not allowed to feel. And I'm telling myself in the mirror now that nothing's going to happen between me and him. Never. Not after what I did.

When I'm ready, I shut the lights off and the fan too. I go out of the door and only get one whole step into the dark hall before I see Jeo standing right in front of me, like he was *waiting* to scare the shit out of me.

I jump right where I am and hiss at him, "Jeo!"

Dinner sounds come at us from around the corner as he whispers at me. "I need you to make a phone call."

And the way he says it, I know I got no choice. It's an order. I know this is me paying him back what I owe.

102

I'm parked outside Polly's in Long Beach with my keys in the ignition. Rush is telling it like things ought to be. I backed into a spot at the end of the lot where I can see as much as possible: the front door on the side, Atlantic beyond it, Thirty-Fifth Street to my right, the back door of the building, the ladder to the roof, the metal trash bin. Most patrons park in the diagonal spots by the side entrance, their cars lit by rectangular floodlights clipped to a curious fence atop the roof. It's dark where I am: better to see and not be seen. I turn the tape off, roll my window down. In the empty lot behind me an oil rig creaks in the dark as I monitor comings and goings. Dinner's over. It's a dessert crowd now: teenagers on dates, Caucasian family with two kids, elderly women. I check my watch. The time is 20:36. We agreed on 21:00.

I came early to do a walk-through of the premises to make certain it wasn't a setup. It's possible I'm being overly cautious, but I know there are risks in pursuing Angela Alvarez, and in some ways, those risks are even greater now. Angela wasn't there the day Dreamer's lawyer slandered me in court by suggesting I planted the gun (she had nursing school, I checked), but I can guarantee she heard about it. I decided to lay low after that, and wait for her to come around. I knew she would, because if she didn't, I'd go see her. It's not like I don't know where she lives.

She paged me, though. It was sooner than I expected. My first thought when it came in with her number on it: she passed my information to somebody else, and the wrong people were trying to find me. I dismissed this after some thought, though. I'm sure Dreamer's fellow gangsters are convinced I did something wrong, but there's no way to prove it, and there's no way they can touch me and conceivably get away with it, so fuck them. I gave it an hour before I returned her call.

She picked up in the middle of the second ring, glad to hear my voice, said she was ready to talk finally. I gave her silence, so she filled it: she missed seeing me in the courtroom when she was on the stand, and for the verdict, but she figured I was working and probably heard. I told her I had. Dreamer's acquittal lifted a weight from her (I judged this to be true from the relief in her voice). She said she never would have forgiven herself for going out with me if he got locked up when she knew he didn't do it, but now that wrong is righted, she wanted to tell me she's leaving Lynwood. She's going to rent out her aunt's house that she has been living in for so long. When she made these decisions, she couldn't help but be motivated by the fact that there was something special about us, and she'd also never forgive herself if she didn't at least give it one more chance. She blamed the kiss (this sounded truthful). She said she has been thinking about it nonstop. She said the date at Disneyland was the best she's ever had (also seemingly sincere). Running into the Lynwood girl who recognized her really had her afraid for her safety at first, but it has all blown over now. People aren't happy with her, but they know she's a grown-up. She's a good person who works hard and can do what she wants, and what she wants is to see her Prince Phillip again (that got me). She sounded so vulnerable and worried I might say no when she said, "Can we? I mean, do you even want to? I get it if you don't." I was always going to say yes, but I wanted to punish her for a few moments before I suggested pie, tonight. She said that would be perfect.

It's 20:41. The family exits the establishment, laughing. They get in a minivan. The father opens the door for the wife before returning to the driver's side.

Traffic is nonexistent on Thirty-Fifth (no new cars have entered from that side), but I spot sidewalk movement: a figure shuffling, weaving, propping himself up with the side of the building. When he pushes off, I could swear it's Augustine Clark.

I say, "What the hell?"

It couldn't be anyone else on earth, and Augie appears to be either inebriated, high, or both (in clear violation of his parole). I have no choice but to run him in for this, and I must admit I'm going to relish sending him back for the way he folded on that stand.

I scan the parking lot: still empty. I watch Augie make it to the trash bin, push off, start back toward the restaurant.

He's Jell-O on two legs. Everything about this scumbucket is sad, predictable. All the Compton and Lynwood trash comes down Atlantic and washes up here. I don't blame him for running south when Kristina refused to pick him up for not upholding the terms of his plea (for such a hard charger, she certainly got soft with him); he was scared of the gang and she found that understandable, even pitiable; she hoped drug court would provide him his last solid chance, but now here he is, stumbling down the county. Fucking dopers. They never change.

I grab the keys out of the ignition, get out, lock the car. I approach Augie as he is halfway across the back of the parking lot, moving toward the entrance.

I say his name and that elicits no response. I close on him.

I say, "Augie, what the level hell are you doing here?"

He turns. His pupils are dilated. He has been using.

He mutters gibberish, finds his feet, leans forward aggressively. I take up a defensive posture.

"You want to fight me, Augie?"

He has to think about that. He looks at the empty parking lot, and then to Atlantic, where cars cruise by fast, before finding words. "You should run."

I laugh. "Run from *you*? Sure."

There's a look in his eyes, though. It's fear, but not of me.

He repeats himself, slower. "You. Should. Run."

It sinks in then: he doesn't mean run from a fight with him.

He means something's coming, for me.

I step back, but I bounce off somebody bigger than me, and I can't set my feet. I attempt to pull my weapon, but something crashes into my face: hard, solid (concrete, or metal). The headache is instant. Ears ring. Things slow. I feel something broken in my mouth. White tooth bits stream out with blood. I reach for my gun again, but my holster's empty. I look down. Something hits my knees, knocks me forward, onto asphalt.

I try to press up, to stand, but wetness slaps my face, smothers me (nose, mouth). Can't breathe. Fumes come fast, harsh. I cough but push nothing out.

Wetness goes away, lights blur. Vision shrinks. *No.* The only word I want to say and it won't come out. *No, no, no.*

A car comes close, idles almost on me. I feel heat. A door opens.

A voice (female) says, "Shit, Vulture! We're gonna have to fuck the front of his face up to cover that now."

103

Little wants me over at the Islands Motel when I got no way of getting there, so Angela takes me in her car. Little told me not to worry about being south of the 105. He said he had an agreement with Scrappy and her clica. That Lynwood was one thing now. It wasn't north and south anymore. Them and us. He said it was all one. And I didn't even know what to make of that shit so I stayed the fuck out of it.

I told Angela I had a bad feeling about it tho. Going over to see him there. And I think she had one too.

Angela told me over dinner at Mrs. Matta's how there was a movie version of *Treasure Island*. She said if I wanted to, I could come over and watch it together with Elisa's kids, Marisela and Rowland, cuz she has to look after them tomorrow. And I told her thanks for thinking of me, but it's only okay if I can be home for dinner with Mrs. Matta cuz I promised.

She said that was cool. She knows I don't break promises to Mrs. Matta anymore. I'm never breaking promises to that woman again for so long as I live. You can kill my ass first.

Cuz I'll never forget how she told me I lost a mom and got a madre. That was the realest shit I ever heard in my life. It was a thing I never knew I needed till someone said it to me. And I been different ever since. New, somehow.

When she parks us by the motel curb, Angela says, "Please don't go, Jacob. I *really* don't like this."

"I know," I say. "But I have to. He asked. And I owe him."

When I go to get out, she grabs my arm. Her fingers clench up on the cotton like she means to hold me there, but I nod at her. When she lets go there's this twist to my sleeve where her hand was.

I say, "Do you want to go to Magic Mountain one of these days? Just as friends."

Before she can even answer, I get out and go. I don't look at her face.

A no is fine. I can take a no. Not before this tho.

This, I just want over first.

Being outside the car is so much louder. Nobody tells you when you get out that the world got louder while you were away. How it's too much some days.

I put my hood up.

The weather's cold. Fifties maybe. I go under the arch to where Little's waiting in the parking lot. As I walk up to him a door goes. A woman pokes her head out.

And Little shouts out to her, "Bitch, go the fuck back inside!"

She does too. She shuts that door.

And I'm swallowing down panic from having somebody yell that close to my face. I feel ashamed at how I want to run. Ashamed at how I still got jail inside me.

And I don't want to tell Little his business. He's changing tho. Shit. He's *changed*. The old Little never would've popped off at somebody like that.

So I guess this is him being Dulce, I'm thinking. A different dude totally.

And right then I get sorry for Mrs. Matta. And I can't even think what it would do to her if she lost her Jeovanni.

Cuz it's all my fault he's like this.

I say, "You got something you want to show me?"

"Yeah, man," he says. He smiles real big.

"What is it?"

"Something. You'll see."

"You got it with you, or . . ."

"It's in this room over here."

He points at a door, #14.

Straightaway, I know something bad's behind it.

You get that feeling enough in jail to know not to walk in somewhere. Only problem is, in jail you can't always keep from doing it. You might get ordered thru. You might have to.

He says, "It's gonna make you happy, I swear."

I'm looking at him hard when I say, "I can't, hermano. Lo siento."

He takes this step back like I hit him.

He says, "The fuck? You got to. Now's the time. With everybody fucked up off of this earthquake. You don't go in now, you're never hav-ing this moment again."

I put my head down like I'm thinking.

I'm not thinking about shit tho . . .

I'm not going thru that door when nobody with cuffs and a gun is ordering me. Cuz I don't have to be the monster anymore. I got my choices back now.

And I won't do this shit.

I say, "I guess I'm not having it then."

His brow drops down over his eyes. It's as mad as I've ever seen him. Mad at me for being stupid. For being ungrateful.

He says, "I did this for you. I tied ends up. I made promises. This thing needs to get done. There's no getting out of it."

I go to grab his shoulder. He rolls away tho.

And I say, "I get how much you did for me. How you've been thru a lot you'll never tell me about."

"You don't get *shit*."

I look at him. At his pain. At this new pride he's got puffing up.

I want to puncture it. Let all its air out. I don't have the heart to tho.

I say, "You're right. I don't. This shit can get done without me."

"It has to be with you there."

"Says who?"

"Says fucking *me*." His face is all red.

I almost think that we might need to throw down. Right here.

So I say, "It's like that?"

And he says right back, "It's like that."

I think about telling him all I did inside. In CJ. In NCCF. How big motherfuckers know my name now. They know I put in work without ever hesitating. Just looking at him now tho? I can see none of that would matter.

So I just say, "We surfed fucking concrete when that earthquake came. The floor was rolling like the ocean."

He don't expect that.

I can see in his eyes how he's torn between wanting to say and want-ing to hear more before he just gives up.

He says, "So what happened?"

"Everybody threw down. *Sixty-five fucking people.* Locked in. Brawling. Fools getting stabbed. Gas coming in . . ."

I see him get to that point where you wonder why somebody's telling you a story, so I just hit his ass with it.

I say, "I could've died in there. I was always getting mixed up in something I didn't want to be in. I had to tho, cuz I was in a fucking cage. And I mean no disrespect to you, hermano. This right here is some shit I don't have to do. I got a choice. It don't mean I don't appreciate you. I got love for all you did, I just . . . I *can't* go in that door."

He's nodding. It's too fast tho. Like he's revving up.

"But I did it for you. For some justice," he says.

"I believe you, hermano." I almost got tears coming. "I already got my justice tho, you know? That jury set me free. For fucking once the system did its thing right."

He's looking at me like I don't got the whole story. Not from his side. And that's cool. Cuz I don't want it.

I know he was out here doing what needed to get done. I read that off his looks.

So I say, "I wouldn't be here without all you did. You don't have to tell me for me to know it."

His nod slows down. He's feeling me. He's getting me. I see tears coming up in his eyes too. He fights that shit down tho.

He says, "I got to do this for the both of us, then."

And he turns. Walks to that door. I watch his back as he goes into #14. And the door shuts.

I know he's gone now. The Little I used to know.

And maybe it's forever.

I know he traded the best parts of himself so I could be free. And I can never fucking repay him for that.

And I'll carry the guilt of that shit till I die . . .

And I must be standing around too long thinking, cuz the woman that poked her head out earlier is poking it out at me again. Telling me to come in where it's warm. Telling me she'll take care of me and even give me a discount.

I say, "Nah. I'm good. Thanks."

She goes back inside. The blinds go tho. And she watches me thru the window.

I nod at her. And then I turn too.

Cuz it's a feeling I have then. That these kinds of places aren't for me anymore. There's too many people that can come at you from every which way. And everybody wants something.

All I really want is to be back with Mrs. Matta. Studying my electrician's manual. Watching movies with Jimena. Eating a fucking donut from Jack's with some coffee.

I want a new book. One that *smells* new. Not like jail. Not one that's been with ten thousand other fingers.

I go in my pocket, to where I know the copy of my CoR is. And I touch it just to touch it. I put my whole left hand over it. The clerk that gave it to me said it was my freedom receipt. That I should carry it with me everywhere in case I ever needed to prove to law enforcement that my warrants no longer apply.

I like those words. *Freedom receipt.* Cuz I did have to pay for it. I paid a lot.

And it's got me thinking that maybe I'm done paying now.

If I can say no to this business right here, I can say no to other things too. Maybe.

I put my head down. I walk back to the car.

And when Angela sees me coming thru the archway, her face lights up. She's never smiled at me like that before. It's new. She's surprised. And happy. And maybe proud too.

She starts the car. The engine turns. And it kicks out some blue smoke on the curb.

It's burning oil. I can get that fixed for her tomorrow if she wants.

Right now tho? It's ready to go. And she's ready. And I'm ready.

So that's it.

We go.

104

Y ahora, I go through the door and close it quick. It's smelling bad in here. No air. No fan. It's a full house for such a little motel room. Vulture's on the bed with his feet up like he don't care how dirty the bedspread is. He's just waiting for this to get done with. No Neck's in the same boat with him, sitting with a towel underneath him on the only chair by the bed. At his feet is Petrillo all knocked out. He has a good scab going on his upper lip from where Vulture popped him with brass knuckles. By the parole officer's knees is Irma, all crouched down, and up by his head is Augie, sweating like he's been running. Behind him, Scrappy's leaning on the wall by the bathroom door. You can't even really see her cane with how she hid it behind one of her legs. She sees the look I got on me before anyone else does.

And she's saying, "I knew he wasn't coming."

"He wasn't about it."

She shrugs at me. "All good. It don't change nothing."

She's right. What needs to be done still needs to be done, whether Jacob sees this shit or not.

I wanted him to. It would've been great if he could see how far I've come, and how this twisted shit that happened to him won't be happening to anybody else around here once they see how we take care of this shit.

Irma slaps Augie's arm. "What you got him on to have him knocked out like this?"

Augie makes a face. "You don't want to know."

She does want to know. She's asked about it three times already. I've been getting the feeling she's trying to figure out what it is so she can hit that shit.

I look to Augie. "Can you bring him back up?"

"Sure," Augie's saying, "I don't really fucking want to, but sure."

Augie's popping smelling salts he lifted from the Thrifty Drugs and waves them in front of Petrillo's face.

At first, nothing happens. No twitching. No eyes moving under eyelids. Nothing.

No Neck laughs. "Isn't that shit supposed to work all at once?"

"Just wait." Augie keeps moving it back and forth under the nose.

The first thing that happens is, Petrillo's nose scrunches up. And the second thing that happens is, he sneezes and blows the little pouch straight out of Augie's hand. It falls on a sticky patch of carpet a foot away and stays there.

"Ha." No Neck's saying it more than he's laughing.

Vulture smiles at him.

On the floor, deep in the dirty-ass carpet, Petrillo's blinking. He's trying to move, but he can't. His arm moves an inch toward his leg.

Vulture leans toward him. "Nothing down there but an empty holster."

And No Neck takes a shot too. "Yeah. We got your gun already, fool."

The rest of Petrillo's face balls up like he's ready to cry, but he takes this big breath in and gets his head turned to Augie and sees him. You can almost hear him deciding how it'll be a good idea to try to plead with Augie's ass, like that hype could ever have a say on this business.

"I was good to you," Petrillo's saying, "I was good to you, Augie. I saved you."

And Augie says nothing, just looks away, and that's pretty much when Petrillo knows it's done with. There's no U-turns here. This street only goes one way.

"You almost got away with your framing shit." I look around the room where he first decided to pick up a gun and try to take Jacob's whole life away. "Now we get to do ours. This shit's for Dreamer. It's justice."

Petrillo doesn't know what I mean. He's got this look of confusion going on in his face. But then he sees Augie getting ready with the needle. It's full of some heroin he already mixed up. Way too much fucking H. So much it could kill a horse. And the only way to get it was to go to Scrappy and pay her for it. But then when she gets paid for it, she decides she wants to see it go down. And she throws Vulture in on top of it for transportation and that's when a plan starts hitting.

The only way to get it in Petrillo's arm is for Augie to mix up a hot shot, aim, and push.

He's wearing this white undershirt and the peacock on his arm dances as he taps for a vein in the middle of Petrillo's left arm.

"No!" Petrillo's as loud as he can get. "No!"

Scrappy laughs. "Nobody cares about screaming around here. You might as well save yourself some fucking dignity. Go out a man. Shit."

Petrillo shuts up but his face is all red as he's fighting to do something to get up and get out, but that's not what's about to happen. Not now. Augie finds a vein and gets that needle in good. He looks to me with his thumb on the stopper part and I give him the nod to do it.

And he does. He pushes that plunger all the way to the bottom.

"Fuck," Irma's whispering, "fuck, fuck."

She's mad about wasting it, no doubt, but she knows there's more where that came from. Way more. Enough to float her forever if she gets her part right. Poor girl doesn't even know she has a hot shot in her future too.

Y ahora, all of us watch Petrillo go. And I don't know what I'm expecting, but it's not crazy. It's not more shouting. His head falls to the side as he nods out, then he flutters his long-ass eyelashes and his breathing gets heavier and slower and then he's gone.

"It's not the worst way to go out." Augie gets a look of pain on his face, like it hurts him to even say it.

And I'm getting the feeling that Augie killing himself slowly is one thing, but putting a needle into somebody else is a whole new kind of shock to him.

A minute goes by, and then we stretch it to two. Petrillo hasn't breathed once.

We decide to wait a little longer but definitely don't feel like staring at him, so Scrappy puts on the TV. She flips it around a bit. Ends up on cable. She stops on an episode of *Growing Pains*. Mike Seaver's caught up in some shit with a girl that likes his ass but he don't like her back. Vulture thinks it's hilarious. He laughs. He repeats lines. The rest of us just put up with it and watch that shit till Scrap flips to *The $25,000 Pyramid*.

It's on a commercial when Irma presses one of her thumbs hard against her forehead before saying, "Can I get the rest of my shit now?"

I let her know. "You get it when you do the thing all the way tomorrow."

Irma looks to Scrappy, like if you don't get what you want from Dad, you go and ask Mom.

Scrap's not having it either. "What the fuck you looking to me for? You heard him, bitch. I only cash you out when you're done with the game."

Everybody waits in their own ways after that. I think about Danny, and how the people I checked up on him with said he was solid, he was good, and maybe I need to call him, how maybe we need to try something, me and him.

Nobody says anything for like twenty minutes, and the whole time Petrillo's just lying there, head off to the side. Not moving. We can all see how his body's just empty now. There's no person to it anymore. No doubt to that.

I look at Scrap and she looks at me. We know it's time.

She pushes herself off the wall and gets going with her cane. "I'm out, then."

"Same," I'm saying as I get that door for her.

But on my way out, I look to No Neck and Vulture and they nod at me. They know where to take Petrillo when it gets real late. They know exactly what the fuck to do.

105

Me and Louis are so close to being done with a ten-shift on the 05:00-to-15:00 when a call comes over to investigate possible human remains in the Los Angeles River basin. We try to duck it since nobody needs to do overtime by babysitting for the coroner, but dispatch checks with other cars, and tells us we're closest—that a body is a body; respond immediately.

We're first on scene. There's a fence between us and the river, and I don't feel like climbing it with my belt and vest on. Neither does Louis, so he stays with the vehicle and I walk a quarter mile up to a break in the fence, navigating broken beer bottles, used hypodermics, and bum trash like newspapers used as toilet paper, before pushing through. Even from my entry point upriver, I see what I'm supposed to see as I work my way south. The body is lying flat-out in the sunshine, with one arm above its head and the other underneath. Its legs are splayed. It is faced away from me. It has no shoes or socks on, just torn pants and an undershirt. When I finally draw up parallel to it, I see the pale face turned to the side. The sight of it gut-punches me.

It's Phil Petrillo.

I wave at Louis to pull the car up closer to me, so he does. As he gets out, he shouts through the fence, "Mirk, is it remains?"

"Yup," I say.

We secure the area as much as is possible when a human body is at the bottom of the biggest concrete ditch on the planet, which means we thread caution tape through the fence near a local bum camp, and Louis and I talk about whether or not I'm going down there, if I can manage not to slip and fall.

"I can vis-ID that it's remains," I tell him. "I see no breathing pattern. He's got livor mortis. Call it in."

While he's doing that, his place at the fence is taken up by a skinny thing—female, wild black hair, bloodshot brown eyes, five-foot-seven.

"Officer," she says to get my attention. "Officer. I know what happened."

I have no choice but to proceed with a field interview at that point. Petrillo's going nowhere. Louis is on with the station seeing how long we need to wait for them to send somebody to look at the body, so I FI the woman. Her name is Irma Sanchez. She sometimes lives at the Islands Motel on Long Beach Boulevard. It's a known prostitution spot, which fits with her appearance and demeanor. She says she parties at this camp sometimes, and that sounds fishy to me, but I let her talk. She knows his name. She calls him Peedro Phil, and says that on occasion he liked to smoke heroin with her and some of the parolees he monitored. I almost bring up the name Augustine Clark, but she's on a roll, so I take down the narrative.

Peedro Phil was broken up last night about a young woman who stopped seeing him, Angela-something. He was hurting so bad that he decided to shoot up for the first time. She warned him about how big that shot was, but he didn't care. He did it anyway, and he died. The local doper council didn't take too kindly to the disrespect of somebody dying at their spot, so they dragged Phil's body to the riverbank—after taking his shoes, socks, jacket, and shirt—and pushed him down. I ask her how they managed it. She said four people went through a hole in the fence. She points to it, and tells me it's not the first time people have pushed a body down that couldn't handle the high. I don't doubt it.

Louis comes back and I tell Irma to tell Deputy Louis what she told me, but I give him the eye to have her empty her pockets and prove to him that she's not carrying drugs or paraphernalia. He gets it. He tells her to go wait by the car, and then tells me there has been a shooting at Ham Park in Lynwood. Some gangbanger folded his last hand. It's an active investigation site, a stone-cold 187, so everybody's over there. We're going to be waiting on services for a while.

"It's not Scrappy, if you're thinking it," Louis tells me. "Decedent is male. No ID yet."

I wasn't thinking it, but I am now. I'm wondering if what's going on at Ham Park is a diversion, but then I look back to Petrillo, and I'm no ME, but it looks like he's been there a long time. The other shooting is likely just a coincidence.

"Harm Park strikes again, huh?" I scratch my nose. Nobody with a badge calls it Ham anymore. "This all smells like a cleanup."

Louis doesn't agree, but he doesn't not-agree either. He goes back to interview Irma as an unmarked cruiser pulls up. It's Willie Montero.

"Isus *Krist*," Montero says as he walks up to the fence. "Why didn't you call Lynwood?"

"Lynwood's already got a body. Harm Park. You didn't hear about that?"

"When it rains, it fucking pours. Which way?"

I point him to the fence break Irma showed me. Willie arrives in half the time it took me. He walks himself to the edge, looks down, recognizes Petrillo, and says, "God-fucking-dammit."

"Yup," I reply. "Somebody sure took long enough to call it in."

"That's how it is around here, Deputy. Nobody ever sees shit. This whole city can turn a blind eye when it needs to."

I nod, mostly at the body.

"Long way down," I say.

"Long way," he agrees. "You think he rolled or what?"

"Logistically, he probably slid."

"Face-first? Hell of a way to go into home plate." Willie cocks his head and looks back at the fence. "You think he was dragged through?"

I point at the back of the unit where Irma Sanchez sits with the door open. The contents of her pockets are spread on the trunk. I tell him, "Got a wit here for you. Says she saw Petrillo regular. Peedro Phil, she calls him."

"Well, fuck, I bet she saw *everything*." Montero's sarcasm is heavy. His way of telling me that everything about this is way too neat and clean to be right.

"Says she did. She'll go on the record."

"I bet. Give me the short version."

"Says a couple old-timers in the bum camp weren't happy about an OD ruining their campsite."

"Naturally." Willie surveys the small camp with half a railroad tie for a bench and a metal fire barrel in the middle. "What else does helpful citizen Irma have to say?"

"Says Petrillo liked to smoke heroin every now and again, but he'd been clean for a while before this episode."

Willie smirks down at his notepad. "Which will conveniently explain why he wouldn't have needlework everywhere, or much prolonged use evident in his system, when we get him on the slab. *Fantastic.*"

I run the rest of my notes down for him. She says she was there when he did it, injected himself. It was his first time. She tried to talk him out of it, but he was real broken up about an Angela—presumably Angela Alvarez—not wanting him anymore.

Montero smirks again. "And he died right over there, and the high bum counsel decided they needed to chuck him."

I watch Montero look down at the middle of the L.A. River. The only running water is in its central channel, no more than eight feet wide. It's a dead river, and now it has a dead man on the Lynwood city side of it.

"I'm going down," he tells me.

I watch him angle his walk down the grade, picking his path on a zigzag. When he gets to the bottom, he moves to Petrillo and inspects everything with the tip of his pen—lifting a leg cuff, checking the arm It takes him a few minutes before he comes back up the same way he went down.

At the top, I put my hand out and he takes it. I pull him up and ask, "What do you think of Irma's account?"

"So far, so square. There's a needle mark on the right arm on the interior elbow. It's an OD, all right." He's a little out of breath, sweat beading on his brow. "*Obvious Death.* No evidence of foul play. We'll need the coroner to tell us if it was heroin. In the meantime, I'll take Irma's story down, just for kicks."

Before he goes, I ask the only thing worth asking. "What do we tell Kristina?"

Willie sighs. "We tell her the truth."

He nods at me, and I nod back. I get where he's going with this. He needs me to back him.

I tell him, "People do fucked-up things when they're not sober. I didn't even know Petrillo used drugs. He hid it so well."

Willie frowns, but he nods again. "We are never privy to the personal pain of others, Deputy."

He turns then, and walks back the way he came.

I raise my voice and ask, "Call the coroner first, or fire?"

He shouts over his shoulder. "Coroner. There's an access road up the way. They can drive down."

Louis's done interviewing Irma, so I call him over. He walks to me without turning his back on her. I tell him to call the coroner. It's not a crime scene now, and the body is just something that needs removing, testing, cataloguing. He says he's on it. After that, I turn back to the river so I can I keep one eye on the body, facedown at the bottom of the grade. Petrillo wasn't the first to take advantage of a badge. He won't be the last. This city breeds them and eats them, and nobody cares when they're gone.

I watch the hills to the south. When there's smog, my little girl says they're smudged, and that's what they are right now. *Smudged*. I watch birds come and go. Three ducks swim the central channel and pass the body without even noticing it. I try not to think about how long it's going to take anybody from the coroner's office to get here. I wonder if they're even at Harm Park yet or if they're still stuck in traffic coming from USC. I look back to the cars to see that Irma has gone, and Louis is talking with Montero. In the riverbed, a lone crow takes an interest in Petrillo, but I find a few bits of nearby concrete to chuck until I scare the thing back into the air. When it's gone, I'm left with the steady buzz of traffic from the 710 and an airplane descending into Long Beach Airport.

That is, until a white bird swoops down to land in the river. It's an egret, or a heron. Which one, I'm not sure, but it's beautiful, this bird— long legs, long neck, yellow beak as long as a switchblade. It couldn't care less about the body. It doesn't even look at him. It only wants the water, and what's in it. I watch it stalk east-west as it fishes, knifing its beak into the current when it sees something and snaps it up, pointing its head at the sky and pumping its neck to swallow. I must stand for twenty minutes like that, watching it until it's done feeding. Afterward, it stops. It faces upriver and stands on one leg in the water—still and tall—a triumphant hunter.

Glossary

#

10-97: Los Angeles Sheriff's Department radio code for "Arrived on Scene."

187: refers to California Penal Code §187, which is the crime of murder.

4700: housing unit usually reserved for general-population inmates at L.A. County's Men's Central Jail.

5150: short for Section 5150 within the California Welfare and Institutions Code that allows an officer or clinician to involuntarily commit a person to a psychiatric hospital if they are suspected to have a mental disorder that makes them a danger to themselves or others.

A

A mal nudo, mal cuño: literally, "For a bad knot [in wood], a bad wedge [a type of woodworking blade that cuts well]"; the widely accepted meaning of the phrase is, "You must meet rough with rough."

abuelita: pet name for grandmother; also: an older woman who looks like a grandmother.

AdSeg: short for administrative segregation, also known as solitary confinement, or "the hole."

ADW: acronym for the crime of assault with a deadly weapon.

AHD: acronym for assistant head deputy; in this case, a title within the L.A. County District Attorney's Office.

Attaboy(s): informal LASD term used at Firestone Park Station to recognize good work.

Awshit: informal LASD term used at Firestone Park Station for a significant mistake that erases any previous recognition of good work.

B

bala: literally, "bullet."

ballistic vest: bulletproof vest.

barrio(s): literally, "neighborhood(s)."

Board of Prison Terms: now-defunct nine-member body in the state of California that weighed issues of parole release for persons sent to prison under indeterminate sentencing laws, suspension and/or revocation of parole in the event of violation, and clemency.

bolsillo(s): literally, "pockets."

brass meeting: meeting of law enforcement higher-ups, i.e., the top brass.

bravada: literally, "brave."

brocha: literally, "brush"; also: a bushy mustache.

bullet: a one-year-long parole violation; the longest punishment for a violation one could do at the time.

bunk status: discipline decided by shotcaller for new, unknown, or untrustworthy inmates, where inmates must spend program time on their bunks, and often give food away to other gang members.

C

Calipatria: city in Imperial County, California most well known for the Calipatria State Prison, a men's-only prison housing four thousand inmates, who make up half of the city's population.

callate: literally, "keep quiet," "be quiet," or "shut up."

car: informal identification of one's race made by inmates that determines which group one will effectively jail with (e.g., spend time with, eat with, be protected by, etc.), which shotcaller one will answer to, and how one will be held accountable to the broader social order within the jail or prison.

cariño: literally, "love," "kindness," or "benevolence"; typically, a form of paying respect by monetary means, but it may also be extortion, depending on context; see also: tax.

carne guisada: type of meat stew typically made with beef, tomato, garlic, onion, and bell pepper.

carnicería: meat market or butcher shop that may sell groceries as well.

casa: literally, "house."

CCB: dated acronym for the Criminal Courts Building on Temple Street in Los Angeles; since 2002, the building has been known as the Clara Shortridge Foltz Center for Criminal Justice.

CDC number: California Department of Corrections inmate identification number. (Note: these typically begin with J; however, R was used in the text so as to eliminate the possibility that Augustine Clark's fictional number could ever reference, or be assigned to, an actual inmate.)

chapín: slang for someone of Guatemalan descent.

chavala: literally, a female child or young person; also: someone who acts or dresses like a gangster (or talks tough) but has little or no substance.

chiba: slang for marijuana.

chingón: literally, "fucker"; also: a slang term for "cool" or "awesome."

chipping: augmenting the use of methadone with heroin to reduce the severity of withdrawals.

Chivas: literally, "the goats," a nickname for Club Deportivo Guadalajara, a fútbol (soccer) team in Jalisco, Mexico.

cholo: typically, a Chicano gangster, but the term is also used broadly by some to include all Latinos.

chorizo: spiced Mexican sausage, typically pork.

chuchito(s): literal translation, "little dog"; Guatemalan tamale wrapped in corn leaves (hoja de elote de máiz).

ciruela: literally, "plum."

Citation 4457: not replacing a stolen, lost, mutilated, or illegible license plate or registration card.

Citation 4464: displaying a license plate that has been altered or modified from its original markings.

clica (or click): either a gang, or a neighborhood portion of a larger gang.

CO: acronym for corrections officer.

collars: informal law enforcement term for arrests.

CoR: acronym for Certificate of Release, a form provided to an inmate after release from custody.

crew: in gang terms, a smaller grouping within a gang or clica.

cuete: literally, "firework"; slang for gun, most often a handgun.

D

dago: ethnic slur for Italians.

doper: user of illegal narcotics, most notably heroin.

DRB: Discipline and Review Board.

drug court: California court program that began in 1994 that allows nonviolent drug offenders with chronic substance abuse issues to undergo supervised treatment and rehabilitation, rather than incarceration; this program's intention is to reduce costs for the criminal justice system, as well as allowing people with addictions to become productive members of society.

E

en serio: literally, "in seriousness."

entiendes: literally, "You understand?"

Es obvio: literally, "It's obvious."

F

FI: acronym for field interview; typically, law enforcement.

fifi: an improvised masturbatory device.

Firestone Park Station: a branch of the Los Angeles Sheriff's Department, which—prior to its closure—was located in the Florence Neighborhood.

fish kit: hygiene supplies provided for new inmates by the county.

Folsom: Folsom State Prison, a maximum-security prison opened in 1880, making it the second oldest in the state of California behind San Quentin State Prison.

fresa: literally, "strawberry"; also: slang for prostitute.

G

G: short for gangster; see also: OG.

gabacho: derogatory term for an English-speaking person of European descent and/or Caucasian.

Gagana Sāmoa: Samoan language course book written by Galumalemana Afeleti Hunkin; it was originally published in 1988.

ganas: literally, "gonads"; it is also a slang term for exhibiting guts or great will.

Garcetti, Gil: the 40th District Attorney of Los Angeles County, serving from December 7, 1992 until December 4, 2000.

gat: slang for firearm, generally a handgun.

gen pop: short for general population.

Guate: short for Guatemalan.

H

hat (most frequently, "the hat"): disciplinary tool that gangs may use either to intimidate a target into compliance, or to identify a target in order to mete out punishment, e.g., one's name can go into the hat.

hermano: literally, "brother."

HG: acronym for hardcore gang.

hilacha(s): literally, "shred(s)"; Guatemalan shredded beef stew.

hood: abbreviation of neighborhood, typically an area with distinctive characteristics relating to the residents' ethnicity or socioeconomic status; often used interchangeably with "ghetto" or "the projects."

hot shot: large, lethal amount of heroin either prepared and given without knowledge, or purposely administered to a victim to make it appear to be an accidental overdose.

hype: heroin user, specifically one who uses hypodermic needles to administer the drug.

I

indecente: literally, "indecent."

IPA: acronym for Inmate Processing Area.

INS: acronym for Immigration and Naturalization Service, an agency under the U.S. Department of Justice that handled immigration services, investigations and deportations, as well as border protection; this agency ceased to exist on March 1, 2003, and the entity known as U.S. Immigrations and Customs Enforcement (ICE) was created to take over its investigation and deportation functions.

Isus Krist: literally, "Jesus Christ," a Croatian swear taking the Lord's name in vain.

J

Jebiga: Croatian exclamation meaning "Fuck it!"

Jebo ti vrag mater: Croatian exclamation meaning, "Devil fucked your mother."

K

K-10: designation for an inmate to be kept away from all other inmates; such inmates are the highest custody priority within the L.A. County institution, either because the inmate is extremely violent, a top-tier gang leader, or because the treatment of this person poses a certain legal risk to the county (e.g., a prisoner of some notoriety).

key(s): slang term for power; though they are not a physical set of keys, they are considered something that is held, similar to the way a boxer holds a title belt; see also: llavero.

kite(s): small paper notes or letters written in microscript by inmates, utilized as a means of undetected communication between incarcerated parties; see also: wila.

L

la maldad: literally, "evil."

LAPD: acronym for the Los Angeles Police Department, the city's policing body.

LASD: acronym for the Los Angeles County Sheriff's Department, the county's policing body.

llavero: literally, "key holder," a term for someone who is the gang's shot-caller, either in prison or on the street; someone who "holds the keys"; see also: keys, shotcaller.

Lo prefiero: literally, "I prefer it."

Lo siento mucho: literally, "I'm very sorry."

locote/lokete/lokita(s): literally, "crazy person," typically a gang member who will go to extreme measures with no regard for consequences.

M

machaca: Northern Mexican spiced beef or pork traditionally dried and re-hydrated.

malias: bodily sickness that occurs from coming down from a hard drug (e.g., heroin), otherwise known as "dope sick."

maricón: derogatory term for a gay man.

marisco(s): literally, "seafood" or "shellfish," typically referring to shrimp, or a restaurant that specializes in the preparation of seafood dishes.

masa: flour prepared by soaking corn in an alkaline solution of lime water before it is washed and hulled, a process called nixtamalization; it is then used to make corn tortillas, tamales, pupusas, and various other dishes.

matón: literally, "killer."

mayate(s): literally, a "black, dung-eating beetle," it is a slang term most frequently used by Mexicans and Chicanos to denigrate dark-skinned people.

MCJ: acronym for the Los Angeles County Sheriff's Department's Men's Central Jail, also known as Central Jail (CJ), built in 1963 and housing approximately forty-three hundred inmates.

ME: acronym for medical examiner.

Mean Streak: a permanent marking stick frequently used in graffiti.

methadone: medication used to treat addiction to opioids, such as heroin.

mierda: literally, "shit."

Mirandize: to inform a recently arrested person of their legal rights (i.e., one's Miranda rights); in *Miranda v. Arizona* 384 U.S. 436 (1966), the United States Supreme Court held that statements made in police custody are only admissible at trial if the defendant was informed of both the right to consult an attorney and the right to remain silent while being questioned by police; informing recently arrested individuals of these two rights is now routine police procedure nationwide.

mostaccioli: penne-like noodle dish that is typically baked with tomato sauce, mozzarella cheese, and Italian sausage.

Muy pequeño el mundo es: literally, "The word is very small."

N

NA: acronym for Narcotics Anonymous.

NCCF: acronym for the North County Correctional Facility, the maximum-security jail also known as the Flagship, which is located on the Wayside Honor Rancho; it was opened on March 10, 1990, with a dedication by then–sitting U.S. president George H. W. Bush.

"Nieves de Enero": literally, "The Snows of January"; it is the title of a folk ballad by Mexican songwriter and performer Chalino Sánchez, and tells of a heartbroken man who hoped to get married to his love in January, but many months have passed since then with no marriage, and he wishes to be told the truth as to why.

O

OD: acronym for overdose, as in drug overdose.

OG: Original Gangster, typically describing someone who has been in the gang life for an extended period of time.

"O.P.P.": song by hip-hop artists Naughty by Nature that provides a shorthand of sorts for learning if one is open to cheating on one's partner; the acronym has multiple meanings, and can stand for other people's property, pussy, or penis.

OSS: acronym for Operation Safe Streets, a bureau within the Los Angeles Sheriff's Department that provides county-wide gang suppression and investigation support.

P

packing: slang for carrying a concealed weapon, most frequently a handgun, but knives as well, particularly in custody environments.

paisa (short for paisano): literally, "countryman" or someone of rural origin.

PAL warrant: acronym for parolee-at-large warrant.

payaso(s): literally, "clown(s)."

PC: acronym for protective custody.

PD: acronym for public defender.

Pero ahora tu tienes una madre: literally, "But now you have a mother."

pička: Croatian expression meaning "pussy," "cunt," or "wimp."

platano(s): literally, "plantain(s)."

pocket: slang for anus (men), or vagina or anus (women).

por supuesto: literally, "Of course."

program time: designated times within an institution for special programs, such as EBI (education-based incarceration).

property bag: a small bag given to an inmate for the purposes of holding personal property; also: race car property bags exist in order to keep various items (e.g., food, books, or even pruno) that each prison racial grouping owns collectively—items from this collection are doled out to new members when they enter the prison, most typically by the shotcaller for the given race.

pruno: prison wine made from whatever fruit might be available, as well as bread, which provides yeast for the fermenting process.

puta/puto: all-purpose vulgarity that can mean "bastard," "asshole," "whore," or "son of a bitch," and the insult can be intensified by changing the gender of the noun to the opposite of the person being targeted; also: it can be a gay slur depending on context.

Q

quebradita: Mexican dance style, one often performed to Sinaloa-style banda music.

R

race car: see definiton for car(s).

Raza (or La Raza): literally, "race," "the Race," or "the People," this term can also express unity and/or racial pride among Latinos.

respeto: literally, "respect."

responsibilidad: literally, "responsibility."

S

Sa-I-Gu: Korean term for the Los Angeles Riots of 1992.

sally port: secure, controlled entrance and exit in a custody facility that consists of two doors; one will not open until the other has closed.

Sánchez, Chalino: Mexican singer and writer perhaps best known for his narcocorridos, North Mexican ballads about life in the illegal drug trade.

Se pueden callar sus pinche bocas: literally, "They can shut their fucking mouths."

shotcaller: leader of a given race car in jail or prison; literally, the one who calls the shots and whom all must answer to.

sleeper: gang member who seeks to remain unidentified to law enforcement, typically lacking any sign of affiliation, e.g., gang tattoos or distinctive clothing.

soft 39: discipline tactic within Sureño jail and prison populations that consists of an under-the-radar attack by multiple gang members upon one victim, focusing punches and kicks mainly on head and upper torso, for 39 seconds (or until broken up).

soldado: literally, "soldier."

soup(s): slang for packets of Top Ramen; for further information on the importance of this commissary staple, see: *Prison Ramen: Recipes and Stories from Behind Bars* by Clifton Collins Jr. and Gustavo "Goose" Alvarez.

speedball(s): intravenously injected mix of heroin and cocaine (more prevalent in the 1990s), or heroin and speed.

spread: meal made by inmates in prison that utilizes any available food-stuffs, e.g., it can include "tortilla" made from mashed-up bread, or "tamale" made from mashed-up corn chips, a Top Ramen base augmented to a specific flavor with additional ingredients, or the term can simply refer to multiple items eaten all together at a single meal, possibly in celebration of parole or release.

spic: dated derogatory term for a Spanish speaker, or someone who may look as if he or she has ancestors from Central or South America, or the Carribean.

store: slang for commissary, where inmates can use the money put on their books by friends or family members to buy small necessities and food.

suerte: literally, "luck."

Sureño(s): Southern California Latino street gangs organized within jails and prisons, potentially associated with the Mexican Mafia.

SVP: acronym for sexually violent predator.

T

tamale(s): pastry made of cornmeal dough, typically filled with meat or cheese and baked in a cornhusk.

tax: extortion generally used upon those conducting illegal business (e.g., drugs or prostitution) that requires a percentage of the profits be paid to the key holder in the given area of operation, either in order to avoid being informed on, for the purposes of protection, or as a show of loyalty to a larger group; see also: cariño.

Te lo prometo: literally, "I promise you."

Telefona ambulanza: incorrect Spanish usage by Augie of "Telefona a la ambulancia"; literally, "Call an ambulance!"

Thunder Dorm: inmates tend to refer to Thunder Dorm as the most violent dorm in a given facility.

tinā: literally, "mother" in Samoan.

Todo está bien: literally, "It's all good."

tranquilo: literally, "Be calm."

U

Uso: literally, "brother" in Samoan; it is the word used for the race car referring to people of Pacific Island origin.

V

Valenzuela, Fernando: former Major League Baseball (MLB) pitcher and Mexican national who played seventeen seasons (1980 to 1997) for six teams, primarily the Los Angeles Dodgers.

Viking(s): a reference to the Lynwood Vikings, a secret gang within the LASD once referred to by U.S. district judge Terry J. Hatter, Jr., as a "neo-Nazi, White supremacist gang" that had engaged in "racial hostility" and "terrorist-type tactics."

Virgencita: affectionate term for the Virgin Mary.

voc shop: short for Vocational Shop, where inmates may work on paper printing presses or sewing machines at a special unit located within NCCF.

W

WAD: acronym for Warrants and Detainments, a division within the Los Angeles Sheriff's Department responsible for setting arraignment dates, among other things.

wet (or getting wet): slang for PCP use, or to add a dose of PCP to a cigarette or joint by dipping it in a vial of the substance.

wila(s): likely the Anglicized version of huila (literally, "kite"); see also: kite.

Wood(s): short for peckerwoods; prison term for inmates belonging to the white race car.

Y

Y ahora: literally, "and now."

Acknowledgments

Álvaro
Deputy Maria Aiken
Gustavo Arellano
Jerry Ballesteros
Rowland Becerra & the Lynwood Union Gallery
Jon Bernthal
Christopher D. Brand
Kate Butiu (née Thomas) & her students at Firebaugh High School
Cap
Deputy Eddie Carter
Jon Cassir
Steph Cha
Deputy Jason Chavez
Chee
Daphne Durham
Espi
Charles Farrell
The Gattis Family
Roly Gonzalez
Sergeant Sterling G. Haley
Simon Lipskar
Nicky Lund
Special Agent Eric Kraus
Lizzy Kremer
Judge Stephen A. Marcus
Steve Martínez
Sean McDonald
Harriet Moore
Deputy District Attorney Louis Morin

Felix Quintana

Michael Raulston

Assistant U.S. Attorney Bruce Riordan

Marisa Roemer & the Roemer Family

Aniela Arlene Russo

Councilwoman Marisela Santana

Evan & Melissa Skrederstu

Deputy Michael Steen

Deputy Lucia Varela

Cristiana Wilcoxon, Research Assistant

Steve Younger

&

The many others who anonymously shared with me concerning either their own incarceration or the incarceration of their loved ones.